The easy Guide to Your Walt Disney World Visit 2018

Dave Shute & Josh Humphrey

Theme Park Press

Theme Park Press publishes its books in a variety of print and electronic formats. Some content that appears in one format may not appear in another.

Editor: Bob McLain
Layout: Artisanal Text
ISBN 978-1-68390-083-2
Printed in the United States of America

Theme Park Press | www.ThemeParkPress.com
Address queries to bob@themeparkpress.com

To my mom and dad, for introducing me to Disneyland, Disney World...and everything else —Dave

To my mom, dad, brother, and friend(s)—without your help and guidance this would probably be a prison memoir rather than a Walt Disney World guidebook —Josh

Contents

Introduction

Congratulations. You are about to embark on a trip filled with magic and memories to one of the world's most popular vacation destinations. But with a Walt Disney World trip comes hundreds of decisions, from when to go to where to stay to what to eat to which attractions to experience. Walt Disney World spans more than 39 square miles and includes four major theme parks, two water parks, an expansive shopping and dining district, a 24-screen movie theater, more than 20 Disney-operated resorts, dozens of restaurants, hundreds of attractions, and a whole lot more.

That's where we come in. Whether this is your first or your fiftieth visit, this book will prepare you and your family to make the best choices, eat at the restaurants that provide the most value, make sure you experience the best Disney has to offer, eliminate as much time waiting in line as possible, and guarantee that your experience at Walt Disney World is magical and stress-free.

This guide is written to help all visitors plan better vacations, whether you're a first-timer still unsure of how Space Mountain and Dumbo the Flying Elephant are different, or if you're an experienced returning visitor trying to decide whether you want to pick Na'vi River Journey or Flight of Passage as your Pandora FastPass+ choice at Animal Kingdom. We'll introduce each topic and then expand on it with tips and tricks so first-time visitors are quickly brought up to speed and returning visitors will learn new strategies to maximize their time and money.

Why this book in particular, you ask? Dave and Josh share thousands of theme park visits, hundreds of hotel room stays, and far more theme park meals than either of them would probably like to remember. Their experience culminates in this carefully crafted guidebook designed to be the framework for every step of your vacation planning. Both are firm believers that a little planning goes a long way. By spending time mulling the many options now, you'll set yourself up for the best vacation possible.

Getting free updates. We will update this 2018 edition several times between its initial August 2017 publication date and the summer of 2018, when our 2019 edition will come out. In the meantime, we are offering free updates!

The paperback and Kindle versions are for sale on Amazon.com, and the PDF version is for sale on Gumroad.com.

- If you bought your 2018 edition on Gumroad.com, you'll **automatically** get an invitation to download an updated version of it when it's available.
- If you bought your 2018 edition on Amazon, then **forward your confirming Amazon email** (that is, the email titled "Amazon.com order of The easy Guide to Your Walt Disney World Visit") to easyguidewdw@gmail.com, and then, whenever an update to the 2018 edition comes out, we will email you instructions on how to get yours (as a PDF).

Sit back, relax, and enjoy the planning!

How to Use This Book

This chapter serves two primary purposes: introducing the topics of the rest of the book, and boiling down our recommendations into an easy-to-digest list. First-time visitors will benefit from clear, actionable advice, while those returning to the Most Magical Place on Earth can compare and contrast our thoughts with their own experiences.

Subsequent chapters offer detailed information on the whys and hows behind the recommendations summarized in this chapter, and add hundreds of detailed and up-to-date thoughts, reviews, and tips. For example, you may be interested only in eating at one or two sit-down restaurants. Instead of forcing you to read through a hundred reviews, we've listed the best values and the most immersive experiences here in an effort to speed up and simplify the planning process. And you never know, as you read the later reviews of our favorite restaurants, something else might catch your eye.

While you can skip around the book, we suggest that returning visitors pay special attention to the material on the new FastPass+ system (much different than the old FASTPASS) in Chapters 6 and 9, and that first-timers should consume the full text from beginning to end—perhaps a chapter per night with the help of a glass of wine and a roasty, toasty fire. The chapters build on each other, with decisions made during Chapters 2 and 3 affecting the choices you make in Chapters 4 and following. Chapters 8 and 9 come full circle and serve as the road map for your entire trip.

Changes, corrections, updates, links to larger color versions of key charts, and such, can be found at YOURFIRSTVISIT.NET/ EASY-GUIDE-2018-CHANGES.

Why Age and Height Matter [Chapter 2]

Children of all ages enjoy wonderful visits to Walt Disney World every single day of the year. However, if this may be your kids' only childhood visit, consider going when your youngest child is at least 8 or 9, and your shortest child at least 48 inches tall.

Many of Walt Disney World's best and most popular attractions require riders to be 44" to 48" tall, and kids around the third-grade-age are mature enough to appreciate the layers and nuances of each Disney experience. Those already planning to return may want to start earlier, when the kids are younger and all aspects of the Disney magic are open to them. While toddlers and younger kids are charmed by and enamored with the Disney princesses, older kids may be less enthusiastic about a sit-down meal with Belle and Cinderella. Starting young offers an opportunity to enjoy many varied trips as the kids get older. But starting too young and too short on a once-in-a-lifetime trip means passing on several of Disney World's best rides. Chapter 2 describes how easy it is to design an itinerary with kids (or adults) of any age.

How Long to Stay [Chapter 3]

Wonderful Walt Disney World vacations come in all shapes and sizes, with guests enjoying trips that last anywhere from just one day to as long as several weeks. However, for a once in a lifetime trip, we recommend spending nine days in Orlando.

Guests planning to return enjoy the ability to ease into visiting the theme parks with shorter trips of four or so days, knowing they can catch missed attractions and experiences in the future. Those planning once-in-a-lifetime style vacations are best served pushing their stay to eight or nine days. This affords the opportunity to enjoy most of the best of Walt Disney World, and also allows a mixture of longer days in the theme parks tempered by more relaxing downtime back at the resort. While a longer trip will be more expensive than a shorter one, fixed travel costs and the way Disney prices tickets make the per-day costs of a longer trip significantly lower.

By booking FastPass+ experiences in advance and touring the theme parks intelligently, those returning to Walt Disney World may experience a wide selection of their favorite attractions during shorter visits. First-time visitors spending just a few days at Disney World will be able to maximize their time and money by putting our advice into action and making carefully thought out decisions in advance of their arrival.

Returning visitors need to know:

- Animal Kingdom has expanded its after-dark hours and offerings, especially with Tree of Life Awakenings and Rivers of Light. Two new rides, the world-class Avatar Flight of Passage and the less interesting Na'vi River Journey, opened in an entirely new land, Pandora: World of Avatar, in May 2017.

- At Epcot, Frozen Ever After, a ride based on the popular movie, has replaced Maelstrom in the Norway Pavilion. Anna & Elsa meet in a new building next door. Wait times for Frozen Ever After routinely eclipse 75 minutes, making it a top FastPass+ priority. Waits for meeting Anna & Elsa have proven to be much shorter, often peaking under 30 minutes. Disney added a third theater to Soarin', in turn raising capacity by 50% and reducing standby waits. It has also received a new film and is now called Soarin' Around the World. New characters have been added to Innoventions West, including Joy & Sadness and Baymax.

- At Hollywood Studios, large swaths of land are closed for construction of all-new lands based on *Toy Story* (opening June 30, 2018) and *Star Wars* (opening 2019). Closures include all of the Streets of America and the old Backlot area. Most of the attractions remain in operation with the exception of Backlot Tour, Honey I Shrunk the Kids Movie Set Adventure, the Great Movie Ride, and Lights Motors Action! Extreme Stunt show. Most returning guests will still want to revisit favorites and Disney has added Star Wars experiences and a new nighttime show in Star Wars: A Galactic Spectacular Fireworks.

- At Magic Kingdom, Disney expanded Fantasyland by adding Storybook Circus, where you'll find the Dumbo ride and Barnstormer roller coaster. Seven Dwarfs Mine Train is also a headlining addition and a top FastPass+ priority, located across from the Winnie the Pooh ride. Mickey's Royal Friendship Faire is the name of the new Cinderella Castle stage show that includes appearances from *Tangled*, *Frozen*, and *The Princess and the Frog* characters, in addition to Mickey and friends. The evening parade is gone, and Wishes was replaced by a new show, Happily Ever After.

- Downtown Disney is now known as Disney Springs and has added more than two dozen new places to eat and over 50 new stores. Parking and traffic are improved with two new multi-level garages, the widening of streets, and the addition of two pedestrian bridges.

When to Go [Chapter 4]

If you can, visit Disney World at some point between the day after Martin Luther King Day in January until the Sunday a week before President's Day in February, or the three weeks beginning the Sunday after Thanksgiving.

In picking dates, it's important to consider crowd levels, pricing, weather, possible refurbishments, and special events. Our specialty is honing in on the less crowded times to visit, when wait times are lower at attractions, lines are shorter at stores and dining venues, and there's less congestion inside the parks. Lower crowds means being able to do more in a less stressful environment. From there, we typically prioritize lower resort pricing, followed by weather, refurbishments, and special events.

Based on these factors—but especially low crowds and lower prices—we recommend the following weeks:

- From the day after Martin Luther King Day in January until the Sunday a week before President's Day in February
- The Sunday after President's Day through the first week of March
- The week that begins the Sunday after Easter until mid-May
- From the day after Labor Day through the rest of September
- The last two weeks of October
- November after Veterans Day until the Saturday before Thanksgiving
- The three weeks beginning the Sunday after Thanksgiving

Josh recommends the late January and early February dates, with the lowest prices (prices go up February 16), comfortable daytime temperatures, and some of the lowest crowds of the year. Dave recommends the three weeks after Thanksgiving, which marry below average-crowds and prices with Disney World's Christmas displays and offerings like Holidays Around the World and Mickey's Very Merry Christmas Party.

Those embarking on a possible once-in-a-lifetime trip should note that the peak of the hurricane season ends in early October, and that a few rides are almost invariably closed for refurbishments in January and early February.

If these dates won't work, Chapter 4 offers a blow-by-blow overview of everything to expect all year long.

Returning visitors need to know:

- Disney World crowds are about as high as they've ever been, and many of the new crowds are coming during periods that used to be much slower. There are still much better and much worse times to go, but starkly low crowds are a thing of the past.

- Price seasons at the values and moderates have changed over the past few years, the net effect being that late summer and fall dates are no longer in the lowest price "Value" (or "Value 2") seasons.
- Disney started charging different prices for different dates for single-day tickets in 2016. In early 2018, it announced that later in the year it would begin charging seasonal prices for multi-day tickets as well. At press time, no further details are available, but we expect seasonal pricing to launch perhaps as soon as April, since Toy Story Land opens in Hollywood Studios at the end of June.

Where to Stay [Chapter 5]

Stay at Disney's Art of Animation, Pop Century, Port Orleans French Quarter, Port Orleans Riverside, Wilderness Lodge, Grand Floridian, Contemporary, or Polynesian Village.

We suggest that you stay in a Disney-owned resort hotel. While more expensive than hotels operated by third parties, they are also typically:

- Much more fun
- Much more convenient
- Much more "Disney"

The Disney-owned hotels also offer unique perks, including:

- The right to book FastPass+ reservations for key attractions beginning 60 days in advance of arrival. At press-time, non-Disney guests (except those at the Swan or Dolphin, and, new for 2018, Shades of Green and the Disney Springs Resort Area hotels—the latter only if booked as a package through the Walt Disney World Travel Company) can only book these 30 days in advance.
- The right to book dining ten days further out than non-Disney guests, which can be critical for high-demand meals like dinner at Be Our Guest Restaurant.
- Free airport transport to and from your hotel via Disney's Magical Express.
- Free and frequent transport from your hotel to the parks, waterparks, and Disney Springs.
- Free parking at both your hotel and the parks.
- Access to the various Disney Dining Plans, a convenient budgeting tool even if they often don't present much actual savings.

Perhaps even more important than any of these quantifiable perks is the comfort and safety of staying inside the "Disney bubble", far removed from the hustle, bustle, and worry of the outside world. Staying on property is the easiest way to forget about life's problems and truly enjoy an immersive experience together. While a vacation staying off-site is generally less expensive at first blush, consider additional expenses like resort fees, car rental, and the price of your time. There is no more convenient way to experience Walt Disney World than staying at one of their resorts. There is a reason Disney commands premium prices and why so many return visitors stay on property over and over again. Strongly consider the additional cost of an on-property stay and find out for yourself.

Disney groups most of its hotels into three price types, which are from least to most expensive Value resorts, Moderate resorts, and Deluxe resorts. Among them we recommend, depending on budget:

VALUE RESORTS
Art of Animation, Pop Century

These resorts are among the least expensive on property, offer dedicated bus service, have great food courts, and offer newer rooms. Art of Animation is the newest Disney resort on property, and Pop Century is a short walk away. Refurbed rooms at Pop Century offer coffeemakers and queen beds—both firsts among standard value resort rooms.

MODERATE RESORTS
Port Orleans French Quarter, Port Orleans Riverside

French Quarter enjoys the smallest footprint of the moderate-level resorts and all rooms are just a few minutes away from the resort's amenities, including the bus stop, food court, boat dock, and resort concierge. Riverside is much larger, but offers better amenities, including a table service restaurant and several quiet pools.

DELUXE RESORTS
Wilderness Lodge, Grand Floridian, Contemporary, Polynesian Village

The Grand Floridian is Disney's flagship resort and its most opulent, providing several of its nicest restaurants, beautiful pool and garden areas, and a convenient location to Magic Kingdom. The Contemporary is a magical space and just a short walk away from Magic Kingdom. Theme park view rooms in the tower look over Cinderella Castle and the monorail zooms through the center of the resort all day. The Polynesian Village combines South Seas theming that kids find fun and adults find charming with great convenience and strong dining. The Wilderness

Lodge with its glorious lobby and lower prices—but smaller rooms—rejoined this list after it completed a multi-year refurb in July 2017. Chapter 5 includes in-depth reviews of every Disney-owned hotel.

Returning visitors need to know:

- In late 2017 and early 2018, Disney added about 10% more rooms to those that can book FastPass+ at 60 days—Shades of Green, and for those booking packages through the Walt Disney Travel Company (for example, through My Disney Experience), the Disney Springs Resort Area hotels. At the same time, it extended Extra Magic Hour privileges to the Disney Springs hotels (Shades guests already had them). In early March 2018, Extra Magic Hours privileges were added to guests staying at the Four Seasons. These changes may be temporary.

- Five person rooms are easier to find, as Caribbean Beach completed a refurb that added many in 2015, and DVC studios that sleep five are now available in the Polynesian, Grand Floridian, Wilderness Lodge Boulder Ridge, BoardWalk Inn, and Beach Club DVC offerings.

- In early 2017 Disney kicked off major construction projects at Coronado Springs and especially Caribbean Beach, with closures of its dining, shopping, and bar areas, supplemented by temporary replacements. Our experiences suggest that guests planning much dining at the hotel avoid Caribbean Beach until permanent dining re-opens there later in 2018. A Pop Century refurb that began in 2017 has yielded the first value resort standard rooms with coffeemakers and queen beds. At press time, half of Pop's ten buildings have completed their refurbs, and two more are being worked on. A minor room refurb project is underway at Port Orleans French Quarter, and at Old Key West as well.

How to Spend Your Time [Chapter 6]

Set daily plans from the example itineraries and "cheat sheets" we provide.

Planning your time at Disney World can be broken down into three parts:

- Dividing your days among the parks
- Picking the best parks for each day
- Setting your plan for each park day

There are two easy ways to use this book to plan your time at Walt Disney World, each designed around Disney's new FastPass+ program:

- For those who can use them as a starting point, we provide sample 9-day, Saturday-arrival itineraries.

- For everybody else, we provide "cheat sheets" for designing your visits that work for both younger and older kids, and for longer and shorter trips.

Here's an excerpt from one of the example itineraries:

Meals:	Wednesday	Thursday
Breakfast	*Hotel Room*	*Hotel Room*
Lunch	Hollywood Studios Counter	**TBD Cinderella's Royal Table****
Dinner	Sunset Ranch Market	Magic Kingdom or Hotel Counter
Parks, Etc:		
Early Morning	Off	At Magic Kingdom by 8.15a
Late Morning	Off	Magic Kingdom
Early Afternoon	At Hollywood Studios by noon	Magic Kingdom
Late Afternoon	Hollywood Studios	Magic Kingdom
Evening	Hollywood Studios	
Late Evening		
Notes:		
Parade		Afternoon Parade
Evening Show	Fantasmic	
Park-Open Target	n/a	Peter Pan
FastPass+ to	Rock 'n' Roller Coaster, Tower of	Seven Dwarfs Mine Train, Haunted
pre-schedule	Terror, Voyage of Little Mermaid	Mansion, Enchanted Tales with Belle
Extra FP+ Target	Fantasmic	Winnie the Pooh

And here's an example from one of the Cheat Sheets:

Hollywood Studios Morning Plan

Use FastPass+ at Tower of Terror 9:15–10:15am, Rock 'n' Roller Coaster 10:15–11:15am, and Star Tours 12:15–1:15pm.

1. Ride Toy Story Midway Mania: 9–9:20am.
2. See the 9:30am Voyage of the Little Mermaid: 9:22–9:45am.
3. Ride Tower of Terror with FastPass+: 9:55–10:20am.
4. Ride Rock 'n' Roller Coaster with FastPass+: 10:22–10:45am.
5. See 11am Beauty and the Beast Live on Stage: 10:50–11:30am.
6. Have lunch: Sunset Ranch Market/Backlot Express/PizzeRizzo are convenient: 11:35–12:20pm.
7. Ride Star Tours with FastPass+: 12:30–12:50pm.
8. Schedule a 4th FastPass+ via the phone app or Muppet*Vision kiosk.

Chapter 6 includes in-depth reviews of all the theme park attractions and explains theme park touring strategy in detail.

Returning visitors need to know:

- Disney's new FastPass+ program, explained in this chapter and in Chapter 9, has profoundly changed the best ways to plan for and tour the parks. Never have advance planning and thoughtful itineraries paid off more, and never has lack of planning (or planning too late...) hurt more. This guidebook is part of the first guidebook series written from scratch for the era of FastPass+.

- FastPass+ allows you—and pretty much requires you—to book well in advance times for specific rides on specific days, beginning 60 days ahead if you are staying at a Disney-owned resort (or the Swan, Dolphin, Shades of Green, or a Disney Springs Resort Area hotel on an eligible package) and 30 days ahead for everyone else.

- So many attractions offer FastPass+, and so much capacity is allocated to it, that standby waits for the majority of the rides are longer than they were prior to the implementation of the FastPass+ initiative.

Where to Eat [Chapter 7]

Target your dining venues based on our recommendations, our reviews, or simply where you are when you're hungry!

First-time family visitors to Walt Disney World need to know three things about dining:

1. Several dining venues are among the most memorable and delightful experiences Walt Disney Word has to offer.

2. Table service reservations open 180 days in advance. Availability at the most sought-after restaurants is taken almost immediately.

3. Disney World dining is expensive. Expect to pay 25 to 40% more on-property than you would for comparable meals off-property. For most (but not all) visitors, the Disney Dining Plan won't save any money.

For families, we recommend:

- The Princess meals: **Cinderella's Royal Table** at the Magic Kingdom and **Akershus Royal Banquet Hall** at Epcot. The first has the better setting, the second is much less expensive.

- Dining with Tigger, Pooh, and friends at the **Crystal Palace** in the Magic Kingdom.

- Dining with Mickey and Friends at **Chef Mickey's** at Disney's Contemporary Resort, **Tusker House** at Disney's Animal Kingdom, and **'Ohana** breakfast at Disney's Polynesian Village Resort.

- Dining in the Beast's Castle at **Be Our Guest Restaurant** in Magic Kingdom.

- Various degrees of wait-staff induced silliness at **50's Prime Time Café** at Disney's Hollywood Studios and **Whispering Canyon Café** at Disney's Wilderness Lodge.
- **The Hoop-Dee-Doo Musical Revue**, a fun, energetic dinner show with interactive elements and plenty of audience participation at Disney's Fort Wilderness Resort.
- Exotic settings in the local versions of national chain restaurants like the **Rainforest Café**, in both Disney's Animal Kingdom and Disney Springs, and **T-REX** in Disney Springs.

For couples looking for the most romantic atmosphere and the best food, we suggest:

- **California Grill**—located on the 15th floor of the Contemporary Resort, it offers breathtaking views of Magic Kingdom during the evening fireworks, in addition to a great menu focused on fresh ingredients, sushi, and contemporary cocktails.
- **Artist Point**—nestled inside Wilderness Lodge, it is themed to the restaurants found in the great National Park lodges of the West. Buffalo, salmon, and a terrific mushroom soup and berry cobbler are menu mainstays.
- **Victoria & Albert's**—offering impeccable service and astonishing attention to detail, dinner at this Grand Floridian restaurant is a truly memorable experience.

Chapter 7 includes advice on the Disney Dining Plan and in-depth reviews of all the major Disney World dining options, plus suggestions on the best quick service options.

Returning visitors need to know:

- Remarkable new dining has opened in the last few years, particularly in Disney Springs (Morimoto Asia, The BOATHOUSE, and Homecoming), but also in Magic Kingdom (Be Our Guest, Skipper Canteen) and Disney's Animal Kingdom (Tiffins).
- While prices are up everywhere, Disney World has seen strong increases in counter service meals, the more expensive of which now approach the price of the least expensive table service options.
- While we still don't particularly recommend the various Disney Dining Plans, they have gotten much more flexible and diner-friendly over the last few years.
- For the first time, 2018 Dining Plans include one alcoholic (or "specialty" for those under 21) drink per meal credit

Which Tickets to Buy and How Much to Budget [Chapter 8]

Big budgets allow for more extravagances, but a vacation can be tailored to just about any budget. Realistically, for a first visit, a family of four is looking at spending more than $4,000.

"What should we budget?" is the hardest simple question for this book to answer. This is because smaller families, families whose kids are younger, families staying at a less expensive hotel, families going during a less expensive week, and families on shorter trips will pay less. Larger families, families where everyone is older than nine, families staying at a more expensive hotel, families going during a more expensive week, and families on longer trips will pay more.

- A parent and one younger child with three days of tickets and three nights in a value resort during one of the less expensive price seasons could spend as little as $1,400 in Orlando.
- Add another parent and another younger child and this trip jumps to $2,400.
- Stretch the visit out to the 8 nights and 9 days we recommend for "only visits" and the in-Orlando price exceeds $4,400.
- Stay this long in one of the more expensive deluxe resorts instead, and the price is more than $7,800.
- Shift to the most expensive times to visit at this deluxe resort and add $2,300 more.

(All the figures are before transportation costs and souvenirs.)

The good news is that budgeting for a specific trip is relatively straightforward, once you've made the key decisions that are outlined in this book.

Returning visitors need to know:

- Hotel, ticket, and dining prices have seen major increases the past few years, at the same time as the range and availability of discounts that Disney offers has been severely scaled back.
- In February 2018, Disney announced that it would move to seasonal pricing for multi-day tickets later in 2018. At press time, there are no further details, but we project the current ticket prices to represent the lowest levels of such seasonal pricing, and that price seasons may be in place before Toy Story Land opens on June 30, 2018. Tickets bought before the new prices come out will be honored until they expire at the end of 2019,

so long as they are unchanged. Guests able to purchase tickets or packages before the new price seasons come into effect may save money by locking in current pricing.

How to Set Everything Up and Get Everything Done [Chapter 9]

Your plans should be firm at least 181 days before your arrival date. Then see the To-Do List for exactly what to do, and when, to prepare for your trip.

There are three key dates to consider:

- Restaurant reservations open for booking 180 days before a potential dining date.
- For those staying at a Disney-owned resort or another eligible hotel, FastPass+ reservations can be booked beginning 60 days before their arrival date.
- For everyone else, FastPass+ reservations can be booked beginning 30 days before planned use.

Building a To-Do List is keyed to these three dates because booking as early as possibly will result in the widest selection of experiences being available. Chapter 9 covers exactly how and when to make these decisions.

Returning visitors need to know:

- FastPass+ reservations are, along with good daily plans, the critical part of designing a lower-wait, lower-stress trip. The most options and best rides will be available at the beginning of your booking window. Which FastPass+ to book is explained in Chapter 6, and how to create FastPass+ reservations is explained in this chapter.
- You make and manage your FastPass+ and other reservations through the My Disney Experience website and app—creating and using a account is also explained in this chapter.
- Finally, for Disney-owned hotel guests, there are no more room keys. Customizable MagicBands, also explained in this chapter, serve as room keys and link to all your other reservations and tickets, and will be shipped before departure to U.S.-based addresses.

Disney World planning may feel like a daunting task. Don't worry. You're in good hands. The following chapters offer a step-by-step walkthrough of the entire planning process, offering just the right amount of detail so you can make informed decisions. When everything goes according to plan and the group asks, "How did you make this trip so wonderful?" you can respond with a smile, "It was pretty easy, actually."

Why Age and Height Matter

2

Children of all ages enjoy Walt Disney World in their own ways, whether by meeting the characters, riding the thrill rides, or blending both roller coasters and princess breakfasts into an overall itinerary. When deciding whether it's time to book a first trip, consider the ages and heights of the kid(s) and what they can and will be able to experience once they arrive. If one or more of the kids are under 48 inches tall, they will run into attractions they aren't able to experience due to height restrictions. If they don't have the intellectual and emotional maturity of the typical eight year old, other rides for which they are tall enough may be too frightening, or just a little too sophisticated for them to fully enjoy.

If your kids aren't eight or older and over 48" tall, and this is a once-in-a-lifetime trip, you need to decide whether you should wait until they are tall enough and mature enough to enjoy everything Walt Disney World offers. Even with height restrictions and the possibility that the content of an attraction like Living with the Land will fly over their heads, younger and shorter kids typically have as much fun as their older counterparts. But while pictures of the kids when they're young enough to sit on Mickey's lap might initially seem like a more precious proposition, trips with the kids when they're older may be more enjoyable and more memorable for all involved. Those already planning on a return visit benefit from enjoying a wider range of experiences over many years, in addition to more flexible planning. The good news is that no matter whether or not you're already planning a return visit, it's easy to design an itinerary around the unique needs of kids of any age.

This chapter first discusses trips with kids of various ages. It then covers handling a single visit with kids of wildly different ages.

Visits by Age and Height

PRESCHOOLERS
• •

Preschool age children especially delight in the magic of meeting the Disney characters. They are young enough that they still believe they are meeting *the* Cinderella and *the* Winnie the Pooh. Pictures of the kids entranced with characters like Snow White and the Seven Dwarfs will turn into memories that last a lifetime. Some kids remain shy or apprehensive about meeting the characters. Mickey is, after all, an alarming five feet tall. Goofy, with his oversize top hat, stretches over

Comprehensive Guide to Rides

Key: **E=Epcot, AK=Animal Kingdom, HS=Hollywood Studios, MK=Magic Kingdom**
Underline: Favorite of older kids; *Italic*: Skippable for older kids

PRE-SCHOOL KIDS

Avoid	**E**: *Gran Fiesta Tour (Mexico)*, Innovations, *Journey into Imagination with Figment*. **MK**: Carousel of Progress, Hall of Presidents.	**E**: Impressions de France, O Canada!, Reflections of China, Agent P's World Showcase Adventure. **MK**: Stitch's Great Escape.	**E**: The American Adventure, Mission: Space, Soarin', Test Track. **AK**: Avatar Flight of Passage, DINOSAUR, Expedition Everest. **HS**: Fantasmic!, Rock 'n' Roller Coaster, Tower of Terror. **MK**: Haunted Mansion, Space Mountain, Splash Mountain.
Other	**E**: Living with the Land. **AK**: *Conservation Station*, Primeval Whirl, *Wildlife Express Train*. **MK**: Country Bear Jamboree, *Enchanted Tiki Room*.	**E**: The Seas with Nemo and Friends, Disney & Pixar Short Films. **AK**: Gorilla Falls, Na'vi River Journey, Exploration Trail. **MK**: The Barnstormer, Swiss Family Treehouse.	**E**: Spaceship Earth. **AK**: It's Tough to Be a Bug, Maharaja Jungle Trek. **HS**: Indiana Jones Epic Stunt Spectacular, Walt Disney Presents. **MK**: Big Thunder Railroad, Pirates of the Caribbean, Seven Dwarfs Mine Train.
Best-Loved	**AK**: *The Boneyard*, Dinorama, Triceratops Spin. **HS**: Disney Junior: Live on Stage. **MK**: Astro Orbiter, Prince Charming Regal Carrousel, Dumbo the Flying Elephant, Magic Carpets of Aladdin, Mad Tea Party, Tomorrowland Speedway, Tomorrowland Transit Authority PeopleMover, Tom Sawyer Island, WDW Railroad.	**AK**: Finding Nemo the Musical, UP: A Great Bird Adventure*. **E**: Frozen Ever After. **HS**: Frozen Sing-Along Celebration, Voyage of the Little Mermaid. **MK**: It's a Small World, Liberty Belle Riverboat, The Many Adventures of Winnie the Pooh, Monsters Inc. Laugh Floor, Under the Sea: Journey of the Little Mermaid	**E**: Illuminations, Turtle Talk with Crush. **AK**: Festival of the Lion King, Kali River Rapids, Kilimanjaro Safari, River of Light. **HS**: Beauty and the Beast, Muppet Vision 3-D, Star Tours, Toy Story Midway Mania. **MK**: Afternoon Parade, Buzz Lightyear, Enchanted Tales with Belle, Happily Ever After, Jungle Cruise, Mickey's PhilharMagic, Peter Pan.
	Skippable	**Other**	**Favorite**

THIRD GRADERS AND UP

*Preliminary ranking of attraction not yet open

six feet. With apprehensive and shy kids, run a search on YouTube for "Disney World characters" and watch some interactions leading up to the trip. This will familiarize the kids with what to expect and reduce many of the first-time jitters and the tears that accompany them. While preschoolers will be too short or young for many of the premier attractions, there's still plenty for them to experience, especially at Magic Kingdom.

But they shouldn't try everything. Some attractions are simply too scary or intense for preschoolers. To help you figure out what is what, we have sorted every attraction based on how well kids of varying ages are likely to enjoy them.

For example, in the bottom left box we have The Boneyard, which is a richly themed playground at Disney's Animal Kingdom. Younger kids love to play there, but most older kids will find it juvenile. The upper right box contains several of Disney's best attractions, many of which aren't suitable for younger children due to height restrictions or scary content. Most older kids (and their parents) love these attractions, which is why they fall into "favorites" for third graders and up, and into "avoid" for preschoolers.

With preschoolers, try to match their interests, stamina, and routines with what the family plans to accomplish...or you'll have the joy of experiencing the same tantrums every other parent is enjoying come 3pm.

When the meltdowns begin, it's not uncommon for Josh to turn to Dave and say, "It must be 3 o'clock." Indeed, even more common than Mickey bars and WDW t-shirts are the afternoon hissy fits. Be realistic about how long the kids are going to be able to go. While Disney World might be a magical place, pixie dust does not seem to increase kids' stamina or reduce their inclination to break down when they're overstimulated and ready for a nap. Plan a daily afternoon break for when crowds, wait times, and heat peak. This will rejuvenate the kids and their parents and prepare them for a fun and relaxing evening back in the parks.

YOUNGER SCHOOL-AGE KIDS

Kids between five and eight are young enough that they still enjoy most character meets and some of the other sillier entertainment that older kids may have lost interest in. They are also beginning to approach the height required to enjoy Disney's more thrilling major attractions.

The chart on the next page illustrates which attractions shorter kids are disqualified from riding. Unfortunately, this chart could double as a list of Disney World's best and most popular attractions (with the exception of Stitch's Great Escape), including almost all of the headliners at each park. With a single trip on the horizon, if you can't wait until the kids are 48" tall, consider waiting until they are at least 44" tall. They'll then be eligible for every ride on property but two. And the two they aren't eligible for aren't necessarily deal breakers. Primeval Whirl is an off-the-shelf carnival ride at Animal Kingdom. Rock 'n' Roller Coaster is located inside a relatively nondescript building at the end of a long road on Sunset Boulevard at Hollywood Studios. Simply avoid it and the kids won't feel like they're missing anything.

Keep in mind that "tall enough for" doesn't necessarily translate into "ready for". Moreover, many of Disney World's best attractions are like a Pixar movie in that there are layers of substance and humor that guests of all ages enjoy for different reasons. Kids between 5 and 8 understand and enjoy the attractions on a basic level, but nuances and deeper meanings are often lost.

Disney World Rides Excluded by Height

Children Less Than 38" Tall Can't Ride	Children Less Than 40" Tall Can't Ride	Children Less Than 44" Tall Can't Ride	Children Less Than 48" Tall Can't Ride
Primeval Whirl	Primeval Whirl	Primeval Whirl	Primeval Whirl
Rock 'n' Roller Coaster	Rock 'n' Roller Coaster	Rock 'n' Roller Coaster	Rock 'n' Roller Coaster
Avatar Flight of Passage	Avatar Flight of Passage	Avatar Flight of Passage	
Expedition Everest	Expedition Everest	Expedition Everest	
Space Mountain	Space Mountain	Space Mountain	
Mission: SPACE Mars	Mission: SPACE Mars	Mission: SPACE Mars	
Mission: SPACE Earth	Mission: SPACE Earth		
Big Thunder Mountain	Big Thunder Mountain		
DINOSAUR	DINOSAUR		
Soarin'	Soarin'		
Splash Mountain	Splash Mountain		
Star Tours	Star Tours		
Stitch's Great Escape	Stitch's Great Escape		
Test Track	Test Track		

KIDS BETWEEN 8 AND 88

Kids who are eight or older are tall enough, old enough, and mature enough to enjoy all of Disney World's rides and entertainment. Unfortunately, they may be getting too old to be swept up in the magic of breakfast with Cinderella inside the Castle. Most remain happy to participate, if for no other reason than it makes mom happy.

With just one planned trip, consider waiting until the kids are around this age. Returning guests that begin visiting when their kids are younger enjoy the widest range of experiences over many years. Cherish the memories of their first visit with Mickey Mouse and look forward to pretending you're not afraid when junior first starts begging to ride Expedition Everest.

Trips with Children of Different Ages

There are several ways to plan trips around kids of wildly different ages and maturity levels. The underlying problem, as discussed, is that kids of varying ages enjoy different things. This is not unique to Disney World. At home, young kids may like playing with Legos, while older kids have moved on to the Xbox One X. At Disney World, kids may occasionally want to or need to split up in order to experience certain attractions. Disney has made this relatively easy by building playgrounds and diversions aimed at younger kids in close proximity to the thrillers. Here are a few other ideas:

Take advantage of Rider Switch. Commonly referred to as "Child Swap", Rider Switch allows those eligible and willing to experience an attraction with a height requirement to ride, while others either wait alongside them in line or do something else. Most attractions require the group to approach the attraction's entrance and present the child too short or too leery to board the ride. The Cast Member will hand the group a Rider Switch pass. The members of the group experiencing the attraction wait in line. Members not experiencing the attraction may wait at the same time or head elsewhere. Once the group has experienced the attraction, up to three people can use the Rider Switch pass to enter the FastPass+ line, eliminating much of the wait. This can include a member or two of the original group. For example, let's say a family of four wants to experience Test Track, but one child is too short. Parent 1 and the older child wait in line and ride, while Parent 2 and the younger child head off to Innoventions to play. Once Parent 1 and the older child are off Test Track, up to three members of the family may use the Rider Switch at the FastPass+ line. That means the older child that previously rode Test Track can ride again alongside Parent 2. Parent 1 can then take the younger child elsewhere—perhaps to the interactive play area at Mission: SPACE's exit.

Have part of the family focus on rides for older kids, and the rest on attractions designed for the youngest. Split the family up, with older kids and a parent on one set of rides, and the littler ones on another age-appropriate set. This works particularly well if one parent has little interest in the thrill rides and coasters anyway. You can build completely different itineraries and FastPass+ selections for the two groups, or have some experiences in common and some different.

Consider childcare services. Disney vets use an independent in-room babysitting service called "Kid's Nite Out" for kids between six months and twelve years old. At press time, rates start at $18 per hour for one child and go up to $26 an hour for four children (four hour minimum).

There's a $2/hour surcharge after 9pm and a one-time transportation fee of $10. Babysitters arrive armed with age-appropriate games, crafts, and books.

In addition, Children's Activity Centers are available for potty-trained kids between 3 (if potty-trained) and 12 at select resorts until July 31, when they will be closing:

- Simba's Cubhouse at Disney's Animal Kingdom Lodge
- Lilo's Playhouse at Disney's Polynesian Village Resort
- Sandcastle Club at Disney's Yacht Club and Beach Club Resorts

At press time, rates per child at Simba's Clubhouse are $15/hour with a two-hour minimum, and Lilo's Playhouse and the Sandcastle Club have a fixed charge of $55 per evening. Call 407-939-3463 for more information or to reserve. Until they permanently close, these services are available to all guests, but are most convenient for those staying nearby or for families that want to drop off a youngster before heading to some of Disney's finer dining choices.

Families visiting with kids of any and all ages thoroughly enjoy their Walt Disney World vacations, but keep in mind that the experience will be quite different depending on who it is you're taking. Groups consisting of families with kids of varying ages will need to make some compromises, but the good news is that the vast majority of your time can and will be spent together as a family.

How Long to Stay

3

This chapter addresses the decision-making process for how long to stay at Walt Disney World. Guests planning to return enjoy the ability to ease into visiting the theme parks with shorter trips of four or so days, knowing they can catch missed attractions and experiences in the future. Those planning once-in-a-lifetime style vacations are best served pushing their length of stay to eight or nine days. This affords the opportunity to enjoy much of the best of Walt Disney World, and also allows a mixture of longer days in the theme parks tempered by more relaxing downtime back at the resort. Shorter stays are often rewarding and enjoyable for everyone involved, but the limited time necessitates skipping key experiences and requires a more ambitious schedule with fewer opportunities to relax.

We'll first cover the basics: budgets, time, and the ages of the kids. Then, in the next section, we'll address the importance of taking time away from the parks to relax, followed by a section about allocating time for an "only" trip.

Budgets, Time Available, and Ages of the Kids

Most prospective guests will choose a length of stay based on three primary factors: budget, time constraints, and kids' ages. Mom might only be able to get a Monday through Wednesday off work, necessitating a shorter five-day trip that begins with travel early Saturday and ends with travel late Wednesday. A budget might be stretched too thin for a seven-night stay at a moderate resort, but work with fewer nights at a value (Chapter 5 explains the difference between "moderates" and "values"). A family with very young kids may find that a delightful trip lasts only three or four days.

The good news is that guests with a wide range of budgets and trip lengths can thoroughly enjoy their visits. The bad news is that, like most things, (within reason) more is better.

A longer trip means more relaxing, more theme park visits, more Mickey ice cream bars, and, ultimately, more flexibility. Longer trips also have lower per-day costs. Most travel costs are fixed regardless of how many days you spend in Orlando. If airfare and related costs are $1500, the per-day travel cost on a five-day vacation is $300. On a ten-day trip, the per-day travel cost drops in half, to only $150 per day. Second, at press time adding the sixth to tenth day is only an additional $10.65 (including tax) per day. A four-day child base ticket costs $383 with tax. That's $96 per day. An eight-day child base ticket costs $431 with tax. That's just $54 per day. Of course, days five through eight come with other costs like dining, souvenirs, and lodging, but one long stay is often much less expensive than two shorter stays. (Note that seasonal pricing of multi-day tickets is expected later in 2018, which will raise some of these costs for many dates.)

If this is a once-in-a-lifetime visit, we recommend trying to stretch your vacation dollars to eight nights and nine days. This allows for the equivalent of a full day or so at each of Animal Kingdom and Hollywood Studios, in addition to two days at Epcot and two or three full days at Magic Kingdom. The longer trip length also offers flexibility in late arrivals and early departures. You may elect to leave Epcot one afternoon at 3pm to head off to the Grand Floridian Resort & Spa for afternoon tea with Alice from *Alice in Wonderland*. With an eight-night stay, there's plenty of time to return to Epcot without fear of missing anything. On a four-night trip, there's more pressure to stay in the park and tour until the last member of the family drops. It's either that or potentially miss out on key attractions that could be made up with a longer stay.

If time and budget don't allow, a shorter trip can be perfectly enjoyable, particularly if you're already planning a trip farther down the road. Two trips spread out over the years offer an opportunity to enjoy two potentially different experiences, while also providing more time to save for the hefty costs. (It also affords a great opportunity to purchase two of our guidebooks, which is pretty fantastic in itself.)

Deciding on a trip length that maximizes value and enjoyment varies a bit based on age:

KIDS FIVE AND YOUNGER tend to enjoy Magic Kingdom the most, where Fantasyland and most entertainment offerings cater specifically to their heights and maturity levels. Kids at that age may have no interest in visiting Disney Springs or Epcot. In this situation, a three- or four-day trip focused on visiting Magic Kingdom offers plenty of time to visit over multiple half days, in addition to affording opportunities to head back to the resort for naps.

MOST KIDS BETWEEN FIVE AND EIGHT will still prefer Magic Kingdom over the other major theme parks, but will get more out of trips to Animal Kingdom, Epcot, and Hollywood Studios. Plan to spend at least a half day at each of these three, pushing the number of theme park days up to five or six.

MOST KIDS EIGHT AND OLDER will be tall enough to ride every major attraction, including the thrill rides at each theme park, and mature enough to enjoy them all. Still plan at least two days at Magic Kingdom, but also include full days at each of the other major theme parks (and, if you can, even more) to take care of attractions like Test Track and Rock 'n' Roller Coaster.

The Value of Time Away from the Parks

Many first-time visitors equate time away from the theme parks as time wasted or value lost. This seems logical on the surface. After all, if theme park tickets are going to cost $350 a pop, we sure as heck better be in the theme parks waiting in line for *something*. But don't make the most common rookie mistake.

Touring the theme parks in Florida, by their very nature, is exhausting—particularly during the unrelenting summer when it's 85 degrees by 10:30am. It's a lot of standing. It's a lot of walking. If the kids are in strollers, it's a lot of pushing. In fact, it's not uncommon at all for guests to rack up five or more miles a day walking through the theme park. Just a quick lap around Epcot's World Showcase Lagoon is 1.2 miles. And that's without doing anything!

Time spent together back at the resort hotel will likely be some of the most fun, most rewarding experiences of the trip. One of Josh's favorite memories from his first visit to Disney World is sitting on the beach at the Polynesian with his brother, mom, and dad holding a Mickey ice cream bar in one hand and a hot cocoa in the other. Dave has fond memories of playing on the beach at the Contemporary with his mom and sister while his dad napped back in the room. Spending time with loved ones is a big part of a vacation and spending relaxing time together with Walt Disney World as the backdrop is an integral part of the experience.

Afternoon breaks are particularly necessary with young kids (or dads) who will be bombarded with sensory overload virtually every moment they spend in the parks. A child that's spent a few hours back at the pool will be a much happier camper when it comes time to stake out a spot for IllumiNations that night. And, as an added bonus, those afternoons are also the busiest and hottest parts of the day at the theme parks. Where would you rather be? In a 25-minute-long line for a $4 Smartwater in the scorching afternoon sun, or back at the resort sipping a Mai Tai on the beach?

If It's Your Only Visit, Aim for Nine Days in Orlando

Returning visitors have the flexibility of choosing to spend less time at the theme parks and more time enjoying their resort and the other amenities Walt Disney World offers. But the four major theme parks—the Magic Kingdom, Epcot, Disney's Hollywood Studios, and Disney's Animal Kingdom—are the heart of a Walt Disney World experience. To fully appreciate the best they have to offer, you need about nine days:

- About a day to a day and a half each at the Animal Kingdom and Hollywood Studios
- At least a full day and an additional evening at Epcot
- Two to three days at the Magic Kingdom
- The equivalent of a day or two taking it easy

Add it up and you're looking at about seven full days in Orlando with a travel day on both ends, bringing the total number of vacation days up to nine. But if you can't make nine days work—don't despair, just move on to the next section!

SHORTER "ONLY" VISITS

Shorter "only" visits are doable with some compromises:

FIVE FULL DAYS To see most of the best of Disney World, five full days in the parks are about the minimum—two in the Magic Kingdom, and one more in each of the other three parks. Working some of this park time into your arrival or departure days will give you some needed time off in the middle of your visit.

SIX FULL DAYS Adding another day lets you have more time off and more time at Epcot or Animal Kingdom.

LONGER "ONLY" VISITS

If you are fortunate enough to enjoy more than nine days in Orlando, first prioritize time spent away from the parks. Time is a luxury at Walt Disney World, and more time means more sleeping in, more late park arrivals, and more time relaxing at the pool. Late arrivals are particularly advantageous with the invention of FastPass+, which offers the ability to schedule three high priority attractions for later in the day, far in advance of setting foot inside the theme park. For example, with two days of late arrivals at Disney's Hollywood Studios, you can schedule afternoon FastPass+ at Toy Story Midway Mania, Star Tours, and Voyage of the Little Mermaid on day one, and Rock 'n' Roller Coaster, Tower of Terror, and the Frozen Sing Along on day two. Show up at 11am and you'll be able to walk on six of the most popular attractions over those two days with minimal waits. Experiencing the same rides just one day will require a very early morning, much more walking, and a carefully crafted plan. It's doable, but it requires a much longer, more intense day.

CONSIDERING ARRIVAL DAYS

If you are planning a nine-day visit, we suggest a trip that spans the nine days from Saturday to the following Sunday because it best fits the typical week off of work. The sample itineraries presented in Chapter Six will guide you through planning such a visit.

Of course, flexible visitors may prefer to arrive another day of the week, for the sake of saving time and money. Disney World tends to be busiest on weekends as local passholders push up attendance. If possible, design your vacation to maximize the number of weekday theme park visits. As a bonus, Disney resort rates are often higher on Friday and Saturday nights by $20 to $150, and typically lowest Mondays, Tuesdays, and Wednesdays. Avoiding the more expensive nights will save money and reduce waits.

Airfare may be cheapest on Tuesdays and Saturdays, and there may be other travel expenses that can be reduced by traveling on certain days. Guests with flexible schedules should use services like KAYAK.COM or GOOGLE.COM/FLIGHTS to search out the cheapest or most convenient itinerary possible.

When deciding how long to stay, keep in mind that most travel costs are fixed, and the per-day cost of theme park tickets goes down as more days are added. Longer vacations allow more flexibility, in addition to providing more opportunities to experience everything Walt Disney World has to offer. Shorter Walt Disney World vacations tend to be more of a whirlwind experience. That isn't necessarily bad, but the go, go, go mentality often leaves first-time visitors thinking they need a vacation from their vacation upon returning home.

When to Go 4

In picking dates, it's important to consider crowd levels, pricing, weather, possible refurbishments, and special events. Our specialty is honing in on the less crowded times to visit, when wait times are lower at attractions, lines are shorter at stores and quick service venues, and there's less congestion inside the parks. Lower crowds means being able to do more in a less stressful environment. From there, we typically prioritize resort pricing, followed by weather, refurbishments, and special events.

CROWDS Historically, Walt Disney World has been the most crowded when hordes of U.S. school kids are out of school: from early June through the third week in August, Thanksgiving week, Christmas and New Year's weeks, President's Day week, the spring break month of March; and the weeks before and after Easter. Recently, however, summer crowds have been more moderate than we would have predicted. Other dates see an ebb and flow of mostly low and moderate crowds, all noted in the month-by-month calendar that follows.

TICKET PRICING Disney has not changed its ticket prices depending on when during a period tickets are used, except for one-day tickets. However, in February 2018, Disney announced that "later this year" it would institute seasonal prices for multi-day tickets. At press time, there are no further details, but we project the current ticket prices to represent the lowest levels of such seasonal pricing, and that price seasons could be in place before Toy Story Land opens on June 30, 2018. Tickets bought before the new prices come out will be honored until they expire at the end of 2019, so long as they are unchanged. In the absence of information about ticket price season dates and levels, in the rest of this chapter when we say "prices," we mean "resort prices."

RESORT PRICING Disney resort pricing is constantly fluctuating, so much so that the same exact room can cost $259 one night and $303 the next night, as it does at Port Orleans Riverside from December 13–14, 2018. Picking less expensive dates may save $150–300 per night at the deluxe resorts. Disney used to name periods of different prices "Price Seasons": value, regular, summer, fall, etc., but seems to have abandoned this practice for 2018. We are sticking to the traditional price season names for simplicity and comparability. Fortunately, the less crowded times are also often the least expensive.

WEATHER The main weather points that concern us are summer heat and humidity, erratic winter highs and lows, and the peak of the hurricane season from mid-August to early October. Many of the least crowded and least expensive stretches suffer from weather issues, but none of these issues is routinely as challenging as the heat and humidity of the crowded summer months.

REFURBISHMENTS Disney announces refurbishments about eight weeks in advance, making it difficult to plan a vacation around an unexpected major refurbishment. Fortunately, refurbishments follow a pattern, and we've identified when they're less likely to occur. In addition, it's rare that more than one or two major attractions are closed at the same time.

SPECIAL EVENTS Certain guests, particularly those returning, may want to plan a vacation around a special event like the Epcot Food and Wine Festival. Our month-by-month calendar identifies these special events and offers some advice on taking advantage of them, or how best to avoid them, depending on your needs.

Based on these factors—but especially low crowds and lower prices—we recommend the following weeks throughout the year:

- From Martin Luther King Day in January until the Sunday a week before President's Day in February
- The Sunday after President's Day through the first week of March
- The week that begins the Sunday after Easter until mid-May
- September after Labor Day through the end of the month
- The last two weeks of October
- November after Veterans Day until the Saturday before Thanksgiving
- The three weeks beginning the Sunday after Thanksgiving

Josh recommends the late January and early February dates, with the lowest prices (prices go up February 11), comfortable day-time temperatures, and some of the lowest crowds of the year. Dave recommends the three weeks after Thanksgiving, which marry below average crowds and prices with Disney World's astonishing Christmas displays and offerings like Holidays Around the World and Mickey's Very Merry Christmas Party.

Disney World 2018 Crowd Calendar

Those embarking on a possible once-in-a-lifetime trip should note that the peak of the hurricane season ends in early October, and that a few rides are almost invariably closed for refurbishments in January and early February.

This chapter begins with summaries of what you can expect of weekly crowds, resort prices, and weather.

Next, it presents detailed overviews of each of the months of the year, discussing prices, weather, crowds, refurbishments, special events, and recommended times to visit that month.

Finally, for first timers who may never return, it presents Dave's chart that ranks all the weeks of the year based on crowds, pricing, weather, and other essential variables.

Crowds and When to Go

When considering "low crowds", remember that Walt Disney World comprises four of the top ten busiest theme parks in the world, by overall attendance. Magic Kingdom averages around 56,000 guests per day. The days with the lowest attendance tend to see slightly north of 30,000 guests, while anything over 55,000 will result in much longer lines. Epcot averages about 32,000 guests per day. It's rare that the park sees fewer than 20,000 people, while anything above 35,000 will result in longer lines.

Each park suffers from bottlenecks and narrow walkways, in addition to succumbing to periodic mass exoduses from shows throughout the day. From there, certain attractions are extremely popular, with demand far outstripping supply. For example, let's take a look at Frozen Ever After, the re-imagining of the old Maelstrom ride in Norway. The attraction moves around a thousand people an hour and Epcot's average attendance is about 32,000 people a day. On an average day with Epcot open from 9am to 9pm, there are 12,000 rides to share with those 32,000 people. And it takes just 1,000 of those 32,000 people (or just 3.1%) in front of you to hit a 60 minute standby wait.

With only four rides and eight more shows and other attractions, the headlining Studios attractions see 40- to 70-minute peak waits even on the least crowded days. Don't be too discouraged, however. Just because everyone else waits 75 minutes in line doesn't mean you have to. Our touring tips and the cheat sheets that follow in Chapter Seven will reduce waits to virtually nothing.

Over the past year or so, Disney World has tried various strategies to try to shift guests away from what would otherwise be naturally crowded times like major holidays and summer vacations. At the same time, the parks have reduced capacity during less popular times of day and cut operating hours during less crowded periods of the year in an attempt to lower costs. Economic and political strife, particularly in some major South American countries, have also contributed to lower international attendance.

The results, so far, have been lower attendance in the summer, higher attendance in the fall, especially the two weeks around Columbus Day, and higher standby waits during many periods of the year.

Prices and When to Go

While until now the major prices at Disney World that vary by season have been hotel room prices, in February 2018 Disney World announced it would begin charging different theme park ticket prices for multi-day tickets at different times of the year. We have no further details at press time—as they unfold, we'll post updates at yourfirstvisit.net and easyWDW.com. Because of that, in the material that follows, "prices" always refer to hotel prices, not ticket prices.

For its resort hotels, Disney traditionally assigned dates to a specific "price season." These resort hotel price "seasons" did not mean anything so simple as fall or winter. Rather, Disney changes prices much more frequently than that. For 2018, it made two changes. First, pricing now changes more often over the course of a given week, so the price for the room on a Monday or Wednesday night is often different than the price paid on a Thursday or Sunday night. Second, Disney World seems to no longer be using its traditional names (or any names) for these price seasons. We believe that each of these changes is a step on a path to much more varied day by day prices over the course of the year.

In the material that follows, for consistency and clarity we will be using the traditional Disney price season names:

- Value
- Fall
- Regular
- Summer
- Peak
- Easter
- Holiday

The first two seasons are always the lowest-priced, and the last three always the highest. Disney groups hotels into value, moderate, and deluxe resorts (more on this in the next chapter). At Disney's value resorts, Summer rates are much higher than Regular rates; at its moderates, Summer and Regular are about the same over a multi-day visit; and at deluxe resorts, Summer rates are lower than Regular rates. Moreover, deluxe seasons change according to a different calendar in the summer and fall than value and moderate seasons do.

For exact prices by day, search for "Mousesavers 2018 Disney World Room Rates" and follow the links. This chart shows different resort prices at Walt Disney World over the year in 2018. It does not refer to the seasons themselves, as it's much more useful to show actual prices. The chart picks an example from each group, and to smooth out fluctuations that come from Sunday, Thursday, and weekend upcharges, averages prices over a seven-night stay.

Average* 2018 Price Per Night
Deluxe Polynesian Village (top), Moderate Coronado Springs (middle), Value All-Star Sports (bottom)

*By arrival date; average of next seven nights; lowest cost room; includes tax

Weather and When to Go

The chart on the following page shows the range of high temperatures at Disney World. The middle line is the average high. There's a 20% chance highs will be lower than the lower line, and a 20% chance that highs will be higher than the higher line. Note the big range of temperatures in the winter months.

Orlando Average, 20th, and 80th Percentile High Temperatures

Month-by-Month Comments on When to Go

JANUARY

COST Most of late January enjoys the least expensive resort pricing of the year, but January 1, 2017, with Holiday season pricing, is among the most expensive nights of the year, and January 2–6 sees higher WDW Marathon pricing. The Friday-Sunday periods of the Martin Luther King Jr. weekend sees average pricing. (See earlier in this chapter for more on pricing.)

WEATHER It's the coldest month in Orlando, with erratic temperatures and an average high of 69 and an average low of 50 degrees. Historically, it rains on 22% of days.

CROWDS Many U.S. school districts continue winter break through the first week, causing some of the highest crowds of the year to persist through the first Saturday of the new year. Crowds are low the rest of the month, with two sure major exceptions and a possible third. Marathon Weekend brings in thousands of runners and their families, but they have surprisingly little impact on theme park crowds, resulting in only average crowds. Martin Luther King Jr. weekend crowds, from January 13–16, are well above average and the highest crowd level we'll see until President's Day weekend in the middle of February. It's best avoided. Finally, the Pro Bowl will be held in Orlando on January 28, with major related festivities at Disney World the week before. This may make the week beginning January 22 more crowded, although we saw little crowd impact from the first Orlando Pro Bowl in 2017.

REFURBISHMENTS January usually sees the most refurbishments, including brief closures at most resort pools and typically lengthier closures at a few other attractions. The vast majority of attractions remain operating. Blizzard Beach will be closed into March.

SPECIAL EVENTS THAT MAY AFFECT CROWDS OR YOUR STAY:

- The WDW Marathon impacts transportation on the morning of the half- and full-marathons. It's best to take Disney transportation.
- Several holiday events continue through the first week in January.
- Beginning in mid-January, avoid the large tour groups that become common.
- The Epcot Festival of the Arts will return in 2018, beginning January 12 and adding to weekend crowds at Epcot. The festival brings presentations, seminars, activities, shows, and kiosks in World Showcase offering food and beverage samples. Part will be open seven days a week, but some entertainment will be focused on Fridays through Mondays.
- Pro Bowl events will occur at the Magic Kingdom, Disney Springs, and especially ESPN Wide World of Sports the days before the game on January 28.

BEST TIME TO VISIT January 16 and later has cool weather, some of the lowest crowds of the year, and the lowest Disney hotel prices of the year.

FEBRUARY

COST The lowest pricing of the year continues up until the Sunday a week before President's Day weekend when prices rise to the Regular season level. On the Thursday before Presidents Day, they rise again to the expensive Peak season. Peak pricing continues through the week following President's Day. Prices fall back to average February 25, 2018, and stay at that level into early March.

WEATHER The average high is 72 degrees and the average low 53, but temperatures are erratic and highs can get into the low 80s or dip well below 60. Precipitation is relatively low, but it does rain on about 23% of days.

CROWDS Crowds are below average to average through the Wednesday before President's Day weekend, when crowds are well above average (as well as in the week following it). Crowds return to average from the last week in February through the first week in March.

REFURBISHMENTS Most refurbishments will be completed by mid-February. Blizzard Beach remains closed.

SPECIAL EVENTS THAT MAY AFFECT CROWDS OR YOUR STAY:

- The Epcot Festival of the Arts will continue until Presidents Day. See "January" for details.
- The Princess Half Marathon (Feb. 22–25) is scheduled the weekend after President's Day. It affects transportation in the early morning on Sunday and keeps crowds above average until the Saturday following President's Day.
- Superbowl Sunday (Feb. 4) sees few locals visiting, reducing crowds.
- Valentine's Day (Feb. 14) makes it harder to secure dinner reservations, but does not affect attendance.
- The Atlanta Braves MLB baseball team returns to the ESPN Wide World of Sports Complex in mid-February for spring training.
- The Epcot International Flower and Garden Festival will begin February 28 and continue until May 28. The festival brings millions of flowers, Disney-themed topiaries, and special activities around the park, in addition to kiosks in World Showcase offering food and beverage samples that generally cost $2–$7 each. The festival does not adversely affect daily crowds.

BEST TIME TO VISIT A trip before peak season pricing goes into effect is best, with these weeks seeing the lowest prices and some of the lowest crowds of the year.

MARCH

COST March 1–9 is Regular season with average pricing across the resorts. The rest is first Peak then Easter season with some of the highest prices of the year.

WEATHER Temperatures warm, but remain erratic. Expect highs anywhere from the mid-60s to the mid-80s with an average high of 77 and an average low of 57 degrees, with minimal precipitation.

CROWDS Expect average crowds the first third of the month, followed by some of the heaviest crowds of the year the rest of the month due to spring breaks.

REFURBISHMENTS Pool closures remain common, and Blizzard Beach will remain closed until March 18. Attraction closures are less common.

SPECIAL EVENTS THAT MAY AFFECT CROWDS OR YOUR STAY:

- The Epcot International Flower and Garden Festival continues through the month. See "February " for details.

BEST TIME TO VISIT February 25 through March 8 will have the lowest crowds and prices of the month.

APRIL

COST High Easter prices will continue until April 7. At the moderates and values, prices return to average on April 8 and stay that way for the rest of the month. The deluxes see a week of Peak pricing and then drop to average prices for the rest of the month on April 15.

WEATHER April warms up to some of the most comfortable weather of the year, with an average high of 82 degrees and an average low of 62. Precipitation remains low with chances at 18%.

CROWDS Heavy spring break crowds continue through one week after Easter Sunday. Beginning Sunday, April 8, average level crowds return through early May.

REFURBISHMENTS Pool closures are rare, and few attractions are closed.

SPECIAL EVENTS THAT MAY AFFECT CROWDS OR YOUR STAY:

- The Epcot International Flower and Garden Festival continues through the month. See "February" for details.
- The Star Wars Half Marathon weekend is April 19–22. It affects transportation in the early mornings, but will have little additional impact on crowds.

BEST TIME TO VISIT Begin a trip at least one week after Easter Sunday when crowds and resort prices fall from some of their highest levels of the year to average.

MAY

COST May 1–24 is Regular season, with average resort pricing, before prices rise slightly from May 25–27 for Memorial Day. Then it's Summer season, when Value resort prices are higher than Regular, but lower than Peak. Moderate resort Summer prices are about the same as Regular, and Deluxe Summer prices can be lower than Regular season by 5–10%.

WEATHER Temperatures rise significantly in May, with an average high of 87 and an average low of 69 degrees. The weather gets wetter and more humid as you move closer to June.

CROWDS Crowds are average to slightly above average through the Thursday before Memorial Day weekend. The earlier in May, the less crowded. The Memorial Day weekend will be busy, but not as busy as other major holidays like Easter. Toy Story Land in Hollywood Studios may open as early as May. When it does, crowds will increase there.

REFURBISHMENTS Rare.

SPECIAL EVENTS THAT MAY AFFECT CROWDS OR YOUR STAY:

- The Epcot International Flower and Garden Festival continues through May 28. See "February" for details.

BEST TIME TO VISIT Any time between May 1–14, with average crowds and resort pricing, cooler and drier days than later in the month, and the Flower and Garden Festival in full swing.

JUNE

COST All of June is Summer season. At the Value resorts prices are higher than Regular, but lower than Peak. Moderate resort Summer prices are about the same as Regular, and Deluxe Summer prices can be lower than Regular season by five to ten percent.

WEATHER June is hot, with an average high of 90 and an average low of 72 degrees. Precipitation inches up with a 38% chance and the highest accumulation of precipitation of the year.

CROWDS June is among the busiest months as schools let out for summer, but 2016 and 2017 summer crowds were lower than expected. South American tour groups can drive crowds significantly upwards, though this effect will be moderated while economies there remain weak. If the summer returns to historical norms, daily crowds will be lower than Easter or Christmas weeks, but busier than just about any other time.

REFURBISHMENTS Rare.

SPECIAL EVENTS THAT MAY AFFECT CROWDS OR YOUR STAY:
- Tour groups are common in June and July. If you see (or hear) a group of young kids walking around behind a 20-year-old carrying a flag, head in the opposite direction.

BEST TIME TO VISIT June 3–9 will have slightly lower crowds than later in the month, in addition to reduced precipitation and slightly lower temperatures.

JULY

COST All of July is Summer season at the Value and Moderate resorts. At the Values, prices are higher than Regular, but lower than Peak. At the Moderates, prices are about the same as Regular. At the Deluxes, the first week is Summer season, with prices that can be lower than Regular season by five to ten percent. After July 5, pricing at the Deluxes is reduced even further to Value Season 2 and some of the lowest prices of the year.

WEATHER July is among the hottest months in Orlando, with an average high of 91 and an average low of 74 degrees. Even worse than the heat is the humidity, which averages about 75%. Rain showers also increase in July, with a 49% chance of precipitation on any given day.

CROWDS Fourth of July crowds are the largest of the summer. Traditionally, the rest of July is the first or second busiest month overall because almost all U.S. kids are out of school, but see the note for "June" about recent lower crowd levels. International visitation is also at its highest point of the year. Most other months have at least some portion where crowds will be significantly smaller, but not July. It is crowded every day. Crowds are slightly lower towards the end of the month.

REFURBISHMENTS Rare.

SPECIAL EVENTS THAT MAY AFFECT CROWDS OR YOUR STAY:
- Magic Kingdom offers a special fireworks show on July 3 and 4. The July 3 show is slightly less crowded. Epcot hosts special events and meet and greets in the United States Pavilion throughout the Fourth, and offers a special IllumiNations show with several extra minutes of intense fireworks. The Magic Kingdom show is the best, but Epcot crowds are more manageable.
- Tour groups remain common.

BEST TIME TO VISIT As late in July as possible is best. International visitation wanes and pricing at the Deluxes is lower.

AUGUST

COST Deluxe prices continue low throughout August, dropping even a bit more on August 24. Summer season at the Values and Moderates continues through August 12. On August 12, the Values and Moderates drop to the Regular season, and then on August 26 drop again to the Fall season, one of the lower priced seasons.

WEATHER August is one of the hottest months in Orlando, with an average high of 91 and an average low of 75 degrees. Peak hurricane season begins in the third week. Hurricanes rarely directly impact Disney World or lead to the park closures we saw in 2016, but they and lesser storms may affect flights and bring nasty weather. Showers and thunderstorms are common in the afternoons, with a 43% chance of precipitation.

CROWDS The first two weeks in August are as crowded as the rest of the summer. Crowds diminish beginning the third week in August as kids start the new school year and are the lowest of the summer in the final week. Guests with flexible schedules are best served waiting until September when crowds are significantly lower.

REFURBISHMENTS Rare.

SPECIAL EVENTS THAT MAY AFFECT CROWDS OR YOUR STAY:
- The Epcot Food and Wine Festival may begin in late August, as it did in 2017. It runs every day through mid-November. It's a fun event with interesting food, educational classes, and several expensive dinners. There are also bands performing throughout the Festival outside at the American Gardens Theater for free.

During the festival, Epcot is extremely busy on weekends, and weekdays in World Showcase are also busier.

- Mickey's Not So Scary Halloween Party may begin in late August, as it did in 2017. It requires a separate ticket to attend. The party runs from 7pm until midnight, with ticket holders typically allowed to enter as early as 4pm. The party's main features are a unique parade, fireworks show, and trick-or-treating throughout the park. Most rides are operating. This event closes the Magic Kingdom at 6 or 7pm for visitors without a ticket to the Halloween Party. The Magic Kingdom is actually less busy on days when there is a Halloween Party because it closes early. If you have park hopper tickets, you may want to start at Magic Kingdom and then hop to another park to end the day. Without a park hopper, consider visiting Magic Kingdom on a party day then a dinner reservation at one of the resorts connected by the monorail. Tuesday parties are the least crowded.

BEST TIME TO VISIT The last week in August is the least crowded since early May.

SEPTEMBER

COST September sees a mixture of Value, Fall, and Regular price seasons. All prices are below average. In a turn that began in 2016, value and moderate resort prices, while still low compared to most other dates, are higher earlier in the month than in years before 2016, as the price season then is now Fall instead of Value.

WEATHER September is just barely cooler than the summer months with an average high of 89 and an average low of 74 degrees. Humidity remains extremely high, and there is a good chance thunderstorms or rain will disrupt most afternoons and some evenings. Historically, it rains 40% of days in September. Peak hurricane season continues.

CROWDS Crowds are at their lowest levels of the year during the first three weeks in September, with the possible exception of the weekend of September 8 and the two days following, as vast swathes of kids in the Northeast have the September 10 and 11 off for Rosh Hashanah. The only time you may find less people in the parks is certain days toward the end of January and the first two weeks in February, making it an excellent time to visit as far as crowds are concerned. September 2–4 will be the busiest days due to the Labor Day holiday, but even those three days will have significantly smaller crowds than any of the days over the summer.

REFURBISHMENTS The frequency of attraction refurbishments increases with the lower crowds. Expect a few rides to be down.

SPECIAL EVENTS THAT MAY AFFECT CROWDS OR YOUR STAY:

- Mickey's Not So Scary Halloween Party includes many September dates. See "August" for details.
- Night of Joy is a contemporary Christian concert series that moved to the Wide World of Sports in 2016, after having taken place inside Magic Kingdom after-hours for years. Attendees will receive admission to Magic Kingdom during the day with bus transportation offered to Wide World of Sports for the event.
- The Epcot Food and Wine Festival continues every day through mid-November. See "August" for details.

BEST TIME TO VISIT The first half of September will have low crowds and some of the lowest prices of the year, especially when considering the likelihood of significant discounts. Any date later in the month to the beginning of October is still more than do-able with well below-average crowds, other than the weekends at Epcot.

OCTOBER

COST Most of October is a mix of Fall season and Regular season, with pricing slightly below average. Columbus Day weekend (Oct. 6–8) is the exception, with average pricing.

WEATHER Weather cools slightly with an average high of 84 and an average low of 68 degrees. Precipitation is much lower than the summer months, with a 26% chance of showers on any given day. Peak hurricane season ends early in the month.

CROWDS Crowds are heavier in October than in past years with domestic school schedules moving towards week-long fall breaks largely before or after Columbus Day. South American attendance is also higher in the first two weeks, culminating in the largest crowds of the month over Columbus Day weekend. If you are flexible with your dates, hold off until after October 15.

REFURBISHMENTS Expect a couple minor attractions to be closed briefly throughout the month.

SPECIAL EVENTS THAT MAY AFFECT CROWDS OR YOUR STAY:

- The Gartner Symposium will likely return to the Swan, Dolphin, Beach Club, and Yacht Club in mid-October. All of the Epcot-area resorts will be sold out, and most of the restaurants in the area will be booked solid for those dates. The convention does not affect theme park attendance, except for Epcot, which is busier in the evenings.
- Mickey's Not So Scary Halloween Party includes many dates throughout October. See "August" for details.

- Epcot's International Food and Wine Festival continues daily through mid-November. See "August" for details.

BEST TIME TO VISIT October 15 through the end of the month is the best time to visit in October, with average crowds, cooler weather, and plenty of opportunities to enjoy Mickey's Not So Scary Halloween Party and the Food and Wine Festival.

NOVEMBER

COST Other than the week of Thanksgiving, prices are average to below average. At the Values and Moderates, with the exception of Thanksgiving week (Nov. 18–25), all of November is Fall season, with pricing slightly higher than Value season 2 and lower than Regular season. At the Deluxes, the Fall season is interrupted with Regular season November 2–11. Thanksgiving week sees pricing about 10% higher than Regular season, which is less than Peak season and other major holidays.

WEATHER It's noticeably cooler than September and October, with an average high of 76 and an average low of 59 degrees. November introduces more variability in high and low temperatures than the summer. Humidity is also substantially lower, with a 23% chance of precipitation. For those who like warm, but not uncomfortably hot temperatures, November is the perfect month to visit.

CROWDS Crowds are surprisingly light for the majority of November, with two major exceptions. The first is November 8–11, due to a phenomenon known as "Jersey Week" combining with, we expect, the Wine and Dine Half Marathon. All New Jersey schools are off the Thursday and Friday of the first full week of November, and many families from the state travel to Disney World during that week and/or weekend. This raises crowd levels significantly, particularly at Epcot and Magic Kingdom. Second, Thanksgiving week is very crowded.

REFURBISHMENTS Typically a few minor attractions.

SPECIAL EVENTS THAT MAY AFFECT CROWDS OR YOUR STAY:

- Mickey's Very Merry Christmas Party begins around November 7 and happens several other evenings throughout the month. It requires a separate ticket to attend. Like Mickey's Not So Scary Halloween Party, it includes a unique parade, fireworks show, and special stage shows. Cocoa and cookies take the place of trick-or-treating candy. It runs from 7pm–12am, with ticket holders able to enter as early as 4pm. Because of the 6 or 7pm closures for regular guests, other nights that have late closures and fireworks are wildly crowded at the Magic Kingdom. Unlike the Halloween Party, where the first few parties typically are the least crowded, the first few Christmas Parties typically sell out due to elevated crowds for Jersey Week and the Wine and Dine Half Marathon.

- Epcot's International Food and Wine Festival continues daily through mid-November. See "August" for details.

- The Epcot International Festival of the Holidays (formerly Holidays Around the World) begins Sunday, November 18, and is fully in place by Friday, November 23. Storytellers tell holiday stories and explain unique traditions in many of the World Showcase countries. Santa Claus meets in the U.S. Pavilion. Beginning November 23 the Candlelight Processional is an amazing stage show featuring the voices of famous celebrities, a large choir, and a 50-piece orchestra. The show, which tells the story of Christmas, is put on three times throughout the night (5pm, 6:45pm, and 8pm) and lasts about 40 minutes. IllumiNations, the nightly fireworks and laser show, also includes several holiday-only effects that you won't want to miss. The festival will increase crowds to the World Showcase in the evening, especially on the weekends.

- The Osborne Family Spectacle of Dancing Lights had its last run in 2015. The new-in-2016 holiday show Jingle Bell, Jingle BAM! will likely return to Hollywood Studios in early November 2018, replacing during its run the evening Star Wars show.

BEST TIME TO VISIT November 11–17 is the best time to visit with the lowest crowds of the month and low resort pricing. You'll have plenty of opportunities to see the Magic Kingdom Castle Lighting and to attend Mickey's Very Merry Christmas Party. Consider a visit over the first week in November if you'd prefer to attend the Food and Wine Festival.

DECEMBER

COST Fall season continues with prices slightly below average through December 8, 2018. Regular season pricing begins December 9; Peak season, with well-above-average pricing, begins December 14; and the highest prices of the year, the Holiday season, begin December 21.

WEATHER Expect erratic temperatures throughout December. It is not uncommon for one day to be in the low 60s and the next day to be in the high 70s. Nonetheless, the average high is 72 and the average low is 53 degrees, making most afternoons comfortable and most evenings a little chilly. Precipitation remains low with a 22% chance.

CROWDS Crowds are slightly below average to average through December 14. Crowds build that week, and beginning December 22, some of the heaviest crowds of the year arrive, with the highest crowds of the year from December 25–31.

REFURBISHMENTS Expect a few minor attraction closures for brief stints.

SPECIAL EVENTS THAT MAY AFFECT CROWDS OR YOUR STAY:

- Pop Warner brings its youth football Super Bowl to Disney World over the first full week of December. Pop Warner does not have a substantial impact on theme park attendance, but it does have a serious impact at the resorts where kids and their families stay. Pop Warner families typically receive hefty discounts at the All-Stars, Coronado Springs, and Caribbean Beach. If planning a trip over the first full week of December, consider booking another resort to avoid thousands of largely unchaperoned kids.

- Mickey's Christmas Party continues through several dates in December, with the last party likely on December 21. See "November" for details.

- The Festival of the Holidays in Epcot runs through December 30. See "November" for details.

- The Jingle Bell, Jingle BAM! show will likely continue until December 30 at the Studios. See "November" for details.

NEW YEAR'S EVE CELEBRATIONS Magic Kingdom hosts identical fireworks December 30 and 31. The 30th is slightly less crowded, but both days should fill to capacity in the afternoon. Epcot hosts a special IllumiNations on the 31st with several minutes of outstanding fireworks at the end. Dance parties throughout World Showcase continue into the late night. Hollywood Studios shoots fireworks off from behind and on top of the buildings around Hollywood Boulevard to live music. The Studios' show is the easiest to see, and Animal Kingdom is the least crowded park to visit during the day.

BEST TIME TO VISIT Try to end the trip by December 15 to take advantage of below-average crowds, average to below-average resort pricing, and everything the Christmas season has to offer.

When to Go If It's Your Only Visit

A family looking at a once-in-a-lifetime trip should aim to visit at a less-crowded time when refurbishments and weather are less likely to negatively impact the trip. Based on both this and the delights of the Disney Christmas program, Dave has ranked all the weeks of the year for first-timers who may never return, in the chart on the following page.

Choosing dates is easiest for those with flexible schedules. For vacationers with school-age children unwilling to take them out of school, or other date constraints, picking a date among the less desirable times of year may be a bit daunting. The good news is that you're in the best possible position to make an informed decision. From there, we'll help you save money and time in the following chapters, regardless of when you ultimately choose to visit.

2018 Weeks to Visit Rankings

Arrival Date	Week Rank	Crowds	Values Prices	Moderates Prices	Deluxe Prices	Other
12/30/17	39	High-	Moderate	High	Moderate+	
1/6/18	53	Low+	Low	Low	Low	Ride Closures Common
1/13/18	52	Low+	Low	Low	Low	Ride Closures Common
1/20/18	51	Low+	Lowest	Lowest	Lowest	Ride Closures Common
1/27/18	50	Lower	Lowest	Lowest	Lowest	Ride Closures Common
2/3/18	48	Lowest	Lowest	Lowest	Lowest	Some Ride Closures
2/10/18	49	Moderate -	Moderate	Moderate+	Moderate	Some Ride Closures
2/17/18	41	High-	High	High	High	
2/24/18	**13**	Low+	Moderate	Moderate+	Moderate	
3/3/18	**6**	Low	Moderate	Moderate+	Moderate	
3/10/18	44	Higher	Moderate+	High	High	
3/17/18	40	High-	Moderate+	High	High	
3/24/18	46	Highest	Highest	Highest	Highest	
3/31/18	45	Highest	Highest	Highest	Highest	
4/7/18	**14**	Low+	Moderate	Moderate+	High	
4/14/18	**8**	Low+	Moderate	Moderate+	Moderate	
4/21/18	**9**	Low+	Moderate	Moderate+	Moderate	
4/28/18	**10**	Low+	Moderate	Moderate+	Moderate	
5/5/18	**11**	Low+	Moderate	Moderate+	Moderate	
5/12/18	**12**	Low+	Moderate	Moderate+	Moderate	
5/19/18	17	Moderate	Moderate	Moderate+	Moderate	
5/26/18	38	High-	High	Moderate+	Moderate-	
6/2/18	19	Moderate+	High	Moderate	Low+	
6/9/18	30	High-	High	Moderate	Low+	
6/16/18	31	High-	High	Moderate	Low+	
6/23/18	32	High-	High	Moderate	Low+	
6/30/18	42	High	High	Moderate	Low+	
7/7/18	37	High-	High	Moderate	Low	
7/14/18	36	High-	High	Moderate	Low	
7/21/18	35	High-	High	Moderate	Low	
7/28/18	34	High-	High	Moderate	Low	
8/4/18	33	High-	High	Moderate	Low	
8/11/18	27	Moderate+	Moderate	Moderate+	Low	Peak Hurricane Season
8/18/18	26	Moderate	Moderate	Moderate+	Low	Peak Hurricane Season
8/25/18	23	Low	Low+	Moderate	Low	Peak Hurricane Season
9/1/18	20	Lower	Low+	Moderate	Low	Peak Hurricane Season
9/8/18	22	Low	Low+	Moderate	Lowest	Peak Hurricane Season
9/15/18	21	Lower	Moderate-	Moderate+	Low	Peak Hurricane Season
9/22/18	24	Low	Moderate	Moderate+	Moderate-	Peak Hurricane Season
9/29/18	25	Moderate -	Moderate-	Moderate+	Moderate-	Peak Hurricane Season
10/6/18	29	High-	Moderate	Moderate+	Moderate-	
10/13/18	16	Moderate	Moderate	Moderate+	Low+	
10/20/18	**7**	Low+	Moderate	Moderate+	Low+	
10/27/18	**5**	Low	Low+	Moderate	Moderate-	
11/3/18	15	Moderate -	Low+	Moderate	Moderate	Some Xmas Program
11/10/18	**4**	Low	Low+	Moderate	Moderate-	Some Xmas Program
11/17/18	28	High-	Moderate	Moderate+	Moderate-	Some Xmas Program
11/24/18	**1**	Low	Low+	Moderate-	Low+	Xmas Program
12/1/18	**3**	Low+	Low+	Moderate-	Low+	Xmas Program
12/8/18	**2**	Low	Moderate	Moderate+	Moderate	Xmas Program
12/15/18	18	Moderate	Higher	High	Higher	Xmas Program
12/22/18	47	Highest	Higher	Highest	Highest	Xmas Program
12/29/18	43	High	Higher	Higher	Higher	Some Ride Closures

Bold=Recommended week for first time visitors who may never return

Where to Stay

5

In this chapter we suggest that first-time visitors stay in a Disney-owned resort hotel, either a value, moderate, or deluxe resort, based on budget. Returning visitors should also consider a Disney-owned resort, in particular because of their FastPass+ advantages compared to most alternatives. Specifically, we recommend:

- **VALUE** Art of Animation, Pop Century
- **MODERATE** Port Orleans French Quarter, Port Orleans Riverside
- **DELUXE** Wilderness Lodge, Polynesian Village, Contemporary, Grand Floridian

The chapter begins by addressing the advantages and disadvantages of staying on-site in a Disney-owned hotel. We then discuss the key differences between Disney's value, moderate, and deluxe classes, and take a look at what specifically differentiates resorts within each class. Next we provide detailed reviews of all the Disney-owned resorts by resort class. The chapter finishes with alternatives to staying in a Disney-owned resort.

Stay at a Disney World Owned Resort

More than 20 Disney-owned resorts dot the 40+ square miles that comprise Walt Disney World.

Another dozen hotels owned by third parties are also on Disney World property. Most of these are located in the far southeast corner of Disney World near Disney Springs (formerly known as Downtown Disney). Third-party hotels much closer to the parks include the Swan and Dolphin, both about a 10-minute walk to Epcot and about 15 minutes away from Hollywood Studios. Another is Shades of Green, an armed forces recreation center with lodging for military personnel and their families, located right across the street from the Polynesian. Finally, the Four Seasons Resort Orlando, between Fort Wilderness and Port Orleans Riverside, is the only five-star resort on property, and it offers luxurious amenities (with pricing to match), including the best pool complex in all of

Disney World. There's more on these non-Disney owned hotels on Disney World property, and also off-site options, near the end of this chapter.

The Disney-owned resorts are usually more expensive than hotels operated by third parties, but they are also typically:

- Much more fun
- Much more convenient
- Much more "Disney"

The Disney-owned hotels offer unique perks that third-party operators could never dream of providing. The most advantageous perks include:

- The right to book dining ten days further out than non-Disney guests, which can be critical for high-demand meals like dinner at Be Our Guest Restaurant.
- The right to book FastPass+ reservations for key attractions beginning 60 days in advance of arrival. All non-Disney guests (except those staying at the Swan, Dolphin, Shades of Green, or who have booked a Disney Springs Area Resort hotel package through the Walt Disney World Travel Company) can book only up to 30 days before use—which may mean some attractions aren't available for pre-booking, and others may be available only at less convenient times.
- Free airport transport to and from your hotel via Disney's Magical Express.
- Free and frequent transport from your hotel to the parks, water-parks, and Disney Springs.
- Free parking at both your hotel and the parks.
- Access to the various Disney Dining Plans, which are a conve-nient budgeting tool if your family eats the way they are designed to feed you, and may save you a bit if your kids are younger than ten and you plan on several character meals.
- While it's easy to read a list of definable resort perks, it's more difficult to describe to a first-time visitor how it feels to be caught up in the immersive atmosphere of the Walt Disney World bubble. There are very few vacation destinations in the world that truly allow visitors to escape the harsh realities of life and instead be immersed in the fun and fantasy of a make-believe world. An inclusive on-property stay offers just that—from the time Magi-cal Express picks you up at the airport to the moment they drop you off again, there's nothing to worry about at Disney World.

The Perk We Rarely Recommend

Extra Magic Hours (EMH) are one of the best-known perks offered to guests staying at Disney-owned resorts, as well as at the Swan, Dolphin, Four Seasons (as of March 2018), Shades of Green, and the Disney Springs Area Resort hotels. EMH are early or late periods—most commonly at one park each day—when only guests at these hotels can ride the open Disney World attractions.

There are two varieties of Extra Magic Hours: morning and evening. Morning Extra Magic Hour is limited to one hour immediately before a park's regular open. Evening Extra Magic Hours are two hours long and begin immediately after a park's regular close. Most popular rides operate during both Morning and Evening Extra Magic, though the selection is wider during the evening. The participating attractions are indicated in Chapter 6. At least one park offers Extra Magic Hours virtually every day. Disney World seems to have settled on the following:

SUNDAY Hollywood Studios morning

MONDAY Animal Kingdom morning

TUESDAY Epcot evening

WEDNESDAY Magic Kingdom evening

THURSDAY Epcot morning

FRIDAY Magic Kingdom morning

SATURDAY Animal Kingdom morning

Seasonal or special events may alter the schedule, so check the park calendars for your dates.

So why is the park with such a great benefit so rarely recommended? Over 25,000 rooms on property have the opportunity to "take advantage of EMH" and every guest checking in will receive a Times Guide with the Extra Magic Hours schedule for the week clearly listed. "Up to two exclusive hours inside the park" sounds so overwhelmingly positive that the majority of the 75,000+ resort guests staying on property choose the park with the "extra magic". In turn, the park(s) with Extra Magic Hours are usually the busiest from 10am–7pm because they attract so many extra people. Simply choosing a different park avoids these resort guests.

In addition, Morning EMHs begin at 8am or even 7am, and it's awfully hard to get the family up, bathed, clothed, fed, and on the way in time to actually take advantage of the extra time. Arriving late to the park with EMH completely negates any benefit. Evening EMHs are often late at night, making it more difficult to arrive at a park the next day before open when waits are often much shorter. Moreover, because Hollywood Studios and Epcot offer so few rides during EMH, wait times at them are usually just as long during evening EMH as they are during the day, negating much of the benefit.

There are a few ways to make Extra Magic Hours work:

- If you actually arrive in time to take advantage of the full morning EMH and can park hop (hopping, and its cost, is explained in Chapter 8) away from it in the afternoon, then you can have a tremendous amount of success during the extra hour, particularly at Magic Kingdom. The morning EMH park will be busier than other days from 10am–7pm, and staying in the park during that time will lessen the benefit of the extra hour.

- Evening EMHs are less busy in the final hour, particularly at Magic Kingdom on nights its regular close is late. Those able to park hop to the evening EMH park at night and stay through EMH close often enjoy themselves if they begin with the "anytime attractions" we identify in Chapter 6.

It's easier to simply avoid the park with EMH and instead visit the less busy parks. You'll also be better rested and better able to enjoy the parks in the morning during a regular day.

How to Pick Your Disney Resort Hotel

The most important factor is budget. Standard value resort rooms range in price from $111/weeknight at the All-Stars during value season all the way up to $260/night at Art of Animation over Christmas. Standard rooms at the deluxes start at $369 at the Wilderness Lodge in the value season and go up to $934/night for a standard view at the Grand Floridian over the holidays. Larger rooms, better locations, and better views cost even more.

There are five different types of Disney resorts:

- **VALUE RESORTS** Lowest prices, smallest rooms, fewest amenities, no table service restaurants. (Value resort "Family Suite" rooms, available at Art of Animation and All-Star Music, come in at about twice the size of a standard room, but cost more than twice as much.)

- **MODERATE RESORTS** Middle-of-the-road prices, room sizes, and amenities. Table service restaurants at all but Port Orleans French Quarter and, during its refurb, Caribbean Beach.

- **DELUXE RESORTS** Highest prices, largest rooms, most amenities, plentiful dining.

- **DISNEY VACATION CLUB RESORTS** There are multiple deluxe-level room types: Studios are similar to deluxe rooms; Villas,

Bungalows at the Polynesian, Cabins at the Wilderness Lodge, and Treehouses at Saratoga Springs are larger and have full kitchens, and, at the two-bedroom and larger sizes, sleep eight people plus.

- **THE CAMPSITES AT DISNEY'S FORT WILDERNESS RESORT** Campgrounds for tent and RV campers (the Cabins at Fort Wilderness are grouped in the moderate class).

The vast majority of first time visitors stay in one of the first three resort types. The table below shows more detailed distinctions among them. Take heed of the notes at the bottom of the table...none of this is as easy as we'd all wish!

What You Can Expect by Price Class

Value Resorts	Moderate Resorts	Deluxe Resorts
Basic, small, ~260 square foot rooms	Good-sized ~314 square foot rooms	Lovely ~344-440 square foot rooms
Cost: $131–$179/night	Cost: $239–$256/night	Cost: $411-$695/night
Two full beds sleeping 4	Most have two queen beds, sleep 4	Most sleep 5 on two queens and a daybed
Split baths	Split baths	Most have split baths
No coffeemakers	Coffeemakers	Coffeemakers
Basic exteriors	Lovely exteriors	Lovely exteriors
Basic landscaping	Lovely landscaping	Lovely landscaping
Basic pools	Nice pools with slides	Great pools with slides
Food court	Food court, plus table servcie at most	Food court at most; table service at all
Basic dining choices	Better dining at most	Best dining for adults and kids
Hourly luggage service	Bell luggage service	Bell luggage service
Buses to parks	Buses to parks	Room service
Pizza delivery	Pizza delivery	Fun park transport at most, also buses
NOTES		
Excludes Family Suites, Cabins, DVC	Some rooms at CB and POR sleep 5	AKL and WL rooms sleep 4
Cost: Average Fall 2018 Price Season	Pirate rooms at CB have full beds	AKL has only bus transport to parks
Rooms can hold in addition one more child younger than 3 at check-in	POFQ has no table service	
	CS has room service	

Once you've set your budget, there's no one size fits all answer, but the material in this section, and detailed reviews later in this chapter, should help paint a clearer picture of which resort is the best fit for your group. The reviews focus on the standard room options at each of Disney's resorts, the Disney Vacation Club Studios, and also the popular family suites at Art of Animation and All-Star Music. For a more comprehensive look at the various Disney Vacation Club Villas and updates on the comings and goings of the resorts throughout the year, visit Dave's YOURFIRSTVISIT.NET.

Dave suggests picking hotels based first on overall kid appeal, mainly visual, and then on transportation convenience in a trip where the Magic Kingdom sees the most visits. Convenience to Epcot is prioritized second.

The chart, next page, is derived from this methodology, with Dave's top picks at the top and on the right. Josh ranks resorts on a wider set of criteria, but largely arrives at the same results.

RESORTS SORTED BY CONVENIENCE AND KID APPEAL

Bold= Value Resort, *Italic* = Moderate Resort, <u>Underline</u> = Deluxe Resort

CONVENIENCE

Very Convenient	<u>Grand Floridian</u>	<u>Contemporary</u>	<u>Polynesian</u>
Convenient	<u>BoardWalk Inn and Villas</u> <u>Beach Club and Villas</u> <u>Yacht Club</u>		<u>Wilderness Lodge and Villas</u> <u>Animal Kingdom Lodge and Villas</u> **Art of Animation** **Pop Century**
Somewhat Convenient	*Port Orleans Riverside* *Port Orleans French Quarter* <u>Old Key West</u> <u>Saratoga Springs</u> <u>Fort Wilderness</u>	*Caribbean Beach* *Coronado Springs*	**All-Star Sports** **All-Star Movies** **All-Star Music**
KID APPEAL	Slight Kid Appeal	Some Kid Appeal	Great Kid Appeal

VALUE RESORTS

Art of Animation and Pop Century are the top two choices.

The distinctive features of the value resorts are their tiny 260-square-foot standard rooms, their terrific—but garish to the eyes of many adults—kid appeal, and their short list of resort amenities compared to what you'll find at the moderates and deluxes. For instance, a lot of first-time visitors are surprised that most standard value rooms don't have coffeemakers. You also won't find many leisure activities or any table service restaurants at the values.

Standard value resort rooms sleep four in two full beds. You may also add a child younger than three in a crib. A refurb at Pop Century that kicked off in March 2017 adds rooms with one queen bed, one fold-down queen bed that sleeps two more, and even coffeemakers. These rooms fit the needs of many first-time family visitors looking for low prices, as they won't be spending much time in them other than sleeping.

Family Suites at the All-Star Music (520 square feet) and Art of Animation (565 square feet) resorts are much larger, sleep six, and include coffee-makers in every room, but cost more than double the price of standard rooms.

Dave favors Art of Animation with its oversized icons of some of Disney's most popular contemporary properties like *Cars* and *Finding Nemo* that are sure to excite kids. Rooms are bright and cheery, from the deep red clam-shell-themed chairs to the oversize Ariel motif on the shower curtain. Josh loves Animation's detailed theming, but all its standard rooms are located in the Little Mermaid section, which is a five to seven minute walk from the main building. This is less of a concern if you're already planning to stay in one of its more convenient family suites. Pop rooms are blander and more generic looking with less in-room decoration. Some families and couples may prefer the subdued room theming at Pop, while others favor the over-the-top décor at Animation. Otherwise, Pop standard rooms average $30 less per night than standard rooms at Art of Animation. Both resorts are newer than the All-Stars, provide dedicated bus service, offer elevated fare at their quick services, and feature more robust Disney-inspired theming.

The other value resorts—All-Star Sports, All-Star Music, and All-Star Movies—average about $15 per night less than Pop, but they're also significantly farther away from Magic Kingdom and Epcot. The three All-Stars sometimes share buses and none of their themes (except Movies) are overtly "Disney", though each features smaller character scenes around the resort. Finally, their food courts offer lower quality, less inspired fare.

MODERATE RESORTS
. . . .

Port Orleans French Quarter and Port Orleans Riverside are the best choices.

Standard moderate rooms are found in all moderates except the Cabins at Fort Wilderness. They cost, on average, about $100/night more than the least expensive standard value rooms and about $350/night less than a standard room at the Polynesian Village. Your extra $100/night buys you about 50 more square feet than value rooms, in addition to queen beds (except in Caribbean Beach's "Pirate Rooms"), double sinks (except in not-yet refurbed rooms at Coronado Springs), a coffee-maker, a table service restaurant (except at French Quarter and Caribbean Beach during its refurb), an indoor lounge (except at Caribbean Beach), a pool slide, and hot tubs. The moderates also provide the most cost-effective way to sleep five (in the Alligator Bayou section of Riverside and in many Caribbean Beach rooms) and the most cost-effective way to get a full kitchen in The Cabins at Disney's Fort Wilderness Resort. Compared to the deluxes, the moderates have limited dining options, no character meals, are less convenient to at least one theme park, and have far fewer services and amenities. Fortunately, living areas are more comparable in size to those in the deluxes than you might expect, especially deluxe resorts with smaller room sizes like those at the Animal Kingdom and Wilderness Lodges.

Major construction and/or room refurbishment is happening or expected in 2018 at each of the moderate resorts except the Cabins at Fort Wilderness. The impact, so far as we can tell, is minor except at Caribbean Beach. We are hesitant to recommend Caribbean Beach for any guests planning much dining at the hotel until permanent dining reopens there—perhaps in later 2018—as its temporary dining is barely adequate.

Of the moderates, all but Port Orleans French Quarter are large and spread out, with dozens of guest buildings spread out over hundreds of acres. All have multiple bus stops (including shared buses at POFQ). All have more amenities than the values, but fewer than the deluxes. Coronado Springs offers the most amenities, including a salon, gym, nightclub, a strong room service menu, and the largest hot tub on property. French Quarter offers the fewest, including no quiet pools, and no sit-down restaurant. Luckily, all those amenities and more are a short walk or boat ride away at Port Orleans Riverside.

Moderate resorts favor tranquility and a more sublime atmosphere when compared to the values, but don't offer the lushness and detail of the deluxes. This may translate to less overt kid appeal. There are no 50-foot-tall Mickey Mouse icons at the moderates, and other than some subtle references, nothing about them screams Disney World. Of the moderates, the vast majority of kids prefer Caribbean Beach Resort, with its beautiful white sand beaches, hammocks, and colorful guest houses. It also features a pirate-themed pool and play area that kids adore.

Our preference for Port Orleans French Quarter comes largely from its being so much easier to get around than any other moderate, and the relative ease in getting from it to the Magic Kingdom. Among the less convenient moderates, Port Orleans Riverside beats out Caribbean Beach because of its better transportation and it beats out Coronado Springs because of its more family-friendly atmosphere and dining. The temporary dining replacements make it hard for us to recommend Caribbean Beach.

(The Cabins at Fort Wilderness are so different than any other moderate that we refer you to the detailed review later in this chapter. However, we do not recommend them for first-time visitors.)

DELUXE RESORTS

The Wilderness Lodge, Polynesian Village, Contemporary, and Grand Floridian are the best choices.

Compared to other Walt Disney World options, the deluxe resorts are distinguished by having the:

- Most amenities, with the Contemporary and Grand Floridian at the top of this list.
- Nicest views, especially at the Contemporary, Polynesian, Grand Floridian, and Animal Kingdom Lodge.
- Best in-resort and nearby dining options, especially at the four Magic Kingdom-area resorts—the Contemporary, Polynesian, Grand Floridian, and Wilderness Lodge. The Epcot resorts—the BoardWalk Inn, Yacht Club, and Beach Club—have access to

many nearby restaurants, but most of them are undistinguished for either kids or parents. The restaurants in the Animal Kingdom Lodge are marvelous, but there's no character dining, and no easy access to more dining at other resorts.

- Best pools, especially at the Beach Club, Yacht Club, Polynesian Village, Wilderness Lodge, and Animal Kingdom Lodge.

- Best transportation, especially at the Contemporary, Polynesian, and Grand Floridian that share the resort monorail to the Magic Kingdom. The Polynesian is most convenient overall. It has resort monorail and boat access to Magic Kingdom, and it's also possible to walk from the Polynesian to the Transportation and Ticket Center (TTC) to catch the Epcot monorail, which eliminates the lengthy monorail ride to the TTC before then having to switch monorails. The Contemporary is just a ten minute walk away from the Magic Kingdom, making it most convenient for a Magic-Kingdom-centric vacation. The Beach Club, located just a five minute walk or boat ride away from Epcot's International Gateway entrance, is the most convenient for an Epcot-centric vacation, particularly during the Food and Wine Festival in the fall.

- Largest standard rooms, with those in the monorail resorts the largest, and those at the Wilderness and Animal Kingdom Lodges the smallest.

- Highest prices for standard rooms, with the monorail resorts the highest, and Wilderness and Animal Kingdom Lodges the lowest.

- Mixed kid appeal, with the Wilderness Lodge and Animal Kingdom Lodge the highest, the Polynesian next, and the Yacht Club and BoardWalk Inn the lowest.

As perhaps is clear by now, there are much bigger differences across the deluxes than in the other price classes. The detailed reviews later in this chapter cover these differences.

In 2018, Disney World made a new perk available to those booking "signature" rooms at the deluxes. Signature rooms are Disney's "club" level rooms—what most others call "concierge" rooms—and also its deluxe-level suites, and the Bungalows at the Polynesian and Cascade Cabins at the Wilderness Lodge. Those booking these already expensive rooms can, for an added $50/person/day (minimum of three days) reserve three additional FastPass+ per day beginning 90 days before their departure date, as well as special seating at an evening show per day. This new offering will be relevant to only a few, so we won't refer to it much in this book, but for those who can afford it, the ability to get six pre-booked FastPass+ per day, three of them bookable before most others have the chance to book their FastPass+, has the promise of real value.

We particularly recommend the Polynesian which combines kid-and adult-pleasing South Seas theming with large rooms, great dining for both kids and adults, and a terrific pair of pools. It also has the most convenient location for trips particularly focused on Magic Kingdom and Epcot. We also recommend the Wilderness Lodge. The overall architecture—especially the lobby—is stunning. Its location across Bay Lake puts it a fun boat ride or just a short bus ride to Magic Kingdom. It offers one of the most family-friendly restaurants in Whispering Canyon Café. Artist Point is a delightful Northwest-inspired signature restaurant away from the hustle and bustle of the monorail resorts. And Territory Lounge, with terrific Northwest beer on draft and a menu that features appetizers that come out of the kitchen it shares with Artist Point, is among the best bars on property. The main pool is fantastically themed and there's even a geyser that erupts throughout the day near the great new outdoor bar and grill, Geyser Point. The second pool, the newly rebuilt Boulder Ridge Cove, is also delightful. One qualifier—rooms are smaller than at most other deluxes, but prices are in turn lower.

Among the rest, Beach Club is the best choice for an Epcot-focused visit—which most first visits aren't. It's closer to Epcot and less uppity than neighboring Yacht Club. It also shares with the Yacht Club the best pool complex at a Disney-owned resort on property (the pools at the Four Seasons are the best overall on-property pool complex) and is more convenient to the limited Epcot resort quick service dining.

Value Resort Reviews

DISNEY'S ART OF ANIMATION RESORT

Disney's Art of Animation Resort ("AofA") is themed on four wildly popular Disney animated films—*Cars*, *The Lion King*, *Finding Nemo*, and *The Little Mermaid*. Like Disney's other value resorts, this theming is partly achieved with larger-than-life sculptures, but much more than the other values, the theming is also suffused into the landscape and into the rooms themselves. This makes it the most "Disney" of any Disney World hotel, wonderfully so to kids, and unrelentingly and garishly so to some adults. In late 2017, AofA became dog-friendly as part of a year-long pilot program.

You'll find at AofA four lodging areas, each with two or three buildings framed around one of the movies, and two distinct room types. Family Suites sleeping six are found in the Cars, Lion King, and Finding Nemo areas, and standard rooms similar to those at the other value resorts (except for their much deeper Disney theming) are in the more distant

Little Mermaid area. Found in Animation Hall near the entrance to the resort are dining, shops, and guest services. The main "Big Blue" pool, just outside Animation Hall, is the best pool among the values. You'll find two smaller pools as well—a tiny one in the Cars area, and a larger one in the Little Mermaid section.

All transport to theme parks, water parks, and Disney Springs is via bus. AofA is one of only two resorts at Walt Disney World with one bus stop and no shared buses, making total transit time shorter—nearby Pop Century is the other. Because at full capacity AofA holds fewer people than Pop does, AofA is the clear convenience winner among the values. AofA (and Pop Century) are just next to and south of the Epcot Area resort Caribbean Beach, but Disney way-finding identifies them as ESPN Wide World of Sports Area resorts. Regardless, these are the two most centrally-located of Disney's value resorts, though neither is particularly close to anything.

AofA's rich and detailed theming gives it the highest kid appeal, by far, among the values, and perhaps of any Disney World resort—at least for kids into one the movies it showcases. As with all the values, adult appeal is mixed, with some finding it fun, and others garish.

At AofA, there are two very different room types in four very different themed areas.

One room type is standard rooms sleeping four on two full beds (almost identical except in decoration to what you'll find at the other value resorts except for newly refurbed rooms at Pop Century). These are all found in

Disney's Art of Animation Resort
Little Mermaid Room   ~260 Square Feet

the Little Mermaid area, which is also the farthest area from the main pool, Animation Hall, and bus stops. At about 260 square feet, these standard rooms may be the smallest four-person rooms you will ever see in the U.S. outside of historic center-city hotels. Besides the two full beds, you'll find in the sleeping area a table and two chairs, a TV/dresser combo, and a mini-fridge. There are no coffee-makers in these standard rooms. In the divided bath, you'll find a clothes hanging area, hair dryer, and single sink separated from the rest of the room by a fabric curtain. Next to this you'll find the toilet and tub in their own room. Unlike the other value resorts, which have little room theming, the *Little Mermaid* gang is quite present in these rooms. No rooms at Art of Animation have balconies. All Little Mermaid rooms are accessed from exterior corridors.

The rest of the rooms at AofA are Family Suites, found in three themed areas—Cars, Finding Nemo, and the Lion King. (No standard rooms are in these three areas, and no family suites are in the Little Mermaid area.) AofA Family Suites sleep six in more than twice the area of standard rooms, and contain a living room with a couch that folds out into a full bed, a dining area with a full bed that folds down, a master bedroom with a queen, two full baths (one connected to the master bedroom) and a kitchenette with a mini-fridge, microwave, and coffee-maker. Each of these rooms is deeply themed to its respective movie. Family Suites are accessed via interior corridors—more comfortable than exterior ones, but potentially more noisy.

Dining is in Animation Hall at the food court, Landscape of Flavors, the most ambitious of Disney's food courts in terms of adventuresome menus and fresh preparation. (Josh finds it unreliable and easily over-pressed by guests—if you do too, the food court at Pop Century is just over the bridge between the two resorts.) There's no indoor bar, but you'll find an outdoor bar by the main pool. There is no table service restaurant at any value, nor any character meals.

Amenities at the resort include movies, jogging trails, playgrounds, and an arcade. Art of Animation and Pop Century are the only value resorts on a lake, but the only water recreation available is bird-watching.

At AofA there are no upcharges for views, but Finding Nemo suites are more expensive than Cars or Lion King suites, because of their convenience.

Standard four-person rooms average $161/night during the 2018 Value season, $207/night during the Regular season, $223/night during the Summer season, and $179 a night during the Fall season. These prices average about $30 per night than Pop Century, and around $45 more per night than the All-Stars.

Six-person Lion King and Cars family suites average $371/night during the 2018 Value season, $453/night during the Regular season,

Disney's Art of Animation Resort
Family Suite Floor Plan ~565 Square Feet

$474/night during the Summer season, and $400 a night during the Fall season. These prices average about $125 per night more than the only other value resort family suites at All-Star Music. Nemo suites average $25 more per night.

DISNEY'S POP CENTURY RESORT

Disney's Pop Century Resort ("Pop") is themed around the toys, cultural icons, and Disney characters popular in the second half of the twentieth century. Think larger-than-life icons of Roger Rabbit, yo-yos, and a Mickey phone with Mickey, too. Pop has five themed lodging areas, each with one to three buildings framed around one decade—the 50s, 60s, 70s, 80s, and one lonely building representing the 90s. All this is more fun than it sounds, and the icons of characters—Roger Rabbit, Mickey, Mowgli and Balou, Lady and Tramp—add Disney sparkle. Found in Classic Hall near the entrance to the resort are dining, shops, and guest services. The main Hippy Dippy Pool is just outside Classic Hall. You'll find two additional, smaller—but still plenty big—pools, the Bowling Pin pool in the 50s area, and the Computer Pool in the 80s and 90s area. Among these three pools, Pop has the largest area of pool and sunbathing space of any value.

All transport to theme parks, water parks, and Disney Springs is via bus. Pop is one of only two resorts at Walt Disney World with one bus stop and no shared buses, making total transit time shorter (nearby AofA is the other). Because at full capacity AofA holds fewer people than Pop does, it is the convenience winner among the values, with Pop a close second. Pop is just next to and south of the Epcot Area resort Caribbean Beach, but Disney way-finding identifies it as an ESPN Wide World of Sports Area resort. Regardless, Pop and AofA are the two most centrally-located of Disney's value resorts, though neither is particularly close to anything.

Not as themed as Art of Animation, especially in the rooms, but more Disney than any of the All-Star resorts except All-Star Movies, Pop has high kid appeal, and is a little less busy to parental eyes than AofA.

Not-yet-refurbed standard rooms at Pop sleep four on two full beds (almost identical to what you'll find in the standard rooms at the other value resorts). At about 260 square feet, these standard rooms may be the smallest four-person rooms you will ever stay in. Besides the two full beds, you'll find in the sleeping area a table and two chairs, a TV/ dresser combo, and a mini-fridge. There are no coffee-makers in these standard rooms. In the divided bath, you'll find a clothes hanging area, hair dryer, and single sink separated from the rest of the room by a fabric curtain. Next to this you'll find the toilet and tub in their own room. The rooms themselves have next to no theming. No rooms at Pop have balconies, and all are accessed from exterior corridors.

A major room refurb project that kicked off at Pop Century in March 2017 should be complete in later 2018. At press time, five of Pop's ten buildings have completed their refurb, and more have started. Refurbed standard rooms include a fixed queen bed, a fold-down queen bed that

Disney's Pop Century Resort
Refurbed Room Floor Plan ~260 Square Feet

eliminates the dining table when it is down, a sliding solid door separating the sink area from the living space of the room, and a coffeemaker. The floor plan shows one of these refurbed rooms. We expect some daytime construction noise, but nothing major. Our sites easyWDW.com and yourfirstvisit.net will have updates as this project unfolds.

Dining is in Classic Hall at the food court Everything Pop. In terms of size and menu, Everything Pop is well above average among the values. There's no indoor bar, but you'll find an outdoor bar by the main pool. There is no table service restaurant at any value, nor any character meals.

Amenities include movies, jogging trails, playgrounds, and an arcade. Art of Animation and Pop Century are the only value resorts on a lake, but the only water recreation available is bird-watching.

At Pop, you can pay extra for "preferred" rooms closer to Classic Hall and for pool views. Standard view, non-preferred four-person rooms average $141/night during the 2018 Value season, $170/night during the Regular season, $181/night during the Summer season, and $151 per night during the Fall season. These prices average about $30 per night less than AofA, and around $15 more per night than the All-Stars.

DISNEY'S ALL-STAR MOVIES RESORT

Disney's All-Star Movies Resort ("Movies") is themed around five movies—*Toy Story, The Mighty Ducks, Fantasia, The Love Bug,* and *101 Dalmatians*—with two accommodation buildings in each theme. These films are represented by much-larger-than-life icons of characters and objects from them. Found in Cinema Hall near the entrance to the resort are dining, shops, and guest services. The main Fantasia Pool is just outside Cinema Hall. You'll find a smaller—but still plenty big—hockey-themed pool in the Mighty Ducks area.

All transport to theme parks, water parks, and Disney Springs is via bus. At lower demand times, Movies shares buses (except to Magic Kingdom) with sister resorts All-Star Music and All-Star Sports. Shared buses stop at Sports first and Movies last—which at times has meant the buses were filled by the time they got to Movies, making this resort the least convenient of the three. The All-Star resorts are Animal Kingdom Area resorts, and are the least conveniently located of the values.

Movies is much more Disney-themed than the other All-Stars, but does not have so rich a set of kid-appealing movies in its themes as AofA, nor are many of its movies as widely kid appealing as the Disney characters and the toys at Pop. The rooms themselves have only the lightest theming related to their area. Adults may find the theming garish, or may warm to the represented movies.

Standard rooms at Movies sleep four on two full beds (almost identical to the standard rooms at the other value resorts, except for newly refurbed rooms at Pop Century). At about 260 square feet, these standard rooms are very, very small. Besides the two full beds, you'll find in the sleeping area a table and two chairs, a TV/dresser combo, and a mini-fridge. There are no coffee-makers in these standard rooms. In the divided bath, you'll find a clothes hanging area, hair dryer, and single sink separated from the rest of the room by a fabric curtain. Next to this you'll find the toilet and tub in their own room. No rooms at Movies have balconies, and all are accessed from exterior corridors.

Dining is in Cinema Hall at the World Premiere food court. Movies has the largest food court among the All-Stars, and is average among the values. The bar is set in the exterior wall between the food court and the pool, and serves guests from both areas. There is no table service restaurant at any value, nor any character meals.

Amenities available at the resort include movies, jogging trails, playgrounds, and an arcade.

At Movies, you can pay extra for "preferred" rooms closer to Cinema Hall. Non-preferred rooms average $124/night during the 2018 Value season, $153/night during the Regular season, $170/night during the Summer season, and $131 a night during the Fall season. These prices are the same as similar rooms at the other All-Stars, are on average about $45 per night less expensive than AofA, and around $15 less per night than Pop.

Disney's All-Star Movies Resort
Standard Room Floor Plan ~260 Square Feet

DISNEY'S ALL-STAR SPORTS RESORT

Disney's All-Star Sports Resort ("Sports") is themed around five sports—baseball, basketball, tennis, football, surfing—with two accommodation buildings in each theme. These sports are represented by much-larger-than-life icons of sports objects, and by the spaces between the two buildings themed to the playing field of the respective sport. Dining, shops, and guest services are in Stadium Hall near the resort entrance. The main Surf's Up pool is outside Stadium Hall. You'll find a smaller—but still plenty big—baseball field-themed pool in the baseball area.

All transport to theme parks, water parks, and Disney Springs is via bus. At lower demand times, Sports shares buses (except to Magic Kingdom) with sister resorts All-Star Music and All-Star Movies. Shared buses stop at Sports first and Movies last—which means that Sports guests are most likely to get a seat, making Sports the most convenient of the All-Stars, and of average convenience among the values. The All-Star resorts are Animal Kingdom Area resorts, and are the least conveniently located of the values.

Sports appeals to kids interested in its specific themes, but is otherwise thin on general kid appeal. The rooms themselves have only the lightest theming related to their area. Adults may find the theming garish, or may warm to the represented sports. All the All-Stars can be overrun with kids competing in events at ESPN Wide World of Sports, and this seems most common at Sports.

Standard rooms at Sports sleep four on two full beds in rooms pretty much identical to what you'll find at the other All-Stars. At about 260

Disney's All-Star Sports Resort
Standard Room Floor Plan ~260 Square Feet

square feet, these standard rooms are teeny but adequate for sleeping. Besides the two full beds, you'll find in the sleeping area a table and two chairs, a TV/dresser combo, and a mini-fridge. There are no coffee-makers in these rooms. In the divided bath, you'll find a clothes hanging area, hair dryer, and single sink separated from the rest of the room by a fabric curtain. Next to this you'll find the toilet and tub in their own room. No rooms at Sports have balconies, and all are accessed from exterior corridors.

Dining is in Stadium Hall at the End Zone food court. Recently renovated, this space is still too small for the guests it tries to serve, and is below average among the values. The bar is set in the exterior wall between the food court and the pool, and serves guests from both areas. There is no table service restaurant at any value, nor any character meals.

Amenities available at the resort include movies, jogging trails, playgrounds, and an arcade.

At Sports, you can pay extra for "preferred" rooms closer to Stadium Hall. Non-preferred rooms average $124/night during the 2018 Value season, $153/night during the Regular season, $170/night during the Summer season, and $131 a night during the Fall season. These prices are the same as similar rooms at the other All-Stars, are on average about $45 per night less expensive than AofA, and around $15 less per night than Pop.

DISNEY'S ALL-STAR MUSIC RESORT

Disney's All-Star Music Resort ("Music") is themed around five musical genres—calypso, jazz, Broadway, rock, and country, with two accommodation buildings in each theme. These genres are represented by much-larger-than-life icons of musical instruments and other objects related to the theme, e.g., cowboy boots in the country music area, and by a bit of theming here and there of the spaces between the two buildings to the musical genre. Found in Melody Hall near the entrance to the resort are dining, shops, and guest services. The main Guitar pool is just outside Melody Hall. You'll find a smaller—but still plenty big—piano-themed pool deeper in the resort.

All transport to theme parks, water parks, and Disney Springs is via bus. At lower demand times, Music shares buses (except to Magic Kingdom) with sister resorts All-Star Movies and All-Star Sports. Shared buses stop at Sports first and Movies last—which means that Music guest are less likely than Sports guests to get a seat, but more likely than Movies guests. This makes Music of average convenience among the All-Stars, and of below-average convenience among the values. The

All-Star resorts are Animal Kingdom Area resorts, and are the least conveniently located of the values.

Music appeals to kids interested in its specific themes, but is otherwise quite thin on general kid appeal. The rooms themselves have only the lightest theming related to their area. Adults will find it the loveliest of the values, and its overall layout the easiest to understand and navigate.

Music has two very different room types: standard four-person rooms found in all its themed areas, and six-person family suites in the Calypso and Jazz areas.

Standard rooms at Music sleep four on two full beds in rooms pretty much identical to what you'll find at the other All-Stars. At about 260 square feet, these standard rooms are really small but adequate for sleeping. Besides the two full beds, you'll find in the sleeping area a table and two chairs, a TV/dresser combo, and a mini-fridge. There are no coffee-makers in these standard rooms. In the divided bath, you'll find a clothes hanging area, hair dryer, and single sink separated from the rest of the room by a fabric curtain. Next to this you'll find the toilet and tub in their own room. No rooms at Music have balconies, and all are accessed from exterior corridors.

Family Suites at Music sleep six in twice the area of standard rooms, and contain a living room with three furniture items that fold out into beds—a couch that folds out into a full, and a chair and an ottoman that each fold out into twins. It also has a master bedroom with a queen and two full baths, each accessible to anyone in the room, plus a kitchenette with a mini-fridge, microwave, and coffee-maker. These rooms are not nearly

Disney's All-Star Music Resort
Standard Room Floor Plan ~260 Square Feet

as much fun as the suites at AofA, and the fold-out beds are not nearly as comfortable for older/heavier guests. But some families will appreciate the more flexible number of sleeping spots, and others the fact that these suites are on average $125 per night less expensive than those at AofA.

Dining is in Melody Hall at the Intermission food court. In late 2017, Intermission began an experiment in which some menu items are ordered at the cashier stations, rather than at the food prep stations, and when they are ready, signaled for pick-up via a pager. This promising approach, a version of which is common at deluxe counter services, limits congestion in the food-ordering area, at the cost of some members of your party (i.e., those ordering the items available only directly at the prep stations) potentially having their food much earlier than others. The bar is set in the exterior wall between the food court and the pool, and serves guests from both areas. There is no table service restaurant at any value, nor any character meals.

Disney's All-Star Music Resort
Family Suite Floor Plan ~520 Square Feet

Amenities available at the resort include movies, jogging trails, playgrounds, and an arcade.

At Music, you can pay extra for "preferred" standard rooms closer to Melody Hall. Non-preferred standard rooms average $124/night during the 2018 Value season, $153/night during the Regular season, $170/night during the Summer season, and $131 a night during the Fall season. These prices are the same as similar rooms at the other All-Stars, are on average about $45 per night less expensive than AofA, and around $15 less per night than Pop.

Family Suites at Music are all the same cost, whether in Jazz or Calypso. Family Suites average $284/night during the 2018 Value season, $347/night during the Regular season, $383/night during the Summer season, and $301 a night during the Fall season. These suites average about $125 less per night than at AofA.

Moderate Resort Reviews

DISNEY'S PORT ORLEANS FRENCH QUARTER RESORT

Disney's Port Orleans French Quarter Resort ("POFQ") is one of two moderates with "Port Orleans" in the name—the other is Port Orleans Riverside Resort. Some mistakenly call these one resort. The only point of commonality most guests will ever notice is that guests at either are welcome to share the other's pools. The confusion comes from Disney shutting down, more than a decade ago, the table service restaurant and bike rentals at what was then known as Port Orleans Resort, and is now POFQ, and then renaming both resorts as Port Orleans—indicating to guests that these amenities weren't really missing, but just more distant, at Port Orleans Riverside, part of the same resort now.

Disney does not much bother with this distinction any more—other than making it clear to guests that they are welcome to partake in everything offered at both. It turns out that despite the missing amenities at Port Orleans French Quarter, it is the most highly valued of the Disney moderates—which is why alone among the moderates it is rarely included in Disney's discounts and other special offers.

POFQ has as its theme New Orleans and Mardi Gras, combining lacy wrought iron, lovely gardens, and cobblestoned streets. Mardi Gras figures and decorations are scattered about, especially near the main pool. POFQ has half as many rooms as Port Orleans Riverside and Coronado Springs, and two-thirds as many as Caribbean Beach, the other traditional moderates, and has—with no lake or river in the middle—a more compact footprint for those rooms. As a result, it is, by far, the easiest moderate to get around. It has no separate areas for its seven accommodations buildings, though you'll see North Quarter and South Quarter signage meant to help you find your building. Near the entrance at the center is dining, shops, and guest services in the Port Orleans Square area. The only pool, the Mardi-Gras themed Doubloon Lagoon, is just steps away, and the sole bus stop is right out front. One pool may seem like not enough, but the main pool area at POFQ has 65% of the area of Port Orleans Riverside's main pool, but serves only half as many rooms. A terrific kids splash pool was added in 2016.

All transport to theme parks and water parks is via buses. POFQ sometimes shares buses (except to the Magic Kingdom) with Riverside, but the single bus stop on the MK route makes it the most convenient of the moderates. Disney Springs is accessible by both boat and bus. POFQ, like Riverside, is labeled as a Disney Springs Area Resort in Disney's way-finding material, but is more centrally located than that implies. The Magic Kingdom, Epcot, and Disney's Hollywood Studios are all close.

There's no special kid appeal at POFQ, and in fact the Mardi Gras theming—including, for example, an enormous depiction of a sea serpent at the pool—wigs some kids out. But POFQ is the loveliest and most romantic of the moderates, and that, when combined with the ease of getting around and to the parks, makes it a great favorite of adults and of returning visitors among the moderates.

Rooms at POFQ are typical of those at the traditional moderates. They sleep four on two queens in about 314 square feet, and all come with a table and two chairs, a dresser/mini-fridge, coffee-maker, hair-dryer,

Disney's Port Orleans French Quarter Resort
Standard Room Floor Plan ~314 Square Feet

and a divided, family-friendly bath. In the bath, the two sinks and closet/dressing area are shielded from the sleeping part of the room by a curtain, and the tub and toilet have their own room. All buildings have elevators. No rooms have balconies. All rooms are accessed from exterior corridors.

In January 2018, POFQ began a room refurb project. Refurbed rooms include wooden floors, added power points, and larger TVs. At press time, one of POFQ's seven buildings has completed this refurb, and another has begun. The refurb activity has little impact on POFQ guests.

The only dining at POFQ is at the food court Sassagoula Floatworks Food Company, which, after its late 2016 refurb, is well above average among the moderates, and has a nice sprinkling of themed offerings—for example, beignets, Po Boys, jambalaya, and BBQ ribs served with collard greens. (You can, of course, walk to the table service Boatwright's at Riverside.) The indoor bar, the Scat Cats Lounge, is not as rollicking as the River Roost Lounge at Riverside, but one should always have the option to not rollick. There are no character meals.

Amenities are thinner than at the other moderates, although most that are missing are nearby at Riverside. On site, you'll find (besides the pool) an arcade, playground, and movies. (Some nights, movies are at Riverside or POFQ, but not both.)

At POFQ there are no "preferred" rooms—itself an indication of how easy it is to get around for a moderate—but you can still pay extra for king beds, for garden views, for pool views, and for water views. Standard view rooms average $233/night during the 2018 Value season, $273/night during the Regular season, $266/night during the Summer season, and $256 a night during the Fall season. Prices are the same as Port Orleans Riverside and typically about $20-$30/night more than Caribbean Beach and Coronado Springs.

DISNEY'S PORT ORLEANS RIVERSIDE RESORT

Disney's Port Orleans Riverside Resort ("POR") is one of two moderates with "Port Orleans" in the name—the other is Port Orleans French Quarter. Some mistakenly call these one resort. The only point of commonality most guests will ever notice is that guests at either are welcome to share the other's pools and other amenities.

POR has as its theme the 19th century American South, particularly the bayou and riverine areas of Louisiana and Mississippi. Rooms in the massive resort are in two areas, Magnolia Bend, with four large buildings meant to be reminiscent of plantation mansions, and Alligator Bayou, with many smaller buildings meant to evoke a more rural feel. Found in the Sassagoula Steamboat Company area near the entrance to the resort are dining, shops, and guest services. The main pool, located on a central island, has a bit of saw-mill theming, and is average among moderate pools. Testifying to the sprawl of the resort and the distance of many rooms from Ol' Man Island, you'll find five additional smaller pools around the resort. The resort proper has four bus stops, but sometimes shares buses (except to the Magic Kingdom) with nearby Port Orleans French Quarter, making it less convenient than either Coronado Springs or Port Orleans French Quarter. The overall accommodations footprint of POR is larger than that of Coronado Springs, but, because it has no lake, the main services at POR are more central than those at Coronado Springs. In late 2017, POR became dog-friendly as part of a year-long pilot program.

All transport to theme parks and water parks is via bus. Disney Springs is accessible by both boat and bus. POR is labeled as a Disney Springs Area Resort in Disney's way-finding material, but is more centrally located than that implies. Before the Animal Kingdom and Blizzard Beach opened, the two Port Orleans Resorts were in fact the most centrally located moderates, and the Magic Kingdom, Epcot, and Disney's Hollywood Studios are still all close—at least after the buses finally get out of the resort. The resort itself is massive, and some rooms are a hike from the main services, and others from the main pool...some from both.

There's no special kid appeal at POR compared to that at Caribbean Beach, and no special adult appeal compared to that at Coronado Springs and POFQ. But even so, POR is likely the best-loved, most frequently recommended, and most loyally defended of all the moderate resorts.

Disney's Port Orleans Riverside Resort
Standard Room Floor Plan ~314 Square Feet

There are three very different room types at POR. All are about the same size as those at the other traditional moderates, about 314 square feet, and all come with a table and two chairs, a dresser/TV/mini-fridge combo, coffee-maker, hair-dryer, and a divided, family-friendly bath. In the bath, the two sinks and closet/dressing area are shielded from the sleeping part of the room by a curtain, and the tub and toilet have their own room. The two story buildings in Alligator Bayou have no elevators, but the taller Magnolia Bend buildings do. No rooms have balconies. All rooms are accessed from exterior corridors.

The Alligator Bayou section of POR is one of only two areas at Disney World with traditional moderate rooms that sleep five—two each in two queens, and the fifth in a small murphy bed (about 66 inches long by 31 inches wide, and meant for a kid ten or younger) that folds down beneath the TV. (Caribbean Beach is the other.)

Rooms in half the Magnolia Bend section have "Royal" theming, and are more expensive. These rooms sleep 4 in two queens, and have much prince and (especially) princess detail, including a lovely headboard light show based on the *Princess and the Frog* triggered by an easy-to-miss button on the side.

Rooms in the other half of Magnolia Bend also sleep 4 in two queens, but do not have the special royal theming—nor its extra cost. They are also largely more convenient than the Royal Rooms, and, if you don't need the fifth sleeping spot, more livable than the Alligator Bend rooms.

We expect rooms at POR to be refurbed in the second half of 2018 and in 2019, beginning in Alligator Bayou. Details are not clear, but the refurb likely will include larger TVs, more power points, and wooden floors. We expect the refurb to have little impact on POR guests.

Dining is at Sassagoula Steamboat Company, with a food court that's average among the moderates and a table service restaurant, Boatwright's Dining Hall, that's also average. The food court is too small for the crowds it faces, but has some menu items that reflect its theming—e.g., a Swamp burger, a Cajun chicken sandwich, fried green tomatoes, etc. The indoor bar, the River Roost Lounge, has a widely loved family-friendly show from "Ye Haa" Bob Jackson most Wednesday through Saturday evenings. There's also a bar at the main pool. There are no character meals.

Amenities available at the resort include movies, campfires, bike rental, fishing, jogging trails, playgrounds, and an arcade. (Some nights, movies are at Riverside or POFQ, but not both.) The main pool is far too small for the resort, and can't fit everyone who would like to be there.

At POR you can pay more for preferred locations that are a closer walk to the Sassagoula Steamboat Company, for the Royal rooms, for king beds, for garden views, and for water views. Standard view, non-preferred rooms average $233/night during the 2018 Value season, $273/night during the Regular season, $266/night during the Summer season, and $256 a night during the Fall season. Prices are the same as POFQ and typically about $20-$30/night more than Caribbean Beach and Coronado Springs.

DISNEY'S CARIBBEAN BEACH RESORT

Disney's Caribbean Beach Resort ("CB") is themed around Caribbean islands, their beaches, and the pirates who once voyaged among them. Rooms in the massive resort are found in five "villages" ringing a lake, all named after Caribbean destinations: Trinidad North, Trinidad South, Martinique, Aruba, and Jamaica. Each colorful village has palm-tree lined beaches, and each has its own pool and bus stop. The central Centertown area includes another bus stop and the main pool at the resort, the pirate-themed Fuentes del Morro Pool—the best pool of the Disney World moderate resorts.

Six pools and six bus stops may sound like an abundance of riches. They are not. Rather, there are this many pools and bus stops because of design flaws that make CB large and hard to get around—especially for guests staying at Trinidad South. All transport to theme parks, water parks, and Disney Springs is via buses. Because of the number of required bus stops, CB is not particularly convenient to anywhere, but is closest to Disney's Hollywood Studios and Epcot.

Caribbean Beach entered a refurb in May 2017 that may eventually solve some of its issues, but in the meantime makes for problems. Disney has closed the table service restaurant, food court, bar, and gift shop, and replaced some of their services with temporary facilities also in the same central area of the resort until a new set of permanent offerings is built and open. Moreover, there's been demolition and/or rebuilding at the resort, including Old Port Royale, Barbados, part of Martinique, and we expect, the Custom House.

Based on our visits since the temporary facilities here opened, we can't recommend Caribbean Beach to anyone expecting to dine much at the resort. Breakfast is fine, lunch weak, and dinner is adequate during good weather, but over-pressed during heavy rain, not uncommon in Florida. The bar replacement is adequate, and the gift shop replacement very weak. Permanent improvements may be in place by late 2018.

Many rooms at CB have Disney theming—a light touch in most, and deep pirate theming in the distant (and overly expensive) Trinidad South area. The combination of Disney-themed rooms, sparkling beaches, bright colors, swaying palms, and the pirate-themed main pool give CB high kid appeal among the moderates. Adults like most of this, too, but can be frustrated by the weak temporary amenities, walking distances, and all the bus stops.

There are three types of standard rooms at CB, all about 314 square feet: Pirate-themed rooms that sleep four on two full beds, and two types of non-Pirate rooms—rooms that sleep four on two queens, and rooms that sleep five on two queens and a murphy bed under the TV that's about 30 inches wide by 64 inches long. (The floor plan, below, depicts a five person room.)

Rooms come with a table and two chairs, a dresser/TV/mini-fridge combo, coffee-maker, hair-dryer, a smaller storage chest in four-person rooms, and a divided, family-friendly bath. In the bath, the sinks and closet/dressing area are shielded from the rest of the room by a curtain in the Pirate rooms and sliding solid doors in all other rooms, and the tub and toilet have their own room. The two-story buildings that hold these rooms have no elevators, and no rooms have balconies. All rooms are accessed from exterior corridors.

During construction, dining is available at an air-conditioned buffet tent in Centertown at breakfast and dinner, from a couple of all-day food trucks, and from room service. Snacks and refrigerated food are available from small markets in converted guest rooms in Jamaica, Aruba, and Martinique. More specifically,

- Breakfast is fine. Supplies for cold in-room dining are easily available, and the hot buffet and food truck offerings are adequate.
- Lunch is weak. Both hot and cold offerings are limited. The quality of the hot food is good, but options and capacity are each slim. Cold food is widely available in limited options and while

Disney's Caribbean Beach Resort
Five Person Room Floor Plan ~314 Square Feet

the fruits and salads are OK, the cold sandwiches are weak.

- Dinner is adequate for a meal or two. Between the buffet, food truck, room service, and other options, most will find something to like, but the offerings at each option are limited, and capacity is tight except at the buffet.

Heavy rain can impede Disney's ability to supply the buffet, force the closure of the food trucks, and overwhelm room service.

Other amenities include movies, campfires, bike rental, fishing, a Pirate Adventure cruise, great jogging trails, and playgrounds. With the elimination in 2017 of more than 550 rooms here, the main pirate-themed pool now more commonly fits everyone who would like to be there.

At CB, you can pay more for preferred locations that are closer to Centertown, for the Pirate rooms that are quite a hike and still have full beds, for king beds, and for water views. Standard view, non-preferred rooms average $198/night during the 2018 Value season, $236/night during the Regular season, $234/night during the Summer season, and $237 a night during the Fall season. This is on average about $20-$30/night less than POR and POFQ.

When Caribbean Beach comes out of this refurb in later 2018, we expect it to be much more livable than during its pre-refurb sprawl. However, until then, we would not stay here if we planned to dine much at the resort.

DISNEY'S CORONADO SPRINGS RESORT

Disney's Coronado Springs Resort's ("CS") theme is based on the American Southwest, Spanish-colonial Mexico, and the architectural remnants of Mesoamerican civilizations. Rooms in the massive resort are found in three areas surrounding a lake: the Casitas, elegant colonnaded three- and four-story buildings; the Ranchos, a sharply contrasting, desert-inspired area; and the Cabanas, a beach-house themed area with beaches, too—fewer than at Caribbean Beach, but more than at any other moderate. The El Centro area, between the Casitas and Cabanas, includes dining, shopping, and guest services, and leads to the Coronado Springs Convention Center. Away from El Centro, and near the actual center of the resort—and most convenient to the Cabanas and Ranchos—is the Mesoamerican-themed main pool, the Lost City of Cibola, in the Dig Site area, the second-best pool among the moderates. Each of the three room areas has its own smaller pool (the Casitas pool is the only lap pool at Disney World), as well as a bus stop. A fourth bus stop is at El Centro.

All transport to theme parks, water parks, and Disney Springs is via buses (or your rental car). CS is labeled as an Animal Kingdom Area

Resort in Disney's way-finding material, but is in fact the most centrally-located of all the moderate resorts. This, combined with its "only" four bus stops, makes it the second most convenient of the moderates—among them, only Port Orleans French Quarter is more convenient for park travel. The resort itself is massive, and some buildings in the Ranchos in particular are quite distant from El Centro.

Coronado Springs is the only moderate with convention facilities. This has led to much fussing, largely unfair. The same number of rooms occupied by conventioneers rather than families means fewer people in total at the resort (because conventioneers average fewer people per room) and fewer people at the bus stops and pools (as the fewer conventioneers are in meetings, not going to the parks or the pools). Most of the time, except breakfast, there's also fewer people in CS's public dining spaces, as most meetings have meals served as part of the meeting program. However, when a thousand people leave a meeting at once, and all want to go someplace, things clot up quickly.

On the other hand, because of the demands of the business travelers at the convention center, Coronado Springs has a much higher level of services and amenities than at the other moderates. There are the usual movies, campfires, bike rental, fishing, playgrounds, and arcade. In addition, uniquely at CS among the moderates, you'll find a health club, spa services, real room service, a main pool menu with real food, the largest hot tub at Disney World, multiple bars, and a business center. The effect of these extra services is to make Coronado Springs quite attractive to adults and to returning visitors looking for better amenities at moderate prices.

Disney's Coronado Springs Resort
Standard Room Floor Plan ~314 Square Feet

Kids like the beach-themed Cabanas, the Dig Site area and main pool, and, if they aren't familiar with the geography, the exotic Southwest theming.

Rooms at Coronado Springs began a refurb early in 2017. Standard not-yet refurbed rooms at CS hold four people on two queen beds in about 314 square feet. They are similarly sized to those at the other traditional moderates, but have no Disney theming—and are in fact the most stark rooms among the moderates. In a concession to convention travelers, they come with a desk rather than the table and two chairs you'll find in the other traditional moderates. Most other room amenities are similar—a dresser/TV/mini-fridge combo, coffee-maker, and hair dryer. The bath is divided and family friendly, but has one sink rather than two, and sliding wooden doors separating it from the sleeping area, rather than the fabric curtains you'll find in the other traditional moderates except the standard rooms in Caribbean Beach. All buildings have elevators, and no rooms have balconies. All rooms are accessed from exterior corridors.

A refurb that began in 2017 includes a second sink, Disney art, and the addition of an easy chair—making these rooms more family-friendly. As part of this refurb, one accommodations building has been demolished, and will be replaced by a multi-story building that will include a new rooftop restaurant. At press time, five of the twelve remaining accommodations buildings have completed the refurb.

Until the new restaurant opens, dining is at El Centro, and, unless you are on the dining plan, is more expensive than at the other moderates. The food court, Pepper Market, used to be the best food court among the Disney World hotels, but while still good has gotten less interesting recently. The main table service restaurant, Maya Grill, has a menu suited to the Southwest theming of the resort, but is overpriced. A smaller table service venue, Las Ventanos, offers a simpler menu. The indoor bar, Rix Lounge, is the closest thing to a club you'll find in a Disney-owned hotel; there's an additional outdoor lakeside bar, and yet another bar by the pool. There are no character meals.

You can pay more for preferred locations that are a closer walk to El Centro, for king beds, for suites, and for water views. Standard view, non-preferred rooms average $215/night during the 2018 Value season, $247/night during the Regular season, $242/night during the Summer season, and $239 a night during the Fall season. Prices typically are comparable to those at CB, and $20-$30/night less than POR and POFQ.

THE CABINS AT DISNEY'S FORT WILDERNESS RESORT

Disney has had some trouble over the years communicating what's in the Cabins at Disney's Fort Wilderness Resort. Now that there are also starkly different "cabins" at the similarly named Wilderness Lodge, we expect even more confusion. The Fort Wilderness cabins—each its own little building—are distinctive spaces, sleeping six in two rooms, and with full kitchens. There used to be a "home away from home" category which the Cabins were in, but everything else in this group was a "deluxe" class room, and the Cabins didn't match up well with them.

So to eliminate the confusion about amenities, in 2009 Disney re-classed these Cabins as "moderates". This is a fair description of room-level amenities and spaciousness, but there's really few other ways that the Cabins are like the other moderates (inconvenience is one, and thin kid appeal another). As a result, the phrase "traditional moderate" started being used for all the moderates except the Cabins.

The Cabins are one of two lodging options at Fort Wilderness—the other being campsites. Fort Wilderness is one of America's great campgrounds, and the Cabins share in all the wonderful recreational activities available in the rest of this resort. The Cabins are each small, standalone buildings, looking on the outside like a nice small wood-paneled mobile home, and on the inside like a rustic cabin. If driving—and you should have a car to stay in these—you park right in front. Each cabin also has an outdoor barbecue grill and a big deck with picnic table. In late 2017, the Cabins became dog-friendly as part of a year-long pilot program.

All of the Cabins except those in Loop 2100 completed a refurb in spring 2016 (Loop 2100 Cabins were removed). As you walk in, you'll find first the full kitchen —diminished by the refurb from a range with

The Cabins at Disney's Fort Wilderness Resort
Cabin Floor Plan ~504 Square Feet

four burners and a full oven, to a two burner stove and a combined microwave and convection oven. The microwave/oven works better as an oven than you might think, but it is short (with only 6 inches of clearance between the rack and the top of the oven) and can't exceed 450 degrees. Adjacent is a small dining table and small living room. A queen bed folds out from a couch, so this space sleeps two—typically the parents. Further back is a full bath. It's not divided, and is short on hot water, so it doesn't always well suit the six people that these cabins can sleep. Beyond this is the back bedroom, with a tight-fitting queen bed on one side and a pair of bunk beds on the other.

The Cabins are not the least expensive way to get a Disney room for six—a family suite at All-Star Music is that. But they are the least expensive way to get moderate-level fittings and fixtures for six, and are by far the least expensive way to get a (mostly) full kitchen.

The challenge, though, is some crowding, especially around the bath, thin kid appeal—unless your kids love campgrounds—and great inconvenience. If you don't have a car, it takes two transport acts to get off Fort Wilderness and to a park—the first bus gets you to another bus stop or boat dock, from which you go to your final destination. We couldn't imagine staying here if you don't have a car. (Much-loved golf carts are also available for rent. They limit walking or bus waits at the Fort proper, but can't be used off the campground.)

Fort Wilderness has some family-friendly table service dining—the storied Hoop-Dee-Doo Revue and Mickey's Backyard Barbecue. There's also Trails End restaurant, with great value for money. Plus you have that kitchen. But there's not much in the way of counter service, and to get to these table service venues from the Cabins, you need to take a bus.

The resort has two pools. One is dull but within walking distance of the Cabins; the other, the main pool, remains the weakest among the moderates. This pool is farther (a bus trip for most), and is in the same Meadows area as where you'll find many of Fort Wilderness's other amenities. At the Settlement end of Fort Wilderness, you'll find (via bus...you can't drive to these) the beach, marina, boat docks (with boat service both to the Magic Kingdom, and also to the nearby Wilderness Lodge and Contemporary resorts), and the dining noted above.

If you need the lowest-priced kitchen you can find, need to sleep six, and have a car, the Cabins are great options. Otherwise, not so much.

The Cabins have no extra price options for views and such. They average $375/night during the 2018 Value season, $489/night during the Regular season, $434/night during the Summer season, and $418 a night during the Fall season.

Deluxe Resort Reviews

DISNEY'S POLYNESIAN VILLAGE RESORT

Disney's Polynesian Village Resort ("Poly"), a monorail resort, is themed around the Pacific islands of Polynesia. Theming at the Polynesian is pervasive and detailed, but more subtle than that of the jaw-dropping Wilderness Lodge and Animal Kingdom Lodge. Lush landscaping, lovely beaches, flaming torches, and exotically styled and named "longhouses" (where you find the rooms) create a delightful impression. In the Great Ceremonial House ("GCH") near the entrance to the resort are dining, shops, guest services, and, on the second floor, access to the resort monorail with service to the Magic Kingdom, the other monorail resorts, and the Transportation and Ticket Center (TTC). Disney Vacation Club Villas are available for booking in the lagoon and east side of the resort. The main Lava Pool is just outside the GCH, and the smaller Oasis pool is between the main resort and the DVC longhouses.

With travel to the Magic Kingdom available via both monorail and boat, and many rooms at the Polynesian within easy walking distance of the TTC and its Epcot monorail, the Polynesian is the most convenient Disney World resort. Transportation to the other parks and Disney Springs is via buses, typically shared with one or two other Magic Kingdom area resorts.

All standard rooms at the Poly sleep five on two queens and a sofa that flips into a twin. Rooms are about 415 square feet, among the largest at Disney World. Besides the two queens and couch, you'll find an easy chair and ottoman, a desk with a small rolling table underneath, desk chair, mini-fridge, TV/dresser combo, two closets, and

Disney's Polynesian Village Resort
Standard Room Floor Plan ~415 Square Feet

a coffeemaker. The spacious bath includes two sinks and a hair dryer, but is not divided, making it a little less family friendly than you'll find in more recently built hotels (the Polynesian was built in the early 70s). Second-floor standard rooms don't have balconies; other floors have patios or balconies. Polynesian DVC offerings available for rent to the general public include Bungalows and Studios. Studios are most comparable to standard Poly rooms, and sleep five on a queen, fold-out couch, and flip-down 72" x 30" Murphy bed. All studios have balconies. All standard rooms and studios are accessed from interior corridors. Like the other deluxe resorts, you can also reserve concierge-supported rooms (Disney calls these "club" rooms) and suites.

The Poly has three table service restaurants and two quick service options. Dining is in GCH, except for the Oasis Pool and the Luau which has its own building at the northwest edge of the resort. 'Ohana is a great family restaurant that features character breakfasts with Mickey, Lilo, and Stitch. Kona Café has terrific and under-appreciated food. The Luau fills any need you may have for a Polynesian-themed dinner show. The main quick service location is Capt. Cook's, too small for the resort but convenient to the larger pool. A second quick service at the refurbed smaller Oasis pool opened in 2016. While it operates during limited hours, often just from 11am to 5pm, the menu is as unique as it is diverse, offering items like sashimi, kalua pork sliders, and grilled sustainable fish tacos that are cumin-spiced with crunchy cabbage and cilantro-lime crema. More great dining is just a monorail ride away at the Grand Floridian and Contemporary. There's a bar outside of 'Ohana, and downstairs you'll find the most distinctive resort bar on property, Trader Sam's.

Amenities available at the resort include beaches, movies, campfires, jogging trails, playgrounds, boat rental, bike rental, fishing, a volleyball court, and an arcade. Poly guests can use the spa and health club Senses on the Poly side of the Grand Floridian. The Poly is one of only three Disney deluxe resorts (the Wilderness and Animal Kingdom Lodges are the others) that are not convention hotels.

At the Poly you can pay extra for views. Standard view five-person rooms average $546/night during the 2018 Value season, $650/night during the Regular season, $592/night during the Summer season, and $579 a night during the Fall season.

DISNEY'S GRAND FLORIDIAN RESORT & SPA

Disney's Grand Floridian Resort & Spa ("GF"), a monorail resort inspired by the Hotel Del Coronado in San Diego, is a lovely mix of gorgeous landscaping, white Victorian shapes and details, and red roofs. It visually enchants adults but does nothing in particular for kids. At opening, it supplanted Disney's Contemporary Resort as Disney World's flagship—and most expensive—hotel, leading some Contemporary Cast Members to refer to GF as the "red roof inn". There are three basic areas at GF: the main building, the outer buildings, and the Disney Vacation Club Villas. The main building has most dining, all shops, guest services, some suites, and several types of "club" rooms (Disney-speak for concierge rooms). The five outer buildings have more club rooms, more suites, all standard rooms, and some smaller but high-ceilinged "dormer" rooms. The Villas are at the southern edge of the resort grounds. From the second floor of the main building, GF guests can access the resort monorail with service to the Magic Kingdom, the other monorail resorts, and the Transportation and Ticket Center (TTC). The uninteresting but large main pool is in a beautifully landscaped area between the main building and the outer buildings, and the smaller but more fun Beach Pool is between the main building and the Villas.

Transportation to the Magic Kingdom is by the resort monorail or a boat shared with the Polynesian. Transportation to Epcot is via the Epcot monorail at TTC, accessible by the resort monorail. Transportation to the other parks and Disney Springs is via buses, typically shared with one or two other Magic Kingdom area resorts. Transportation convenience is above average among the deluxes for a Magic Kingdom focused trip, but not as good as sister monorail resorts the Contemporary and Polynesian.

Adults generally love the exterior and grounds of GF, while reactions to interior decorating choices are mixed, with some finding them stuffy. Kids often don't get the theme—a hotel themed as a hotel?—or it fails to delight them.

Disney's Grand Floridian Resort & Spa
Standard Room Floor Plan ~440 Square Feet

All standard rooms at GF sleep five on two queens and a sofa that flips into a twin bed. Standard rooms are about 440 square feet—larger than the standard rooms at any other Disney-owned hotel. Besides the two queens and couch, you'll find an easy chair, a desk with a small rolling table underneath, a desk chair, mini-fridge, TV, dresser, closet (with robes!), and a coffee-maker. The spacious divided bath includes two sinks and a hair dryer, and a toilet and tub in a separate room. Rooms in the nearby Villas are also available for rent to the general public. Of the four room types at the Villas, studios are most comparable to standard GF rooms. They sleep five in a smaller overall space, but one with a better bath, on a queen, fold-out couch, and flip-down 72" long murphy bed. All rooms are accessed from interior corridors, and all rooms have balconies or patios.

The Grand Floridian has the best adult dining of any Disney resort, some attractive kid dining, and easy access to other great options at the other monorail resorts. GF has five table service restaurants and one quick service option. Two are on the second floor of the main building. Victoria and Albert's is by far the best and most expensive restaurant at Disney World. Kids under ten are not allowed, and jackets are required. Citricos is a seafood-focused establishment with inspired modern fare. "Resort casual" is the appropriate dress. On the first floor is 1900 Park Fare, with character meals at breakfast and dinner—Mary Poppins and others in the morning, and Cinderella and her family in the evening. Also on the first floor is the unpretentious and unambitious Grand Floridian Café—with no dress code, no characters, and no fancy dining, it's usually the easiest to book, but also the least interesting for kids or adults. The fifth table service restaurant, Narcoossee's, fronts the Seven Seas Lagoon near the boat dock, specializes in steak and seafood, and has a resort casual dress code. The quick service option is in the main building but only accessible from outside, and is one of the best quick service options among the deluxes. There's a bar on the second floor of the main building, and another at each pool.

The Grand Floridian has an extensive set of amenities, including beaches, movies, campfires, jogging trails, playgrounds, a pirate cruise, boat rental, fishing, a great spa and fitness center, hot tubs, a sports court, and an arcade.

At the Grand Floridian you can pay extra for views. Standard view (Outer Building Garden View) five-person rooms average $661/night during the 2018 Value season, $718/night during the Regular season, $699/night during the Summer season, and $695 a night during the Fall season.

DISNEY'S WILDERNESS LODGE *Nov 2018*

Disney's Wilderness Lodge ("WL"), near the Magic Kingdom, completed a major refurb in mid-July 2017. Inspired by the great U.S. National Park Lodges, it celebrates them and the mountain West. Its astonishing theming begins with its jaw-dropping lobby and continues with extensive detail everywhere in the resort. Half of the main lodge is the new Disney Vacation Club Copper Creek Villas, and nearby in a separate building is the Disney Vacation Club Boulder Ridge Villas. These villas are also available to all for rent. Guest services, a shop, and most dining are accessed from the lobby. Most rooms and villas are in two wings off the lobby that enclose a mountain-stream-themed courtyard that ends in the delightful main pool. A smaller pool between the WL and the Boulder Ridge Villas re-opened in July 2017.

The Wilderness Lodge is on Bay Lake near Magic Kingdom, a ten-minute boat ride away. Boats also connect the Wilderness Lodge with the nearby Contemporary Resort and Fort Wilderness, giving easy access to the great dining options at those resorts. The other theme parks, water parks, and Disney Springs are accessed via shared buses that can take a while. The Wilderness Lodge is well located for a Magic Kingdom-focused trip. The quality of the exterior architecture, lobby, detailing, and pools make the Wilderness Lodge an astonishingly kid-appealing resort. Adults will enjoy it as well, although they might find its rooms smaller than expected.

Standard guest rooms at WL, with about 340 square feet, are tied with those at Disney's Animal Kingdom Lodge as the smallest deluxe rooms on property (they are also the least expensive such rooms). No five-person rooms are available except in the Boulder Ridge Villas—standard rooms sleep four on two queens. Four person rooms with one queen and a set of bunk beds are also available. You'll also find a table

Disney's Wilderness Lodge
Standard Room Floor Plan ~340 Square Feet

and two chairs, mini-fridge, TV, dresser, closet, and a coffee-maker. The divided bath includes two sinks and a hair dryer, and a toilet and tub in a separate room. Of the room types at the two Villas, studios are most comparable to standard WL rooms. Boulder Ridge studios sleep five in a slightly larger space, on a queen, a fold-out couch, and a fold-down smaller bed that's 32 inches by 75 inches. These five-person studio rooms are great choices for five-person families looking for Wilderness Lodge kid appeal who can fit in their beds. Copper Creek studios are the same size as standard Wilderness Lodge rooms, and sleep four on a queen and a fold-out couch. Rooms have balconies or patios, and are accessed from interior corridors. Like the other deluxe resorts, you can also reserve concierge-supported rooms ("club" rooms) and suites, and WL also has larger "deluxe rooms" that sleep six.

There are two table service restaurants at WL. Artist Point has a resort casual dress code, and offers a Pacific Northwest inspired menu. Whispering Canyon Café provides raucous fun and family-friendly dining. There are no character meals here, but these and other kid and adult-appealing meals are available at the Contemporary and Fort Wilderness—each just a boat ride away. WL has one of the better counter service options among the deluxes, and the best bar of the Magic Kingdom resorts. There's another bar and grill, Geyser Point, between the two pools.

Amenities include movies, campfires, jogging trails, fishing, a spa/ fitness center, hot tubs, volleyball, a playground, and boat rental. More water sports and a pirate cruise are at the nearby Contemporary. WL is one of three deluxe resorts (the Polynesian and Animal Kingdom Lodge are the others) that are not convention hotels.

At the Wilderness Lodge you can pay extra for views. Standard view rooms average $374/night during the 2018 Value season, $457/night during the Regular season, $435/night during the Summer season, and $423 a night during the Fall season.

DISNEY'S CONTEMPORARY RESORT

Disney's Contemporary Resort ("Contemporary"), a monorail resort, is essentially un-themed but still iconic, and, on first impression, visually striking. The massive concrete A-frame with monorails passing through the middle is stunning at first view. However, the spare masses and geometric landscaping quickly fade from notice, and there's not much interesting detail earning a second glance. There are three basic areas at the Contemporary—the main Tower, which is what most people mean when they think of it; the South Garden Wing, low-rise rooms mostly without balconies; and Bay Lake Tower, the Disney Vacation

Club offering. Found in the main Tower are dining, shops, guest services, and, from a dedicated escalator and elevator on the fourth floor, access to the resort monorail with service to the Magic Kingdom, the other monorail resorts, and the Transportation and Ticket Center (TTC). The dull but large main pool is outside the Tower, and there's a second dull and somewhat smaller pool between the main pool and Bay Lake. The Contemporary is the only Disney resort from which you can walk to and from the Magic Kingdom. With travel to the Magic Kingdom available via both monorail and walking, the Contemporary is, by far, the most convenient Disney World resort for trips focused particularly on that park.

Transportation to Epcot is via the Epcot monorail at TTC, accessible by the resort monorail. Transportation to the other parks and Disney Springs is via buses, typically shared with one or two other Magic Kingdom area resorts. There's also boat service among the three Bay Lake resorts—the Contemporary, Wilderness Lodge, and Fort Wilderness.

The Contemporary has nothing of the visual kid appeal of the Polynesian or the Wilderness or Animal Kingdom Lodges, but it does make a strong first impression, and some kids continue to be fascinated by the monorail running through the middle.

Standard rooms at the Contemporary sleep five on two queens and a sofa that flips into a twin bed. Most rooms are about 400 square feet, among the largest at Disney World. Besides the two queens and couch, you'll find a very large L-shaped desk that is too large to fit gracefully where it is placed, with a small rolling table underneath, a desk chair, mini-fridge, TV, two closets, and a coffee-maker. Clothes storage drawers are in the corner of the desk area, making them a little less usable than those in rooms with more central storage. The spacious bath

Disney's Contemporary Resort
Standard Room Floor Plan ~394 Square Feet

includes two sinks and a hair dryer, but only the toilet section is divided, making it less family friendly than you'll find in more recently built hotels (the Contemporary was built in the early 70s). Views from the higher main Tower rooms of the Magic Kingdom or Bay Lake are marvelous, and, because it is Disney World's only high-rise hotel, guests in Tower rooms will also find it the most compact Disney hotel to navigate. All Tower rooms have balconies. Garden Wing rooms have similar size and furnishings to Tower rooms, but are much more spread out, and without the views—or balconies—of the Tower rooms. They are also much less expensive. Of the four room types in the Disney Vacation Club at Bay Lake Tower, studios are most comparable to Tower rooms, but sleep only four in a cramped space with a queen and fold-out couch. All rooms are accessed from interior corridors. Like the other deluxe resorts, you can also reserve concierge-supported Tower rooms ("club" rooms) and suites in both the Tower and the Garden Wing.

The Contemporary has three table service restaurants and one quick service option. All dining is in the Tower. The first floor Wave of American Flavors focuses on locally grown and organic offerings. Chef Mickey's on the fourth floor offers a wildly popular buffet attended by Mickey, Minnie, Donald, Goofy, and Pluto. The top-floor California Grill offers fine modern American and sushi dining with a great view of the Magic Kingdom, especially if you are there during the fireworks. The quick service location is the fourth-floor Contempo Café. More great dining is just a monorail ride away at the Grand Floridian and Polynesian, and a boat ride away at the Wilderness Lodge and Fort Wilderness. There's a weak-looking and mis-placed bar on the fourth floor, a fine setting for a bar at the California Grill, and a pool bar.

The fourth floor of the Contemporary is the center of much of its action, and elevators there can be quite crowded. Guests headed from there to the first floor should consider the escalators.

The Contemporary has as broad a set of amenities as you will find at a Disney resort. They include beaches, movies, campfires, jogging trails, playgrounds, boat rental, bike rental, parasailing, waterskiing, wakeboarding, tubing, tennis, fishing, a spa and fitness center, hot tubs, a Pirate cruise, a volleyball court, and an arcade.

At the Contemporary, you can pay extra for views. Standard (Bay Lake) view five-person main tower rooms average $645/night during the 2018 Value season, $700/night during the Regular season, $700/night during the Summer season, and $672 a night during the Fall season.

DISNEY'S BEACH CLUB RESORT

Disney's Beach Club Resort ("BC"), an Epcot resort, is themed to recollect images of Victorian seaside cottages and hotels from Stone Harbor and other Cape May, New Jersey, settings. The exterior architecture is particularly charming, and of high appeal to adults. Kids don't much get its theming until they see the Stormalong Bay pool and its associated beaches and playgrounds. After that, that's all they see... The Beach Club occupies half of an enormous, long-corridored building, with sister resort The Yacht Club taking up the other half. Nearby you'll find the DVC Beach Club Villas. In the center of the building are kitchens and other back-of the house areas, then on either side the table service restaurants of the two resorts, then the guest service areas (one for each) and shops. Near Crescent Lake you'll find Stormalong Bay pool, shared with the Yacht Club—actually three separate pools, each with its own focus: a sand-bottomed shallow pool delightful for little ones; a pool perfect for drifting or tubing; and a pool for swimming. The larger of two fun water slides accessed from a shipwreck on a Crescent Lake beach splashes down at one end of this pool. Some call Stormalong Bay a "mini water park". That's a stretch, yet does capture the difference between it and every other Disney World pool except those at the Four Seasons. There's one smaller pool at the far west end of YC, and two smaller ones near the east end of BC.

The Beach Club is near the back entrance to Epcot, the International Gateway. For Epcot, walk or take a boat. For most BC rooms, the boats are a long walk away, so walking is often the better choice. Hollywood Studios is best accessed by boat, and the other theme parks, water parks, and Disney Springs via shared buses that can take a while. The Beach Club is wonderfully located for trips centered on Epcot, and a favorite of many returning family visitors. It's not so well located for a Magic Kingdom-focused trip.

Disney's Beach Club Resort
Standard Room Floor Plan ~381 Square Feet

Adults generally love the architecture and convenience to Epcot of BC, while kids often don't get the theme—a hotel themed as a cottage?—but just don't care after they see the pool.

Most standard rooms at BC sleep five on two queens and a daybed (some rooms omit the daybed— the floor plan shows such a room). Standard rooms are about 380 square feet—in the middle of the deluxe range, but well-appointed and proportioned. Five-person rooms have beside the beds a desk with a small rolling table underneath, a desk chair, mini-fridge, TV, dresser, closet, and a coffee-maker. The divided bath includes two sinks and a hair dryer, and a toilet and tub in a separate room. Four-person rooms have the same size, omit the daybed, but add an easy chair. Rooms in the nearby Villas are also available for rent to the general public. Of the three room types at the Villas, studios are most comparable to standard BC rooms. They sleep five in a smaller overall space, on a queen, a fold-out couch, and a fold-down bed that was added in a 2016 refurb. All rooms are accessed from interior corridors. Most BC standard rooms have small balconies or patios that seat two, but many BC rooms have tiny balconies with barely room to stand. This choice adds interest and grace to the façade, but impedes livability. Like the other deluxe resorts, you can also reserve concierge-supported rooms (Disney call these "club" rooms) and suites.

BC has two table service restaurants. Cape May Café offers a character breakfast with Goofy, and other characters like Minnie, Chip and Dale, but not Mickey. In the evening, Cape May converts to a no-character "clambake" buffet. Seafood can be good from a buffet—but it can't be great. By the pool is the Beaches and Cream ice cream and burger-focused establishment, with not remotely enough seats. There's no real counter service, just a few options in the back of the gift shop and at Hurricane Hanna's, the pool bar and grill. You can walk to sister resort the Yacht Club and find in the Market nice shelf-stable snacks and a few minor hot options or go to the BoardWalk for sandwiches. Dining in Epcot is also an option, but may be impractical for families without hopper tickets. There's an indoor bar and another at the pool.

Among them, the three Epcot resorts—the Beach and Yacht Clubs, and BoardWalk Inn—provide within walking distance access to almost any amenity, including beaches, movies, campfires, jogging trails, play-grounds, a pirate cruise, boat rental, fishing, a spa/fitness center, tennis, hot tubs, volleyball, a business center, and arcades.

At the Beach Club you can pay extra for views. Standard view rooms average $455/night during the 2018 Value season, $560/night during the Regular season, $529/night during the Summer season, and $525 a night during the Fall season.

DISNEY'S ANIMAL KINGDOM LODGE

Disney's Animal Kingdom Lodge ("AKL"), near the Animal Kingdom theme park, shares with the Wilderness Lodge astonishingly detailed theming and a jaw-dropping lobby, based in its case on African park lodges. It is also near-surrounded with parklands (Disney calls them "savannas") displaying animals. These animals are visible from savanna-view rooms and also from multiple public viewing areas. On several upper floors of the main building (Jambo House) you'll also find Disney Vacation Club spaces, the Jambo House Villas, and, a long walk or short bus ride away, even more DVC Villas at Kidani Village, all available for rent. Guest services and a shop are accessed from the main AKL Jambo lobby. Dining is at a lower level. (Kidani has another lobby, shop, and restaurant.) Most Jambo rooms are in two long-corridored semi-circular wings off the lobby that enclose animal savannas. The main pool is as good as any Disney-owned pool except Stormalong Bay at the Yacht and Beach Clubs. A slightly smaller but still wonderful pool serves Kidani.

The Animal Kingdom Lodge is at the far southwest corner of Walt Disney World. Uniquely among the deluxes, all transport to the theme parks, water parks, and Disney Springs is via buses shared with Kidani. Included in this is the Animal Kingdom park—you can't walk there. AKL thus is not particularly well located.

The animals, exterior architecture, lobby, detailing, and pools make AKL an astonishingly kid-appealing resort. Adults enjoy it as well, although they might find its rooms smaller than expected.

Standard guest rooms at AKL, with about 340 square feet, are tied with those at Disney's Wilderness Lodge as the smallest deluxe rooms on property (standard view rooms also are—for a Disney

Disney's Animal Kingdom Lodge
Standard Room Floor Plan ~340 Square Feet

deluxe—inexpensive). Most first-time visitors ought not to pay for views, as they won't be in their rooms enough, but they absolutely should pay for savanna views at AKL. No five-person rooms are available—standard rooms sleep four on two queens. Four-person rooms with one queen and a set of bunk beds are also available. You'll also find a table and two chairs, mini-fridge, TV, dresser, closet, and a coffee-maker. The divided bath includes two sinks and a hair dryer, and a toilet and tub in a separate room. Of the four room types at the Disney Vacation Club Jambo and Kidani Villas, studios are most comparable to standard AKL rooms. They sleep four in a slightly larger space, on a queen and a fold-out couch. Jambo studios are the better choice than Kidani studios, even though smaller, as the Jambo building is much better themed, and dining is much more convenient. Rooms have balconies, and are accessed from interior corridors. Like the other deluxe resorts, you can also reserve concierge-supported rooms ("club" rooms) and suites.

There are two table service restaurants at in the main Jambo building, and another at Kidani. In Jambo, Jiko nears the top of many "best Disney dining" lists, has a resort casual dress code, and offers an eclectic African-inspired menu. Next-door Boma is more family friendly, with a wide-ranging buffet. At Kidani, the underappreciated gem Sanaa has an African/Indian inspired menu. In 2016, Sanaa began serving a counter-service style breakfast, making mornings much simpler here. AKL also has one of the better counter service options among the deluxes, and one of Disney World's best bars. There's another bar at each pool. Unlike the other deluxes, there's no easy access to more dining at another hotel.

Amenities include movies, campfires, jogging trails, playgrounds, a spa/fitness center, hot tubs, and arcades. AKL is alone among the Disney deluxe resorts in not being on water, having no beach, and offering no easy access to water sports. AKL is one of three deluxe resorts (the Polynesian and Wilderness Lodge are the others) that are not convention hotels.

At the Animal Kingdom Lodge, you should pay extra for savanna views. Savanna view rooms average $553/night during the 2018 Value season, $647/night during the Regular season, $620/night during the Summer season, and $593 a night during the Fall season. These prices are around $150–$225/night more than standard view rooms.

DISNEY'S YACHT CLUB RESORT

Disney's Yacht Club Resort ("YC"), an Epcot resort, is themed as a formal New England yacht club. The dull gray exterior does little to accomplish this, but there are some nautical decorative elements in the public areas and rooms. Neither kids nor adults much get its theming, but kids are delighted by Stormalong Bay pool and its beaches and playgrounds. The Yacht Club occupies half of a long-corridored building, with sister resort The Beach Club—warmer, more charming and inviting—taking up the other half. In the center of the enormous building are kitchens and other back-of the house areas, then on either side the table service restaurants of the two resorts, then the guest service areas (one for each) and shops. Near Crescent Lake you'll find Stormalong Bay pool, shared with the Beach Club—actually three separate pools, each with its own focus: a sand-bottomed shallow pool delightful for little ones; a pool perfect for drifting or tubing; and a pool for swimming. The larger of two fun water slides accessed from a shipwreck on a beach splashes down at one end of this pool. Some call Stormalong Bay a "mini water park". That's a stretch, yet does capture the difference between it and every other Disney World pool except those at the Four Seasons. There's one smaller pool at the far west end of YC, and two smaller ones near the east end of BC. In late 2017, YC became dog-friendly as part of a year-long pilot program.

The Yacht Club is near the back entrance to Epcot, the International Gateway. You can walk or take a boat to Epcot. Hollywood Studios is accessed by a long walk or by boat, and the other theme parks, water parks, and Disney Springs via shared buses that can take a while. The Yacht Club is well located for trips centered on Epcot, but not so well located for a Magic Kingdom focused trip.

All of Disney's marketing material stresses the "formality" of the Yacht Club and the "fun" of the Beach Club. Both points are overstated, but result in families self-selecting into the prettier Beach Club, and conventioneers (both hotels are convention hotels) into the duller Yacht Club. This is fine—the Beach Club is the better family choice on any relevant measure except balconies: all YC rooms have large balconies, while BC rooms have either small or almost uselessly tiny ones.

Guest rooms at the YC completed a much-needed refurb in late 2017. Most standard rooms at YC sleep five on two queens and a daybed (some rooms omit the daybed and sleep four). Standard rooms are about 380 square feet—in the middle of the deluxe range, but well-appointed and proportioned. Five-person rooms have, beside the beds, a desk with a small rolling table underneath, a desk chair, mini-fridge, TV, dresser, closet, and a coffee-maker. The divided bath includes two sinks and a hair dryer, and a toilet and tub in a separate room. Four-person rooms have the same size, omit the daybed, but add an easy chair. All rooms are accessed from interior corridors. Like the other deluxe resorts, you can also reserve concierge-supported rooms (Disney call these "club" rooms) and suites.

YC has two table service restaurants. The Yachtsman Steak House is a top-notch venue with steaks as good as any Disney restaurant. It has a resort casual dress code. The other table service restaurant, Ale & Compass, has little theming and average fare, and because of that is easy to get as a walk-up or last-minute reservation. Minor counter service offerings and nice snacks are available in the newly opened Market. You can walk to the nearby Beach Club and find a character breakfast at Cape May Café, burger and ice cream dining at Beaches and Cream, and more weak counter service. The nearby BoardWalk Inn has neither meaningful counter service nor any kid-appealing table service restaurants except for the new in April 2017 breakfast at Trattoria al Forno featuring Rapunzel, Flynn Rider, Ariel and Prince Eric. Dining in Epcot is also an option, but may be impractical for families without hopper tickets. There's a bar inside and another at the pool.

Among them, the three Epcot resorts—the Beach and Yacht Clubs, and BoardWalk Inn—provide within walking distance access to almost any amenity, including beaches, movies, campfires, jogging trails, playgrounds, a pirate cruise, boat rental, fishing, a spa/fitness center, tennis, hot tubs, volleyball, a business center, and arcades.

At the Yacht Club you can pay extra for views. Standard view rooms average $455/night during the 2018 Value season, $560/night during the Regular season, $529/night during the Summer season, and $525 a night during the Fall season.

Disney's Yacht Club Resort
Standard Room Floor Plan ~381 Square Feet

DISNEY'S BOARDWALK INN
• •

Disney's BoardWalk Inn ("BWI"), an Epcot resort, has a split visual personality. One part of it, facing Crescent Lake, is themed to recall Atlantic coast boardwalk vacation settings. The rest—including the areas with the most rooms—is themed to recall a quieter and more peaceful Colonial-revival style resort with garden courtyards. The BoardWalk Inn is Disney's smallest deluxe resort, but some corridors are as long as those at sister Epcot resorts the Yacht and Beach Clubs. Cutting across the courtyard can save much walking. Connected through the lobby of the BoardWalk Inn is the enormous Disney Vacation Club property Disney's BoardWalk Villas, also available to all for rent. Guest services and a small shop are in the lobby, and more shopping is downstairs on the BoardWalk. Dining is a little weird—there's next to none "in" the BoardWalk Inn, but several restaurants are accessible just outside on the Boardwalk. In the Villas area you'll find the fun amusement-park themed main pool and a second smaller pool. A third pool, also small, is in an internal courtyard of the Inn.

The BoardWalk Inn is near the back entrance to Epcot, the International Gateway, and is as near Epcot as is the Beach Club, and nearer to Disney's Hollywood Studios. You can walk to either park from it, though most take the boat to the Studios. The other theme parks, water parks, and Disney Springs are reached via shared buses that can take a while. The BoardWalk Inn is well located for trips centered on Epcot and the Studios, but not so well located for a Magic Kingdom-focused trip.

From its interior courtyards, the BoardWalk Inn is the loveliest and most compact of the Epcot resorts, and is highly popular with honeymooners. Kids don't get its theme, and the main pool, while fine, isn't at the standard of the pool at the Beach Club, making the Beach Club a better choice for most families. But adults love it, and the resulting demand means BWI is typically as much as $90 a night more expensive than the Beach Club.

Standard guest rooms at BWI, with about 370 square feet, are similar to those in the Yacht Club and Beach Club, mid-sized among the deluxes but well-proportioned and appointed, sleeping four on two queens or five with an added couch. Rooms also have a desk with a small rolling table underneath, a desk chair, mini-fridge, TV, dresser, closet, and a coffee-maker. The divided bath includes two sinks and a hair dryer, and a toilet and tub in a separate room. Four-person rooms have the same size, omit the couch, but add an easy chair. Of the four room types at the Villas, studios are most comparable to standard BWI rooms. After a recent refurb, they sleep five in a similar space on a queen, a fold-out couch, and a fifth fold-down sleeping spot, but can be quite a hike. Rooms have balconies or patios, and are accessed from interior corridors. Like the other deluxe resorts, you can also reserve concierge-supported rooms (Disney call these "club" rooms) and suites, and BW also has larger "deluxe rooms" that sleep six, and Garden Cottages best suited to couples.

The BoardWalk Inn itself has next to no dining, but several restaurants with little kid appeal are right outside on the BoardWalk itself. These include the sports-bar style ESPN Club; the Italian restaurant Trattoria al Forno which in April 2017 added a character breakfast featuring Rapunzel, Flynn Rider, Ariel, and Prince Eric, improving the kid appeal of this area a bit; high-end, expensive seafood at the Flying Fish Café; and the brew pub Big River Grille. There's no real counter service other than limited offerings at the Bakery and at stalls on the BoardWalk itself. More table service dining is at the Yacht and Beach Clubs, and dining in Epcot is an option, but may be impractical for families without hopper tickets. There's a great bar inside and another at the pool.

Among them, the three Epcot resorts—the Beach and Yacht Clubs, and BoardWalk Inn—provide within walking distance access to almost any amenity, including beaches, movies, campfires, jogging trails, playgrounds, a pirate cruise, boat rental, fishing, a spa/fitness center, tennis, hot tubs, volleyball, a business center, and arcades.

At the BoardWalk Inn you can pay extra for views. Standard view rooms average $490/night during the 2018 Value season, $564/night during the Regular season, $535/night during the Summer season, and $518 a night during the Fall season.

Disney's BoardWalk Inn
Standard Room Floor Plan ~370 Square Feet

DISNEY'S OLD KEY WEST RESORT

Disney's Old Key West Resort ("OKW") is a Disney Vacation Club Resort, but unlike those discussed so far it is not paired with a deluxe resort, but rather stands on its own. Like all the other DVC offerings, its accommodations are available to Disney Vacation Club members, to others who have rented points from them, and to anyone using cash just like at any other Disney World resort. Except for dining and convenience, its offerings and amenities are comparable to those at Disney deluxe resorts, which is why we discuss it here.

OKW is themed to recall Key West, which it does a bit here and there. But with dozens of three-story buildings winding among water and fairways, it mostly comes across as a pastel-colored example of a vacation condominium community. Neither kids nor adults much get its theming, and there is little to visually signal you are in Disney World.

Old Key West's two- and three-story accommodations buildings—most of which have no elevators—are scattered across a large expanse, with the central services (dining, shops, check-in, and the main pool) located near the entry to the resort, far from most accommodations buildings. The main pool has a great slide and sandcastle theme, and is fun, but a hike for most guests. Three other pools with fewer amenities serve those who don't wish to walk, drive, take a bus, or get a taxi to the main pool.

OKW is located just south of POFQ and is identified in Disney way-finding material as a Disney Springs Area Resort. Often derided for being isolated, it's actually not that far from Epcot, Disney's Hollywood Studios, and Magic Kingdom. Rather, what makes it inconvenient is the five bus stops needed to serve its sprawl, the bus backtracking that comes from dead-end roads, and the walking distances within it. All transportation to the theme parks and water parks is via bus; there's also a boat to Disney Springs. A car is handy here. We wouldn't stay at OKW without one.

Of the four types of accommodations available at OKW, its studios are most comparable to standard rooms at the deluxe resorts, so they are the focus here. All Disney studios are distinguished from deluxe standard rooms by having a microwave and toaster in addition to the standard coffeemaker and mini-fridge found in both studios and deluxe rooms. Most are also different by having a queen bed and a fold-out couch. Old Key West studios are unique in offering two queens, rather than a queen and sleeper sofa. A sofa creates a more flexible studio; two queens, more comfortable sleeping. OKW studios are about 380 square feet—larger than most other studios—sleep four and have, beside the beds and kitchenette appliances, a table and chairs, TV, dresser, and closet. The bath is not divided, but with a second sink available in the nearby kitchenette the room functions as though it were. Studios here also come with a large patio or balcony.

Larger spaces are also available at OKW. One Bedroom Villas hold five in about twice the space of a studio and Two Bedroom Villas hold nine in about three times the space of a studio. These One and Two Bedroom Villas are among the largest and the most home-like of the DVC offerings. Grand Villas at OKW hold 12 in about five times the space of a studio.

First-timers are often surprised by how thin the dining is at OKW. However, everyone staying here either has a kitchenette, as in the studios, or has the full kitchen that the other OKW accommodations come with. The gift shop is also well-stocked with food. OKW has only one table service restaurant, Olivia's. Much loved among families who return to Old Key West year after year, Olivia's is bright, colorful, and fun, and worth a visit from those staying at OKW—but is by no means destination dining. There's a small counter service venue outside that also serves as the grill for the main pool, and a small bar next to it. Dining in Disney Springs is also an option, but the boats there are slower and less frequent than ideal.

OKW offers most amenities, including movies, campfires, jogging trails, playgrounds, bike rentals, fishing, a spa/fitness center, tennis, basketball, hot tubs, volleyball, and an arcade.

Because of the layout of the accommodations buildings, almost all OKW spaces have nice views, and there are no extra charge options for views or preferred areas. OKW and Saratoga Springs are usually the lowest priced DVC options (other than some not-recommended standard view and "value" studios at the Animal Kingdom Lodge). Studios at OKW average $388/night during the 2018 Value season, $441/night during the Regular season, $436/night during the Summer season, and $425 a night during the Fall season.

DISNEY'S SARATOGA SPRINGS RESORT & SPA

Disney's Saratoga Springs Resort & Spa ("SS") is a Disney Vacation Club Resort, but, like Old Key West, it is not paired with a deluxe resort—it stands on its own. As with all the other DVC offerings, its accommodations are available to Disney Vacation Club members, to others who have rented points from them, and to anyone using cash just like at any other Disney World resort. Except for dining and convenience, its offerings and amenities are comparable to those at Disney deluxe resorts, which is why we discuss it here.

Saratoga Springs is themed to recall the vacation, spa, and horse country around Saratoga Springs, New York, and it does do this a bit here and there. But with large three-story buildings winding among water and fairways, it mostly feels like a golf condominium development. You really could be anywhere.

Saratoga Spring's almost 20 accommodations buildings (all with elevators) are scattered in several named areas across a large expanse, with the main services—dining, shops, check-in, and the main pool—located near the center of the resort, and distant from many accommodations buildings. Uniquely, Saratoga Springs has two full-service pools with slides, bars, food and such: the High Rock Spring pool in the central Springs area, and the Paddock pool in the Paddock area. Another pool, the Grandstand pool, has no slide but is otherwise sound, and two smaller pools with few amenities are in the Treehouse and Congress Park areas.

SS is located just east of OKW and is identified in Disney way-finding material as a Disney Springs Area Resort. Often derided for being remote, it's actually not that far from Epcot, Disney's Hollywood Studios, and Magic Kingdom, but is the most isolated resort after the Animal Kingdom Lodge. What makes it particularly inconvenient is the walks to the central services and the five bus stops needed to serve its sprawl (plus two more at the Treehouse Villas—don't even ask). All transportation to the theme parks and water parks is via bus; there's also a boat and a walking path to Disney Springs. A car is handy here—we wouldn't stay at SS without one.

Of the four types of accommodations available at SS, its studios are most comparable to standard rooms at the deluxe resorts, so they are the focus here. All Disney studios are distinguished from deluxe standard rooms by having a microwave and toaster in addition to the standard coffeemaker and mini-fridge found in both studios and deluxe rooms. Most are also different by having a queen bed and a fold-out couch. SS studios are much like most other Disney World studios, except at about 355 square feet are a little smaller. They sleep four and have, beside the bed, sofa bed and kitchenette appliances, a table and chairs, TV, dresser, and a closet. The divided bath has a sink and closet in one part, and toilet and tub in their own room. Studios also come with a patio or balcony.

Disney's Saratoga Springs Resort & Spa
Studio Floor Plan
~355 Square Feet

Larger spaces are also available at SS. One Bedroom Villas hold four in about twice the space of a studio and Two Bedroom Villas hold eight in three times the space of a studio. Grand Villas at SS hold 12 in about five times the space of a studio. These are among the smaller of these room types at Disney World, so another DVC venue will be a better choice for most. A unique additional offering at SS is the Treehouse Villas—woefully isolated, with their own buses that go only to Saratoga Springs itself, but a great three-bedroom option for a group of nine with a car or two.

First-timers are often surprised by how thin the dining is at SS. However, everyone staying here either has a kitchenette, as in the studios, or has the full kitchen that the other SS accommodations come with. The gift shop is also well-stocked with food. SS has only one table service restaurant, The Turf Club. Much loved among golfers and romantic for couples, it's less interesting for kids. There's a small counter service venue in the gift shop so that you can apply mustard directly to your stuffed Mickey rather than waiting to stain it by chance, and several of the pools have substantial bar and grill menus. Dining in Disney Springs is also an option, but the boats there are slower and less frequent than ideal, and the walking path is a hike from everywhere except the Congress Park area.

SS offers most amenities, including movies, campfires, jogging trails, playgrounds, bike rentals, fishing, a wonderful spa/fitness center, tennis, basketball, hot tubs, and an arcade. It's also the only Disney resort with a pro shop and golf course start, underneath the Turf Club —and outside the pro shop is another minor dining option, Chips and Slices, with a window serving a limited menu for breakfast and lunch.

Because of the layout of the accommodations buildings, almost all SS spaces have nice views, and there are no extra charge options for views or preferred areas. Saratoga Springs and OKW are usually the lowest priced DVC options (other than some not-recommended standard view and "value" studios at the Animal Kingdom Lodge). SS studios average $384/night during the 2018 Value season, $436/night during the Regular season, $432/night during the Summer season, and $424 a night during the Fall season.

Other Disney World Lodging Options

Besides the Disney-owned value, moderate and deluxe resorts, there are other options as well:

- The Disney-owned multi-room spaces at the Disney Vacation club resorts.
- The Disney-owned Campsites at Fort Wilderness.
- The on-property, non-Disney-owned hotels: the Swan, Dolphin, Shades of Green, Four Seasons, and the hotels of the Disney Springs Resort Area. Many of these gained access to valuable perks for 2018.
- Everything else—the offsite hotels and vacation homes.

The positives and negatives of these choices vary, so we'll comment briefly on each.

MULTI-ROOM VILLAS AT
DISNEY VACATION CLUB RESORTS

The Disney Vacation Club ("DVC") Resorts at Walt Disney World are time-shares with rooms that can also be booked via cash reservations, just like any other Disney World resort hotel room.

Except for the studios, which we've already discussed in the "Deluxe Resorts" section, above, what's distinct about the accommodations in these DVC resorts is the extra space and large kitchens—neither of which will be used much during a first visit, but which can be quite comfortable and convenient for returning visitor.

These villas can also be reserved (usually at a huge cost saving) by privately renting "points" from Disney Vacation Club members.

For most first-time family visitors, the multi-room villas in the DVC resorts are worth considering only under a few circumstances:

- Large families, especially those aimed at a deluxe property, who are not willing to bet on actually getting connecting rooms. (You can request connecting rooms at WDW, but getting them is not guaranteed.) Villas which can sleep 8, 9, and 12 people are available.
- Smaller families looking to spread out into a One or Two-Bedroom Villa, despite the higher price.
- Families aimed at a deluxe hotel, but who can only pull it off through the cost savings of renting DVC points.
- Families who have targeted a resort with which a DVC property is paired, find it is sold out, but can get into the DVC resort.
- People who already are DVC owners.

All of the DVC resorts except Saratoga Springs and Old Key West are paired with a deluxe resort and mostly share the pros and cons of that resort in terms of convenience, kid appeal, dining, amenities, and such.

There are, however, some real variances across the DVC resorts in the livability of their rooms.

Studios add to the routine amenities of a deluxe room a microwave and toaster, and generally sleep four in a queen and a fold out-sofa. Old Key West Studios have two queens. Studios in the Boulder Ridge Villas at the Wilderness Lodge ("BR"), the Polynesian, the BoardWalk Villas, the Villas at the Grand Floridian ("VGF"), and the Beach Club Villas sleep five—the third sleeping spot is a short fold-down murphy bed that's 72ish inches long and sleeps shorter than that. Studios in Bay Lake Tower at Disney's Contemporary ("BLT") sleep four, but we think the room is too cramped when the fold-out couch is opened. All Studios except those at the Polynesian have one bath. Polynesian Studios have one full bath, and a second bath space with sink and shower.

One Bedroom Villas sleep four or five, depending on the resort. They have a king bed bedroom that sleeps two and also a combined full kitchen, dining, and living space that typically sleeps two on a fold-out couch. Old Key West, Bay Lake Tower, and the Villas at the Animal Kingdom Lodge (at Jambo House and Kidani Village, "VAKL") add a third sleeping spot to this area with a fold-out chair; at the Villas at the Grand Floridian, this space gets a third spot from a fold-down murphy bed. All One Bedroom Villas except those at Kidani Village and Bay Lake Tower have a single large divided bath; at those two, there's a small bath in the living/dining/kitchen area and another larger one in the king bedroom.

Two Bedroom Villas come in two flavors:

- One type simply combines a Studio and a One Bedroom through a connecting door, and is known as a "lock-off". These lock-off Two Bedroom Villas combine the capacity and merits of the spaces that make them up. Most sleep eight, but those that combine five-person spaces will sleep nine (BCV, BWV, OKW, BLT, VAKL, BR) or, at the Villas at the Grand Floridian, ten.

- A second type, designed as a Two Bedroom Villa from the start, is called in the jargon a "dedicated" villa, sleeps eight or nine, and will have minor variations in the second bedroom compared to a Studio, typically losing the kitchenette, swapping the fold-out couch of the Studio for another queen, and getting another closet instead of an exit to the corridor. At the Grand Floridian, such villas also lose the fold-down bed in the second bedroom and sleep nine.

Two Bedroom Villas don't really have the living or dining space to support the eight or nine people they will hold—a problem particularly acute at the Beach Club Villas, Saratoga Springs, Boulder Ridge Villas at the Wilderness Lodge, and BoardWalk Villas. See the floor plan, below—a Saratoga Springs example. In this space that sleeps eight, note the seats for four in the living area and three at the dining table.

Chairs can be moved around to add seats in these smaller spaces, but larger groups will find the Two Bedroom Villas at Old Key West, the Villas at Disney's Grand Floridian, Kidani Village, and Bay Lake Tower much more livable.

Bungalows at the Polynesian and Lakeside Cabins at Copper Creek are unlike any other DVC two-bedroom spaces, but are too expensive for you to even think about.

Grand Villas, available at all the DVC resorts except the Beach Club Villas and the Polynesian Villas and Bungalows, sleep 12 in a king room, two rooms with two beds each, and some sofa beds. They have twice the living/dining/kitchen space of Two Bedroom Villas, and sometimes—at Jambo House, VGF, and most of the BoardWalk Grand Villas—even more.

There's more variation among the Grand Villas than in any other DVC accommodations, so for more on these huge spaces that can go for more than $2,000 a night, see YOURFIRSTVISIT.NET.

Disney's Saratoga Springs Resort & Spa
Two-Bedroom Villa Floor Plan ~1075 Square Feet

CAMPSITES AT FORT WILDERNESS

Fort Wilderness offers three lodging options—Cabins, group campsites, and individual campsites.

The Cabins were discussed earlier in this chapter, among the Moderates. You'll also find there an overview of the dining, extensive amenities, and inconvenience of Fort Wilderness. Neither of us has enough friends to have rented a group campsite, but they are particularly appropriate for scouts and other youth groups. The individual campsites can be booked for ten people and come in four basic types:

- "Tent or Pop-Up Campsites"
- "Full Hook-Up Campsites"
- "Preferred Campsites", and
- "Premium Campsites"

The key distinction is that Premium Campsites are designed for very large RVs, and have no tent pad. So tent campers, and campers with both an RV and a tent, should avoid them. Full Hook-Up sites have both a large RV spot and also a small tent pad. Tent campers are allowed in the Full Hook-Up campsites, but will find themselves in a sea of rumbling

RVs should they choose one, and most commonly will be best served by a Tent or Pop-Up loop. Preferred sites have the same configuration as Full Hook-Up sites, but are closer to Magic Kingdom transportation and Fort Wilderness dining.

Anyone planning for tents at Fort Wilderness should keep three points in mind, all related to the commonly intense weather—heat and storms—in Orlando:

- Bring extra flys to serve as sun shades and rain protection. Your tent, ideally, will have a full coverage fly and a mesh inner body.
- Since the tent pads are sand, few traditional stakes will hold in weather. See the Fort Wilderness review on YOURFIRSTVISIT.NET for suggested alternative stakes. If you can walk comfortably around your site, you don't have enough guy lines out.
- All Fort Wilderness sites, including the Tent or Pop-Up sites, have power. So bring extension cords and multiple fans.

The Campsites at Disney's Fort Wilderness Resort, while wonderful for returning visitors who like to camp or own an RV, are not recommended for typical first-time family visitors to Walt Disney World. The wilderness and backwoodsy theming of this resort, while charming, is so subtle that it will fly over the heads of most kids. Mickey and other Disney themes are almost entirely absent.

Also, the Campsites at Disney's Fort Wilderness Resort are remarkably inconvenient compared to the other Walt Disney World resorts. See the review of the sister Cabins at Fort Wilderness in the Moderates section of this chapter for details.

OTHER ON-PROPERTY HOTELS

There are two groups of resorts operated by third parties on Disney property. First, there's a group of four that are comparable to the Disney deluxe resorts in room size, quality, amenities, and location. These are Shades of Green, the Swan, the Dolphin, and the Four Seasons. Full reviews follow, but here's the key points:

- **Shades of Green** is an inexpensive deluxe-level resort near the Polynesian for U.S. service members, career military retirees, other eligible guests, and their families and sponsored friends. Shades of Green guests are eligible for EMH and for FastPass+ at 60 days.
- **The Swan and Dolphin** are deluxe hotels near the Epcot resorts—a little closer to Hollywood Studios than Epcot, compared to the other Epcot resorts. Guests at the Swan and Dolphin

are eligible for EMH and for FastPass+ at 60 days. Both resorts are very competitively priced, but suffer from a daily $28 resort fee, in addition to $20 per day for parking.

- **The Four Seasons Resort Orlando** opened in 2014 as the first five-star resort at Walt Disney World. It has the largest standard rooms on property, great dining for adults, a character breakfast a couple of times a week with Goofy, and the best pool complex at Walt Disney World. At press time, Four Seasons did not participate in any Disney hotel perks, except for EMH (as of March 2018).

Second, there's a group of hotels in the Disney Springs Resort Area. While their prices may initially seem attractive, high resort and parking fees typically push the price up by $30 or more per night. The Disney Springs Resort Area isn't convenient to anything but shopping and dining, and these hotels have their own, often disappointing, park transportation. New in 2018, guests at these seven hotels are eligible for EMH, and, if they book a package through the Walt Disney Travel Company, for FastPass+ at 60 days. These new perks may be limited to 2018 visits.

THE DISNEY WORLD SWAN AND DOLPHIN

The Disney World Swan and Disney World Dolphin ("Swan and Dolphin") are paired, connected Marriott (formerly Starwood) convention resorts that share all amenities and have easy access to Epcot and Disney's Hollywood Studios. The two resorts have unusual exterior decorations—off-putting to some and delightful to others—and lovely but un-themed interiors. The larger Dolphin has more amenities just an elevator ride away, but offers full beds in its standard rooms. The smaller Swan is more of a walk to some amenities, but has queen beds in its standard rooms.

The Swan and Dolphin are not owned by Disney, but even so share in the most valuable perk available to guests staying at a Disney-owned resort: they can book FastPass+ at 60 days. Swan and Dolphin guests also are eligible to attend Extra Magic Hours, and the two hotels are fully integrated into the same transportation system that serves Disney's own Epcot resorts—the Yacht Club, Beach Club, and BoardWalk Inn. Guests here don't get free parking at their hotel (but do at the parks), can't use the Dining Plan, and can't use Disney's Magical Express.

The Swan is a long mid-rise building with a curved roof that has enormous statues of swans on top. The Dolphin is larger and taller, rising to a pyramid flanked by enormous statues of a curious nondescript fish. Each hotel has its own amenities which guests at either can use, and the two are connected centrally by a covered walkway, and are connected at the side by a sweep of pool after pool after beach after pool that collectively are the third best pool complex at Disney World.

The Swan and Dolphin are just beyond the BoardWalk Villas and Yacht Club. Guests can use either Disney boats or a walking path to get to Disney's Hollywood Studios and Epcot. The other parks and Disney Springs are served by shared buses which can take awhile. This location makes them a fine choice for a visit centered on Epcot, but not so much for a trip focused especially on the Magic Kingdom—as most first visits are.

Standard rooms at the Swan were refurbed in 2015, and a refurb of Dolphin rooms was completed in 2017. Swan rooms offer two queen beds and a divided bath with two sinks, and the slightly larger (360 vs. 340 square feet) Dolphin rooms offer two full beds and a divided bath with a single sink. The queens and extra sink make Swan rooms better for most families.

Other amenities are similar. These rooms have beside the beds and bath a dresser, desk, mini-fridge, TV, closet, and a coffee-maker. All rooms are accessed from interior corridors, and only some have

Walt Disney World Swan
Standard Room Floor Plan ~340 Square Feet

Walt Disney World Dolphin
Standard Room Floor Plan ~360 Square Feet

balconies. As is typical of convention hotels, many suites are also available in addition to the standard rooms.

The Swan and Dolphin have great adult dining at Kimonos, Shula's Steak House, and Todd English's bluezoo, and some OK kid dining including a character meal at Garden Grove. Casual dining is much better than that at Disney's Epcot resorts. More dining is easily accessible in the Disney hotels, along the nearby BoardWalk, and, for those with hoppers, in Epcot itself.

Amenities at the Swan and Dolphin are comparable to those at Disney deluxe resorts, missing only water sports. Besides the great pool complex, they include playgrounds, spas, fitness centers, tennis, hot tubs, and arcades.

The lack of Disney theming and relative inconvenience to the Magic Kingdom makes us less than keen on the Swan and Dolphin for first-time visitors, and the masses of conventioneers can make them even less fun. (Disney's Epcot resorts are all convention hotels as well, but at a much smaller scale.) But the Swan in particular can be a great choice for a later, more Epcot-focused trip. Dining is better than at Disney's Epcot resorts, the pools are better than those at the BoardWalk Inn (though not as good as those shared by the Yacht and Beach Club), and standard rooms prices are typically lower than what you'd pay for Disney Epcot resort standard rooms.

Prices at the Swan and Dolphin are less transparent than those at the Disney resorts, and sometimes obscure that fact that unlike at the Disney-owned hotels you pay a required resort fee and also have to pay for parking if you have a car. But even with these extra costs, rooms are often less than the Disney-owned Epcot resorts.

SHADES OF GREEN

Shades of Green Resort ("Shades") is a military-owned Armed Forces Recreation Center in the heart of Walt Disney World. The resort overall is un-themed and bland—it could be anywhere—but eligible guests who stay here will find some of the nicest rooms at Disney World at very low prices—prices here vary by rate/rank, but generally are competitive most of the year with Disney's least expensive resorts. Eligibility is complicated—see Steve Bell's MILITARYDISNEYTIPS.COM for the full scoop—but its rooms can be booked by eligible "sponsors" who are currently serving or career retired, or the spouses of such folk, plus a host of other classes detailed on Steve's site. (Veterans who are not career retired can stay in September and January.) Sponsors can book a room for themselves as well as 2–5 additional rooms (depending on the time of year and whether a spouse is involved) for their family and friends at the same low rates.

While Shades is not owned by Disney, its guests do have access to the most valued Disney World perks—Extra Magic Hours and, new beginning late 2017, access to FastPass+ at 60 days. They don't get free parking at the hotel ($7/day) or the parks ($22/day), aren't eligible for Disney's Magical Express airport transportation, and can't use the Dining Plan.

Shades has a large wood and stone lobby building where guest services, the bus stop, and most dining are located. Guest rooms are in two wings off the lobby. The Palm wing is newer, prettier, and closer to parking. The less attractive Magnolia Wing is closer to the two pools at the resort, one near the lobby and another at the far end of the Magnolia wing that has a kids play area, water slides, and easy access to a sports bar and grill.

Shades is nestled between two golf courses in the Magic Kingdom area, across the street from Disney's Polynesian Village Resort. Park transport is via its own bus system that is not as good as the buses serving the Disney-owned resorts. Buses commonly start too late, run too infrequently, and don't directly serve the Magic Kingdom or Epcot, instead dropping guests headed to those parks off at the Transportation and Ticket Center. Many Shades guests walk to the Polynesian to take advantage of its transportation—it's about half a mile from the lobby at Shades to the Poly's monorail stop.

Standard rooms at Shades sleep five on two queens and a couch that converts into a single bed. These rooms are about 480 square feet—larger than those in any Disney-owned resort. Rooms have beside the beds and couch a large table with two chairs, mini-fridge, TV, dresser, closet, and a coffee-maker. The divided bath includes two sinks and a hair dryer, and a toilet and tub in a separate room. All rooms are accessed from interior corridors, and all have large balconies. A few suites are also available.

Shades of Green Resort
Standard Room Floor Plan ~480 Square Feet

Shades has multiple dining options, none of them particularly fun, distinctive or memorable compared to Disney alternatives, but all providing good value for the money. Additional dining is easily accessible at the Polynesian, and from the monorail stop there at other resorts.

Amenities at Shades are a little thin compared to those at the more expensive Disney-owned resorts, but stronger than those in Disney's less expensive resorts, and include playgrounds, a spa, a fitness center, tennis, hot tubs, and an arcade.

You won't find a better room for the money anywhere else at Disney World, making Shades a great choice for returning visitors, especially with its new access to FastPass+ at 60 days, but the combination of bland theming and not-so-convenient transport makes us hesitant to recommend it for first-time visitors. Many eligible first-timers will be better served by staying at a Disney-owned resort using Disney's Armed Forces Salute discount.

Prices at Shades are based on rank/rate. At press time, standard rooms range from $115/night to $145/night. Unlike the Disney resorts, Shades prices don't vary over the course of the U.S. government fiscal year. Discounts are often available. For more on these and everything Shades or military, see MILITARYDISNEYTIPS.COM.

FOUR SEASONS RESORT

The Four Seasons Resort Orlando at Walt Disney World Resort ("Four Seasons") opened in 2014 as Walt Disney World's first five star resort. Lovely but essentially un-themed (it could be anywhere), the 17-story hotel has elements of Spanish Colonial Revival architecture, with inadvertent references to the Tower of Terror. A wonderful respite for returning visitors who plan extensive hotel or pool time, Four Seasons has the nicest standard rooms on property, the best pool complex at Disney World, and fine dining for adults (and a bit of playful dining for kids). But transportation, theming, and FastPass+ issues make it hard for us to recommend it for first-timers.

Four Seasons is not owned by Disney, and its guests don't have access to the perks that those staying in Disney-owned resorts receive except for Extra Magic Hours. For example, they don't get free parking at the hotel or the parks, can't use the Dining Plan, can't use Disney's Magical Express, and, most importantly, can't book FastPass+ at 60 days. Four Seasons guests book FastPass+ at 30 days.

Four Seasons is a mid-sized high rise with guest services on the lower floors and rooms and suites on the upper floors. One of its long sides overlooks its parking lots, and the other has distant vistas of the Magic Kingdom and Epcot, and near views of its wonderful pool complex—the best at Disney World—which includes an adult-only pool, large lazy river pool, pool slide complex, and family pool.

Four Seasons is deep in the Golden Oak residential area, between Fort Wilderness and Port Orleans Riverside. Park transport is via its own motor coach system that is more comfortable but less convenient than the buses serving the Disney-owned resorts. Coaches run too infrequently, and (as of Dave's last stay) begin their schedules too late and end too early.

There's two flavors of standard rooms at Four Seasons, identical except on their bed side, where one offers two full beds and an easy chair, and the other a king bed and a couch that converts into a queen sized bed that is, by far, the most comfortable sofa bed Dave's ever slept on. (The floor plan is of the king bed variant.) All but the shortest and most slender of families seeking one room should choose the king/sleeper sofa floor plan over the full beds. The most common layout pairs one of each of these room types with connecting doors and a deep entry alcove that can also be closed off at the corridor end—making for an easy, albeit expensive, set-up for families seeking more than one room's worth of space or beds.

These standard rooms are about 500 square feet—the largest on property—and have beside the beds and chair or couch, a large table with two chairs that can serve as a desk as well, TV, dresser, enormous closet with more drawers, and a coffee-maker/mini-fridge set up all ready for you to order in a full bar. The overly open bath includes two sinks, a hair dryer, a tub and a separate shower, and a toilet in a separate glass-walled room. All rooms are accessed from interior corridors, and all have large balconies. Suites of all flavors are also available, including a nine-bedroom option going for more than $10,000 a night—add taxes and tips, and pretty soon you are talking about real money.

Four Seasons has multiple dining options, including Capa, a distinctive rooftop Spanish steakhouse with distant views of the Magic

Four Seasons Resort Orlando
Standard King Bedroom Floor Plan ~500 Square Feet

Kingdom and Epcot fireworks; Ravello, a more casual lower level Italian option; character meals with Goofy certain mornings; and other pool-side and casual options. Unlike at the Disney deluxe resorts (except the Animal Kingdom Lodge), there's no easily accessible nearby hotels offering additional dining venues.

Four Seasons offers all the amenities you'll find at any other Disney World hotel except for beaches and water sports. You won't find a more relaxing, delightful, or peaceful resort anywhere else at Disney World, but the combination of bland theming, not-so-convenient transport, and 30 day FastPass+ makes us hesitant to recommend it for first-time visitors. Most first-timers who could afford Four Seasons will be better served by staying at one of the monorail resorts (Contemporary, Grand Floridian, or Polynesian), and saving Four Seasons for a return trip when relaxing at the hotel is as important a priority as is visiting the parks.

Future pricing at Four Seasons is not so easy to uncover as it is at the Disney-owned resorts, but the least expensive rooms at Four Seasons are easily competitive with the Disney monorail resorts, especially if your dates are flexible.

THE DISNEY SPRINGS RESORT AREA HOTELS

The seven hotels of the Disney Springs Resort Area are on Disney World property but owned and operated by third parties. These are a mix of small and larger hotels (though none is as large as the largest Disney hotels), some aimed at conventioneers, others at families, others at couples, some all suites, and some with just small regular rooms with full beds. For 2018, perhaps as a time-limited experiment, guests at all of these gained access to the two most valued Disney World perks: Extra Magic Hours and FastPass+ at 60 days. All guest at these hotels are eligible for EMH; only those who booked a package through the Walt Disney World Travel Company are eligible for 60 day FastPass+ (those who book via other venues get their FastPass+ access at 30 days).

For more on these hotels, see disneyspringshotels.com. To book them through the Walt Disney World Travel Company, start on your My Disney Experience account on the Disney World website, click at the top "Places to Stay," and then under "More Great Accommodations" click "Disney Springs Resort Area Hotels."

OFF-PROPERTY HOTELS AND VACATION HOMES

We think first-timers should stay at a Disney-owned resort, and that returning visitors—especially if their last visit was before

FastPass+—should strongly consider doing so. However, an off-site stay may remain attractive due to significantly lower prices, especially when considering the cost for a family of five to stay on property. While it's theoretically possible for a family of five to stay in the Murphy bed rooms at Caribbean Beach or Riverside, we're still talking about five people sharing a single bathroom and 314 square feet of total space. Disney's idea of a value-priced family suite at Art of Animation starts at $338 per night and skyrockets up to $570/night over the holidays.

However, staying off-site presents another set of costs and challenges. First, any scheduled shuttle transportation from most off-site resorts can be as weak as one bus in the morning and one bus at night. These times are often rigid and inconvenient, whether the bus arrives after park opening or departs long before the nighttime entertainment or the park closes. Miss the bus and it's an expensive cab ride. Off-site guests often rent cars, but that reduces convenience and increases costs. Parking at the theme parks is $22 per day (due only *once* per day, if you keep your receipt), in addition to potential parking costs back at the hotel. Second, resort fees that typically cost $15-$20 per night are another concern. For some families, the price discount may be too much to overlook this trip, and there's nothing wrong with that. But be sure to consider all the costs associated with a stay that may not be included in the initial price.

There are literally thousands of off-site hotels, motels, campgrounds, vacation homes, condos, etc., in and around Orlando. Returning visitors who know their way around can stay anywhere, but we suggest that first timers target their search to the Highway 192/West Irlo Bronson Highway and/or the Disney Springs Resort Area. The value of honing in on these two areas is simple: from almost any place in Walt Disney World, you can find directional signage to 192, and directional signage to Disney Springs.

Walt Disney World is much more complicated than many first-time visitors imagine, and your first few days of finding your way around will be made simpler by this signage.

- The street address of hotels on 192 will include either "Highway 192" and/or the words "Irlo Bronson Highway".
- The street address of hotels in the Disney Springs Resort Area will include "Hotel Plaza Boulevard" (or, in the case of the Hilton Orlando Buena Vista Palace, "Buena Vista Drive".)

It's possible to find multiple-bedroom vacation homes available for short-term rentals in the Orlando area for a fraction of the price you'd pay to stay in some of the deluxe large family options at Walt Disney

World, even counting your rental car costs. Airbnb is also becoming more accepted in Orlando.

First-time visitors benefit most from staying on property at a Disney owned and operated resort. While more expensive than their off-site counterparts, it's hard to put a price on the convenience and peace of mind that an on-site stay in a Disney resort offers.

How to Spend Your Time

This chapter:

- Provides example, pre-made itineraries for guests arriving on a Saturday and planning to spend nine days in Orlando.
- Presents introductions to touring each of the major theme parks, with reviews and insight into every single theme park attraction.
- Follows with Cheat Sheets that cover everything you need to bring with you to the theme parks. These include what to expect at park open, detailed touring plans including when you can expect to arrive and depart each attraction, FastPass+ priority so you know which experiences will save you the most time, and advice on how to see the nighttime spectaculars with the least hassle. Color copies of the newest versions of these Cheat Sheets are available at yourfirstvisit.net/easy-guide-2018-changes.

We open with a discussion of one of Disney's newest innovations, FastPass+, and how it has transformed the theme park experience in positive and negative ways. Maximizing FastPass+ is an important strategic advantage and we'll cover the best methods to save you hours in line every day.

Next, we focus on itinerary planning, including:

- Deciding how many days to visit each park.
- Picking the best park to visit each day based on crowds and entertainment offerings.
- Creating a daily touring plan that blends easy morning touring, strategically chosen FastPass+ experiences, and the best dining choices.

Example itineraries are provided to give you an idea about how best to plan your vacation in its entirety. Modifications can easily be made depending on where you want to go and what you want to do.

This is the lengthiest chapter because the theme parks are what a Walt Disney World vacation is all about. Plan to digest it over several sessions.

FastPass+ at Walt Disney World

Disney's digital FastPass+ system replaced legacy paper FASTPASS in early 2014. More attractions than ever before offer FastPass+, including nighttime spectaculars like IllumiNations at Epcot and character meet and greets like Rapunzel and Cinderella at Magic Kingdom.

Each attraction has one or two entrances. At attractions that do not offer FastPass+, there is a single line called the "standby queue". Here, guests simply get in line and wait their turn. At FastPass+ enabled attractions, there are two separate lines—the standby queue and the FastPass+ return queue.

At attractions with both types of entrances, guests with a FastPass+ can experience an attraction with priority boarding. Attractions like Tower of Terror and Toy Story Mania admit as many as seven FastPass+ riders for every one standby rider. Thus, those with FastPass+ wait much less than those in standby lines, and push up standby waits because they receive priority boarding, even if they arrive long after a standby rider.

Disney bills FastPass+ as an "easy way to reserve some of your must-do fun before you leave home". Indeed, all guests with tickets may book three FastPass+ experiences in advance. Guests staying at Disney-operated resorts, in addition to the Swan and Dolphin resorts, may book up to 60 days in advance of a given date. And as of January 2018, guests staying in Shades of Green, or in a Disney Springs Resort Area hotel with packages booked through the Walt Disney World Travel Company, may also book up to 60 days in advance. Guests staying in all other accommodations may book up to 30 days in advance. This is one of the most positive features of the program—guests may schedule headlining attractions like Toy Story Mania, Test Track, Space Mountain, and the Princess Fairytale Hall Meet and Greets from the comfort of their home long before they arrive in Orlando, or even the day of a visit to the theme park from their smartphone or in-park kiosk. But there are two major negatives:

1. Guests must select a specific one-hour window on a specific day. Based on the attraction reviews that follow, you may decide that the group wants to meet Ariel at Ariel's Grotto in Magic Kingdom. But you'll need to pick a specific date and time—August 27 from 2:15–3:15pm, for example. (The rest of this chapter helps with all these choices—which days, which rides, which FastPass+, and which times.)

2. Some attractions distribute a very limited number of FastPass+ opportunities, making booking 30–60 days in advance necessary.

Later in this chapter, we'll discuss the importance of choosing which theme park to visit based on crowds and entertainment. This goes hand in hand with Chapter 7, which discusses restaurant reservations, some of which must be booked a whopping six months in advance. Combined with the FastPass+ priority discussion next, picking attractions and theme parks is easy, but being forced to select specific hour-long windows for each ride can feel like too much micro-managing and reduce spontaneity.

There is no such thing as legacy FASTPASS inside the theme parks anymore, which—for those who have visited before—means no more paper FASTPASS tickets. Legacy FASTPASS tickets were generally distributed at each attraction that offered it, necessitating backtracking and long walks to collect FASTPASSes over the course of the day. The good news is that FastPass+ eliminates the need to visit each attraction for which you'd like a FastPass+. Gone are the days of sending Dad to Splash Mountain with everyone's park tickets while the rest of the group rides Buzz Lightyear's Space Ranger Spin 20 minutes away.

The introductions to each theme park below, along with the Cheat Sheets, include a list of the attractions that offer FastPass+. Attractions are ranked based on how much time and hassle using FastPass+ will save. For example, Toy Story Mania and Rock 'n' Roller Coaster are the top priorities at Hollywood Studios because using FastPass+ at either will save 60 or more minutes in line most of the day. Muppet Vision 3D is ranked near the bottom because using FastPass+ won't save any time since everyone that shows up for the next show will be admitted. There are a few other considerations also taken into account. For example, the queue for Tomorrowland Speedway at Magic Kingdom is outdoors and exhaust from the cars permeates through the entire area. Speedway is prioritized over several other attractions because it will not only save 20 or more minutes in line, but also bypass much of the stench.

Because FastPass+ experiences can be booked in advance, the new program adds certainty to your schedules and also makes arriving late at a theme park much easier than with the legacy FASTPASS system. Prior to FastPass+, Toy Story Mania legacy FASTPASSes would typically be gone before 11am, with return times well into the evening by 9:45am most days. This meant guests needed to arrive early to secure FASTPASSes with an unknown return time, or find themselves in a 75+ minute standby line at some point later in the day. Now you can leave home knowing you have Toy Story Mania booked in the afternoon, and no longer need to arrive at the park early to assure you can enjoy it.

Unfortunately, Disney has instituted a tiering system at Animal Kingdom, Epcot and Hollywood Studios, which means guests at those parks can initially reserve only one high priority attraction in advance. At Animal Kingdom, guests can pick only one of the two Pandora rides. At Epcot, guests choose between Frozen Ever After, Test Track, Soarin', and IllumiNations. At Hollywood Studios, the major decision is between Toy Story Mania and Rock 'n' Roller Coaster, where guests can only initially choose one. Riding more than one priority Tier 1 ride in a single day is easy if you head to one right at park open and then use FastPass+ for the other later in the day. But riding both over the course of one day with a late arrival will be more difficult. It's possible that these attractions will be available to book as a fourth FastPass+ selection at a kiosk or via the My Disney Experience app in the afternoon, but it's unlikely on busier days and return times will be severely limited.

Choosing the Best FastPass+ Time Slots

When considering when to schedule your FastPass+ experiences, there are two main schools of thought. The first is to schedule FastPass+ beginning right at park opening, with the goal of scheduling a 4th FastPass+ as early as possible. To book a 4th FastPass+, you must use the initial three or the window on the third must pass. So if you book Space Mountain for 9–10am, Buzz Lightyear's Space Ranger Spin for 10–11am, and Peter Pan's Flight for 11am–12pm, you would be eligible to schedule a 4th FastPass+ immediately after you use the 3rd or any time after 12pm should you not use the Peter Pan FastPass+.

Initially, Disney required all guests to book three FastPass+ in advance, but now guests may book just one FastPass+ experience at a time up to three total experiences so long as each is at the same theme park. But guests may initially select one, two, or three FP+ experiences. Most guests visiting just one park each day will want to select the maximum number of three in advance for the best selection.

Also, keep in mind that at Epcot and Hollywood Studios, guests must use or let expire all three of their initial FastPass+ selections in order to book a second Tier 1 FP+. So you can't book just Toy Story Mania from 9–10am, use it right at 9am, and then try to book a second FP+ for Toy Story Mania or another Tier 1 selection like Rock 'n' Roller Coaster. You would be able to book either after using your two Tier 2 selections. Guests planning to park hop could schedule and use just one FastPass+ at one park and then immediately schedule their second FastPass+ at another park, regardless of tier, but based on availability. So you could book and use Toy Story Mania in advance and after using it, immediately book Soarin' so long as times are availabile.

The benefit to booking earlier times is that each additional FastPass+ selection is based on availability, and availability is better earlier in the day when fewer people have had the opportunity to select additional FastPass+. The downside is that on busier days, there may be very little availability for the priority attractions even at 11am, particularly at

Epcot and Hollywood Studios where there are only two or three attractions most people are interested in booking.

Another downside is that using FastPass+ earlier in the day when standby waits are shorter will save less time than using the same FastPass+ later. For example, a Space Mountain FastPass+ used at 9:30am might save 15 minutes in line. A Space Mountain FastPass+ used at 12:30pm might save 60 or more minutes in line because afternoon crowds are so much heavier.

The second school of thought is to schedule FastPass+ in the late morning and afternoon when it will save the most time and take advantage of short standby waits at most attractions in the early morning. Our advice is to begin scheduling FastPass+ as early as 10:30am at a high priority attraction like Test Track or Seven Dwarfs Mine Train. While availability for a 4th FastPass+ will be worse later in the afternoon, it's likely that the same attractions that were available at 11:30am will be available at 1:30pm.

If you're planning to schedule your first FastPass+ for 9–10am, plan to use it as close to 10am as possible to save the most time and take advantage of short standby waits elsewhere before then.

Also note that scheduling a nighttime spectacular in advance inhibits your ability to make additional FastPass+ selections earlier in the day. For example, if you select IllumiNations, Mission: SPACE, and Spaceship Earth as your initial three selections, you won't be able to select a 4th FastPass+ choice because you won't use your third selection until the very end of the night. So there are some tradeoffs should you wish to take advantage of the reserved FastPass+ viewing areas at the nighttime entertainment.

Finally, keep in mind that FastPass+ does not operate during morning or evening Extra Magic Hours. That's mostly good news for those visiting during the extra time because it means FastPass+ returners won't bog down standby queues unnecessarily, in effect leveling the playing field for all on-site guests in attendance.

Designing Your Own Walt Disney World Itinerary

The art of itinerary design has three parts: dividing your time among the parks, picking the best days to visit each park, and shaping what you do each day to minimize time spent waiting in line.

ALLOCATING YOUR TIME AMONG THE PARKS

Chapter 3 covered in-depth how to divide your time depending on party size, makeup, and length of vacation. As a refresher, most guests will spend the most time at Magic Kingdom, with Epcot being a close second except for those traveling with the youngest children. Most guests spend about a day each at Hollywood Studios and Animal Kingdom, though guests spending just a few days at Disney World may not have time for all four parks.

PICKING THE BEST DAYS TO VISIT THE PARKS

There are several factors that contribute to the decision on which theme park to visit each day, including expected crowds and nighttime entertainment. We used to offer daily advice about six-and-a-half months ahead, but Disney has so limited the information it publishes that far in advance that we can no longer be precise in this advice. For imprecise guidance for your dates, leave a comment on any page of Dave's yourfirstvisit.net, or create a thread in Josh's forums at easywdw.com/forums/forum.php.

In general, the longer a theme park is open and the more nightly entertainment it offers compared to the other parks, the busier it will be. This is especially true at Magic Kingdom, which can see wildly different operating hours and entertainment offerings, particularly during Mickey's Party Season from late August through the third week in December. It's not uncommon for Magic Kingdom to be open to regular tickets only from 9am–7pm and offer no evening fireworks three or four days per week, while the other days it's open as late as 1am with fireworks. The days with longer hours are significantly more crowded because people equate longer hours with more bang for their buck. This isn't necessarily true. While a longer day does offer more time in the park, it also brings with it longer lines, increased congestion in common areas, and a more stressful overall experience. With two days at Magic Kingdom, most guests will want to visit on one less crowded day to hammer out the priority attractions and also visit on a day that they can enjoy the nighttime entertainment.

- Animal Kingdom is typically least busy on Sundays and Fridays. It's busiest on Mondays, Thursdays, and Saturdays, particularly on days with morning Extra Magic Hours.
- Epcot is generally least busy on Mondays, Wednesdays, and Fridays. Saturdays are typically busiest with most Tuesdays and Thursdays seeing longer waits than other weekdays.
- Mondays, Wednesdays, and Saturdays are usually best for Hollywood Studios. Sundays and Fridays typically see higher attendance.
- Magic Kingdom is typically least busy on Tuesdays and Thursdays and busiest on Saturdays and Mondays.

One reason why Magic Kingdom tends to be busiest on weekends and Mondays, and the other theme parks less crowded on those days, is the number of people that arrive over the weekend and head to the Most

Magical Place on Earth first thing. We recommend putting off Magic Kingdom for a Tuesday, not only because it's less crowded and more enjoyable, but also because seeing it first might spoil the very different experiences at the other theme parks. While much of Magic Kingdom is an exercise in excitement and sensory overload, Epcot in particular takes more time and thought to discover its richness. This isn't to say the other theme parks are "bad", but it can be difficult to get young kids excited about an educational boat ride about horticulture after experiencing the 50-foot plunge on Splash Mountain the day before.

Once you've sorted out which parks you will visit on which days, begin entering the details in the planning sheet, on the following page. (There's room in it for dining as well, which is coming in Chapter 7.)

DESIGNING YOUR PARK APPROACH FOR EACH DAY

After you've divided your days among the parks, and picked days to visit each park, your final step is designing your approach for each day.

There are two easy ways to go about this:

1. Model your visit around the daily agendas you'll find linked to from the itineraries on yourfirstvisit.net/itineraries. We give two examples of these itineraries after the worksheet.

2. Use the park overviews and ride reviews that come just after the example itineraries, to tailor the easyWDW Cheat Sheets at the end of this chapter to a trip that's perfectly adapted to your group and the length of your trip!

Example Itineraries for Disney World

If you have chosen to do an eight-night, nine-day trip with a Saturday arrival, and your kids are at least 8 years old and 48 inches tall, then you'll find an itinerary for dates within the next six or so months (they are released as Disney releases its operating calendar) at yourfirstvisit. net/itineraries. Scan down the dates at that link and click to the itinerary suggested for that date—taking special note of words like "but see this for required changes...".

When you do so, you'll find an itinerary like one of the two examples that follow, and with it links to daily touring plans based on that itinerary and a tailored To-Do List with suggested FastPass+. While the examples below will give you an idea about what we're looking at, they do change based on different weekly schedules. The list at yourfirstvisit. net/itineraries will be updated with itineraries for each specific week.

Disney World Itinerary Planning Worksheet

Meals:	_____day	_____day	_____day	_____day
Breakfast				
Lunch				
Dinner				
Parks, Etc:				
Early Morning				
Late Morning				
Early Afternoon				
Late Afternoon				
Evening				
Late Evening				
Notes:				
Parade				
Fireworks				
Park-Open Target				
FastPass+ Target				

Underline =
Counter/Quick Service

Bold =
Table Service

Italic =
Cash, not Dining Plan

Red =
Character Meal

Meals:	_____day	_____day	_____day
Breakfast			
Lunch			
Dinner			
Parks, Etc:			
Early Morning			
Late Morning			
Early Afternoon			
Late Afternoon			
Evening			
Late Evening			
Notes:			
Parade			
Fireworks			
Park-Open Target			
FastPass+ Target			

"FastPass+ Target" is the Tier One Fastpass+ to aim for; at time of writing, only Epcot and Hollywood Studios have tiered FastPass+

EXAMPLE ITINERARY: TYPICAL HIGHER-CROWD WEEKS

Disney World Higher Crowd Itinerary

This does not work for all dates! See yourfirstvisit.net/itineraries

	Saturday	**Sunday**	**Monday**	**Tuesday**
Meals:		*Hotel Room*	*Hotel Room*	*Hotel Room*
Breakfast	Travel	Hotel Room	Hotel Room	Hotel Room
Lunch	Travel	Flame Tree Barbecue or Hotel	Hollywood Studios or Hotel Counter	11a Chef Mickey's
Dinner	6p Akershus or San Angel Inn	5.30p Tusker House ROL Dining*	Sunset Ranch Market	6.15p Hoop-Dee-Doo Revue**
Parks, Etc.:				
Early Morning	Travel	At Animal Kingdom by 8.15a	At Hollywood Studios by 8.15a	At Magic Kingdom by 8.15a
Late Morning	Travel	Animal Kingdom	Hollywood Studios	Magic Kingdom
Early Afternoon	At Epcot ASAP	Off	Off	*Magic Kingdom*
Late Afternoon	Epcot	Off	Off	Magic Kingdom
Evening	Epcot	Animal Kingdom	At Hollywood Studios by 5.45p	Cash, not Dining Plan
Late Evening			Hollywood Studios	
Notes:				
Parade				
Evening Show	IllumiNations	Rivers of Light	Fantasmic	
Park-Open Target	n/a	Kilimanjaro Safaris	Rock 'n' Roller Coaster	Buzz Lightyear
FastPass+ to pre-schedule	Frozen Ever After, Spaceship Earth	Na'vi River Journey, Finding Nemo, Kali River Rapids	Tower of Terror, Indiana Jones, and a third	Space Mountain, Tomorrowland Speedway, Jungle Cruise
Extra FP+ Target			Fantasmic	

	Wednesday	**Thursday**	**Friday**	**Saturday**	**Sunday**
Meals:	*Hotel Room*	*Hotel Room*	*Hotel Room*	*Hotel Room*	*Hotel Room*
Breakfast	Hotel Room	Hotel Room	Hotel Room	Hotel Room	Hotel Room
Lunch	Hollywood Studios Counter	TBD Cinderella's Royal Table**	Sunshine Seasons	Magic Kingdom or Hotel Counter	Animal Kingdom Counter or Travel
Dinner	Sunset Ranch Market	Magic Kingdom or Hotel Counter	Epcot or Hotel Counter	6p Crystal Palace	Travel
Parks, Etc.:					
Early Morning	Off	At Magic Kingdom by 8.15a	At Epcot by 8.15a	At Magic Kingdom by 8.15a	At Animal Kingdom by 8.15a
Late Morning	Off	Magic Kingdom	Epcot	Magic Kingdom	Animal Kingdom
Early Afternoon	Off	Magic Kingdom	Epcot	Off	Off
Late Afternoon	At Hollywood Studios by 2p	Magic Kingdom	Epcot	Off	Off
Evening	Hollywood Studios			At Magic Kingdom by 5.30p	Travel
Late Evening	Hollywood Studios			Magic Kingdom	Travel
Notes:					
Parade		Afternoon Parade			
Evening Show	Star Wars Fireworks			Happily Ever After	
Park-Open Target	n/a	Peter Pan	Soarin' Around the World	Splash Mountain	Expedition Everest
FastPass+ to pre-schedule	Toy Story Midway Mania, Star Tours, Frozen Sing-Along	Seven Dwarfs Mine Train, Haunted Mansion, Enchanted Tales with Belle, Winnie the Pooh	Test Track, Turtle Talk with Crush, Mission: SPACE	Big Thunder Mountain, Pirates of the Caribbean, and a third	Avatar Flight of Passage, Festival of the Lion King
Extra FP+ Target			Re-rides	Re-rides	Re-rides

Underline = Counter/Quick Service
Bold = Table Service
Italic = Cash, not Dining Plan
Red = Character Meal

* As Rivers of Light Dining Package   **Two table-service credits

EXAMPLE ITINERARY: TYPICAL LOWER-CROWD WEEKS

Disney World Lower Crowd Itinerary from yourfirstvisit.net

This does not work for all dates! See yourfirstvisit.net/itineraries

Legend:
- Underline = Counter/Quick Service
- **Bold** = Table Service
- *Italic* = Cash, not Dining Plan
- Red = Character Meal

	Saturday	Sunday	Monday	Tuesday
Meals:				
Breakfast	*Travel*	*Hotel Room*	*Hotel Room*	*Hotel Room*
Lunch	*Travel*	Flame Tree Barbecue or Hotel	Backlot Express	**11a Chef Mickey's**
Dinner	**7p Akershus or San Angel Inn**	**5.30p Tusker House ROL Dining***	Sunset Ranch Market	**6.15p Hoop-Dee-Doo Revue****
Parks, Etc:				
Early Morning	*Travel*	At Animal Kingdom by 8.15a	Off	Off
Late Morning	*Travel*	Animal Kingdom	Off	Off
Early Afternoon	At Epcot ASAP	Off	At Hollywood Studios by noon	At Magic Kingdom by noon
Late Afternoon	Epcot	Off	Hollywood Studios	Magic Kingdom
Evening	Epcot	Animal Kingdom	Hollywood Studios	
Late Evening				
Notes:				
Parade				
Evening Show	IllumiNations	Rivers of Light	Star Wars Fireworks	
Park-Open Target	n/a	Kilimanjaro Safaris	n/a	n/a
FastPass+ to pre-schedule	Frozen Ever After, Spaceship Earth	Na'vi River Journey, Finding Nemo, Kali River Rapids	Toy Story Midway Mania, Star Tours, Frozen Sing-Along	Space Mountain, Buzz Lightyear, Jungle Cruise
Extra FP+ Target				

	Wednesday	Thursday	Friday	Saturday	Sunday
Meals:					
Breakfast	*Hotel Room*	*Hotel Room*	*Hotel Room*	*Hotel Room*	*Hotel Room*
Lunch	Hollywood Studios Counter	Magic Kingdom or Hotel Counter	Sunshine Seasons	Magic Kingdom or Hotel Counter	Animal Kingdom Counter or Travel
Dinner	Sunset Ranch Market	**TBD Cinderella's Royal Table****	Epcot or Hotel Counter	**6p Crystal Palace**	*Travel*
Parks, Etc:					
Early Morning	Off	At Magic Kingdom by 8.15a	At Epcot by 8.15a	Off	At Animal Kingdom by 8.15a
Late Morning	Off	Magic Kingdom	Epcot	Off	Animal Kingdom
Early Afternoon	At Hollywood Studios by noon	Magic Kingdom	Epcot	At Magic Kingdom by noon	Animal Kingdom
Late Afternoon	Hollywood Studios	Magic Kingdom	Epcot	Magic Kingdom	*Travel*
Evening	Hollywood Studios			Magic Kingdom	*Travel*
Late Evening					
Notes:					
Parade		Afternoon Parade			
Evening Show	Fantasmic			Happily Ever After	
Park-Open Target	n/a	Peter Pan	Soarin Around the World	n/a	Expedition Everest
FastPass+ to pre-schedule	Rock 'n' Roller Coaster, Tower of Terror, Voyage of Little Mermaid	Seven Dwarfs Mine Train, Haunted Mansion, Enchanted Tales with Belle	Test Track, Turtle Talk with Crush, Mission: SPACE	Big Thunder Mountain, Splash Mountain, Pirates of the Caribbean	Avatar Flight of Passage, Festival of the Lion King
Extra FP+ Target	Fantasmic	Winnie the Pooh	Re-rides	Re-rides	Re-rides

* As Rivers of Light Dining Package   **Two table-service credits
version 5/17

Disney's Animal Kingdom

With the opening of Pandora: The World of Avatar, and the addition of plentiful nighttime entertainment, touring Animal Kingdom is more complicated than it was prior to Pandora's debut on May 27, 2017. First, the new land brings two rides in Na'vi River Journey and Avatar Flight of Passage, each of which boasts 60+ minute peak waits and incredibly limited FastPass+ availability. Guests able to book FastPass+ for Flight of Passage will have the easiest time as Na'vi River Journey is easy to ride with a short wait first thing in the morning or last thing at night. But Flight of Passage FastPass+ are typically unavailable 30 days before a given date, meaning off-site guests won't find any availability. Flight of Passage also sees wait times take off immediately after opening, which necessitates an arrival at least 60 minutes before the park opens in order to be among the first couple hundred people to arrive at the ride.

Furthermore, the addition of the Rivers of Light nighttime spectacular, Tree of Life Awakenings projection show, and the novelty of experiencing Kilimanjaro Safaris, Expedition Everest, and Pandora after dark, may be cause to stay later into the evening than past visits. With regular summer hours being as long as 8am–11pm, it would be difficult or impossible to spend all 15 hours in the park with the heat and the crowds. Guests with longer trips may elect to spend parts of two days at Animal Kingdom or otherwise plan a lengthy afternoon break over the course of a single day. Some guests with a limited number of attractions that they would like to experience may also be able to make a late arrival work.

Overall, it's possible to enjoy the majority of Animal Kingdom's best attractions in a single day, but those who would like to see all of the shows, walk the nature trails, and slow down a bit to take in all of the sights and sounds should consider spending two days. That's particularly true much of the year when seeing Rivers of Light and experiencing the other nighttime attractions is difficult due to operating hour restraints. The introductions, reviews, and cheat sheets that follow will help guide you through the planning process.

FASTPASS+ PRIORITY

FastPass+ at Animal Kingdom is divided into two groups. One group includes the two rides that opened with the new Pandora: World of Avatar land. From these two you can pick just one. The other group includes all other Animal Kingdom FastPass+ attractions, and from these you can pick two more.

1. Avatar Flight of Passage
2. Na'vi River Journey

Everything else (choose two):
1. Kilimanjaro Safaris
2. Expedition Everest
3. Kali River Rapids (when highs are less than 80 degrees)
4. DINOSAUR
5. Rivers of Light (primarily first show; last show is easier to see in standby)
6. Adventurers Outpost Mickey and Minnie (due to fewer experiences available)
7. Kali River Rapids (when highs are under 80 degrees)
8. Festival of the Lion King
9. Finding Nemo the Musical
10. Primeval Whirl
11. It's Tough to Be a Bug

Guests may initially select only one Pandora ride in advance. Avatar Flight of Passage wait times average 160 minutes, while Na'vi River Journey's average wait is closer to 80 minutes, making the choice of which to select obvious when both are available 60+ days in advance. From among the other choices, Kilimanjaro Safaris and Expedition Everest typically save the most time and have relatively limited availability most afternoons. Kali River Rapids and DINOSAUR in the afternoon also save 30-60 minutes most days, but availability as a 4th or subsequent FastPass+ is usually higher.

Rivers of Light may be a good choice for those arriving later in the day, but choosing the nighttime show will result in the inability to make other FastPass+ selections until after the show, thus limiting the day's FastPass+ opportunities to just three. The Adventurers Outpost Mickey and Minnie Meet has limited availability, but wait times are usually under 30 minutes, which is less time savings than the major rides. During cooler days, there is far less demand for Kali River Rapids because fewer people are interested in getting wet.

Time savings at Festival of the Lion King and Finding Nemo the Musical is negligible with FastPass+ since it requires the user to arrive at the shows early enough that a similar seat in standby should be available. On the plus side, using FP+ guarantees a seat, which makes an arrival closer to show time possible, even if the seat is unlikely to have a great view. Finally, Primeval Whirl and It's Tough to Be a Bug have availability almost all day, making it easy to secure FastPass+ for these experiences after using the day's initial allotment.

ARRIVING AT ANIMAL KINGDOM

Guests headed to Avatar Flight of Passage first want to arrive at least one hour before official park open to be among the first couple of hundred people to arrive at the attraction. Posted waits will hit 100+ minutes within 15 minutes of opening. Those headed anywhere else, including Na'vi River Journey, can safely arrive 30 minutes before open and find short waits at any other attraction.

Almost all guests arrive by Disney bus or their own transportation. Guests parking early can easily walk to the main entrance. Guests arriving later and parking farther out have the option of walking or taking a tram. Those arriving via Disney bus will be dropped off just a minute or two walk away from the main entrance.

Bag check precedes the ticket windows. Since Pandora opened, Animal Kingdom ticket windows have seen longer lines, but they're still typically shorter than Magic Kingdom or Epcot. Guest Services is located on the far left both inside and outside the main entrance. Stroller and wheelchair rentals are located on the right just inside the main entrance.

Rainforest Café sits on the left with an entrance/exit both inside and outside the park. Theme park admission is thus not required to dine at the restaurant, which is only convenient as you enter or exit the park.

THE OASIS

Unlike the entry into any other Disney theme park, The Oasis is nearly devoid of shops, restaurants, and loud stimuli. Instead, the area works to transition visitors into the lush, tropical, animal-filled surroundings that set the tone for the rest of the park. Expansive animal habitats display iguanas, anteaters, macaws, ducks, and a variety of other animals amidst rushing waterfalls, dense vegetation, and a burgeoning canopy. Guests arriving prior to park opening will want to breeze through the Oasis with plans to return either in the afternoon or on the way out. Time spent here at open will only result in thousands of people passing you and filling the queues for the major attractions, in turn pushing up wait times. With an afternoon arrival, plan to slowly meander around the winding pathways, taking in the various exhibits for 15–30 minutes.

DISCOVERY ISLAND

After The Oasis, guests cross a bridge to Discovery Island, the central hub for the entire park. Discovery Island circles the 14-story hand-carved Tree of Life, the park's central icon and an easy marker for guests trying to make their way back to the main drag from one of the peripheral lands.

DinoLand and Asia are off to the right, in addition to the Adventurer's Outpost Mickey and Minnie meet and greet, It's Tough to Be a Bug 4D show, and Flame Tree Barbecue, one of the park's best quick services. Off to the left is Pizzafari, another quick service option offering flatbread pizzas and garlic knots in a bright, air-conditioned space. Attached to Pizzafari is a new signature restaurant called Tiffins, which specializes in African, Asian, and South American flavors in an atmosphere that celebrates Disney Imagineers' exploration of those continents as they planned and conceptualized the construction of the park. Nomad Lounge, located inside Tiffins, offers what is probably the most relaxing air-conditioned respite for a drink in any Disney theme park. Past Pizzafari is the park's Starbucks location, followed by Africa, one of the three major lands. Pandora: The World of Avatar officially opened on May 27, 2017, and replaces Camp-Minnie Mickey. The land's main entrance is down the path to the left of Pizzafari and Tiffins.

Discovery Island is where you'll find the bulk of the shopping opportunities, with Island Mercantile and Discovery Trading Company supplying the widest selection. Virtually anything you would find in any of the smaller stores can be found here. Plan to return in the afternoon for some air-conditioned perusing when few people are shopping and the waits at the attractions are longer. Like the major stores at the other theme parks, Island Mercantile and Discovery Trading Company remain open for at least 30 minutes after close, allowing for last-minute impulse buys.

Adventurers Outpost

RANKING Don't miss for those that want to meet Mickey and Minnie together; skippable otherwise. **EMH** No. **FP+** Yes. High priority for guests wanting to meet the characters. **TYPE** Meet-and-greet. **REQUIREMENTS** None.

WHAT TO EXPECT Guests line up outside the winding queue before entering a small air-conditioned room prior to the meet and greet. Mickey and Minnie greet together in their safari outfits with a fun adventurer's background. This is the only regular meet-and-greet where both Mickey and Minnie greet and take pictures together. **SCARY FACTOR** None.

WHEN TO GO Before 9:45am, during the last hour they meet, or with Fast-Pass+. **EXPECT TO WAIT** Peak afternoon waits are typically 25 to 40 minutes. **LENGTH** About two minutes of signing, mingling, and picture taking.

It's Tough to Be a Bug

RANKING Minor attraction. **EMH** Morning. **FP+** Yes. Low priority. **TYPE** 4D Show. **REQUIREMENTS** None.

WHAT TO EXPECT The theater is dark, loud, and there are a number of effects that "add" to the experience. Otherwise, It's Tough to Be a Bug is a fun 3D theater show (in-theater special effects make it "4D") based on *It's a Bugs Life* that most guests enjoy. **SCARY FACTOR (WITH MINOR SPOILERS)** Low for those 12 and older, but it may frighten younger kids. Animatronic spiders, termites, beetles, hornets, and more make appearances; several effects add to the anxiety: smoke, a "sting" from the back of the seat, insects dropping from the ceiling, and the sensation that bugs are running under your feet. If you're scared of bugs, this show may not be for you. At the same time, all of the bugs are "cartoony" like in the movie and not particularly realistic.

WHEN TO GO Afternoon when waits have peaked elsewhere. **EXPECT TO WAIT** Only as long as it takes for the next show to start. **LENGTH** 8 minutes. **WHERE TO SIT** Target the back few rows and let guests fill about half the row before entering. With apprehensive kids, instead sit at the end of a row for an easy exit.

Rivers of Light

Rivers of Light is the park's nighttime spectacular that's scheduled at least once most nights with the first show after dark and the last show typically scheduled at or just past park close. If a show is scheduled after official close, anyone is welcome to stay and see it. It takes place on Discovery River with stadium seating in Asia (FastPass+) and DinoLand (dining package and standby).

RANKING Debatable. The avant-garde show relies heavily on unconventional visuals and whimsical music without fireworks or, arguably, a coherent storyline or anything resembling a true climax. See it and decide for yourself. It's several years in the making. **EMH** No. **FP+** Yes. It's a high priority for those that need to see the first show and don't want to use a dining package. Those able to use a dining package or see a later show in standby will probably want to make their initial three FastPass+ selections elsewhere. **TYPE** Outdoor theatrical production. **REQUIREMENTS** None.

WHAT TO EXPECT The 15-minute show relies heavily on the storytelling ability of the four performers that appear on one of two boats and large floats that glide effortlessly through the water. For the first show, plan to arrive with FastPass+ or dining package reserved seating at least 30 minutes before show time. To see the first show in standby, arrive at least one hour before show time as there's only room for about 1,000 people in that section. For the second show, arrive 30 minutes early with FastPass+ or 30 minutes before show time in standby. **SCARY FACTOR** Just the standby wait. While dark, the show doesn't feature overtly scary visuals.

WHEN TO GO Usually one show shortly after dark and, if offered, a second show scheduled 75–90 minutes later. **LENGTH** 15 minutes.

PANDORA

Animal Kingdom's newest land, with a reported price tag north of $500 million, is a breathtaking sight to behold. Towering mountains that appear to float in midair greet guests with bright flora, cascading water-falls, and thousands of details spread out around the 12-acre expanse. It's one of the most immersive areas in any theme park worldwide. Avatar Flight of Passage is the marquee attraction. A state-of-the-art motion simulator, riders actually feel like they've mounted a banshee before taking a ride through the lush landscape of Pandora. Na'vi River Journey is its much tamer cousin, featuring a scenic, slow-moving boat ride through a dark, bioluminescent rainforest.

Windtraders, Pandora's principal retail store, offers interactive expe-riences in addition to the thousands of items available for sale. Visitors have the opportunity to "adopt" a banshee that sits playfully on the owner's shoulder, complete with a remote control that moves the limbs of the bird-like predator. Guests may also elect to have their own Avatar action figure made based on their likeness. After being scanned by a technician, the figure will be available to take home shortly after.

Satu'li Canteen, the land's major quick service, offers some of the best and most unique fast food at Walt Disney World. Best are the various bowls filled with steak, chicken, fish, or tofu on top of several different base choices, including quinoa and vegetable salad or red and sweet potatoes. Other choices include steamed pods filled with vegetable curry or cheeseburger. Kids can choose from a smaller version of the bowl, in addition to a hot dog or cheese quesadilla. Pay special attention to the blueberry cheesecake dessert.

A takeaway bar named Pongu Pongu sits next to Windtraders, offering alcoholic and non-alcoholic frozen beverages, in addition to pineapple-filled cream cheese lumpia, which are like spring rolls with a sweet, tropical flavor.

Unsurprisingly, virtually none of the merchandise or anything else you see in Pandora focuses on the characters or plot of the first Avatar film. Seeing the movie will enhance your experience a bit, but the rides are perfectly enjoyable with virtually no previous knowledge of James Cameron's alien world.

Avatar Flight of Passage

RANKING Don't miss. **EMH** Morning, Evening. **FP+** Yes, highest priority. **TYPE** 3D flight simulator. **REQUIREMENTS** 44" or taller.

WHAT TO EXPECT The lengthy standby queue is a spectacle in its own right, winding around a mountain outdoors before arriving at the laboratory inside. Guests enter the first of two pre-show rooms, where riders are introduced to the Avatar link process. Next, guests are instructed on how to mount the ride vehicle, which is similar to getting on a bicycle. Some larger and/or taller guests have had trouble fitting on the seat. There is a test seat in front of the entrance that you can try if there's any concern. The trick is to sit as far forward as possible with your legs against the front restraints. The theater where the ride takes place is split into two rooms on each floor with three floors per theater. Eight riders in a single file line will board in each room, for a total of 16 people per floor or 48 people per theater. Unlike Soarin', the ride vehicles aren't lifted into the air in dramatic fashion—each row is already situated where it needs to be. After takeoff, the theater and ride vehicles move to simulate flight to great effect with the 3D images working in tandem with physical effects to create a real feeling of soaring through the world of Pandora. Even those that suffer from motion sickness typically report few problems. It's a tremendous move forward in flight simulation and a don't miss. **SCARY FACTOR** The ride vehicle restraints are a bit strange and some of the effects are surprising, but most riders should be at ease upon takeoff. Only those extremely scared of heights should be put off. The theater drops a few feet from time to time to simulate a mild plunge, but there is nothing overtly scary about the experience. Almost everyone leaves proclaiming it as one of their favorite rides, making it worth any initial unease. Motion sickness is much less of a problem than at imulators like Star Tours due to the smoothness of the ride and the high frame rate of the film.

WHEN TO GO Absolutely first thing in the morning if you arrive at least an hour before open. Standby waits are shortest during the day between 1:30–4pm and riding last thing at night is a viable alternative with actual waits that should be 45–70 minutes. Use FP+ if possible. **EXPECT TO WAIT** Posted waits are typically 150+ minutes within 15 minutes of opening. Other than absolutely first thing in the morning, expect to wait between 75–120 minutes in the afternoon and 50–75 at park close. Peak waits are typically in the vicinity of three hours. **LENGTH** 5 minutes. **WHERE TO SIT** Seats in the middle of each row (seats 6–10) have a more straight-on view with the middle row experiencing the most movement.

Na'vi River Journey

RANKING Major attraction. **EMH** Morning, Evening. **FP+** Yes, but it's a much lower priority than Avatar Flight of Passage and guests may select only one or the other. If Flight of Passage isn't available, Na'vi River Journey is a better choice than any other Animal Kingdom attraction. **TYPE** Boat ride. **REQUIREMENTS** None.

WHAT TO EXPECT Na'vi River Journey is a scenic, indoor boat ride with an intensity similar to it's a small world or Living with the Land. The queue is all outdoors, though at least half is covered. Riders board small boats with just two rows each. Each row seats a maximum of four people. The ride is dark, but never ominous, with bright bioluminescent flora lighting the path and an incredibly detailed, 8-foot tall animatronic Na'vi Shaman of Songs at the end. The ride is pleasant enough, but it's sparse on story and at under five minutes, feels short. **SCARY FACTOR** Only for the intensely scared of the dark. Nothing pops up or is intended to startle.

WHEN TO GO Within 45 minutes of the park opening, during the last hour of operation, or with FastPass+. **EXPECT TO WAIT** Waits are typically under 15 minutes during the first and last half hour of operation, but should hit 45 minutes within an hour of open and typically peak between 70 and 100 minutes. **LENGTH** 5 minutes. **WHERE TO SIT** Request the front row for the best view.

AFRICA

Home to Kilimanjaro Safaris, Festival of the Lion King, Gorilla Falls Exploration Trail, and the Wildlife Express Train to Rafiki's Planet Watch, Africa is Animal Kingdom's largest land. Guests enter through Harambe, a rural African marketplace surrounded by buildings inspired by the ones Disney Imagineers saw during their travels across the continent. You'll see everything from a fortress reminiscent of Zanzibar to thatched huts built by the Zulu in South Africa.

Tusker House Restaurant (a Mickey-hosted character meal), Mahindi Popcorn, Dawa Bar, and Tamu Tamu Refreshments are the first buildings guests see as they cross the bridge over to Africa. Farther back, Mombasa Marketplace is the large store on the right, offering authentic African crafts, Animal Kingdom merchandise, and African wines. Kusafiri Bakery is on the left, serving baked treats and beverages. The entrance to Kilimanjaro Safaris is straight back with the entrance to Gorilla Falls Exploration Trail to the right near the Wildlife Express Train station. Harambe Market is the area's principal, open-air quick-service venue. Here, you'll find a nice variety of tasty entrees like the ground beef kabob flatbread, sausage fried in curried corn batter, and spice-rubbed Karubi-style ribs. The area is most pleasant in cool weather, as there is little to protect guests in line from the elements, and all seating is outdoors.

Festival of the Lion King

RANKING Major attraction. **EMH** No. **FP+** Yes. Low priority. FastPass+ users enter the theater before standby if they arrive 20+ minutes early and have their choice of seats. **TYPE** Musical theater show. **REQUIREMENTS** None.

WHAT TO EXPECT Lion King reopened in a new theater on June 1, 2014, though few things changed from its original run in Camp Minnie-Mickey. The show reprises songs and characters from the movie and features acrobatics, Animatronics, singing, dancing, fire, theater, and the most elaborate costumes and sets you'll find at Disney World. With more than 50 performers, there is almost too much to take in. **SCARY FACTOR** Low, the theater is dark and sometimes loud, but there is little to frighten youngsters.

WHEN TO GO First and last shows are least crowded. **EXPECT TO WAIT** Arrive 10 to 20 minutes early. **LENGTH** 30 minutes. **WHERE TO SIT** The section you choose isn't as important as the row you select. Higher than the eighth row provides a better view of the various floats and sets.

Kilimanjaro Safaris

RANKING Don't miss. **EMH** Morning. **FP+** Yes. High priority. **TYPE** Safari ride. **REQUIREMENTS** None.

WHAT TO EXPECT Riders board a 32-passenger open-air safari truck and take a mildly bumpy, fully narrated trip through the 100-acre Harambe Wildlife Reserve. It's basically a simulated, shortened safari through life-like savannas populated with rare animals, including black and white rhinoceroses, cheetahs, flamingos, lions, giraffes, warthogs, zebras, wildebeests, ostriches, crocodiles, antelopes, and more. The animals aren't always "out" and your viewing may be limited by the time of day and simple luck of the draw. Disney extended the Safaris' hours through park close in May 2016 to mixed results. We recommend a ride that begins a few minutes after sunset when the animals are still active and the savannas are dimly lit. Once the sun goes down, it's difficult to see the few animals that remain and the storyline does little to keep the ride engaging. **SCARY FACTOR** None during the day and it's not much darker than other areas at night. **CAN WE HANDLE IT?** Mild jostling. If you have back or neck problems, request a front row where it's less bumpy.

WHEN TO GO During the first hour of operation, around sunset, or with FastPass+. Try to ride during the day and later at night for the best of both experiences. **EXPECT TO WAIT** 20–60 minutes in the afternoon. **LENGTH** 20 minutes. **WHERE TO SIT** Those sitting on the ends of the rows have the most unobstructed views. Otherwise, the driver's side has the best view.

Gorilla Falls Exploration Trail

RANKING Minor attraction. **EMH** Morning. **FP+** No. **TYPE** Self-guided walking tour, zoo exhibit. **REQUIREMENTS** None.

WHAT TO EXPECT Visitors walk along the path and enter various enclosures and exhibits that show off the animals in their native habitats. Expect to see hippopotamuses, meerkats, naked mole rats, gorillas, okapi (the only known relative of the giraffe), and an extensive number of rare African bird species. **SCARY FACTOR** Zero.

WHEN TO GO Last hour of operation, which may be earlier than park close. Kilimanjaro Safaris spits out thousands of guests an hour right at the doors to Gorilla Falls, causing crowding from 9:30am to 4pm along the narrow paths. The gorillas are also out more consistently in the late afternoon. Closes shortly before dusk. **EXPECT TO WAIT** No waits. **LENGTH** Gorilla Falls is a little less than a half mile long. Most visitors spend about 30 minutes moving through the trail and the various exhibits.

Rafiki's Planet Watch

RANKING Fun but skippable. **EMH** No. **FP+** No. **TYPE** Zoological exhibits and interactive experiences. **REQUIREMENTS** None.

WHAT TO EXPECT Rafiki's Planet Watch is a collection of nicely air-conditioned diversions from long waits in the hot sun. You'll find a variety of exhibits that you'll need to take some time with if you want to get anything out of them. There are no rides or thrills at Planet Watch—just educational exhibits. Here's what's available:

- *Affection Section*, a petting zoo. The animals here are mostly species that are endangered or otherwise at risk.
- *Sounds of the Rainforest*, a five-minute auditory exhibit narrated by Grandmother Willow from *Pocahontas*.
- *Conservation Station*, the main building at Rafiki's Planet Watch housing the majority of the live and hands-on exhibits. Veterinarians and wildlife experts will answer questions and give insight into how the Animal Kingdom operates. You can view live-camera feeds of backstage areas where the animals are kept, as well as a variety of other exhibits featuring a wealth of information on conservation efforts around the globe. Exhibits and activities can change on a daily basis because the area is actually used for live preparation and animal surgeries, so you never know what you'll see.
- *Character Meet and Greets*: Rafiki and Doc McStuffins are often on hand to meet guests to short lines.

SCARY FACTOR Minimal. There is a snake or two and the mornings may feature intensive veterinary procedures on the wildlife, but both can be avoided.

WHEN TO GO Between 11am and 3pm when crowds and temperatures peak elsewhere. There are no waits and the main building offers plentiful air conditioning. Closes shortly before dusk. **EXPECT TO WAIT** Riders must board the Wildlife Express in the back right corner of Africa. Expect to wait up to ten minutes to board the train and another seven minutes to ride over. **LENGTH** As little or as long as you want. Most guests spend about 30 minutes.

Wildlife Express Train

RANKING Fun but skippable. **EMH** No. **FP+** No. **TYPE** Slow-moving transportation. **REQUIREMENTS** None.

WHAT TO EXPECT Guests wait at the station for the slow-moving, open-air train that arrives every eight-or-so minutes. All guests seated on the train sit facing the sights as it slowly travels through backstage areas where riders have an opportunity to see where the elephants sleep, among other things. This is the only way to travel to and from Rafiki's Planet Watch. **SCARY FACTOR** Zero.

WHEN TO GO Between 11am and 3pm when crowds and temperatures peak elsewhere is best. Begins operation 30 minutes after regular park open and closes shortly before dusk. **EXPECT TO WAIT** Between two and ten minutes. **LENGTH** The trip lasts about seven minutes.

ASIA
....

Home to perhaps Disney's best roller coaster, in addition to a white water rafting ride, jungle trek, and the underrated Flights of Wonder, Asia has a lot to offer underneath its dense vegetation and gorgeously detailed theming. Asia is accessible via Discovery Island, a path from Africa, or DinoLand. Guests arriving from Africa or Discovery Island will first happen upon UP! A Great Bird Adventure, at least after the show debuts in place of Flights of Wonder on April 22, 2018. Continuing on, Yak & Yeti Restaurant and quick service are located on the left. The table service restaurant, which is operated by the same parent company as Rainforest Café, serves very good pan-Asian food at relatively reasonable prices, but the quick service arm has reduced offerings and the quality has come down considerably in recent memory. Still, the honey chicken, chicken fried rice, and egg rolls are all very good, though the all-outdoor seating can be uncomfortably hot and humid during the summer months. Just past Yak & Yeti on the left is the walkway to Kali River Rapids and Maharajah Jungle Trek. Free lockers are available near Kali River Rapids to keep belongings dry while enjoying the ride. Continue ahead and Expedition Everest is unmistakable in the distance. The ride entrance is again on the left. Passing Everest will take you to The Theater in the Wild, home of *Finding Nemo–The Musical*, and then on to the rest of DinoLand.

Shopping is thin through Asia, though you don't want to miss the clever Yak & Yeti-themed merchandise to the right of the quick service, or all the Expedition Everest-themed merchandise at the attraction's exit.

Expedition Everest

RANKING Don't miss. **EMH** Morning. **FP+** Yes. High priority. **TYPE** Roller coaster. **REQUIREMENTS** 44" or taller.

WHAT TO EXPECT Interesting artifacts in the queue create the back story of a mysterious beast that resides in the sacred mountains. Riders board (two per row) a train that traverses high speed twists, turns, and drops before a final confrontation with the Yeti. **SCARY FACTOR** Medium-High. Guests plummet down an 80-foot drop at speeds up to 50 miles per hour in the dark, but it could be worse. **CAN WE HANDLE IT?** If you enjoyed Rock 'n' Roller Coaster, or any other "big coaster", you shouldn't have a problem. It is more intense than Space Mountain, but not so intense that the younger crowd won't be jumping up and down begging to ride. Some motion sickness risk, but no loops or inversions. Little jostling or jerkiness.

WHEN TO GO At park open, after dark, or with FastPass+. **EXPECT TO WAIT** 25 to 50 minutes in the afternoon. **LENGTH** 3 minutes. **WHERE TO SIT** The first row provides the best view, but the last provides the wildest ride. There really isn't a bad seat on the train. **SINGLE RIDER LINE**: Yes, to the right of standby entrance. Waits are typically under ten minutes.

Kali River Rapids

RANKING Major attraction. **EMH** Morning. **FP+** Yes. High priority when temperatures are 80+. **TYPE** Flume ride. **REQUIREMENTS** 38" or taller.

WHAT TO EXPECT Expect to get drenched on Kali, which follows a story about the destruction caused by illegal forestry. Riders board large rafts that seat 12 people in a circle around the outside perimeter of the raft. Your raft will be pulled up a 90 foot hill and then be released to freely but briefly float down the rapids, passing through geysers, waterfalls, and beautiful tropical jungles before plummeting down a 30-foot waterfall. The drop isn't fast or particularly thrilling, but it is still fun. Our opinion is that it's not worth the wait or the possible discomfort of wet socks and clothes. Complimentary lockers are located across from the entrance. Put everything you don't want getting wet inside before riding. **SCARY FACTOR** The ride starts off with a 90 foot uphill ascent, but there are no steep drops.

WHEN TO GO When it's hot, ride in standby before 10am or after dark. FastPass+ is useful in the afternoon. In cooler temperatures, anytime. **EXPECT TO WAIT** 35 to 70 minutes in the afternoon when it's hot; 15 to 20 minutes when temperatures are under 70. **LENGTH** 5 minutes total, 2 of which are spent on the initial lift. **WHERE TO SIT** Anywhere.

Maharajah Jungle Trek

RANKING Minor attraction. **EMH** No. **FP+** No. **TYPE** Self-guided walking tour, zoo exhibit. **REQUIREMENTS** None.

WHAT TO EXPECT Maharajah Jungle Trek does not suffer from several of the problems that plague the Pangani Trail—the trail is wider, there is more room to view the animals, and the walkways aren't as crowded. This makes Maharajah more pleasant in the afternoon. Otherwise, like Pangani, Maharajah is a trail that takes visitors through several zoo-like exhibits and enclosures. You'll see Bengal tigers, Malayan tapirs, Blackbuck and Elds deer, and hundreds of exotic birds. Bats are located in a separate house that's easy to skip if you prefer. **SCARY FACTOR** None.

WHEN TO GO Much of the Trek is shaded and cooler than other areas in the Animal Kingdom, which makes it a good choice during the afternoon heat when attraction lines elsewhere are longest. Closes shortly before dusk. **EXPECT TO WAIT** No waits. **LENGTH** Maharajah is a little longer than a third of a mile and most visitors spend about 20 minutes walking through it.

UP! A Great Bird Adventure

Set to debut on April 22, 2018, UP! replaces Flights of Wonder in the Caravan Stage to the left of the Yak & Yeti restaurant. Senior Wilderness Explorer Russell will be accompanied by his canine friend Dug as they discover species of birds from around the world in a show that should blend humor and education in a fun, vibrant setting. The Pixar tie-in should increase interest, but we expect Disney to schedule enough shows that arriving 20 minutes before one starts should still be plenty of time to find good seats together.

DINOLAND USA

By far the least appreciated land in any domestic Disney theme park, DinoLand follows the story of the Dino Institute and their Time Rover Tours. The fictitious backstory is that, in 1947, researchers found dinosaur fossils in Diggs County and "Dino fever" took hold of the area, bringing in thousands of tourists. A local entrepreneurial couple, Chester and Hester, took advantage of the influx by building Chester and Hester's Dino-Rama, a collection of cheap carnival games, gaudy colors, and off-the-shelf rides.

Indeed, much of DinoLand is themed to a cheap carnival built on top of a parking lot—on purpose. Whether it works is another debate, but the Imagineers that designed the park would tell you it took more time and energy to make the parking lot look old and decrepit than it did to install much of the vegetation around the park.

Guests walking from Asia will first see The Theater in the Wild on their left. This houses one of Disney's most elaborate stage shows, *Finding Nemo–The Musical*. In the center of DinoLand sits Primeval Whirl and TriceraTop Spin. TriceraTop Spin is a spinner similar to Dumbo and The Magic Carpets of Aladdin, while Primeval Whirl is an off-the-shelf wild-mouse-style coaster. Farther back to the left of Restaurantosaurus is DINOSAUR, the land's major attraction and a fun dark ride that transports lucky riders back to the end of the late Cretaceous period. Restaurantosaurus itself is a burger-and-nugget quick service option with fun theming, plentiful air conditioning, and refillable fountain beverages.

Chester & Hester's Dinosaur Treasures shop is located near TriceraTop Spin's exit. There's nothing here that isn't available elsewhere. Another small store is located at DINOSAUR's exit. Here, you'll find some fun dinosaur-themed merchandise.

DINOSAUR

RANKING Don't miss. **EMH** Morning. **FP+** Yes. Medium priority. **TYPE** Dark ride. **REQUIREMENTS** 40" or taller.

WHAT TO EXPECT DINOSAUR is located in the Dino Institute, an elaborately themed queue area with authentic dinosaur fossils. After you move through the queue, you will be taken to watch a short video where the storyline is explained. Once the pre-show concludes, you will move to the next area where you board a 12-person (three rows with four people in each row) Time Rover vehicle. Once strapped in, you will embark on your wild ride through time and space. **SCARY FACTOR** High. DINOSAUR is one dark, loud, bumpy ride. Although there are no drops more than a few feet and the vehicles don't move particularly fast, this may still prove to be the scariest ride at Animal Kingdom. **CAN WE HANDLE IT?** Besides being scary and bumpy, DINOSAUR is rough on those with even moderate motion sickness.

WHEN TO GO Before 10:30am or two hours before park close. **EXPECT TO WAIT** 25 to 40 minutes in the afternoon. **LENGTH** 4 minutes. **WHERE TO SIT** Put apprehensive kids in the middle seats. The front row affords the best view.

Finding Nemo the Musical

RANKING Major attraction. **EMH** No. **FP+** Yes. Low priority. **TYPE** Musical theater show. **REQUIREMENTS** None.

WHAT TO EXPECT Featuring the *Finding Nemo* characters, the show is housed in an air-conditioned theater with fairly comfortable bench seats with backs. Tony Award-winner Robert Lopez and his wife Kristen Anderson-Lopez (now of "Let It Go" fame) penned 16 original songs for the show, and Michael Curry, who helped design the wildly successful *Lion King* Broadway show, served as lead designer. The actors and puppeteers wear costumes and are just as much a part of the show as the puppets themselves. Don't be put off by this being "just a puppet show" because it's much, much more than that. **SCARY FACTOR** Low. Nemo gets into some trouble with a shark puppet, but that's about it.

WHEN TO GO First and last shows are least crowded. **EXPECT TO WAIT** You'll want to be lined up about 20 minutes before it begins. **LENGTH** 40 minutes. **WHERE TO SIT** Plan to sit at least half way up in the middle seating section. Sitting any closer may result in a cropped view of the stage that requires a lot of head turning to see the action. FastPass+ users who arrive 20+ minutes early file into the theater before standby guests.

Primeval Whirl

RANKING Fun but skippable. **EMH** Morning. **FP+** Yes. Medium priority. **TYPE** Wild mouse coaster. **REQUIREMENTS** 48" or taller.

WHAT TO EXPECT Riders board four-person spinning ride vehicles reminiscent of Mad Tea Party. The vehicles travel up a steep incline before being unleashed on a track that features no serious drops or g-forces. It is a herky-jerky ride with the occasional neck-snapping stop. **SCARY FACTOR** Medium. While technically less intense than other coasters, the spinning can be disconcerting and it "feels" like you're higher up than you are. **CAN WE HANDLE IT?** The ride can be incredibly hard on necks and backs. Anyone with pain should skip the ride.

WHEN TO GO Before 10:30am or two hours before park close. **EXPECT TO WAIT** 15 to 30 minutes in the afternoon. **LENGTH** 3 minutes. **WHERE TO SIT** The common advice is to evenly distribute weight on each side of the vehicle for less spinning. Or conversely, stick two heavier people on one side and two lighter people on the other for more spinning. Does it have an effect? Probably not, but it might make you feel better.

The Boneyard

RANKING Fun for kids, skippable for everyone else. **EMH** No. **FP+** No. **TYPE** Playground. **REQUIREMENTS** None.

WHAT TO EXPECT The Boneyard is an elaborately themed playground aimed at young kids and has several stories of sand pits, swings, and things to climb on. **SCARY FACTOR** None.

WHEN TO GO Visit with youngsters when the bigger kids are riding Primeval Whirl and DINOSAUR. Otherwise, visit in the late morning or afternoon when waits elsewhere peak. The Boneyard does get hot, so save it for the end of the day during the summer. **EXPECT TO WAIT** Very rarely any wait. **LENGTH** As long as it takes to pry Junior away.

TriceraTop Spin

RANKING Fun diversion, especially with kids. **EMH** Morning. **FP+** No. **TYPE** Spinning ride. **REQUIREMENTS** None.

WHAT TO EXPECT Riders enter four-person dinosaur-themed vehicles with two rows of two people. Each row has a joystick that can slightly alter the way the vehicle moves: either up and down or back and forth. The ride vehicles slowly move around the base of the ride in a circle. **SCARY FACTOR** Minimal. Although the ride does move up, down, and side to side, it's geared towards young children and it shouldn't frighten anyone. **WHEN TO GO** Before 11am or about two hours before park close. **EXPECT TO WAIT** Peak waits of 10 to 15 minutes are common. It's a walk-on, early and late. **LENGTH** 90 seconds. **WHERE TO SIT** Your choice, though young kids will be asked to sit on the inside so they won't accidentally fall out. Riders in the front can reach behind and use the joystick in the back row if there's nobody back there.

Epcot

Epcot is Walt Disney World's second most popular theme park and a quintessential part of any theme park vacation. Most guests with older kids will want to prioritize a second day here over a second day at Animal Kingdom or Hollywood Studios due to Epcot's vast size and the time it takes to experience many of its attractions. Epcot is unlike any other theme park, and many of its attractions take time and a little effort to enjoy.

Epcot consists of two very different pieces: Future World and World Showcase. Future World is where you'll find two of the park's three headlining rides, Soarin' and Test Track, in addition to the bulk of the secondary attractions. It's the area located just inside the main entrance and consumes the north half of the park. World Showcase is home to most of the dining and shopping experiences, in addition to the emphasis on the cultures of the world that the park is so famous for providing. Frozen Ever After, which replaced Maelstrom in the Norway Pavilion in June 2016, is also found here. Peak waits are typically 90 minutes.

Future World usually operates from 9am (rarely, from 8am) through regular park close, although the Imagination Pavilion, Energy Pavilion, Innoventions, and the attractions inside them typically close at 7pm, in addition to Living with the Land in the Land Pavilion.

Most of World Showcase opens at 11am with two exceptions. The bakery in France opens daily at park open, though most guests will want to visit later in the day and focus first on attraction priorities. The Norway Pavilion, including the Frozen Ever After ride and Royal Sommerhus Anna/Elsa Meet and Greet, also opens with the park. While waits to meet Anna and Elsa typically peak under 30 minutes thanks to a healthy hourly capacity, Frozen Ever After is a major priority. We recommend riding with FastPass+ later in the day to avoid the morning rush.

FASTPASS+ PRIORITY

FastPass+ at Epcot is divided into two tiers. In Tier 1 are Frozen Ever After, Soarin', Test Track, and Illuminations. Eight selections comprise Tier 2 with only a few offering much value in most situations.

Tier 1 (choose one)

1. Frozen Ever After
2. Test Track
3. Soarin'
4. Illuminations

Tier 2 (choose two)

1. Character Spot (only offered for the Mickey side; Joy/Sadness do not offer FastPass+)
2. Spaceship Earth
3. Mission: SPACE
4. Turtle Talk with Crush
5. Journey into Imagination with Figment
6. The Seas with Nemo and Friends
7. Living with the Land
8. Pixar Short Film Festival

ARRIVING AT EPCOT

Guests aiming to take advantage of shorter morning waits should arrive at the main entrance at least 45 minutes before open, or at the International Gateway at least 30 minutes before open.

Most guests arrive at the main entrance via Disney bus or their own automobile. Guests staying at the Beach Club, Yacht Club, BoardWalk Inn, Swan, and Dolphin have the option of walking from their resort or taking the boat to the International Gateway entrance in the World Showcase between the United Kingdom and France Pavilions. Guests transferring from Magic Kingdom or the Magic Kingdom parking lot (Transportation and Ticket Center) arrive at the main entrance via the monorail.

Guest Services outside the main entrance is on the far right, while Guest Services inside is on the far left past Spaceship Earth. Wheelchair and ECV rental are on the left just inside the entrance. At the International Gateway, Guest Services is located next to the ticket booths on the left outside bag check. Wheelchairs and EVCs are available for rental inside on the left.

FUTURE WORLD EAST
••

Future World East is where you'll find two of Future World's three top priority attractions: Test Track and Mission: SPACE. Most guests visiting only for one day will want to start on this side, and guests spending two or more days will also want to plan a morning starting with Test Track or a late arrival with Test Track as a FastPass+ selection.

Bypass Spaceship Earth, the park's icon, first thing in the morning. The iconic structure that looks like a giant golf ball enjoys lower peak waits than the headliners and sees shorter waits after 6pm. Many uninformed guests ride Spaceship Earth first thing, putting them at a great disadvantage as they won't arrive at Test Track until at least 9:30am, when waits will already be hitting 30+ minutes.

Dining choices are slim—Electric Umbrella is really it, and it serves a limited menu featuring Disney's standard burgers, chicken nuggets, and sandwiches. Various stands serve snacks like pretzels, churros, and beer.

Mouse Gear is the largest store in Epcot, offering the widest assortment of theme park merchandise outside of World of Disney at Disney Springs.

Innoventions East

RANKING Afternoon diversion. **EMH** No. **FP+** No. **TYPE** Exhibits and interactive experiences. **REQUIREMENTS** None.

WHAT TO EXPECT There are only two experiencing remaining, both of which are skippable for most guests. Colortopia introduces guests to how color changes feelings and mood. The first ten minutes are dull, but kids enjoy the interactive digital coloring exercise at the end. The SpectacuLAB is a 30-minute presentation featuring a variety of live experiments that are not nearly as exciting as the hosts would lead you to believe. It's fun for kids around the ages of 4–9, but is less engaging for older kids and adults. Only visit with a lot of extra time. **SCARY FACTOR** None.

WHEN TO GO In the afternoon. Usually closes at 7pm. **EXPECT TO WAIT** Just a few minutes for the next experience to begin. **LENGTH** 15–45 minutes.

Mission: SPACE

RANKING Major attraction. **EMH** Morning, Evening. **FP+** Yes. High priority. **TYPE** Simulator. **REQUIREMENTS** Must be 44" tall to ride the Mars mission; 40" for Earth. Mission: SPACE has more warnings than any other ride at Disney World, and is the only ride where you will be handed a card with all of the various warnings on it. Consider skipping if you have suffered motion sickness on any other ride, or are claustrophobic.

WHAT TO EXPECT Mission: SPACE is a space flight simulator, where riders board small four-person capsules that are intended to mimic the inside of a space shuttle. There are two versions of this ride. Mars features a spinning takeoff with G-forces up to 2.5, and is much more thrilling and much more risky for those with physical or motion sickness issues. The Earth version debuted in August 2017 with a storyline that revolves around circling the green planet. There is no spinning takeoff, and thus, no G-forces to worry about. After the initial takeoff, the rest of the ride is rather tame with only slight movements by the simulator while you watch a small screen in front of you. During the Mars mission, the intense aspects last for about 15 seconds at takeoff and again for a short amount of time when the spacecraft travels through an asteroid field. Those that have previously experienced Mission: SPACE Orange may want to try Earth for a new experience. **SCARY FACTOR** Medium. The ride itself is not particularly scary, but there are some iffy moments. Mission: SPACE does induce anxiety due to negative hype over people getting sick from the spinning. **CAN WE HANDLE IT?** Apprehensive riders should begin with the Earth mission.

WHEN TO GO Before 10:30am, after 7pm, or with FastPass+. **EXPECT TO WAIT** Peak waits of 30-45 minutes are common. **LENGTH** 5 minutes. **WHERE TO SIT** Experience is the same from any of the four seats.

Spaceship Earth

RANKING Don't miss. **EMH** Morning, Evening. **FP+** Yes. High Tier 2 priority. **TYPE** Dark ride. **REQUIREMENTS** None.

WHAT TO EXPECT Spaceship Earth is a slow moving, dark omnimover ride that takes guests as high as 16 stories inside Epcot's famous geodesic sphere. Visitors ride past more than 20 Animatronic displays featuring scenes from the past 40,000 years that depict how communication techniques have changed with time. A classic. **SCARY FACTOR** Low. The ride is dark, but there are no startling elements.

WHEN TO GO After 6pm or with FastPass+. **EXPECT TO WAIT** Peak waits of 30 minutes are common. Expect to wait less than 10 minutes after 6pm. **LENGTH** 15 minutes. **WHERE TO SIT** Each row seats two to three people. The view from the left is arguably better.

Test Track

RANKING Don't miss. **EMH** Morning, Evening. **FP+** Yes, high Tier 1 priority. **TYPE** Dark/thrill ride. **REQUIREMENTS** 40" or taller.

WHAT TO EXPECT After a 2012 renovation, riders are to imagine themselves to be "inside" a computer simulation of a car being tested. Guests first design their own prototype automobile at a kiosk. The design process takes about three minutes and riders choose what they want their automobile to look like and whether they want to favor capability, efficiency, responsiveness, or power. In a surprise to many, this design step does not affect the ride in any way. Riders then board six-person vehicles with two rows of three seats each and embark on their journey with several sharp turns and increases and decreases in speed before launching outside at speeds up to 65 miles per hour. **SINGLE RIDER**: Test Track offers a single-rider line with the entrance to the left of standby. Waits are usually shorter than standby or FastPass+ because single riders don't go through the design process and the seating arrangement creates more openings. **SCARY FACTOR** Low. Test Track is just a little more intense than normal driving.

WHEN TO GO Immediately after park opening, in the final hour of operation, or with FastPass+. **EXPECT TO WAIT** 60–100 minutes in the afternoon. **LENGTH** 5 minutes. **WHERE TO SIT** Request the front row for the best view.

FUTURE WORLD WEST

Three large pavilions make up the bulk of Future World West. Soarin' on the lower level of the Land Pavilion is its headlining attraction that remains a top morning priority after receiving a new film and the addition of a third theater in June 2016. Most other attractions can safely be saved for the afternoon or early evening. Prior to its 2013 refurbishment, Character Spot was a top priority. Now that it has doubled its capacity, afternoon waits usually hover between 20 and 40 minutes.

Starbucks is located in the old Fountain View Café building to the right of the fountain. Club Cool, situated behind it, offers free samples of Coca-Cola products from around the world. Sunshine Seasons is arguably the best quick service in any theme park. You'll find it in between Soarin' and Living with the Land in the Land Pavilion. Coral Reef and Garden Grill are the two table service restaurants. Coral Reef receives mixed reviews, but the view of The Seas aquarium is intriguing. Garden Grill is a fun family-style character meal hosted by farmers Mickey, Pluto, Chip, and Dale inside the Land Pavilion.

Retail is light, with small stores and kiosks popping up at most attraction exits.

Character Spot—Baymax and Joy/Sadness

RANKING Don't miss for those who wish to meet the characters; skippable for others. **EMH** Morning, Evening. **FP+** No. **TYPE** Meet and greet. **REQUIREMENTS** None.

WHAT TO EXPECT Baymax meets separately from Joy & Sadness with a fun workshop backdrop. Because he isn't able to interact much with guests, waits are typically under 20 minutes and the meet and greet isn't necessarily a high priority. Joy & Sadness on the other hand spend a lot of time with each group and wait times rise to 30+ minutes almost immediately after park open. If this is a must-do for your group, you'll either need to visit first thing at park open, right before park close, or be prepared to wait 45+ minutes at some other point in the day. Both queues are at least completely indoors and air-conditioned. **SCARY FACTOR** None.

Character Spot—Mickey, Minnie, and Goofy

RANKING Don't miss for those who wish to meet the characters; skippable for others. **EMH** Evening. **FP+** Yes. High Tier 2 priority. **TYPE** Meet and greet. **REQUIREMENTS** None.

WHAT TO EXPECT Guests line up indoors with televisions playing old cartoon clips. Guests then meet Mickey, Minnie, and Goofy individually in their classic outfits. **SCARY FACTOR** None.

WHEN TO GO Late in the evening—ideally after 7pm. Waits are also short before 10:15am. **EXPECT TO WAIT** Peak waits are typically 40 minutes. **LENGTH** About five minutes of signing, mingling, and picture taking.

Disney and Pixar Short Film Festival

RANKING Relaxing, but skippable. **EMH** Evening. **FP+** Yes, lowest priority. **TYPE** 4D film. **REQUIREMENTS** None.

WHAT TO EXPECT Located in the Imagination Pavilion alongside Journey into Imagination with Figment, this is a straightforward set of three shorts from Disney and Pixar projected in 3D with a couple of in-theater effects. The shorts are available on YouTube and a variety of other media, but the theater is air-conditioned with comfortable seating, making it a good choice if you have 20 minutes to burn during a hot afternoon. **SCARY FACTOR** None.

WHEN TO GO Go in the afternoon when waits are longer elsewhere. **EXPECT TO WAIT** Up to 15 minutes for the next show to begin. **LENGTH** 15 minutes. **WHERE TO SIT** Like any movie theater, the middle is a good choice.

Journey into Imagination with Figment

RANKING Minor attraction. **EMH** Evening. **FP+** Yes. Low priority. **TYPE** Dark ride. **REQUIREMENTS** None.

WHAT TO EXPECT Narrated by Dr. Nigel Channing with frequent interruptions by Figment the purple dragon, Journey takes riders slowly through a variety of rooms, each designed to stimulate the senses. **SCARY FACTOR** Low. This will only startle the young that are extremely prone to attraction anxiety.

WHEN TO GO In the afternoon or with a shorter child while the rest of the group rides the thrill rides. Usually closes at 7pm. **EXPECT TO WAIT** Peak waits of 20 to 30 minutes are common. **LENGTH** 5 minutes. **WHERE TO SIT** Any row is fine.

Living with the Land

RANKING Minor attraction. **EMH** Morning, Evening. **FP+** Yes. Low priority. **TYPE** Slow boat ride. **REQUIREMENTS** None.

WHAT TO EXPECT Living with the Land is a meandering, educational boat ride about crop cultivation. It's more fun than it sounds! **SCARY FACTOR** Low, unless you have a fear of genetically modified organisms.

WHEN TO GO By 10:30am or after 5pm is best. Usually closes at 7pm. **EXPECT TO WAIT** Less than ten minutes in most scenarios. **LENGTH** 15 minutes. **WHERE TO SIT** Request the first row for the best view.

Soarin' Around the World

RANKING Don't miss. **EMH** Morning, Evening. **FP+** Yes. High priority. **TYPE** Simulator. **REQUIREMENTS** Must be 40" tall to ride.

WHAT TO EXPECT Disney added a third theater in June 2016, in addition to installing a new film featuring scenes from around the world, including flyovers of the Eiffel Tower and Taj Mahal. Now known as Soarin' Around the World, the ride system and overall experience are largely the same, though the new film demands a re-ride for anyone that enjoyed the California version and is a favorite of many first-time visitors. Riders are led into a large room with an 80-foot-tall concave movie screen and three ride vehicles, each of which has three rows. Once all riders are seated, the vehicles are lifted into the air so that each row is above the row below it. A series of scenes are projected onto the screen and the ride vehicles move with the scenes to simulate a hang-gliding flight. **SCARY FACTOR** Minimal. The ride takes visitors 40 feet in the air, which may be frightening for those intensely scared of heights. Motion sickness is much less of a problem than "hang glider" might imply. The ride is gentle and there are no significant drops or sharp turns.

WHEN TO GO Immediately after park open, in the final hour of operation, or with FastPass+. **EXPECT TO WAIT** Afternoon waits are typically in the 40–60 minute range and peak around 75 minutes most days. **LENGTH** 5 minutes. **WHERE TO SIT** The best seats are in the front row of the middle vehicle because other people's feet won't be dangling in front of your face. This is one of the rare rides where your request will actually make a major difference in how much you enjoy it. Strongly consider requesting the first row.

The Seas with Nemo and Friends

RANKING Minor attraction. **EMH** Evening. **FP+** Yes. Low priority. **TYPE** Dark ride. **REQUIREMENTS** None.

WHAT TO EXPECT Nemo & Friends is a slow "clam-mobile" ride through a long *Finding Nemo* themed tunnel. The neatest part of the attraction is when the characters from *Finding Nemo* are shown swimming with real fish inside of the 5.7 million gallon salt-water tank. The ride lets visitors out at The Seas Pavilion, which is full of hands-on activities and places to view the 6,000+ underwater animals that live within one of the largest undersea environments in the world. **SCARY FACTOR** Low. There is a friendly shark Animatronic and it's dark, but that's about it.

WHEN TO GO Before 11am or after 7pm. **EXPECT TO WAIT** Peak waits of 30 minutes are common. Expect to wait less than 15 minutes before 10:30am and after 7pm. **LENGTH** 5 minutes. **WHERE TO SIT** Each clam-mobile seats three across a single row.

Turtle Talk with Crush

RANKING Don't miss for those with young kids, major attraction for everyone else. **EMH** Evening. **FP+** Yes. Medium priority. There are no reserved seats, but FastPass+ guarantees admittance to the next show. **TYPE** Interactive show. **REQUIREMENTS** None.

WHAT TO EXPECT Turtle Talk is a live, interactive show featuring Crush, the turtle from *Finding Nemo* and in a summer 2016 update, characters from *Finding Dory* as well. The theater is small and the kids are asked to sit up front. Crush moves, chats, and fields audience questions in real time, and every show is unique and drop-dead cute. **SCARY FACTOR** Zero.

WHEN TO GO Shows usually begin at 9:40am and run until 8:40pm. Visit before 10:30am or after 7pm. **EXPECT TO WAIT** Up to 30 minutes in the afternoon, but usually just as long as it takes for the next show to begin. **LENGTH** 15 minutes. **WHERE TO SIT** Kids should sit on the floor up front. Adults file into the bleacher-style seating in back.

WORLD SHOWCASE
• •

World Showcase is a collection of 11 pavilions, each themed to a country or collection of countries. The emphasis is on eating, drinking, and shopping, but each pavilion offers authentic entertainment and shows, in addition to the occasional ride. International cast members brought in to fill most roles help introduce guests to their respective cultures and add an additional layer of authenticity. It's truly a world's fair.

With the Frozen Ever After ride now open in place of Maelstrom, the Norway Pavilion should play a major part in most visitors' day(s) at the park. Because of its limited capacity and the popularity of Anna and Elsa, afternoon waits often peak at 75+ minutes. We recommend using FastPass+ when possible, which usually cuts actual waits down to fewer than 15 minutes. Norway is also home to the Royal Sommerhus meet and greet where guests have an opportunity to meet Anna and Elsa inside their air-conditioned summer home. While waits used to exceed two or three hours, thanks to increased capacity, waits for the Sommerhus rarely peak over 30 minutes and should be under 20 minutes most afternoons.

In addition to new attractions in Norway, Disney has installed a variety of interactive experiences designed to make kids more excited about visiting World Showcase. The most popular is Agent P's World Showcase Adventure themed to the popular Phineas and Ferb television show. Guests have an opportunity to pick up a handset or sign up using their own smart devices at a kiosk on the bridge over to World Showcase from Future World to embark on a kind of scavenger hunt throughout World Showcase. Kids also have the opportunity to sit down with Cast Members in each pavilion and decorate drawings. Even if you're not interested in the Frozen ride or meet and greet, moving up to World Showcase as close to 11am as possible guarantees low crowds at the various stores, exhibits, entertainment, and food outlets and the least amount of hassle overall.

IllumiNations

IllumiNations is the park's nighttime spectacular, scheduled every night, almost always at regular park close, and lasting for about 15 minutes. It takes place on World Showcase Lagoon with viewing available from around World Showcase. Detailed advice on where to see the show is in the Epcot Cheat Sheet at the end of the chapter.

RANKING Don't miss. **EMH** No. **FP+** Yes. Low Tier 1 priority. The Fast-Pass+ viewing location is at the base of World Showcase across from the United States Pavilion in an area called Showcase Plaza. It's a low priority because the show is easy enough to see outside the viewing area and using FastPass+ elsewhere will save more time. Note that the view is excellent and using FP+ eliminates much of the wait required for one of the prime viewing locations. Those skipping the priority rides or planning to arrive late for dinner and the show may find use in selecting it. **TYPE** Fireworks show. **REQUIREMENTS** None.

WHAT TO EXPECT Guests begin to fill in along the railing as far as two hours in advance, but most guests will find satisfying viewing locations as few as 15 minutes before show time. The action takes place on World Showcase Lagoon as fireworks explode above a massive rotating globe. **SCARY FACTOR** Low. The fireworks are occasionally loud, particularly at the end.

TYPICAL SCHEDULE: Begins at regular park close. **LENGTH** 15 minutes.

Our World Showcase reviews begin in Mexico and run clockwise around World Showcase Lagoon.

Mexico Pavilion

Framed by a giant Mesoamerican pyramid, Mexico is home to a boat ride, two sit-down restaurants, a quick service outlet, a tequila bar, a margarita stand, a Donald Duck meet and greet, and a live mariachi band.

Most of what Mexico offers is located inside the dark, air-conditioned pyramid that acts as a cool respite from the heat. Grab a margarita and enjoy the heritage exhibits, stores, ambiance, and music.

San Angel Inn, nestled along the water and immersed underneath the perpetual twilight inside the pyramid, is one of our favorite restaurant experiences. While the menu descriptions may seem a bit exotic at first, the flavors should be familiar. La Cantina de San Angel is the pavilion's quick service, offering an array of tacos, empanadas, and salads for lunch and dinner. We like the very shareable nachos, but more unique food can be found in other pavilions and outdoor seating is inadequate after 4pm. La Hacienda de San Angel, a second table service restaurant that's open for dinner at 4pm, is located on the lagoon and offers picturesque views to those that request window seats. The menu is limited and on the expensive side, but some guests may prefer the air-conditioned, homey atmosphere. Margaritas are best inside the pyramid at La Cava del Tequila, which also serves small bites and chips and salsa. Overall, most guests that stop for food and drinks should leave satisfied, but our preference is to search out something more unique.

Minor attraction: Gran Fiesta Tour is a relaxing, slow-moving boat ride through the world of *The Three Caballeros*. The ride lasts about seven minutes and follows Jose Carioca and Panchito as they hunt down Donald before a big gig. Waits are under five minutes most of the time. On busier days, visit before 12:30pm or after 7pm.

Norway Pavilion

Themed to a Viking-era village, Norway features a replica of the 14th century Akershus Fortress, originally built to protect Oslo from attack. Disney's version is sanitized—you'll find a princess-hosted character meal inside. The richly detailed stave church features a *Frozen* tie-in with artwork and artifacts that show how reality influenced the movie. Kringla Bakeri, the pavilion's quick service, offers excellent, inexpensive treats. At the Puffin's Roost, guests can peruse fun Norway-themed merchandise alongside authentic (and expensive) hand-knit apparel, perfume, and toys.

Norway is also home to the highest FastPass+ priority in Epcot: Frozen Ever After. While the attraction faced an uphill battle with a lot of fans due to the intellectual property it introduced to World Showcase and love for the ride that it replaced, reviews are largely positive. That's good news because it means that it's a fun ride that most guests will enjoy, but it also means that you're going to want to ride it, which can be a hassle for those with only one day to visit or for those unable to secure FastPass+.

Frozen Ever After

RANKING Don't miss for anyone able to secure FastPass+ or willing to wait in line. **EMH** Morning, evening. **FP+** Yes. Highest priority Tier 1 FastPass+. All FastPass+ experiences are typically booked 30+ days in advance of a given date, though cancellations do happen. **TYPE** Boat ride. **REQUIRE-MENTS** None.

WHAT TO EXPECT Once inside, the queue walks guests throughout the port town of Arendelle during its summer season celebration before a quick visit inside Oaken's Tokens and then onto the boat that will whisk riders through scenes that include the frozen Willow Forest, Troll Valley, and Queen Elsa's Ice Palace high atop the North Mountain. Olaf, Elsa, Anna, Kristoff, and Sven make multiple appearances as they sing a variety of everyone's "favorite" songs from the movie. The animatronics should impress even the most cynical and kids eat it up. **SCARY FACTOR** Low. It's dark at times and there are a couple of small drops, but anyone that made it through Pirates of the Caribbean or any similar ride will be just fine.

WHEN TO GO With FastPass+ if at all possible, which will reduce 60–120 minute actual waits to fewer than 15. Otherwise, those able to get in line right before park close should do so, when actual waits of fewer than 30 minutes are common. Getting to the ride first thing in the morning is a chore, but those that arrive at least 45 minutes before park open and walk quickly should find short waits first thing. **EXPECT TO WAIT** Peak waits are typically 60–120+ minutes. Ride during a recommended time or with FastPass+. **LENGTH** 5 minutes. **WHERE TO SIT** Boats have four rows with up to three adults fitting in each. The view from the far left seats is arguably better.

Royal Summerhus (building to the left of Norway just past Mexico)

RANKING The best opportunity to meet Anna and Elsa up close. **EMH** Morning, Evening. **FP+** No. **TYPE** Meet and greet. **REQUIREMENTS** Just the inclination to get in line.

WHAT TO EXPECT Those familiar with Maurice's Cottage at Enchanted Tales with Belle inside Magic Kingdom will recognize the quaint aesthetics of Anna and Elsa's summertime home. Guests have a lot to look at as they wait for their turn to meet Anna and Elsa. While the sisters meet separately, there is just one line for both. **SCARY FACTOR** None, unless you are a Disney World guidebook author that has to go through the line over and over in the name of "research."

WHEN TO GO Surprisingly, this is a good choice in the afternoon or evening. Waits typically peak early as guests hurry to the ride and then over to the meet and greet. Try after 11am. **EXPECT TO WAIT** 15–20 minute waits are common. **LENGTH** The sisters are among the most personable of the princess characters. Expect to spend a minute or two with each.

China Pavilion

An intricately detailed triple-arched ceremonial gate welcomes visitors to China. Immediately past the gate is a replica of the Temple of Heaven, inside of which guests can view *Reflections of China*, a 15-minute Circle-Vision 360 film that covers the more positive Chinese traditions and culture (as in all World Showcase shows except the American Adventure, no negative aspects of the culture appear). Visit the air-conditioned, standing-room-only theater at your leisure. While you wait for the next film to begin, check out the Shanghai Disneyland exhibit through the door on the left. Chinese acrobats perform most days either in the courtyard or inside the Temple of Heaven in the Hall of Prayer for Good Harvests.

Nine Dragons is the pavilion's table service restaurant, serving up traditional and contemporary Chinese food at prices lower than most other restaurants on property. It has a lousy reputation, but the food has improved in recent memory and the portions are large. Lotus Blossom is the quick service arm, serving some of the fastest, no-fuss food in World Showcase. With so many other options it's difficult to recommend it strongly, but portions are typically large with prices lower than a lot of other venues. The Joy of Tea stand on the water is a surprisingly good spot to pick up a strong drink or fruity cocktail depending on the group's mood at the time.

Shopping in China is above average at the expansive House of Good Fortune on the left side of the pavilion. You'll find silk robes, traditional fans, tea sets, jewelry, puppets, and more.

Germany Pavilion

Featuring a statue of Saint George slaying a dragon, and a clock tower with a glockenspiel that chimes on the hour, the architecture in Germany is interesting and varied. The main attraction is Altenmunster Oktoberfest beer on draft—though the pavilion did add a stage and live entertainment in July 2016. Also, take a moment to peruse Karamell-Kuche (Caramel Kitchen), in addition to the stores that offer made-in-Germany toys, cuckoo clocks, beer steins, toys, apparel, and other fun items. As you walk toward Italy, pay special attention to the outdoor model train set on the left.

Biergarten is the table service restaurant, featuring a smorgasbord of traditional German salads, roasted meats, pretzel bread, soups, and more. A traditional oompah band plays intermittently throughout the day inside the restaurant. Lunch is priced well. Sommerfest is the pavilion's quick service, offering a variety of bratwurst, frankfurters, and other traditional German foods. Seating for it is scarce.

Italy Pavilion

The focal point of the Italy Pavilion is the 105-foot-tall functioning replica of St Mark's Campanile, the bell tower that looks out over the World Showcase Lagoon. Also prominently featured is a replica of the Doge's Palace, originally built by the Venetians in the early 14th century. In typical Disney fashion, the Palace is full of fine Italian perfume, handmade masks, soccer jerseys, pasta, and other items Italia. Italy is otherwise mostly restaurants and bars. Best is Via Napoli in the back of the pavilion, serving authentic Neapolitan pizzas. Without a reservation, try Tutto Gusto, the wine bar attached to the Tutto Italia restaurant with hundreds of Italian wines, rare Italian beer on draft, and an appetizer and dessert menu that's hard to beat. Tutto Italia is more formal, but still perfect for families and couples, serving regional Italian fare. A mime entertains guests most days.

United States Pavilion

The United States Pavilion is mostly housed inside of a single Colonial-style mansion that was built using 110,000 hand-made Georgian clay bricks.

Major attraction: *The American Adventure*, a 30-minute theater show blending film and Animatronics, is the principal attraction. The patriotic show briefly retells the history of America and runs on a set schedule with the next show listed on posters outside the pavilion. The theater seats over a thousand in comfortable air-conditioning, making it a perfect respite from the afternoon heat. The show is often preceded in the afternoon by the Voices of Liberty a cappella group inside the mansion.

Outside, the America Gardens Theater is home to various free concerts throughout the year with space-available seating, including Flower Power, Sounds like Summer, Eat to the Beat, and the Candlelight Processional.

Liberty Inn is the quick service outlet. Recent menu overhauls have brought steak and fried shrimp, in addition to salads, chicken sandwiches, burgers, hot dogs, and chicken nuggets. Seating is plentiful indoors and outdoors. Fife & Drum Tavern outside serves beer, pretzels, turkey legs, popcorn, and other snack items.

Japan Pavilion

The red torii gate and the 85-foot-tall Goju-no-to pagoda welcome guests to the Japan Pavilion. These and other buildings are surrounded by beautiful gardens made up of native Japanese plants, bamboo, and evergreen, maple, and monkey puzzle trees. The large courtyard in the middle of the pavilion makes Japan feel more open, relaxed, and less cluttered than other pavilions. Be sure to cross the bridge leading to the White Heron Castle and check out the koi fish below.

There are no rides or theater shows in Japan, but it is rich with entertainment and culture. Enjoy the athletic Taiko drummers on the pagoda steps and the cultural exhibits inside the castle. The Mitsukoshi Department Store on the right side of the pavilion is among the best in Disney World, offering more than 50,000 unique products. Kimonos, Samurai swords, Bonsai trees, chopstick sets, calligraphy brushes, toys, and everything in between are available. Check out the popular Pick-a-Pearl where guests can pick an oyster and discover what's inside. Hundreds of relatively inexpensive food and drink items are offered in the final room, in addition to a sake bar with samples available by the glass.

Dining options are even more plentiful. Teppan Edo, a traditional hibachi-grill experience similar to Benihana, is one of the more consistent restaurants on property, offering grilled meat, fish, and vegetables. Tokyo Dining focuses on sushi and tempura in a contemporary setting. Outside, Katsura Grill serves quick service sushi, teriyaki, and other traditional food. Indoor air-conditioned seating is available, in addition to the beautiful outdoor garden setting. Food at Katsura is merely okay, but it's a relaxing location. A sake bar also serving cocktails and beer is located outside across from Mitsukoshi Department Store. Also outside, Kabuki Café serves kaki gori (snow cones) with traditional toppings, in addition to smoothies, beer, and other snacks.

Morocco Pavilion

Morocco is represented by architecture and monuments from three famous Moroccan cities: Casablanca, Fez, and Marrakesh. Koutoubia Minaret, the focal point of the pavilion, is a replica of the 12th century Marrakesh prayer tower. Morocco is the only state-sponsored World Showcase pavilion, and the country played an integral part in the design and construction of the buildings, gardens, and Bab Boujeloud arch. The King of Morocco actually sent his personal craftsmen to construct and lay tile in much of the pavilion, making this one of the most authentic areas in Epcot. Because of the religious significance of many of Morocco's buildings, lights are not shined on the pavilion during IllumiNations.

Morocco is the most-passed-over pavilion, which is unfortunate because there is a lot to see and do, despite it not offering a major show or ride. An authentic musical act entertains guests with live music and dancing most days on the outdoor stage. We highly recommend taking 20–30 minutes to explore the marketplace, museum, and art gallery. Restaurant Marrakesh is the under-rated Moroccan restaurant in the pavilion, specializing in couscous and anything with a shank. A belly dancer appears inside the restaurant throughout the day. Spice Road Table opened in late 2013, offering small Mediterranean tapas, wines, cocktails, and desserts, and adding more sizable entrees in 2015. It's a beautiful restaurant that overlooks the picturesque lagoon. While reservations are offered, it's virtually never necessary to book one in advance. Tangierine Café is the quick service, featuring shawarma and falafel. While the food is a bit more expensive, portions are large and the food is freshly prepared. It's our favorite World Showcase quick service.

France Pavilion

The replica of the Eiffel Tower is the most recognizable feature of the France Pavilion. The buildings are themed like those found in Paris between 1870 and 1910, otherwise known as La Belle Epoque, or The Beautiful Time. France features a gorgeous courtyard area with a fountain and immaculately maintained gardens.

France's main attraction is an 18-minute film titled *Impressions de France*. Projected onto five large screens, *Impressions* provides a 200-degree panoramic view of France, its people, and its culture. You'll experience many of France's most popular destinations, including the gardens at Versailles, the Eiffel Tower, and the breathtaking French Alps. Unlike the films at China or Canada, you'll be able to sit and relax during the air-conditioned show. In addition, the fun Serveur Amusant comedy/acrobat show is scheduled throughout the afternoon most days.

France is home to two sit-down restaurants, a quick service boulangerie patisserie (bakery), and an ice cream parlor. Chefs de France downstairs is themed to a casual Parisian bistro and while the charm remains, the more-expensive, single all-day menu may be more money than most families want to spend for lunch. If you do visit, consider a meal around sunset when $30+ salmon and steak dishes are comparable to other options. Upstairs is the ritzier Monsieur Paul, serving a more expensive dinner-only menu catered toward adults. Les Halles Boulangerie Patisserie, located in the back of the pavilion, serves sandwiches, quiche, salads, desserts, and other French specialties. It's an excellent spot to pick up a snack or a meal. Finally, L'Artisan des Glaces serves freshly prepared sorbet and ice cream with the option of a shot of liquor poured on top.

Shopping includes wine, perfume, and fun French-themed Disney merchandise.

During Disney's D23 Expo in July 2017, Disney announced that a new ride based on *Ratatouille* would be built in the France Pavilion with an expected opening date of sometime in 2021. The experience should be similar to the ride that opened at Walt Disney Studios Park in Paris in 2014. Construction should not adversely affect 2018 visits.

United Kingdom Pavilion

The United Kingdom Pavilion is one of the more architecturally diverse World Showcase pavilions, with the Hampton Court Palace, Anne Hathaway's (William Shakespeare's wife) thatched roof cottage, two castles, and a miniature version of Hyde Park represented. You'll see replicas of the red phone booths England is so famous for, as well as a variety of beautiful garden areas.

The British Revolution, playing hits from The Who, Beatles, Led Zeppelin, and others, is the entertainment here. Several shops carry a range of British goods, including tea, perfume and makeup, apparel, and a lot of Guinness- and Beatles-related merchandise.

Rose & Crown Dining Room is the pavilion's table service restaurant. It's casual, low key, and your best opportunity to watch IllumiNations from a restaurant while you dine. The Pub next door is an excellent spot to grab a pint. Yorkshire County Fish Co. outside serves excellent fast food fish and chips with limited picturesque seating along the lagoon.

Canada Pavilion

Gorgeous Victoria Gardens and a replica of the Canadian Rockies complete with a 30-foot waterfall lead guests into the Canada Pavilion. The Hotel du Canada, modeled after Ottawa's Fairmont Chateau Laurier, is the pavilion's largest and most magnificently detailed building. Canada features a Circle-Vision 360 film similar to *Reflections of China*. The 18-minute *O' Canada!* show is projected onto nine individual screens that surround the theatre. The film is presented in such a way that each screen shows the view looking out in that particular direction, so you feel like you're right in the middle of the shot. While it's standing-room-only, the theater is large and air-conditioned. A 15-minute Canadian musical act is scheduled most days at the outdoor stage.

Le Cellier is the pavilion's table service restaurant, primarily offering steak. Like Monsieur Paul in France, it's a signature restaurant, which means it will set you back two Dining Plan credits and is more expensive out of pocket than most restaurants.

Shopping is limited to stuffed animals and other toys, along with apparel items and some food and beverages.

Disney's Hollywood Studios

Disney's Hollywood Studios opened as a combined theme park and working production studio under the name Disney-MGM Studios on May 1, 1989. The name changed to Disney's Hollywood Studios in 2008. While several famous shows and movies were filmed or animated on site, it's been more than ten years since any serious studio work has happened here.

It's now "just" a Disney theme park, but several of Hollywood Studios' rides and shows are among the best in Walt Disney World. Even with just a few rides and about a dozen shows currently operating, what the park does offer will satisfy most guests and fill an entire day

Touring the Studios is more complicated than one might expect due to long lines at the headliners and several lengthy stage shows that run on a limited schedule. The layout is also a bit confusing for first-time visitors. The Cheat Sheet map at the end of the chapter will make traversing the park significantly easier.

WHAT THE FUTURE MAY BRING

On August 15, 2015, Disney announced two major new lands headed for Hollywood Studios. Originally referred to as "Star Wars Land," the new expansion opening in 2019 will be called Star Wars: Galaxy's Edge. Toy Story Land's opening will precede it by about a year, opening on June 30, 2018. Disney followed with an announcement during 2017's D23 Expo that the Great Movie Ride would close to make way for Mickey and Minnie's Runaway Railway, with a probable opening sometime in 2019.

The additions mean a lot of changes and a lot of construction walls. The Streets of America section is now completely walled off, which means Lights, Motors, Action! Extreme Stunt Show is closed, in addition to Honey I Shrunk the Kids Movie Set Adventure, and Studio Catering Co. quick service. Backlot Tour is also permanently closed with that entire area walled off.

Guests visiting during the first half of 2018 should experience much of what Hollywood Studios currently offers, including major rides like Toy Story Mania, Rock 'n' Roller Coaster, Star Tours, and Tower of Terror. Disney has already replaced some attractions with others, like the Frozen Sing-Along Celebration going in the American Idol space and Star Wars Launch Bay replacing Magic of Disney Animation. In addition, an all-new show featuring BB-8, Chewbacca, Boba Fett, and others is scheduled multiple times daily and Captain Phasma leads a march of First Order Stormtroopers at regular intervals. Star Wars: A Galactic Spectacular Fireworks debuted in June 2016 and serves as a nightcap to the day's proceedings most evenings. Heavy on projections on the old Great Movie

Ride façade with accompanying fireworks, it's a favorite of many guests. A holiday show may replace the Star Wars fireworks from the middle of November through the end of December, as it did in 2017. In addition, Disney debuted a new projection show in May 2017 that precedes the nighttime fireworks called Disney Movie Magic. This 10-minute show largely serves to entertain guests as they wait for the main event, but it includes hundreds of clips and animations from popular Disney movies.

Guests visiting during the second half of 2018 will enjoy all of that, in addition to Toy Story Land. Joining Toy Story Midway Mania! will be two new rides. Slinky Dog Dash is a family-friendly roller coaster that we expect to be a mix of Seven Dwarfs Mine Train and Barnstormer. Alien Swirling Saucers is akin to Mater's Junkyard Jamboree at California Adventure and should prove to be a fun, albeit slow-loading, whip-around ride. Both should prove popular, and the capacity additions should help reduce waits elsewhere and increase the number of FastPass+ experiences distributed each day.

FASTPASS+ PRIORITY

Like Epcot, FastPass+ enabled attractions are broken up into two tiers and guests may initially select only one Tier One attraction, which makes it a struggle for those arriving late to ride both Toy Story Mania and Rock 'n' Roller Coaster. Most guests want to select either Toy Story Mania or Rock 'n' Roller Coaster and ride the other in standby first thing. Rock 'n' Roller Coaster offers a single rider line, though waits are usually in the 15–20 minute range due to the way the vehicles are loaded and it's impossible to gauge how many people are in line until the final loading area. We expect Slinky Dog Dash to be a Tier 1 FastPass+ option, while Alien Swirling Saucers will likely fall into Tier 2.

Tier 1 (choose one)

1. Toy Story Mania
2. Rock 'n' Roller Coaster
3. Fantasmic!
4. Beauty and the Beast Live on Stage

Tier 2 (choose two)

1. Tower of Terror
2. Star Tours
3. Voyage of the Little Mermaid
4. Frozen Sing-Along
5. Indiana Jones Epic Stunt Spectacular

6. Disney Jr. Live on Stage
7. Muppet Vision 3D

Tower of Terror FastPass+ is a no-brainer if you're interested in riding with average peak waits of 60+ minutes. A second Tier 2 selection may be less obvious. FastPass+ is largely useless at the shows, requiring users to arrive very early to enjoy any benefit and with the possibility that the reserved seats will actually be worse than standby. Star Tours is the second-highest priority with peak waits that typically hit 30+ minutes and less availability than other attractions. Voyage of the Little Mermaid is another priority due to its small theater and the likelihood that guests arriving in the afternoon will have to wait through at least one complete show before entering the theater, resulting in actual waits of 15–30 minutes. FastPass+ allows users to walk right in to the specified show even as it nears being full with less lead time. The Frozen Sing-Along is prioritized over the other shows because it's least likely to be available as a 4th FP+ and shows are most likely to be full, making FastPass+ more useful.

ARRIVING AT THE STUDIOS

Arriving at least 45 minutes prior to park opening is essential for guests interested in signing up their 4–12 year old for the Jedi Training Academy without a significant wait. Arriving closer to regular open will mean thousands of guests in line in front of you at the priority attractions.

Most guests arrive via Disney bus or their own automobile at one of the Studios' two entrances. The bus stops are just minutes away from the main entrance, while guests driving have the option of walking or taking a tram from the parking lot. Guests staying at the BoardWalk Inn, Yacht Club, Beach Club, Swan, or Dolphin either walk or take the boat that begins service one hour before regular open. Walking or taking the boat both take about 25 minutes, but walking cuts down on the wait for the first boat and allows you to arrive much earlier in the morning.

Guest Services is located on the left inside and outside of the main entrance. Ticket booths in front of the entrance can handle any purchases or upgrades, usually with non-existent lines. Wheelchair and stroller rental are just inside on the right.

HOLLYWOOD BOULEVARD

Hollywood Boulevard, the Studios' main drag, is similar to Main Street, U.S.A. at Magic Kingdom. The left side consists almost entirely of retail with Mickey's of Hollywood and Keystone Clothiers carrying the widest selection of merchandise in the park. PhotoPass and a couple smaller stores are on the right, followed by Trolley Car Café, the park's sizable Starbucks location. Hollywood Brown Derby, a pricey signature restaurant that costs two credits on the Dining Plan, serves the best food in the park on the right near the end of the Boulevard. Starring Rolls, the popular quick service eatery specializing in sandwiches, cupcakes, and other baked goods, closed unceremoniously in early 2017, perhaps to make way for additional lounge space for Brown Derby. An assortment of similar pastries and other treats is available across the street at Trolley Car Café. Grauman's Chinese Theater, which used to house the Great Movie Ride and will soon contain Mickey and Minnie's Runaway Railway, stands tall at the end of the street.

March of the First Order

RANKING Star Wars fans should make the effort to catch it. **EMH** No. **FP+** No. **TYPE** Parade and stage show. **REQUIREMENTS** None.

WHAT TO EXPECT Captain Phasma leads a group of stormtroopers from just inside the main entrance on the left as you look up Hollywood Boulevard to the stage in front of Grauman's Chinese Theatre. A brief show takes place on the stage before the group marches back to the same area where they entered. **SCARY FACTOR** Low. They are stormtroopers, but it's unlikely they're going to drag you to a trash compactor.

WHEN TO GO There are typically six shows scheduled daily on the hour beginning at 10am and ending in the late afternoon with a break in the middle of the day. See whichever show is convenient. **EXPECT TO WAIT** Arrive on Hollywood Boulevard five minutes before the start. **LENGTH** 15 minutes. **WHERE TO SEE IT** There are two good options. If you don't want to move, watch from near the stage area in front of the Chinese Theatre. If you don't mind walking, see it on the Trolley Car Café side of Hollywood Boulevard in front of the Five & Dime store. The stormtroopers typically stop here for a brief show of strength. After they pass, follow them to the stage.

Star Wars: A Galaxy Far, Far Away

RANKING Star Wars fans may enjoy seeing the characters on stage. **EMH** No. **FP+** No. **TYPE** Stage show. **REQUIREMENTS** None.

WHAT TO EXPECT On the stage in front of Grauman's Chinese Theatre, Kylo Ren, Darth Vader, Darth Maul, Boba Fett, BB-8, C-3PO, R2D2, and others appear on stage in what may seem more like a fashion show than anything else. But this is the only time several of these characters appear. **SCARY FACTOR** Low. Some of the characters are purposefully intimidating, but there's little danger involved. A few fireworks go off toward the end.

WHEN TO GO There are typically six shows scheduled daily on the half hour beginning in the morning and ending in the late afternoon with a break in the middle of the day. See whichever show is convenient. **EXPECT TO WAIT** For front row spots, arrive at least 20 minutes early. Arrive a minute or two before show time to see it from further back. **LENGTH** 15 minutes. **WHERE TO SEE IT** The main problem is the low height of the stage and the number of kids that will be hoisted on shoulders ahead of you. We like to see the show from further back off to the side where there are typically fewer of these shoulder kids. For a more intimate experience, stand near the ramp on the left side of the stage where the characters enter and exit the stage. You'll get a much better look, but will miss most of what happens on stage. Big fans may want to see a show from both vantage points.

ECHO LAKE

Star Tours is the standout in this land, which is also home to Indiana Jones Epic Stunt Spectacular, Frozen Sing Along, and Jedi Training Academy, in addition to several eateries. 50's Prime Time Café, with its comfort food and fun atmosphere, is Dave's favorite Studios restaurant. Hollywood & Vine next door is a buffet featuring Disney Jr. characters during breakfast hours. A seasonal meal hosted by Minnie and featuring Mickey, Goofy, Donald, and Daisy follows for lunch and dinner. Backlot Express is the quick service, now sporting a menu with Star Wars tie-ins. Instead of the usual fries that accompany the chicken nuggets, you'll receive Darth Vader waffles. Also look out for the Star Wars-themed cupcakes. The food at Backlot still isn't great, but there's nicely themed air-conditioned seating inside. Dockside Diner on Echo Lake serves hot dogs and a rotating selection of other entrees, in addition to beer and boozy lemonades. Tatooine Traders sits adjacent to Star Tours and is the best location for *Star Wars* merchandise. *Indiana Jones* merchandise is available at the show's exit and to the right of 50's Prime Time.

With no high priority attractions, Echo Lake is best saved for the late morning or afternoon, particularly with a FastPass+ for Star Tours.

Celebrity Spotlight Olaf Meet and Greet

Olaf meets all day across from Backlot Express to waits that often peak no higher than 20 minutes, making it a good stop before or after lunch.

Frozen Sing-Along

RANKING A must for fans of Frozen, surprisingly enjoyable for everyone else. **EMH** No. **FP+** Yes. FastPass+ guarantees the user a seat at a specific show, but there is no reserved section for FastPass+ users. Because all guests are allowed into the theater about 15 minutes before show time, FP+ users need to arrive at least 20 minutes before the show starts to see any advantage, which is usually early enough that there would be plenty of availability in standby. In other words, using FP+ here is only beneficial if you plan to arrive about five minutes before show time and don't care where you sit—only that you'll be able to. **TYPE** Stage show. **REQUIRE-MENTS** Nothing more than your patience.

WHAT TO EXPECT Guests enter a comfortable, air-conditioned theater for an engaging stage show featuring Anna, Elsa, and the newly-appointed "Royal Historians" of Arendelle. Anna appears briefly at the beginning and Elsa joins her for a powerful number at the end of the show, but the bulk of the time is spent enjoying the genuinely funny banter between the historians with a crowd that intermittently bursts out into song. **SCARY FACTOR** Only your neighbor's singing voice.

WHEN TO GO Most guests will want to see an afternoon show to enjoy some air conditioning and a comfortable seat, perhaps as a 4th or 5th FastPass+ selection. Those already planning a short day may elect to see the first and least crowded show of the day, which typically begins at 10:30am. **EXPECT TO WAIT** Arrive 20–30 minutes before show time. **LENGTH** 25 minutes. **WHERE TO SIT** In the middle section about halfway up.

Indiana Jones Epic Stunt Spectacular Show

RANKING Major attraction. **EMH** No. **FP+** Yes. Low priority. **TYPE** Show. **REQUIREMENTS** None.

WHAT TO EXPECT A large theater seats about 2,000 people on bleacher-style seating. In the show, actors perform a series of stunts that mirror those from the movie *Raiders of the Lost Ark*, and the director explains how they are executed so they are safe and seem real. You'll see large explosions, sword fights, car chases, gun battles, and a number of other exciting stunts. **SCARY FACTOR** Low. While there are some thrilling moments on stage, the audience is never in any danger, real or imagined.

WHEN TO GO The first and last shows of the day are typically least crowded. **EXPECT TO WAIT** Arrive at least 20 minutes early. **LENGTH** 30 minutes. **WHERE TO SIT** At least half way up, in the center section.

Star Tours

RANKING Major attraction. **EMH** Morning, Evening. **FP+** Yes. Moderate priority. **TYPE** Motion simulator show. **REQUIREMENTS** 40" or taller.

WHAT TO EXPECT Riders sit in a large 40-person simulator themed like the inside of a StarSpeeder 1000 spaceship. A 3D movie plays in the front and the ride vehicle tilts, bumps, vibrates, sways, etc., so it feels like you're actually inside of the StarSpeeder making the journey that you see in front of you. Disney advertises that the attraction has "more than 50 story combinations" because there are four scenes during the ride, each of which has a few different character or destination possibilities. For example, you might visit Chewbacca's home planet of Kashyyyk or the icy planet of Hoth after being directed by Yoda, Admiral Ackbar, or Princess Leia. Star Wars fans may wish to ride two or three times over the course of the day to see as many of the scenes as possible. In addition, Disney added a scene from the planet Jakku and a transmission from BB-8 in late 2015, followed by another new addition in late 2017. **SCARY FACTOR** Low. There is a moderate amount of danger involved, but it isn't realistic enough to be scary. **CAN WE HANDLE IT?** The biggest problems are motion sickness and the jerkiness of the ride. Avoid if similar attractions have caused problems.

WHEN TO GO After the priority attractions, in the last two hours of operation, or with FastPass+. **EXPECT TO WAIT** 20–40 minute afternoon waits are common. **LENGTH** 5 minutes. **WHERE TO SIT** Views are similar from most seats. You'll experience the most motion in the far left or right seat in the back row.

GRAND AVENUE

Once part of the now defunct Streets of America, Grand Avenue is home to Muppet Vision 3D, PizzeRizzo, BaseLine Tap House, and Mama Melrose's Ristorante Italiano, in addition to a few stores. Muppet Vision is the epitome of an anytime attraction and a fantastic opportunity to get off your feet in the afternoon heat. PizzeRizzo replaces Toy Story Pizza Planet with a menu that still focuses on reheated pizzas, in addition to salads and meatball subs. Mama Melrose is not Disney's best Italian restaurant, but it still offers serviceable pizzas in a calmer setting than next door for not a whole lot more money. The pricier pasta and meat options are inconsistent and best skipped unless Disney Dining Plan credits are being used. BaseLine Tap House opened in the middle of 2017, offering a menu of draft beers hailing from the great state of California, in addition to a couple of wines and cocktails on tap. The charcuterie board is surprisingly good and we like to stop from time to time for a snack and a customizable beer flight.

Muppet Vision 3D

RANKING Don't miss. **EMH** Morning, Evening. **FP+** Yes. Low priority. **TYPE** 4D show. **REQUIREMENTS** None.

WHAT TO EXPECT A 12-minute pre-show video in a room full of Muppet gags welcomes viewers. The theater is large, air-conditioned, and comfortable. The 4D film follows the Muppets as they prepare for a show and features a live-action Sweetums character at the end. **SCARY FACTOR** Low. At times the show is loud.

WHEN TO GO Afternoon when crowds have peaked elsewhere. **EXPECT TO WAIT** Only as long as it takes for the next show to start. **LENGTH** 12-minute pre-show, 17-minute show. **WHERE TO SIT** Let guests stream in and fill about half of a row at least half way back from the front before entering in order to sit in the middle.

COMMISSARY LANE

Located behind Grauman's Chinese Theatre, Commissary Lane is home to the Red Carpet Dreams Mickey and Minnie meet in addition to the ABC Commissary and Sci-Fi Dine-In. ABC Commissary is a decent quick service with plentiful air-conditioned seating, but a limited lunch menu. Beginning at 4pm, a fast casual concept takes over with higher priced steaks, salmon, burgers, and more. Guests still order at the register, but food is delivered to the table. Sci-Fi, with its fun drive-in theater theme, is Josh's favorite Studios restaurant, serving reliably good sandwich and burger fare. The more expensive options at Sci-Fi are over-priced given the quality, and best skipped by those paying cash.

Red Carpet Dreams Mickey and Minnie Meet and Greet

Mickey and Minnie greet guests at this glamorous location that opened in spring 2016. Mickey is in his classic sorcerer's robes and hat while Minnie meets separately in her iconic pink dress. There is just the one line for both characters and waits typically top out at 30 minutes, making this a decent stop in the late afternoon when you'd spend at least that long to do most other attractions. If possible, meet before 10:30am or with two hours to close to minimize waits further.

PIXAR PLACE

Pixar Place was once the most congested area in the park as guests clamored to ride Toy Story Mania, a ride that used to post the longest wait times of any WDW attraction, in addition to those just trying to pass through to reach Backlot Tour or the Streets of America. Now that construction walls block access to both areas and Disney has added a third track that has dropped Toy Story standby waits by about 40%, congestion is eased and access improved. Still, just about everyone that visits the Studios will pass this way either for the ride or for the Woody and Buzz meet and greet across the way.

When Toy Story Land opens on June 30, 2018, Pixar Place should close with the entrance to Toy Story Mania opening inside the new land.

TOY STORY LAND

Home to what will be two new family-friendly rides and the new entrance for Toy Story Mania when it opens on June 30, Toy Story Land should play a prominent role in most guests' visits. Wait times are hard to gauge as neither ride will likely enjoy a hefty hourly capacity inside of a park currently operating with four rides, but we expect Slinky Dog wait times to peak around 75 minutes with Alien Swirling Saucers often sporting 45-minute waits. Expect a dramatic shift in crowd flow when Star Wars: Galaxy's Edge opens in 2019.

Toy Story Midway Mania!

RANKING Don't miss. **EMH** Morning, Evening. **FP+** Yes, except April 9 through May 7. High Tier 1 priority. **TYPE** Interactive 3D shooting game. **REQUIREMENTS** None.

WHAT TO EXPECT Riders enter slow-moving vehicles and shoot targets to score points with toy guns attached to the front of the ride vehicle. Toy Story Mania is in 3D (with required 3D glasses) and also includes 4D elements. There are five midway style games to play during the ride, none of which are violent. It's a lot more fun to experience than to read about! **SCARY FACTOR** Mild spinning should not upset even the most prone to motion sickness.

WHEN TO GO Within 20 minutes of opening, in the last hour of operation, or with FastPass+. **EXPECT TO WAIT** Until Toy Story Land opens on June 30, 2018, Toy Story Mania will be operating a reduced capacity and will see the highest waits in the park. Visit it absolutely first thing or use FastPass+ if available. (We expect FastPass+ to be unavailable from April 9 through May 7.) **LENGTH** 5 minutes. **WHERE TO SIT** Pairs of riders sit next to each other and compete with the pair facing the opposite direction in the same vehicle.

MICKEY AVENUE

Mickey Avenue is the corridor that connects Pixar Place with the Animation Courtyard behind Grauman's Chinese Theatre, now home to just one attraction: Walt Disney Presents.

Walt Disney Presents

RANKING Minor attraction. **EMH** Morning, Evening. **FP+** No. **TYPE** Walk-through exhibit with an optional film and meet-and-greet opportunity. **REQUIREMENTS** None.

WHAT TO EXPECT A sincere, interesting look at the man behind the Walt Disney Company, featuring memorabilia and artifacts from Walt Disney's life and models of Disney park attractions from around the world. When available, the optional 15-minute film at the end is highly recommended, but more often than not, Disney uses the space to promote a preview of one of their new feature films. Disney also uses the space as a temporary meet and greet location for characters like Moana. **SCARY FACTOR** None.

WHEN TO GO See it when waits are long at other rides, or you simply are nearby. **EXPECT TO WAIT** No wait to enter the exhibit, but the character meet and greet wait usually peaks around 30 minutes and it may be five to ten minutes until the next film begins. **LENGTH** As long as you like—most guests spend about 30 minutes, including the film.

ANIMATION COURTYARD

Star Wars Launch Bay, located in the back of the courtyard, anchors this area. Inside, you'll find *Star Wars* character meet and greets, props from the movies, interactive games, and a large store filled with high-end merchandise. Back outside, the area is lined with character meet and greets including Doc McStuffins, Sofia the First, Pluto, and Jake from *Jake and the Neverland Pirates*. Voyage of the Little Mermaid, an enchanting stage show featuring a live Ariel, is arguably the land's best attraction. Disney Jr. Live on Stage, aimed specifically at preschoolers, is a favorite of most of them. There are no dining options here, but two shops are located on the Voyage of the Little Mermaid side, including one that's almost entirely princess merchandise.

Disney Jr Live on Stage

RANKING Don't miss for young kids, skippable for everyone else. **EMH** No. **FP+** Yes. Low priority. **TYPE** Musical stage show. **REQUIREMENTS** None.

WHAT TO EXPECT Features characters from *Mickey Mouse Clubhouse*, *Handy Manny*, *Little Einsteins*, and *Jake and the Never Land Pirates* in a fun musical stage show. There is no conventional seating in the theater except for in the very back where there are several benches. Parents and kids are expected to sit on the floor throughout the show—at least until the singing, dancing, and clapping start. There is a lot of audience participation throughout, and little ones really get into it. **SCARY FACTOR** None.

WHEN TO GO Try to see one of the first two or last two shows. **EXPECT TO WAIT** Arrive at least 15 minutes early. **LENGTH** 22 minutes. **WHERE TO SIT** With seating on the floor, there isn't an outstanding place to sit.

Star Wars Launch Bay

RANKING Minor attraction. **EMH** Morning, Evening. **FP+** No. **TYPE** Part exhibit, film, and character meet and greets. **REQUIREMENTS** None.

WHAT TO EXPECT The Launch Bay is made up of several pieces. Guests first have the option to wait and watch a short film about how much of an impact *Star Wars* has made on popular culture and what it means to the filmmakers, or skip ahead and enter the exhibit portion of the attraction. Here, guests have an opportunity to look at a variety of props and models from the movies. In the next room, Chewbacca, BB-8, and Kylo Ren greet guests in separate lines. Finally, guests exit through a gift shop with a number of high-end goods. **SCARY FACTOR** Just hope Kylo is having a good day.

WHEN TO GO Character waits are shortest before 10am and in the last hour of operation. Otherwise, visit in the afternoon. **EXPECT TO WAIT** Up to ten minutes to see the film. Chewbacca and BB-8 waits typically peak at 30 minutes while Kylo's line is rarely longer than 20 minutes. **LENGTH** With the film, most guests will spend about 30 minutes. Add more time if the characters are of interest.

Voyage of the Little Mermaid

RANKING Major attraction. **EMH** Evening. **FP+** Yes. Moderate priority. **TYPE** Musical stage show. **REQUIREMENTS** None.

WHAT TO EXPECT A mixture of puppets, Animatronics, and live actors tell the story of the Little Mermaid inside of a comfortable, relatively small theater. **SCARY FACTOR** Medium for young kids. Ursula, the wicked octopus, may frighten young children. She is 12-feet tall, 10-feet wide, and accompanied by loud effects and darkness. You might want to prepare youngsters by reminding them that she can't leave the stage.

WHEN TO GO The first two or last two shows of the day are least crowded. **EXPECT TO WAIT** Up to 30 minutes in the afternoon. **LENGTH** 15 minutes. **WHERE TO SIT** Let half of a row file in first to be in the center. Sit at least half way back for a full view of the stage.

SUNSET BOULEVARD
. . . .

Here, you'll find two of Hollywood Studios' best rides: Rock 'n' Roller Coaster and Tower of Terror. The entrance to the Hollywood Hills Theater, where Fantasmic! takes place, is located on the right before Tower of Terror. Nearby *Beauty and the Beast* is an excellent stage show that has been running longer than any other WDW show.

Sunset Boulevard is primarily lined with retail on the left and right sides of the street before the attractions. On the right is a store offering merchandise based on whatever property Disney is currently pushing, followed by a store offering Planet Hollywood merchandise, and then a store selling mostly apparel and higher-end watches and purses. On the left is Sweet Spells, offering freshly baked treats similar to those found at Main Street Confectionery at Magic Kingdom, in addition to other packaged edibles. Further up is Reel Vogue, which is currently offering Toy Story merchandise, "Made with Magic" items like the Sorcerer Mickey Wand, and generic character merchandise. At the exit to Rock 'n' Roller Coaster is a store selling a smorgasbord of rock 'n' roll-inspired merchandise. The shop at the exit to Tower of Terror features over a hundred items themed to the attraction, including Hollywood Tower Hotel robes and bells.

Sunset Ranch Market, an outdoor collection of six individual stands, serves all kinds of food—barbecue, burgers, sandwiches, salads, ice cream, fruit, snacks, and more. The common seating area is outdoors. Hollywood Hills Theater offers snacks and drinks, in addition to heartier items like hot dogs for about 90 minutes before Fantasmic! starts.

Beauty and the Beast Live on Stage

RANKING Major attraction. **EMH** No. **FP+** Yes. Low priority. **TYPE** Stage show. **REQUIREMENTS** None.

WHAT TO EXPECT This 25-minute Broadway-style musical features characters, music, and scenes from *Beauty and the Beast*. The sets are elaborate, the costumes are first-rate, and the acting is excellent. **SCARY FACTOR** None.

WHEN TO GO The first and last shows are typically least crowded. **EXPECT TO WAIT** Arrive at least 20 minutes early. **LENGTH** 30 minutes. **WHERE TO SIT** At least half way up in the center section.

Rock 'n' Roller Coaster

RANKING Don't miss. **EMH** Morning, Evening. **FP+** Yes. High Tier 1 priority. **TYPE** Roller coaster. **REQUIREMENTS** 48" or taller.

WHAT TO EXPECT An Aerosmith video pre-show explains why you are about to drive really fast. Next you board a limousine-themed roller coaster vehicle that seats 24 people in rows of two. The vehicle will then propel out of the gate with the force of a supersonic jet. **SCARY FACTOR** With max speeds over 60 miles per hour, three inversions, and multiple corkscrews, this is arguably Disney's most intense roller coaster. The dark setting may actually ease fears as the track is never fully visible to riders. **CAN WE HANDLE IT?** The initial launch is the most intense part—the rest of the ride is relatively tame compared to any major coaster at Six Flags or Universal. Anyone that made it through Everest or Space Mountain should be fine.

WHEN TO GO First thing or immediately after Toy Story Mania, in the final hour of operation, or with FastPass+. Rock 'n' Roller Coaster offers a single-rider line, but because it's impossible to know how many people are ahead of you in it before you actually get to the indoor pre-show area, it's not recommended. **EXPECT TO WAIT** 50 to 100 minutes in the afternoon. **LENGTH** 90 seconds. **WHERE TO SIT** Request the front row for the best view, the middle if you're apprehensive, or the back to see all the twists and turns.

Twilight Zone Tower of Terror

RANKING Don't miss. **EMH** Morning, Evening. **FP+** Yes. Highest Tier 2 priority. **TYPE** Elevator drop. **REQUIREMENTS** 40" or taller.

WHAT TO EXPECT A pre-show video in the dilapidated hotel's library explains the circumstances surrounding your unfortunate visit. After a tense five- to ten-minute wait in the boiler room, you board your elevator, which will embark on an eerie journey through the hotel. Anyone going down? **SCARY FACTOR** High. The most obviously frightening ride at Disney World, and one of few that puts an emphasis on fear. There are no particularly scary images or scenes, but Disney does an excellent job of building tension up to the final drop, which begins at 170 feet above ground at a speed faster than gravity would naturally pull. **CAN WE HANDLE IT?** Motion sickness can be an issue, but otherwise walk the nervous past the ride exit and note that almost everyone leaves with a smile on their faces.

WHEN TO GO Immediately after Toy Story Mania and/or Rock 'n' Roller Coaster, in the final hour of operation, or with FastPass+. **EXPECT TO WAIT** 50–100 minutes in the afternoon. **LENGTH** 5 minutes. **WHERE TO SIT** All seats are good, but the view from the front row is the least obscured.

NIGHTTIME FIREWORKS AND SHOWS

Disney Movie Magic

RANKING Good filler before nighttime fireworks. **EMH** No. A show may be scheduled to start during or after evening EMH begins, but anyone is welcome to attend. **FP+** No. **TYPE** Projection show. **REQUIREMENTS** Ability to arrive in the Center Stage area in front of Grauman's Chinese Theatre at least ten minutes before show time.

WHAT TO EXPECT This 10-minute projection show on the Chinese Theatre façade features hundreds of clips and animations from Disney movies to entertain guests waiting for the nighttime fireworks. It's worth staking out a spot in time to see it as the same spot will also guarantee a good spot for the main event. **SCARY FACTOR** There are no fireworks or scary scenes.

TYPICAL SCHEDULE: Usually begins 30 minutes before fireworks. **LENGTH** 10 minutes. **WHERE TO SIT**: About halfway in between the Chinese Theatre entrance and the two tall projection towers.

Fantasmic!

RANKING Don't miss. **EMH** No. A show may be scheduled to start during or after evening EMH begins, but anyone is welcome to attend. **FP+** Yes, low priority in most situations. There is dedicated FastPass+ seating near the center, but getting a good seat within the section requires an early arrival. And choosing Fantasmic! in advance means you won't be able to schedule a 4th FP+ because the show is so late and you won't have an opportunity to use your Fantasmic! FastPass+ until the end of the night. **TYPE** Fireworks and live action show. **REQUIREMENTS** None.

WHAT TO EXPECT The theater seats about 9,000 people on bleacher seating without backs. Mickey is the star of the show as he appears on stage with over 50 live performers as film sequences featuring many best-loved Disney moments and characters, plus Pocahontas, play on screens made of water, fireworks shoot overhead, and fire and magic potions abound. **SCARY FACTOR** Moderate for the young. Mickey is in a considerable amount of danger with a 40-foot-tall dragon and all the villains. Sit near the back with anxious toddlers for a quick escape if it gets to be too much.

TYPICAL SCHEDULE: Presented once or twice per evening almost every evening of the year. Show times vary, depending on when it gets dark, and may be as early as 7pm or as late as 10.30 pm. The second show, if scheduled, will be less crowded. **LENGTH** 30 minutes. **WHERE TO SIT**: Arrive at least 45 minutes early for the first show. Arriving 20 minutes early is sufficient for the second show. Sit at least half way up, as close to the center as possible.

Star Wars Galactic Spectacular

RANKING Don't miss for avid Star Wars fans; entertaining for everyone else. **EMH** No. A show may be scheduled to start during or after evening EMH begins, but anyone is welcome to attend. **FP+** No. **TYPE** Projection show and fireworks. **REQUIREMENTS** None.

WHAT TO EXPECT This is now predominantly a projection show on the Grauman's Chinese Theatre façade with the addition of fire, lasers, and fireworks. Many clips from the Star Wars franchise are played along with some of the films' most iconic music. It's a stirring mixture of visuals, sound, and effects. **SCARY FACTOR** Low for anyone but the most susceptible to darkness and loud noises. The audience is never in any danger and the fireworks are typically shot low to the ground.

TYPICAL SCHEDULE: Usually begins at park close. Anyone is welcome to stay and enjoy the show. **LENGTH** 10 minutes. **WHERE TO SIT**: About half way in between the Chinese Theatre entrance and the two tall projection towers. If you're seeing Disney Movie Magic, the same spot should be fine for this show.

The Magic Kingdom

The original Walt Disney World theme park and the most popular theme park in the world, Magic Kingdom offers more attractions, entertainment, and atmosphere than any of the other theme parks. Its offerings are varied, from elaborate stage shows to classic dark rides to roller coasters. Magic Kingdom is best toured over two or more days, but guests with limited time still have the opportunity to visit the highlights and take in the fabulous nighttime entertainment.

FASTPASS+ PRIORITY

There are far more FastPass+ opportunities at Magic Kingdom than at any of the other theme parks, making the decision on which to pick difficult. Consider picking three high-priority attractions in a Land that you don't plan to visit until the afternoon or evening. For example, if you plan to start your day with The Magic Carpets of Aladdin, Jungle Cruise, Big Thunder Mountain, and Splash Mountain, then you may want to use FastPass+ in the afternoon in Fantasyland at Peter Pan's Flight, Cinderella, and the Mine Train, or in Tomorrowland at Space Mountain, Tomorrowland Speedway, and Buzz Lightyear.

FastPass+ Priority

1. Seven Dwarfs Mine Train
2. Peter Pan's Flight
3. Space Mountain
4. Splash Mountain (when high temperatures are 80+ degrees)
5. Meet Mickey at Town Square Theater
6. Big Thunder Mountain Railroad
7. Meet Cinderella and a Visiting Princess
8. Meet Rapunzel and a Visiting Princess
9. Enchanted Tales with Belle
10. Meet Ariel at Ariel's Grotto
11. Buzz Lightyear's Space Ranger Spin
12. Tomorrowland Speedway
13. Jungle Cruise
14. Haunted Mansion
15. Pirates of the Caribbean
16. The Many Adventures of Winnie the Pooh
17. Splash Mountain (when high temps are less than 80 degrees)
18. Meet Tinker Bell at Town Square Theater
19. Magic Carpets of Aladdin
20. it's a small world
21. Barnstormer
22. Under the Sea ~ Journey of the Little Mermaid
23. Dumbo the Flying Elephant
24. Mad Tea Party
25. Monsters Inc. Laugh Floor
26. Mickey's PhilharMagic

ARRIVING AT MAGIC KINGDOM

Magic Kingdom's parking lot is located at the Transportation and Ticket Center (TTC) across Seven Seas Lagoon. Guests arriving via their own automobile or buses from non-Disney-owned resorts (except the Swan and Dolphin) will need to transfer from the TTC to Magic Kingdom via the resort monorail, express monorail, or ferry boat. The express monorail is the fastest because it's a direct route that takes about three minutes. There are also more monorails on the express beam, so a fresh monorail arrives every 3–5 minutes. The resort monorail is often less crowded, but the trip takes about 20 minutes with stops at the Polynesian and Grand Floridian resorts first. The five-minute ferry ride is scenic and less cramped because there's more room to spread out. Our preference is the ferry, though the express monorail is often a few minutes faster. Guests traveling from Epcot will also transfer at the Transportation and Ticket Center. Occasionally, guests will instead take buses if other methods of transportation are unavailable.

Most guests from Disney-owned resorts and the Swan and Dolphin arrive at Magic Kingdom via Disney buses, which pick-up and drop-off just a couple minutes walk from the park's main entrance. Guests from the Contemporary have the option of walking about ten minutes or taking the resort monorail. Guests at the Polynesian and Grand Floridian may take the resort monorail or watercraft. Guests at the Wilderness Lodge and Ft. Wilderness may take a bus or watercraft. Watercraft trips are usually slower, but more scenic.

Guest services is located on the far right outside the entrance and on the left at City Hall inside the entrance. Lines are often shorter inside at City Hall. Wheelchair and ECV rentals are located on the right just inside the entrance. Stroller rental is located underneath the train station.

MAIN STREET, U.S.A.

Main Street, U.S.A. is themed to a small town at the turn of the 20th century. The train station blocks the view of what's inside as guests pass underneath. Once through, the magnificent Cinderella Castle shines in the distance. To the right in Town Square Theater is a Magician Mickey Mouse meet and greet. Tinker Bell meets separately in the same building. Next door is the below-average Tony's Town Square restaurant themed to *Lady and the Tramp*, with Italian food that's generally done better at Olive Garden.

On the left is package pickup and Guest Services. Inside the fire station, guests can sign up to play the interactive Sorcerers of the Magic Kingdom game. Five playing cards per person may be picked up daily. Next to it is Harmony Barber Shop with surprisingly reasonable prices. Stop in for a fun first haircut or some "pixie dust" for a lot less money than the Bibbidi Bobbidi Boutique in Fantasyland. Also on the left, the Emporium stretches for much of Main Street, offering just about every piece of theme park merchandise from toys and plush to Mickey Crocs.

On the right, The Chapeau offers a wide selection of hats, and Main Street Confectionery is your best spot for handmade treats and cupcakes. Further up on the right is Main Street Bakery, which now hosts the park's Starbucks. Past that is Main Street Cinema, Uptown Jewelers, and Crystal Arts, all offering upscale items like Dooney and Bourke bags and Ray-Ban sunglasses. Uptown Jewelers is also home to the Pandora store that offers theme park-exclusive charms.

At the end of Main Street on the left is Casey's Corner, serving hot dogs with intereesting toppings like barbecue pork and coleslaw. Farther on the left is Crystal Palace, which hosts a Winnie the Pooh and friends buffet for all three meals. On the right is Plaza Ice Cream Parlor, a great spot for a sundae in the afternoon. To the right of it is The Plaza Restaurant, serving the most inexpensive table service sandwich fare on property.

Mickey Mouse at Town Square Theater

RANKING Don't miss for little kids who need to meet Mickey; skippable for others. **EMH** No. **FP+** Yes. High priority for guests wanting to meet Mickey. **TYPE** Character meet-and-greet. **REQUIREMENTS** None.

WHAT TO EXPECT Magician Mickey greets guests inside Town Square Theater with a fun backstage backdrop. **SCARY FACTOR** None.

WHEN TO GO First two or last two hours of operation, during a parade, or with FastPass+. Skip first thing in the morning for higher priorities. **EXPECT TO WAIT** 35–50 minutes in the afternoon. **LENGTH** A minute or two of exchanging pleasantries and taking pictures.

Tinker Bell at Town Square Theater

RANKING The only place (normally) to meet Tink. **EMH** No. **FP+** Yes, low priority. **TYPE** Character meet-and-greet. **REQUIREMENTS** A willingness to be shrunk down to fairy size.

WHAT TO EXPECT Tinker Bell meets alone in a location that doesn't make a lot of thematic sense, but it does feature a nice backdrop and it is air-conditioned. **SCARY FACTOR** None.

WHEN TO GO In the first two or last two hours of operation or with FP+. **EXPECT TO WAIT** 25–40 minutes in the afternoon. **LENGTH** About a minute of one-on-one time.

The Walt Disney World Railroad

RANKING Minor attraction. **EMH** No. **FP+** No. **TYPE** Steam train tour around the outer perimeter of the park, with additional stops in Frontierland near Splash Mountain and Fantasyland near Barnstormer. **REQUIREMENTS** None.

WHAT TO EXPECT The Disney World Railroad is a relaxing way to see parts of the Magic Kingdom that you might miss by walking around in a hurry. Some minor vignettes are only visible from the train (and the steamboat). You board at any of the three stations and ride for as long as you like around the 1.5 mile track. If you are walking between areas near two of the stops, the train is a nice break. The strollers Disney rents at the park are not allowed on the train. You will need to remove your belongings, name card, and have your receipt handy to pick up a new stroller at your final destination. Skippable for those on shorter visits. **SCARY FACTOR** None.

WHEN TO GO Anytime attraction. See it when waits are long at other rides, or when you want to use it as transport to save walking. The train stops operating prior to Happily Ever After in the evening and does not usually resume service. **EXPECT TO WAIT** Only for the next train—7–10 minutes. **LENGTH** A full circle around the Magic Kingdom takes about 20 minutes. **WHERE TO SIT** Views are best from the side where you board.

ADVENTURELAND

Split into two distinct areas—the Arabian Village and Caribbean Plaza—Adventureland is distinctively adventure-y. In the Arabian section, you'll find most of the attractions—Tiki Room, Jungle Cruise, Magic Carpets of Aladdin, and Swiss Family Treehouse—as well as the cult favorite Citrus Swirl, a blend of frozen orange juice and vanilla ice cream, at Sunshine Tree Terrace. The Jungle Skipper Canteen restaurant, themed to the nearby Jungle Cruise attraction, opened in December 2015 in the old Adventureland Veranda space to the right of Sunshine Tree Terrace. The immersive atmosphere offers plenty of fun little details and the menu is a little out there with appetizers like falafel or shu mai and entrees like whole fried fish, though other dishes like grilled steak and crispy chicken should be more familiar. Because of its large size and the perceived exoticness of the menu, reservations are easy to secure, particularly for lunch. We like it more for the atmosphere and fun overall experience than the food, which typically sounds bolder than it ends up being flavorful.

Agrabah Bazaar is the primary, smallish store offering wares perfect for adventurers. A store sponsored by Sunglass Hut is across from Swiss Family Robinson Treehouse, offering sunglasses that mostly cost hundreds of dollars. To the right of the Pirates entrance is the signup building for the fun Pirate's Adventure Treasures of the Seven Seas interactive game. It includes a free, high-quality souvenir map that sends players around Adventureland unlocking secrets and setting off surprises. Visit in the afternoon as a fun diversion when waits peak elsewhere.

Arabian Village opens up to Caribbean Plaza on the Frontierland side, hosting the Pirates of the Caribbean attraction with an expansive store at its exit offering everything pirate. Tortuga Tavern is the land's quick service, currently offering primarily hot dogs and sandwiches. Aloha Isle behind The Magic Carpets of Aladdin, which recently relocated from its spot now occupied by Sunshine Tree Terrace, serves the popular Dole Whip, a frozen pineapple-flavored treat.

Enchanted Tiki Room

RANKING Minor attraction. **EMH** Evening. **FP+** No. **TYPE** Audio-Animatronics show. **REQUIREMENTS** None.

WHAT TO EXPECT A groundbreaking attraction when it originally opened at Disneyland in the early 60s, the Enchanted Tiki Room entertains with singing Animatronic birds. Today it feels quaint—kids don't enjoy it a lot, and while adults are charmed, it's not a priority. Many Disney fans love it because of its history, but it's ultimately skippable for those immune to nostalgia. **SCARY FACTOR** Not much—just a bit of thunder and lightning.

WHEN TO GO Anytime attraction. See it when waits are long at other rides, or you need to get out of the weather. **EXPECT TO WAIT** 10–15 minutes. **LENGTH** 10 minutes. **WHERE TO SIT** Sit in the last row, towards the center.

Jungle Cruise

RANKING Don't miss. **EMH** No. **FP+** Yes. Medium priority. **TYPE** Comedy disguised as a river cruise. **REQUIREMENTS** None.

WHAT TO EXPECT This boat ride takes you through areas themed as several of the world's great rivers, inhabited by Audio-Animatronic people and animals. Your (human) skipper guides the tour, making corny jokes and telling silly puns along the way. The effects are dated, but the skipper can make the ride so much fun that it's not to be missed. **SCARY FACTOR** Low. There is a short section in dark ruins, but that's it.

WHEN TO GO First two or last two hours of operation, or with FastPass+. **EXPECT TO WAIT** 35–70 minutes in the afternoon. **LENGTH** 10 minutes. **WHERE TO SIT** Anywhere along the edge of the boat—avoid the interior seats.

Magic Carpets of Aladdin

RANKING Skippable but fun. **EMH** Evening. **FP+** Yes. Low priority. **TYPE** Spinning ride. **REQUIREMENTS** None.

WHAT TO EXPECT This slow-loading, low capacity ride raises four-person magic-carpet themed vehicles and then spins riders in the air over Adventureland. You can control how high you go. The ride is fun and offers some spectacular views, but most guests won't want to spend more than a few minutes waiting. **SCARY FACTOR** Low. **CAN WE HANDLE**

IT? Motion sickness is rarely an issue. A camel may spit water in your general direction.

WHEN TO GO Anytime attraction. See it when waits are long at other rides, or you simply are nearby. **EXPECT TO WAIT** 10–20 minutes in the afternoon. **LENGTH** 2 minutes. **WHERE TO SIT** Cast Members will assign your group a carpet—the experience is the same from all. The front seat controls height, the back seat tilt.

Pirates of the Caribbean

RANKING Don't miss. **EMH** Evening. **FP+** Yes. Low priority. **TYPE** Boat ride through pirate-themed Audio-Animatronics and settings. **REQUIREMENTS** None.

WHAT TO EXPECT One of the most famous rides at the park, Pirates sends riders floating through a Disneyfied version of a town ransacked by pirates. In a reversal of what usually happens, the Jack Sparrow films were based on the ride, and Jack and others from the films are present in many scenes. **SCARY FACTOR** This is a lighthearted, playful ride, yet one with lots of skeletons and implied violence. Skip it if Haunted Mansion was too much. **CAN WE HANDLE IT?** There's a mild drop towards the beginning of a few feet that may result in a bit of water splashing over the first row, but that's it.

WHEN TO GO In the first two or last two hours of the day is best. **EXPECT TO WAIT** 30–50 minutes in the afternoon. **LENGTH** 10 minutes. **WHERE TO SIT** All seats have a similar experience. The front row has slightly better views, and a better chance of getting a little wet.

Swiss Family Treehouse

RANKING Skippable but fun. **EMH** Evening. **FP+** No. **TYPE** Self-guided walking tour. **REQUIREMENTS** There are a lot of stairs up and down.

WHAT TO EXPECT The Treehouse replicates the living conditions from the popular film that few probably remember. While interesting, the attraction is not particularly compelling and guests visiting over one day usually have higher priorities. **SCARY FACTOR** Low. **CAN WE HANDLE IT?** The top of the tree is high; the stairs all the way up and down can be tough on cranky knees or hips.

WHEN TO GO Anytime attraction. See it when waits are long at other rides, or you simply are nearby. **EXPECT TO WAIT** No wait to 5 minutes in the afternoon. **LENGTH** 10 minutes or so.

FRONTIERLAND

Home to Big Thunder Mountain, Splash Mountain, and one of the park's most popular quick services, most guests will spend a considerable amount of time here. Fortunately, both rides enjoy hefty capacities that make it possible to visit them in the second hour of operation. You'll also find two anytime attractions: the comfortable serenading of bears in Country Bear Jamboree, and Tom Sawyer Island, where adventures await.

Pecos Bill is the principal quick service, now offering a menu featuring burritos, fajitas, nachos, salads, and burgers with an expansive toppings bar. Diamond Horseshoe's offerings depend on the season, but will be somewhere between forgettable snacks or an all-you-care-to-enjoy meal featuring barbecue food that you don't want any part of. Golden Oak Outpost is located at the Pecos' side exit, serving chicken nuggets and waffle fries to normally non-existent lines when it's open. Westward Ho alongside the river serves snacks and drinks. Two to three carts also position themselves along the river across from Diamond Horseshoe, serving hot dogs, churros, and pretzels. Lines are usually shorter at similar stands around the corner in Liberty Square.

Of course, you'll find several merchandise opportunities here, too. Splash Mountain's exit offers some attraction-branded merchandise, in addition to several shops between Pecos Bill and Diamond Horseshoe that offer everything from freshly baked treats to limited-edition pins.

Big Thunder Mountain Railroad

RANKING Don't miss. **EMH** Evening. **FP+** Yes. High priority. **TYPE** Runaway train-themed roller coaster. **REQUIREMENTS** 40" or taller.

WHAT TO EXPECT Prospective miners board trains consisting of five cars, each with three rows that seat two to three people each. With top speeds under 30 miles per hour, Big Thunder is not an intense experience, but the theming is first rate. **SCARY FACTOR** Minimal for a roller coaster—there are two scenes inside caves that are loud and dark, but anyone that made it through any other Disney coaster will be just fine. **CAN WE HANDLE IT?** Some motion sickness issues for the highly susceptible, and jostling.

WHEN TO GO First or last two hours of operation, or with FastPass+. **EXPECT TO WAIT** 40–60 minutes in the afternoon. **LENGTH** 4 minutes. **WHERE TO SIT** The back provides the wildest experience. Sit up front for a tamer ride.

Country Bear Jamboree

RANKING Minor attraction. **EMH** Evening. **FP+** No. **TYPE** Audio-Animatronics show. **REQUIREMENTS** None.

WHAT TO EXPECT A musical review and show with country-and-western songs performed by Animatronic bears. Wildly popular when it opened, it is now attended largely by roots/country music fans, diehard Disney fans, and visitors looking for a bit of a rest and some air conditioning. The characters are fun but the jokes are hokey, and the songs, while fun to those with wide musical tastes, aren't everyone's favorite. Skippable for many on shorter visits. **SCARY FACTOR** None. **CAN WE HANDLE IT?** The music is more bluegrass/western than modern country.

WHEN TO GO Anytime attraction. See it when waits are long at other rides, or you need to get out of the weather. **EXPECT TO WAIT** 10–15 minutes for the next show. **LENGTH** 15 minutes. **WHERE TO SIT** Sit in the middle row, toward the center. Wait for 25 people or so to enter a row first, and follow them.

Splash Mountain

RANKING Don't miss. **EMH** Evening. **FP+** Yes. High priority on hot days, medium on cool days. **TYPE** Mostly a gentle log ride, with fewer thrills than you'd guess from outside. **REQUIREMENTS** 40" or taller.

WHAT TO EXPECT Splash Mountain is the ride that most showcases all of the best of Disney. You float past brilliantly executed scenes based on the Br'er Rabbit character from Disney's (unavailable) *Song of the South*. And here and there—especially towards the end—there's some thrilling drops. **SCARY FACTOR** The very visible final drop, from 52 feet up and at 40 miles per hour at a 45-degree angle, is greatly misleading. Most of this ride is gentle floating through darling settings. But besides the final drop, there are several much shorter drops. **CAN WE HANDLE IT?** You may get wet—especially if you sit in the front, but possibly from any seat. The visible final drop scares many off who would absolutely love this ride. Trust us and give it a chance.

WHEN TO GO First two or last two hours of operation, or with FastPass+. **EXPECT TO WAIT** 15–90+ minutes in the afternoon (the longer waits on crowded hot days, the shorter on cold low-crowd days). **LENGTH** 12 minutes. **WHERE TO SIT** The front seat has the best view, but is most likely to get wet. Those seated on the left side of the log enjoy the best views of the Animatronics.

Tom Sawyer Island

RANKING Minor attraction. **EMH** No. **FP+** No. **TYPE** Self-guided walking tour and playground. **REQUIREMENTS** None.

WHAT TO EXPECT Tom Sawyer Island is only accessible via motorized rafts that board near the entrance to Big Thunder Mountain Railroad. Once on the island, visitors can explore numerous areas themed to Tom Sawyer and Huck Finn—caves, a mine, two bridges, a working water wheel, and Fort Langhorn, a play area. Benches are plentiful and the Island is a terrific spot to take a break. Skippable for those without kids, or on a short visit. **SCARY FACTOR** None.

WHEN TO GO Anytime attraction. See it when waits are long at other rides, or you simply are nearby. Afternoons tend to be best, but note that it closes before dusk. **EXPECT TO WAIT** 5–15 minutes to get raft transport in the afternoon. **LENGTH** Allow 30–45 minutes+ including time spent waiting for the rafts, more if your kids really need to run around.

The Walt Disney World Railroad

See the "Main Street" entry on the railroad, which stops in Frontierland near the exit to Splash Mountain.

LIBERTY SQUARE
....

To the left of Cinderella Castle, Liberty Square offers the fewest attractions and eateries of any land, but what is offered is mostly above average in quality. Hall of Presidents is a perfect way to spend a hot afternoon, while Haunted Mansion is quintessential Disney. In October 2016, Disney added a fantastic Muppets show that plays in the windows above Heritage House and The Hall of Presidents.

Columbia Harbour House across from Haunted Mansion is our favorite quick service, offering a delicious fried shrimp platter, in addition to salads, unique sandwiches, grilled salmon, and excellent soups. Sleepy Hollow Refreshments serves funnel cakes, waffles, and other ice cream treats. We prefer lunch to dinner at Liberty Tree Tavern for guests paying cash. While the number of lunch entrees was reduced in October 2016, relatively inexpensive options are still available in the hamburger, pot roast, fish and chips, pasta, and salad. The all-you-care-to-enjoy platter, featuring turkey, pot roast, pork loin, and all the fixings, is available for lunch and dinner. For dinner, the fixed-price, per-person platter is the only option on the menu. It includes a non-alcoholic beverage and dessert.

Across from Hall of Presidents is Ye Olde Christmas Shoppe, which offers primarily Christmas-related merchandise. Memento Mori near Haunted Mansion's exit offers the full line of Haunted Mansion merchandise, along with kitchen-related items.

Hall of Presidents

RANKING Minor attraction. **EMH** No. **FP+** No. **TYPE** Audio-Animatronics show. **REQUIREMENTS** None.

WHAT TO EXPECT A theater show featuring film clips and animatronics of all of the U.S. Presidents. The show is patriotic and expounds on the hardships and triumphs of the United States through the years. The theater is air-conditioned, comfortable, and seats over 700 people, which makes it a nice and easy attraction to enjoy in the afternoon heat. Enjoyed most by adults and patriotic Americans, dull for most kids. Skippable for those on shorter visits. **SCARY FACTOR** None, other than it's full of politicians.

WHEN TO GO Anytime attraction. See it when waits are long at other rides, or you need to get out of the weather. **EXPECT TO WAIT** Arrive either at 20 or 50 minutes past the hour and your wait should be just ten minutes. **LENGTH** 25 minutes. **WHERE TO SIT** In the middle row, toward the center.

The Haunted Mansion

RANKING Don't miss. **EMH** Evening. **FP+** Yes. Medium priority. **TYPE** Light-hearted, slow-moving ride through a haunted house and its grave-yard. **REQUIREMENTS** None.

WHAT TO EXPECT One of the most famous rides at the park, the Haunted Mansion is one of Disney's best and most enduring attractions. Intended to be a fun and goofy ride, not a frightening experience, you won't see anything truly gruesome or disgusting. This is a must-ride for almost all guests. **SCARY FACTOR** Haunted Mansion is much more spooky than it is scary, but a lot of kids are going to be apprehensive about entering the foreboding building. Rest assured that it's a lot of fun. **CAN WE HANDLE IT?** Yes, those brave enough to enter enjoy the experience.

WHEN TO GO First two or last two hours of operation, or with FastPass+. **EXPECT TO WAIT** 20–50 minutes in the afternoon, longer if the Hall of Presidents and Liberty Square Riverboat have just let out guests, as they do every thirty minutes. **LENGTH** 10 minutes. **WHERE TO SIT** Each Doom Buggy seats two to three. Sit apprehensive youngsters (or dads) in the middle.

The Liberty Square Riverboat

RANKING Minor attraction. **EMH** No. **FP+** No. **TYPE** Steamboat tour around the Rivers of America. **REQUIREMENTS** None.

WHAT TO EXPECT The Liberty Square Riverboat is a stately three-tiered paddle-wheel boat that slowly circles Tom Sawyer Island and offers fan-tastic views of Splash Mountain, Big Thunder Mountain Railroad, and several other popular attractions. Some minor vignettes otherwise visible only from the Walt Disney World Railroad also appear. The voice of Mark Twain narrates the journey. Skippable for those on short visits. **SCARY FACTOR** None.

WHEN TO GO Anytime attraction. See it when waits are long at other rides, or you need to get out of the weather. **EXPECT TO WAIT** Arrive either at 20 or 50 minutes past the hour and your wait should be just ten minutes. **LENGTH** 17 minutes. **WHERE TO SIT** Bow and stern locations where you can easily see both riverbanks are best. Otherwise sit on the port side. (That's left when facing the bow—the end without the paddlewheel.)

The Muppets Present...
Great Moments in American History

RANKING Don't miss. **EMH** No. **FP+** No. **TYPE** Stage show. **REQUIRE-MENTS** None.

WHAT TO EXPECT The Muppets, including Sam Eagle, Miss Piggy, Kermit, and Fozzie Bear, take over the windows above Heritage House and The Hall of Presidents for one of two shows scheduled intermittently throughout the morning and early afternoon. The shows are surprisingly and authentically entertaining with fun songs and an appreciation for American history. **SCARY FACTOR** None.

WHEN TO GO There are typically 6–8 shows scheduled daily and any is fine. Check the My Disney Experience app for exact times. **EXPECT TO WAIT** Arrive ten minutes before the start. **LENGTH** 8–10 minutes. **WHERE TO SIT** A rope will be placed on the ground to identify the front of the viewing area. Sit or stand somewhere directly behind it.

FANTASYLAND
....

With the longest list of attractions, this is where most guests will spend the majority of their time. Fortunately, most attractions enjoy short durations and healthy capacities, making it relatively easy to bang out the majority of rides in under an hour first thing in the morning or when crowds ease in the late evening. Mickey's PhilharMagic is an outstanding 3D anytime attraction, and Enchanted Tales with Belle is an afternoon FastPass+ priority.

Be Our Guest Restaurant remains one of the most popular places to eat on property, serving quick service breakfast and lunch, in addition to table service dinner. Reservations are usually required for any of these meals and can be made up to 180 days in advance. We like breakfast for those that can secure a reservation close to 8am with a 9am park open. Diners will be able to beat the rush to a priority Fantasyland attraction like Seven Dwarfs Mine Train so long as they exit the restaurant by 8:45am. Later breakfasts are not recommended because they take up precious morning touring time. Lunch is mostly soups, salads, and sandwiches, in addition to quiches and braised pork. Average entrée prices have climbed to around $15, but most guests find value in the enchanting atmosphere and food is delivered to the table for added convenience. Through July 26, 2018, dinner is a typical table service experience with a menu featuring steaks, salmon, chicken, lamb, and a vegetarian ratatouille, with cupcakes and cream puffs for dessert, just like at lunch. Beginning July 27, the restaurant will exclusively serve a 3-course prix-fixe menu with each guest choosing appetizer, entrée, and dessert. More information is available in Chapter 7: Where to Eat.

Pinocchio Village Haus is the primary dinnertime quick service, located to the left of the entrance to New Fantasyland. The flatbread pizzas and salads are above average and there's plentiful air-conditioned seating in addition to outdoor patio seating. Gaston's Tavern between Be Our Guest and Journey of the Little Mermaid serves cinnamon rolls, snacks, and an apple-flavored frozen beverage called LeFou's Brew.

Indoor seating is minimal, but the theming is exquisite throughout. Friar's Nook, located across from the entrance to Seven Dwarfs Mine Train, serves tater tots with a variety of toppings. Storybook Treats is Fantasyland's version of the Plaza Ice Cream Parlor, serving decadent sundaes and other ice-cream treats. Cheshire Café serves snacks, drinks, and treats next to Mad Tea Party, while Prince Eric's Village Market serves drinks, lemonades, and snacks across from the Journey of the Little Mermaid ride in New Fantasyland. Finally, Big Top Souvenirs across from Dumbo is yet another spot to find freshly made treats, including caramel corn, candied apples, and fudge, in addition to the frozen Goofy's Glacier drinks.

Shopping is plentiful in and around Fantasyland. Castle Couture to the left of Mickey's PhilharMagic is one of the best spots for princess merchandise. Across the way is Sir Mickey's, primarily offering toys and apparel. Two great stores are located back in New Fantasyland: Bonjour Gifts, to the right of Gaston's Tavern, offers unique glassware, goblets, and other upscale items, and Big Top Souvenirs offers toys and apparel.

Ariel's Grotto

RANKING Don't miss for little kids who need to meet Ariel; skippable for others. **EMH** Morning, Evening. **FP+** Yes. High priority for guests wanting to meet Ariel. **TYPE** Character meet and greet. **REQUIREMENTS** None.

WHAT TO EXPECT After winding through a line themed to undersea rockwork, meet Ariel in her picturesque grotto. **SCARY FACTOR** None.

WHEN TO GO First or last hour of operation, or with FastPass+. **EXPECT TO WAIT** 25–45 minutes in the afternoon. **LENGTH** About a minute with everyone's favorite undersea princess.

The Barnstormer

RANKING Minor attraction. **EMH** Morning, Evening. **FP+** Yes. Low priority. **TYPE** Roller coaster. **REQUIREMENTS** 35" or taller.

WHAT TO EXPECT This slow-loading, low-capacity ride with some light theming around Goofy's stunt plane is the tamest coaster at Disney World, and best thought of as a "starter" roller coaster. Fun, swoopy, and brief, its features are fully visible, so there's no surprises. Great fun for little kids, but skippable for others. **SCARY FACTOR** Low. Mild speeds and heights. **CAN WE HANDLE IT?** If your kids decide after it begins that they aren't ready for coasters, it will be over within seconds. Ride vehicles are low to the ground with just enough room for two average-size adults to sit side by side.

WHEN TO GO First two or last two hours of operation, or with FastPass+. **EXPECT TO WAIT** 25–40 minutes in the afternoon. **LENGTH** Less than 1 minute. **WHERE TO SIT** The front seat has the best view, but no seats are bad.

Dumbo the Flying Elephant

RANKING Minor attraction. **EMH** Morning, Evening. **FP+** Yes. Low priority. **TYPE** Spinning ride. **REQUIREMENTS** None.

WHAT TO EXPECT Charming Dumbos with two riders side by side rise from their delightfully decorated base and slowly spin. Riders control how high or low their Dumbo flies. A favorite of little kids, but skippable for adults. Those not using FastPass+ have the option to wait in an air-conditioned play area instead of the typical queue. **SCARY FACTOR** Low. The mild heights may trouble the most severely acrophobic. **CAN WE HANDLE IT?** Spinning is too slow to affect motion sickness. Little kids can't ride alone.

WHEN TO GO First two or last two hours of operation, or with FastPass+. **EXPECT TO WAIT** 30–50 minutes in the afternoon. **LENGTH** Less than 2 minutes. **WHERE TO SIT** All seats are good.

Enchanted Tales with Belle

RANKING Major attraction. **EMH** Morning, Evening. **FP+** Yes. High priority. **TYPE** Combined walk-through tour, Audio-Animatronic show, interactive show, and character photo op. **REQUIREMENTS** None.

WHAT TO EXPECT This experience starts as a tour of Maurice's cottage, magically shifts to the Beast's Mansion where audience volunteers are recruited by Madame Wardrobe for a show, moves to the Beast's Library where under Lumiere's direction the volunteers act the show out for Belle, and ends with the show volunteers getting a chance to meet and have pictures with Belle. Only show volunteers get photos by default, so if your kids aren't picked for a part, have them volunteer at the last "anybody else?" casting call. Drop dead cute, it's Disney at its best. **SCARY FACTOR** None.

WHEN TO GO During the afternoon parade, in the final hour of operation, or with FastPass+. **EXPECT TO WAIT** 20–40 minutes in the afternoon. **LENGTH** 25 minutes.

it's a small world

RANKING Minor attraction. **EMH** Morning, Evening. **FP+** Yes. Low priority. **TYPE** Boat ride. **REQUIREMENTS** None.

WHAT TO EXPECT Boats seating 20 or so float past miniatures of singing children from around the world, colorfully attired and accompanied by toys and representations of their cultures. A world-famous tour-de-force of design, song writing, and artistic unity. **SCARY FACTOR** None.

WHEN TO GO Before 11am, in the final two hours of operation, or with FastPass+. **EXPECT TO WAIT** 20–35 minutes in the afternoon. **LENGTH** 11 minutes. **WHERE TO SIT** Seats at the sides of the boat have the best view.

Mad Tea Party

RANKING Minor attraction. **EMH** Morning, Evening. **FP+** Yes. Low priority. **TYPE** Spinning ride. **REQUIREMENTS** None.

WHAT TO EXPECT Spinning tea cups lightly themed to *Alice in Wonderland* delight kids, annoy most adults. Skippable for those on shorter visits. **SCARY FACTOR** None. **CAN WE HANDLE IT?** There's three simultaneous spins: the whole ride, a group of cups, and individual cups. Don't ride if you are subject to motion sickness.

WHEN TO GO Anytime attraction. See it when waits are long at other rides, or you simply are nearby. **EXPECT TO WAIT** 5–15 minutes in the afternoon. **LENGTH** 90 seconds. **WHERE TO SIT** In a different cup than your children, who will wish to spin much more than you do.

The Many Adventures of Winnie the Pooh

RANKING Minor attraction. **EMH** Morning, Evening. **FP+** Yes. Low priority. **TYPE** Dark ride. **REQUIREMENTS** None.

WHAT TO EXPECT Four-person "honey pots" make their way through multiple, richly-detailed Winnie the Pooh-themed scenes featuring Pooh, Eeyore, Piglet, Owl, Tigger, and others. **SCARY FACTOR** Low—a briefly blustery day where the ride vehicle tips up and down slightly for a few seconds.

WHEN TO GO First two or last two hours of operation, or with FastPass+. **EXPECT TO WAIT** 30–40 minutes in the afternoon. **LENGTH** 3 minutes. **WHERE TO SIT** All seats are good.

Mickey's PhilharMagic

RANKING Don't miss. **EMH** Morning, Evening. **FP+** Yes. Lowest priority. **TYPE** 4D show. **REQUIREMENTS** None.

WHAT TO EXPECT This 3D film (supplemented by in-theater effects—hence 4D) tells the tale of Donald getting in trouble, with Mickey ultimately to the rescue. Interwoven between are some of the best bits from some of Disney's most popular films: *Peter Pan*, *Aladdin*, *Little Mermaid*, *Lion King*, and more. It's a must-see because of its fun and diabolically creative celebration of some of Disney's best-loved animation. **SCARY FACTOR** Low. 3D effects and typical cartoon mayhem spook some little ones. Take off their 3D glasses if this happens.

WHEN TO GO Anytime attraction. See it when waits are long at other rides, or you simply are nearby. **EXPECT TO WAIT** Up to 15 minutes for the next show. **LENGTH** 12 minutes. **WHERE TO SIT** Sit in a middle row, towards the center. Wait for 25 people or so to enter a row first, and follow them.

Peter Pan's Flight

RANKING Don't miss. **EMH** Morning, Evening. **FP+** Yes. High priority. **TYPE** Dark ride. **REQUIREMENTS** None.

WHAT TO EXPECT Pirate ships seating 2–3 people fly through scenes from *Peter Pan*. Kids love it, but teens and adults are mixed. For some, the flight over London instantly makes it among their favorite rides at Disney World; others find it pedestrian, a little dull—especially the middle section—and overrated. It's a "Don't miss" so that you can discover for yourself where you stand. **SCARY FACTOR** Dark, but not scary.

WHEN TO GO At park open, in the final hour of operation, or with FastPass+. **EXPECT TO WAIT** 50–70+ minutes in the afternoon. **LENGTH** 3 minutes. **WHERE TO SIT** All seats are good.

Pete's Silly Sideshow: Goofy and Donald

RANKING Don't miss for little kids who need to meet Goofy or Donald; skippable for others. **EMH** No. **FP+** No. **TYPE** Character meet and greet. **REQUIREMENTS** None.

WHAT TO EXPECT Goofy and Donald in elaborate circus costumes greet guests in a tent at Pete's Silly Sideshow. Minnie and Daisy greet in the same tent, but their line is separate. **SCARY FACTOR** None.

WHEN TO GO Anytime attraction. See it when waits are long at other rides, or you simply are nearby. **EXPECT TO WAIT** 10–20 minutes in the afternoon. **LENGTH** About a minute with each character individually.

Pete's Silly Sideshow: Minnie and Daisy

RANKING Don't-miss for little kids who need to meet Minnie or Daisy; skippable for others. **EMH** No. **FP+** No. **TYPE** Character meet and greet. **REQUIREMENTS** None.

WHAT TO EXPECT Minnie and Daisy in elaborate circus costumes greet guests in a tent at Pete's Silly Sideshow. Goofy and Donald greet in the same tent, but their line is separate. **SCARY FACTOR** None.

WHEN TO GO Anytime attraction. See it when waits are long at other rides, or you simply are nearby. **EXPECT TO WAIT** 20–30 minutes in the afternoon. **LENGTH** About a minute with each character individually.

Prince Charming Regal Carrousel

RANKING Minor attraction. **EMH** Morning, Evening. **FP+** No. **TYPE** Slowly spinning carousel. **REQUIREMENTS** None.

WHAT TO EXPECT As stately and lovely a carousel as you will ever see, the essence of this ride is obvious from simply looking at it. Ride it if you have kids that wish to; just watch it otherwise. **SCARY FACTOR** None, other than getting the spelling right (two r's in carrousel). **CAN WE HANDLE IT?** Spins too slowly to bother most.

WHEN TO GO Anytime attraction. See it when waits are long at other rides, or you are nearby. **EXPECT TO WAIT** 5–10 minutes in the afternoon. **LENGTH** 2 minutes. **WHERE TO SIT** Along the outside for the best photo opportunities.

Princess Fairytale Hall: Cinderella and a Visiting Princess

RANKING Don't miss for those who need to meet Cinderella; skippable for others. **EMH** Morning, Evening. **FP+** Yes. High priority for those who want to greet these characters. **TYPE** Character meet and greet. **REQUIREMENTS** None.

WHAT TO EXPECT Cinderella and another princess greet guests in Princess Fairytale Hall. Rapunzel greets in the same building, but her line (and FastPass+) is entirely separate. **SCARY FACTOR** None.

WHEN TO GO At park open, in the final hour of operation, or with Fast-Pass+. **EXPECT TO WAIT** 30–60 minutes in the afternoon. **LENGTH** 3–5 minutes of signing, mingling, and picture taking.

Princess Fairytale Hall: Rapunzel and a Visiting Princess

RANKING Don't miss for those who need to meet Rapunzel; skippable for others. **EMH** Morning, Evening. **FP+** Yes. High priority for those who want to greet these characters. **TYPE** Character meet and greet. **REQUIREMENTS** None.

WHAT TO EXPECT Rapunzel and another princess greet guests in Princess Fairytale Hall. Cinderella greets in the same building, but her line (and FastPass+) is entirely separate. **SCARY FACTOR** None.

WHEN TO GO At park open, in the final hour of operation, or with Fast-Pass+. **EXPECT TO WAIT** 30–60 minutes in the afternoon. **LENGTH** 3–5 minutes of signing, mingling, and picture taking.

Seven Dwarfs Mine Train

RANKING Don't miss. **EMH** Morning, Evening. **FP+** Yes. High priority. **TYPE** Combined roller coaster and dark ride. **REQUIREMENTS** 38" or taller.

WHAT TO EXPECT This ride combines the swoops and curves of a moderate roller coaster with richly detailed scenes from *Snow White*, focusing especially on the Dwarfs. The vehicles are small and seating may be uncomfortable for guests over six feet tall. **SCARY FACTOR** Low—the roller coaster parts are mild and the dark scenes brief. **CAN WE HANDLE IT?** A new ride system (cars that swing side to side) both increases the impression of speed and makes the ride smoother and more comfortable for those with motion sickness.

WHEN TO GO Immediately at park open, in the final hour of operation, or with FastPass+. **EXPECT TO WAIT** 50–90+ minutes in the afternoon. **LENGTH** 3 minutes. **WHERE TO SIT** The front row provides the best views while the back row offers the wildest ride.

Under the Sea ~ Journey of the Little Mermaid

RANKING Major attraction. **EMH** Morning, Evening. **FP+** Yes. Low priority. **TYPE** Dark ride. **REQUIREMENTS** None.

WHAT TO EXPECT Two-to three person "clamshells" take you under the sea into a fairly literal re-telling of the *Little Mermaid*. There's much color and movement, and the party scene is particularly well-done, but those who are not Little Mermaid fans may find it dull. If just one Little Mermaid attraction is enough for you, see the one at Disney's Hollywood Studios instead. **SCARY FACTOR** Low. It has its moments shrouded in darkness, but it's not in any way scary.

WHEN TO GO First two or last two hours of operation, or with FastPass+. **EXPECT TO WAIT** 30–40 minutes in the afternoon. **LENGTH** 5 minutes. **WHERE TO SIT** All seats are good.

The Walt Disney World Railroad

See the "Main Street" entry on the railroad for more details. The Fantasyland stop is near the entrance to The Barnstormer.

TOMORROWLAND
....

One of the most popular lands, and the one located just off the Hub to the right, Tomorrowland is home to several of Magic Kingdom's most popular attractions, including the venerable Space Mountain and Buzz Lightyear's Space Ranger Spin. Several anytime attractions are also situated here, including the Carousel of Progress, Tomorrowland PeopleMover, and Monsters Inc. Laugh Floor. Expect to see construction walls over the next couple of years as Disney begins construction on a Tron roller coaster similar to the ride that debuted in Shanghai. It will be situated in between Space Mountain and Tomorrowland Speedway

Tomorrowland has no table service restaurants, but Cosmic Ray's Starlight Café is one of Magic Kingdom's most popular quick services. Unfortunately, the menu options have been cut recently and ribs are no longer available. You will still find hamburgers topped with bacon and pulled pork, chicken nuggets, chicken sandwiches, salads, and rotisserie chicken, among other items. Tomorrowland Terrace is another major quick service, located closer to the Plaza Restaurant on Main Street than the rest of Tomorrowland, but it's only open when Magic Kingdom is crowded. If it is open, the menu consists of a surprisingly decent mixture of interesting takes on the usual Disney standards. Lunching Pad is located underneath Astro Orbiter in the center of Tomorrowland, serving hot dogs, Mickey Pretzels, frozen beverages, and snacks. Also near Astro Orbiter, Cool Ship serves beverages and snacks. Joffrey's Coffee opened Revive, a fun-looking kiosk in front of Space Mountain, in March 2017. It's a nice change of pace for those that have sworn off Starbucks as it offers a variety of coffee and tea beverages, like the specialty Mission to S'Mores Latte, in addition to pastries and other snacks. Rounding out the choices is Auntie Gravity's Galactic Goodies, serving smoothies, snacks, and ice cream treats.

Mickey's Star Traders and Merchant of Venus near Stitch's Great Escape are the two primary stores, though most everything sold here is available elsewhere. There are small shops at the exits to Buzz Lightyear and Space Mountain as well.

Astro Orbiter

RANKING Skippable but fun. **EMH** Morning, Evening. **FP+** No. **TYPE** Spinning ride. **REQUIREMENTS** None.

WHAT TO EXPECT This slow-loading, low capacity ride spins riders high over Tomorrowland. Twelve "rocket ships" load from an elevated platform (two to a vehicle), raise up, and spin. You can control how high you go. Views are nice, and being high is bit of a thrill, but not worth long waits. **SCARY FACTOR** Medium. This is the most intense spinner attraction at WDW, with the high altitude and rocket ships that slant inward. **CAN WE HANDLE IT?** Put a parent with each kid to help with any fears about height. Those with severe fear of heights should sit this out. Motion sickness is rarely an issue. Note that the seating situation is different than other spinner rides. Riders sit one in front of the other with their legs spread out to the sides. Two adults may want to split up as parties of one for a more comfortable ride. The brief elevator ride before and after the ride is packed full and cramped.

WHEN TO GO At park open or in the final hour of operation. **EXPECT TO WAIT** 20–40 minutes in the afternoon. **LENGTH** 2 minutes. **WHERE TO SIT** Seat adults in back with the kids up front.

Buzz Lightyear's Space Ranger Spin

RANKING Don't miss. **EMH** Morning, Evening. **FP+** Yes. Medium priority. **TYPE** Dark ride shooting gallery. **REQUIREMENTS** None.

WHAT TO EXPECT In this slow-moving ride, prospective space rangers protect the universe by turning their ride vehicle and shooting an "ion cannon" at targets as they traverse a series of *Toy Story*-themed spaces. Vehicles hold more than two, but have only two cannons. Scores are tallied, so you compete with your ride-mate. The simple concept—being inside a Toy Story-themed video game—delights almost everyone. **SCARY FACTOR** None. **CAN WE HANDLE IT?** A joystick controls much of the spinning. Keep youngsters away to enjoy a ride with less motion.

WHEN TO GO First two or last two hours of operation, or with FastPass+. **EXPECT TO WAIT** 25–80 minutes in the afternoon. **LENGTH** 5 minutes. **WHERE TO SIT** All vehicles and seats give the same experience.

Monsters Inc. Laugh Floor

RANKING Minor attraction. **EMH** Evening (usually first hour only). **FP+** Yes. Low priority. **TYPE** Interactive show. **REQUIREMENTS** None.

WHAT TO EXPECT Mike Wazowski, the one-eyed green monster from *Monsters Inc.*, puts on a comedy show to collect laughs from the audience to power Monstropolis. Cool technology allows the monsters to directly interact with the audience. The laughs typically are weak—though often fun for kids. Turtle Talk with Crush at Epcot uses similar technology much, much better. Those on shorter visits may elect to skip. **SCARY FACTOR** None, if your kids have seen the movies. **CAN WE HANDLE IT?** Avoid if you already have had enough Billy Crystal in your life.

WHEN TO GO Anytime attraction. See it when waits are long at other rides, or you need to get out of the weather. **EXPECT TO WAIT** 10–20 minutes in the afternoon. **LENGTH** 10 minutes. **WHERE TO SIT** As in most shows, the center of the theater seating, midway back, give the best views.

Space Mountain

RANKING Don't miss. **EMH** Morning, Evening. **FP+** Yes. High priority. **TYPE** Roller coaster in the dark. **REQUIREMENTS** 44" or taller.

WHAT TO EXPECT In one of the park's most popular rides, small three-person rockets, coupled together in flights of two, blast into the darkness of space and traverse sharp curves and minor dips past planets, stars, moons, and meteors, before returning to the launch facility. **SCARY FACTOR** Moderate. Because the ride is in the dark, speed seems much higher than it is, and everything that happens is unexpected. This scares some. But otherwise it's a very mild coaster. **CAN WE HANDLE IT?** Motion sickness typically is not an issue, but the ride's jerkiness can aggravate back/neck/shoulder pain.

WHEN TO GO At park open, in the final hour of operation, or with Fast-Pass+. **EXPECT TO WAIT** 45–120+ minutes in the afternoon. **LENGTH** 3 minutes. **WHERE TO SIT** The six seats in each coupled-together ride vehicle are single file. Front seats are the most fun. If you are concerned a kid might panic, sit behind them so you can comfort them by touch. The third and fourth seats are the least jerky.

Stitch's Great Escape!

RANKING Skippable. **EMH** Morning, Evening. **FP+** No. **TYPE** Audio-Animatronics show. **REQUIREMENTS** 40" or taller.

WHAT TO EXPECT Stitch's Great Escape replaces a prior show that was great, but far too scary to be in the Magic Kingdom—or perhaps anywhere at Disney World. However, Stitch's Great Escape replaced only one of the many scary elements of the old show, added the annoyances of Stitch—animatronic belching, anyone?—and now scares kids and bores adults. **SCARY FACTOR** High. Guests are trapped in separated individual seats while scary things happen around them, often in the dark. This attraction has the highest potential to scare kids tall enough for it of any Disney World attraction, and because of the seat design, parents can't comfort kids until the end of the "show". **CAN WE HANDLE IT?** Don't go if your kids have been scared by anything else at Disney World.

WHEN TO GO Stitch was moved to "seasonal" status during the fall of 2016 and only operates during very busy times of the year. If it is operating when you visit, chances are that you want to visit in the afternoon when waits are high elsewhere. **EXPECT TO WAIT** 5–10 minutes in the afternoon. **LENGTH** 10 minutes. **WHERE TO SIT** On a different ride.

Tomorrowland Speedway

RANKING For little kids: don't miss. For everyone else: skippable. **EMH** Morning, Evening. **FP+** Yes. High priority only if you have little kids. **TYPE** Slow, go-cart-style ride on a highly constrained track. **REQUIREMENTS** 32" or taller to ride, 54" or taller to drive.

WHAT TO EXPECT An opportunity for kids to drive or ride along a speedway-themed track in a small two-seater car, at speeds of less than 8 mph along a guide rail that prevents getting out of their lane. Go-cart-style rides can be fun for adults, but this isn't. Young kids tall enough to drive love it, and waits can be long. **SCARY FACTOR** A reminder that Junior is turning 16 far too soon. **CAN WE HANDLE IT?** Both the queue and the ride reek of exhaust and are largely unprotected from the sun. Getting rear-ended by a gleeful 6 year old is common, which can be rough on your back and neck.

WHEN TO GO At park open, in the final hour of operation, or with Fast-Pass+. **EXPECT TO WAIT** 20–40 minutes in the afternoon. **LENGTH** 5 minutes. **WHERE TO SIT** All vehicles give the same experience. If the kids are tall enough (54"+), let them drive. Then keep whining at them, "Are we there yet?"

Tomorrowland Transit Authority PeopleMover

RANKING Minor attraction. **EMH** Morning, Evening. **FP+** No. **TYPE** Tour above and through Tomorrowland. **REQUIREMENTS** None.

WHAT TO EXPECT This slow-moving elevated attraction sends four-person magnetically powered vehicles around Tomorrowland and through parts of several rides, providing a bit of a tour of the land's attractions, and a rest for weary feet. Skippable for those on short visits. **SCARY FACTOR** None.

WHEN TO GO Anytime attraction. See it when waits are long at other rides, or you need to get out of the weather. **EXPECT TO WAIT** No wait to 10 minutes in the afternoon. **LENGTH** 10 minutes. **WHERE TO SIT** All vehicles and seats give the same experience.

Walt Disney's Carousel of Progress

RANKING Minor attraction. **EMH** Morning, Evening. **FP+** No. **TYPE** Audio-Animatronics show. **REQUIREMENTS** None.

WHAT TO EXPECT The theater-style seating area rotates through four charming scenes of American family life, highlighting changes in home technology from the turn of the last century until the mid-90s. Designed for, and an enormous hit at, the New York World's Fair of 64/65, the ride suffers from the lack of a recent update and is dull for many kids. Many diehard Disney fans love it—and it's the only ride in the park that Walt Disney touched. Unlike most theater shows, leaving midway through is not allowed due to the theater's movement. **SCARY FACTOR** None.

WHEN TO GO Anytime attraction. See it when waits are long at other rides, or you need to get out of the weather. **EXPECT TO WAIT** 5–10 minutes in the afternoon. **LENGTH** 20 minutes. **WHERE TO SIT** As in most shows, the center of the theater seating, midway back, give the best views.

PARADES, FIREWORKS, AND SHOWS
....

Afternoon Festival of Fantasy Parade

RANKING Don't miss. **EMH** No. **FP+** No. **TYPE** Parade. **REQUIREMENTS** None.

WHAT TO EXPECT Featuring astonishing floats, a great mix of characters, and wonderful walking entertainers, this parade (which debuted in early 2014) is a don't miss. **SCARY FACTOR** None.

TYPICAL SCHEDULE: Begins at 3pm most days. May show at 2pm in the fall. Unusual events, e.g., tapings of shows on Main Street, may result in different times. The busiest days of the year often see two parades. **LENGTH** 15 minutes once it arrives.

WHERE TO SEE IT: The parade begins in Frontierland to the left of Splash Mountain, takes a turn near Hall of Presidents, and continues down Main Street, exiting between the firehouse and the Emporium. People begin staking out spots on Main Street more than an hour before showtime, but most days there are great spots still available in Frontierland 15–30 minutes before the parade. The height of the floats means that even little kids don't need to be right in front, but the great entertainers and walking characters will be hard for them to see from farther back. See it across from Pecos Bill where crowds are lighter and you can leave sooner. Tony's Town Square offers a fixed price, 3-course meal that includes a ticket to see the parade in a reserved viewing section in Town Square. While there is some value if you order the most expensive items on the menu, we don't recommend it as the food is subpar and seeing the parade from another area, including right across from the reserved section, is usually easy enough.

Evening Castle Show: Once Upon a Time

RANKING Don't miss. **EMH** No. **FP+** No. **TYPE** Projection show. **REQUIRE-MENTS** Decent eyesight.

WHAT TO EXPECT Once Upon A Time, which has nothing to do with the fairytale soap opera of the same name, is a 15-minute animated show that's cleverly projected onto the front of Cinderella Castle. In addition to all of the characters and stories, including scenes from Frozen, Beauty and the Beast, Winnie the Pooh, Alice in Wonderland, Pinocchio, Cinderella, and a whole lot more, special effects and pyrotechnics help complete this nighttime spectacular. **SCARY FACTOR** None.

TYPICAL SCHEDULE: Double check the Times Guide. It's currently scheduled 45 minutes after Happily Ever After begins. **LENGTH** 15 minutes.

WHERE TO SEE IT: Somewhere between the Casey's Corner area on Main Street and the Partners statue in the hub is best. The projected images are large enough that they can be seen from further back more easily than previous shows.

Happily Ever After: Evening Fireworks

RANKING Don't miss. **EMH** No. **FP+** No. Dessert parties are offered and the courtyard viewing makes seeing the show much easier. The more expensive terrace seating provides an off-center view, and is not recommended. **TYPE** Fireworks show. **REQUIREMENTS** None.

WHAT TO EXPECT Happily Ever After debuted on May 12, 2017, and combines more pyrotechnics than the former show, Wishes, with colorful, emotionally evocative projections on Cinderella Castle. **SCARY FACTOR** The show may prove too loud for some kids.

TYPICAL SCHEDULE: Usually one show nightly scheduled between 8pm and 10pm. **LENGTH** 15 minutes.

WHERE TO SEE IT: The best viewing location is in the Casey's Corner area of Main Street, where it's possible to take in the panoramic view of the fireworks and see the projections on the castle clearly. The fireworks bursts are visible from a variety of locations in Adventureland, Fantasyland, Liberty Square, and Tomorrowland.

The Cheat Sheets

The Cheat Sheets are designed to break down all of our touring advice and principles into an easy guide you can bring along to the theme parks. Print out the newest versions in color at EASYWDW.COM/EASY-GUIDE.

Each Cheat Sheet covers one park, and includes:

- Coded maps
- Touring overviews
- General FastPass+ priorities
- Daily touring plans that include specific FastPass+ suggestions

The maps are shaded based on the best time to visit the various attractions:

- The dark gray attractions are your top morning priorities, or best saved for the very end of the day or FastPass+.
- Medium gray attractions are best visited in the first/second hour of operation, or in the last two hours the park is open. They're a lower priority than the dark attractions because waits build slower and peak lower.
- Light gray attractions are designated "anytime", which is another way of saying they're best saved for the afternoon when waits at the higher priority attractions are longer. Most shows are designated "light gray" because you want to save them for the afternoon or evening when waits are longer at the major attractions.

Attractions that offer FastPass+ are followed by a +. FastPass+ kiosks are noted with the FP+ symbol. Also included are bathrooms, quick services, restaurants, and the larger stores.

Several touring plans are included with each Cheat Sheet. You may need to make changes based on the previous reviews (which is why we offer them), particularly with kids too short or too easily scared to experience certain attractions. For example, you may want to avoid roller coasters, character meets (at press time, no rides include both), or motion simulators, etc. Once you've picked your plan, it's easiest to simply cross off attractions the group isn't interested in experiencing. That will only result in shorter waits at the next attraction. Also consider substituting attractions coded the same. For example, you may want to substitute a second ride on Toy Story Mania over Rock 'n' Roller Coaster if coasters are problematic.

Animal Kingdom Cheat Sheet

PARK MAP

TOURING AT ANIMAL KINGDOM

GENERAL TOURING PHILOSOPHY The May 2017 opening of Pandora: World of Avatar complicates touring at what before then was an easy park to visit, but it's still possible to experience most or all of Animal Kingdom's attractions in one day—and all in one hard day. A visit over parts of two days doubles the number of FastPass+ available to you and greatly simplifies seeing everything at Animal Kingdom. How you go about your visit comes down to whether you can acquire FastPass+ for Avatar Flight of Passage, which are typically not available 59 or less days from a given date. That means little or no availability for those staying off-site or planning a trip less than 60 days in the future.

- **If you are able to acquire Flight of Passage FP+**: With one day, the easiest way to do most everything is to arrive at least 45 minutes before open and head straight to Pandora to ride Na'vi River Journey in standby. After, head to priority attractions outside of Pandora where waits will be short. If you can't arrive that early but can stay late, get in line for Na'vi River Journey about 5 minutes before park close. If neither is possible, ride Na'vi sometime between 1pm and 5pm when waits are actually shorter than the morning or evening. Use FastPass+ at Flight of Passage and other priority attractions in the late morning and earlier afternoon. With two days, book FastPass+ for Flight of Passage on one day and Na'vi River Journey on the second, in addition to two other selections each day.

- **If you are unable to acquire Flight of Passage FP+**: With one day, the easiest way to do most everything is by arriving at least 90 minutes before open and heading straight to ride Flight of Passage in standby. After, head to Na'vi River Journey or priority attractions outside of Pandora where waits will be short. If you can't arrive early but can stay late, get in line for Flight of Passage a few minutes before park close. If neither is possible, ride sometime between 1pm and 5pm when waits are shorter than the morning or evening. Use FastPass+ in the late morning and afternoon at Na'vi River Journey and other priority attractions. Visiting over two days will allow more FastPass+ usage and an easier time seeing the nighttime entertainment.

Either way, with an early arrival and plans to stay for the nighttime entertainment, including the Tree of Life Awakenings and Rivers of Light, most guests will want to plan a lengthy afternoon break to rest. Without interest in the nighttime entertainment, a three-quarters day should work. For a single-day visit with a late morning or early afternoon arrival, some compromises will need to be made as it will be difficult to experience both Pandora rides and all of the headliners with short waits, in addition to the evening entertainment. Plan to use FastPass+ upon arrival and then make as many subsequent selections as possible after using the initial three.

CHARACTERS Mickey & Minnie in Adventurers Outpost and the Wilderness Explorers meet to the left of It's Tough To Be A Bug are the only priorities and both usually see actual waits under 20 minutes.

ROPE DROP Animal Kingdom has recently had its official open at both 8am and 9am. Because of that, in the morning parts of the touring plans later in this section, we offer both 8am and 9am variants. Either way, the park usually begins letting guests inside the park 30-45 minutes prior to the scheduled open and holds guests in three places inside the park. Those headed to Asia or DinoLand wait at the Tree of Life. Those waiting for Pandora are held just outside the land along the bridge leading into it. Those heading to Africa are held in the Pizzafari/Starbucks area. Guests are typically walked into Pandora 20-30 minutes before official open with guests headed elsewhere held until closer to official park open.

The main rope drop priority is Avatar Flight of Passage, where it's essential to arrive at least an hour before open and hurry as fast as possible to the holding area. For Flight of Passage, stay to the right. The walk can be a congested experience. The walk to Na'vi River Journey on the left is much less stressful. Very few people will be heading anywhere other than Pandora first thing.

ANIMAL KINGDOM AT NIGHT AND RIVERS OF LIGHT Disney began keeping Animal Kingdom routinely open past dark in mid 2016, adding plentiful nighttime entertainment and, in February 2017, a new after-dark show, Rivers of Light, which we consider subtle rather than spectacular but still not-to-be-missed.

Rivers of Light during busy periods is shown daily, one to three times a night, but during less busy periods is scheduled as infrequently as once a night on just four nights a week--typically Saturday, Sunday, Tuesday and Thursday.

Many nights it has capacity for many fewer people than would enjoy seeing it, and while it is bookable as a FastPass+, the problem with booking FP+ in advance for it is that the show is late at night and because of that, you'll be limited to just two FP+ during the day without the ability to book more. The easiest way to see the show is with the dining package, which guarantees a seat in the reserved section and allows booking FP+ elsewhere. Without the package, on a single-day visit afternoon/evening arrivers probably want to book FP+ in advance as doing so won't much limit using FP+ elsewhere. Morning arrivers may want to see the last show in standby when applicable or refresh FP+ availability to try to score additional FP+ that someone else canceled closer to show time.

Those uninterested in the show still ought to take advantage of Animal Kingdom's later hours, when wait times drop substantially at priority attractions. Expedition Everest at night is a whole new experience and the Tree of Life Awakenings, which happen sporadically from sundown through about 30 minutes after park close, are not to be missed.

FASTPASS+ AT ANIMAL KINGDOM

FASTPASS+ PRIORITY FastPass+ at Animal Kingdom is divided into two groups. One group includes the two rides that opened with the new Pandora: World of Avatar land. From these two you can pick just one. The other group includes all other Animal Kingdom FastPass+ rides, and from these you can pick two more.

Pandora (choose one):

1. Avatar Flight of Passage
2. Na'vi River Journey

Everything else (choose two):

1. Kilimanjaro Safaris
2. Expedition Everest
3. Kali River Rapids (when highs are 80+ degrees)
4. DINOSAUR
5. Rivers of Light (primarily the first show; last show is easier to see in standby)
6. Adventurers Outpost Mickey and Minnie Meet (due to fewer experiences available)
7. Kali River Rapids (when highs are less than 80 degrees)
8. Festival of the Lion King
9. Finding Nemo the Musical
10. Primeval Whirl
11. It's Tough To Be A Bug

4TH FASTPASS+ SELECTION AVAILABILITY Avatar Flight of Passage and Na'vi River Journey will have no day-of availability outside of cancellations. "Everything Else" attractions 1–9 will have limited availability on busier days by noon, but with so much capacity at most attractions, each will become available when refreshing availability. Primeval Whirl and It's Tough To Be A Bug have plenty of availability.

FASTPASS+ KIOSKS Add or change FastPass+ on your device or at the following locations:

- *Island Mercantile.* On the left just after crossing the bridge into Discovery Island
- *Kali River Rapids.* To the left of the entrance across from the lockers
- *Kilimanjaro Safaris.* To the left of the entrance

TWO DAY TOURING PLAN
WITH AN EARLY AND A LATE ARRIVAL

Use FastPass+ at Avatar Flight of Passage or Na'vi River Journey 12:30–1:30pm, Kilimanjaro Safaris 1:30–2:30pm, and Kali River Rapids 3–4pm.

Two Day Early and Late Arrival Plan, Day One (8am Open)

1. Ride the Pandora ride for which you were unable to acquire a FastPass+: 7:45–8:25am.
2. Ride Expedition Everest, twice if time allows: 8:40–9am.
3. Ride Primeval Whirl: 9:05–9:20am.
4. Ride DINOSAUR: 9:23–9:40am.
5. Ride TriceraTop Spin: 9:42–9:55am.
6. See It's Tough to Be a Bug and/or meet a character: 9:57–10:40am.
7. See Finding Nemo the Musical: 11–11:40am.
8. Have lunch (your choice): 11:45am–12:45pm
9. Ride Avatar Flight of Passage or Na'vi River Journey with FP+. Explore Pandora: 1–2pm.
10. Ride Kilimanjaro Safaris with FastPass+: 2–2:40pm.
11. See Festival of the Lion King: 2:40–3:30pm.
12. Ride Kali River Rapids with FastPast+: 3:40–4pm.
13. Visit additional attractions you'd like to experience, then depart.

Two Day Early and Late Arrival Plan, Day One (9am Open)

1. Ride the Pandora ride for which you were unable to acquire a FastPass+: 8:45–9:25am.
2. Ride Expedition Everest, twice if time allows: 9:40–10am.
3. Ride DINOSAUR: 10:05–10:30am.
4. Ride TriceraTop Spin: 10:32–10:45am.
5. See Finding Nemo the Musical: 11–11:40am.
6. Have lunch (your choice): 11:45am–12:45pm
7. Ride Avatar Flight of Passage or Na'vi River Journey with FP+. Explore Pandora: 1–2pm.
8. Ride Kilimanjaro Safaris with FastPass+: 2–2:40pm.
9. See Festival of the Lion King: 2:40–3:30pm.
10. Ride Kali River Rapids with FastPast+: 3:40–4pm.
11. Book Primeval Whirl as a 4th FastPass+ and ride as soon as return window opens
12. Visit additional attractions you'd like to experience, then depart.

Two Day Early and Late Arrival Plan, Day Two

With variable closing times, the plan below goes by hour after arrival rather than time of day. With a 9:30pm close and 8:45pm Rivers of Light, the plan starts around 5:30pm.

Use FastPass+ at an attraction of your choice, Avator Flight of Passage or Na'vi River Journey, and Rivers of Light.

1. Use FastPass+ at desired attraction and eat dinner: 00:00–01:30.

2. Ride a Pandora ride with FastPass+ and look around: 01:30–02:30.

3. See Rivers of Light with FastPass+: arrive at least 30 minutes before show time.

4. Ride Expedition Everest or Kilimanjaro Safaris or visit Pandora after dark: 03:35–04:15.

5. See Tree of Life Awakenings: 04:20–04:45.

With Animal Kingdom closing anywhere between 7pm and 11pm moving forward and the potential for zero, one, or two Rivers of Light shows per night, how you go about your evening depends on the Rivers of Light schedule and how late the park is open. Modify the loose plan above to work with the actual operating hours and whether or not you'd like to see Rivers of Light. If you don't, it opens your evening up to experience other attractions at night and spend more time in Pandora after dark.

ONE DAY RIDE-FOCUSED TOURING PLAN
WITH OPTIONAL EVENING RETURN

Use FastPass+ at Avatar Flight of Passage or Na'vi River Journey 10–11am, Kali River Rapids 12:30–1:30pm, and Expedition Everest 1:30–2:30pm.

Morning Plan (8am Open)

1. Ride the Pandora ride for which you were unable to acquire a FastPass+: 7:45–8:25am.

2. Ride Kilimanjaro Safaris: 8:30–9:10am.

3. Ride Expedition Everest: 9:20–9:40am.

4. Ride Primeval Whirl: 9:45–10am.

5. Ride DINOSAUR: 10:02–10:30am.

6. Ride Avatar Flight of Passage or Na'vi River Journey with FP+. Explore Pandora: 10:40–11:40am.

7. Have lunch. Satu'li Canteen is easy: 11:45am–12:45pm.

8. Ride Kali River Rapids with FastPass+: 1–1:20pm.

9. Ride Expedition Everest with FastPass+: 1:30–1:45pm.

10. Experience anything else you'd like, make a fourth FastPass+ reservation for the evening, and return to resort.

Morning Plan (9am Open)

1. Ride the Pandora ride for which you were unable to acquire a FastPass+: 8:45–9:25am.

2. Ride Expedition Everest: 9:35–9:50am.

3. Ride Primeval Whirl: 9:55–10:15am.

4. Ride DINOSAUR: 10:17–10:45am.

5. Ride Avatar Flight of Passage or Na'vi River Journey with FP+. Explore Pandora: 11am–12:00pm.

6. Have lunch. Satu'li Canteen is easy: 12–12:55pm.

7. Ride Kilimanjaro Safaris with FastPass+: 1–1:40pm.

8. Ride Kali River Rapids or Expedition Expedition with FastPass+: 1:50–2:05pm.

9. Experience anything else you'd like, make a fourth FastPass+ reservation for the evening, and return to resort.

Evening Plan

Time your evening return based on what you'd like to accomplish. Pandora, Expedition Everest, and Kilimanjaro Safaris are completely different, recommended experiences after dark. To do all three, arrive at least three hours before close. Rivers of Light and Tree of Life Awakenings will add at least another hour.

TWO DAY, TWO LATE ARRIVALS TOURING PLAN

Two Day, Two Late Arrival Plan, Day One

With variable closing times, the plan below goes by hour after arrival rather than time of day. With a 9:30pm close and 8:45pm Rivers of Light, the plan starts around 3pm.

Use FastPass+ at Expedition Everest 00:00–01:00 (the first hour after arrival), Kilimanjaro Safaris: 01:00–02:00, and Avatar Flight of Passage or Na'vi River Journey 03:00–04:00.

1. Ride Expedition Everest with FastPass+: 00:00–00:15.

2. Walk Maharajah Jungle Trek or see a show: 00:15–01:00.

3. See It's Tough to Be a Bug or meet a character: 01:05–01:30.

4. Ride Kilimanjaro Safaris with FastPass+: 01:40–02:20.

5. See Festival of the Lion King: 02:25–03:10.

6. Ride Flight of Passage or River Journey with FP+. Explore Pandora: 03:15–04:15.

7. Have dinner. Satu'li Canteen is convenient: 04:15–05:00.

8. Ride Kilimanjaro Safaris: 05:00–05:40.

9. Ride Expedition Everest: 05:50–06:10.

10. See Tree of Life Awakenings: 06:15–06:30.

Two Day, Two Late Arrival Plan, Day Two

With variable closing times, the plan below goes by hour after arrival rather than time of day. With a 9:30pm close and 8:45pm Rivers of Light, the plan starts around 4:30pm.

Use FastPass+ at DINOSAUR 01:00–02:00 (the second hour after arrival), Kali River Rapids or Expedition Everest 02:30–03:30, and Rivers of Light (arrive at least 30 minutes before show time).

1. See a show, meet a character, or look around: 00:00–01:00.

2. Ride DINOSAUR with FastPass+: 01:10–01:35.

3. Ride TriceraTop Spin: 01:37–01:50.

4. Ride Primeval Whirl: 01:52–02:30.

5. Have dinner. Restaurantosaurus, Flame Tree, Yak & Yeti are convenient: 02:30–03:30.

6. Ride Kali River Rapids or Expedition Everest with FastPass+: 03:30–03:50.

7. See Rivers of Light with FastPass+: arrive at least 30 minutes before show time.

8. Ride Expedition Everest or another ride if time allows.

9. See Tree of Life Awakenings.

TYPICAL ANIMAL KINGDOM WAIT TIMES IN MINUTES

Low Crowds, 8pm Close

	9:30am	10am	11am	12pm	1pm	2pm	3pm	4pm	5pm	6pm	7pm	8pm
Avatar Flight of Passage	120	90	90	90	90	90	90	90	90	70	70	60
DINOSAUR	10	10	20	20	20	20	20	20	10	10	5	5
Expedition Everest	10	15	20	20	20	20	20	20	15	10	5	5
It's Tough to be a Bug	5	5	5	5	5	5	5	5	5	5	5	5
Kali River Rapids (hot)	10	15	25	40	40	40	40	30	30	20	15	10
Kali River Rapids (cool)	5	10	10	10	10	10	10	10	5	5	5	5
Kilimanjaro Safaris	10	20	30	30	20	20	20	20	15	30	20	10
Na'vi River Journey	50	60	60	60	50	50	50	50	50	60	50	40
Primeval Whirl	10	10	15	20	20	20	20	20	10	10	10	5
TriceraTop Spin	5	5	5	5	5	5	5	5	5	5	5	5

Moderate Crowds, 8pm Close

	9:30am	10am	11am	12pm	1pm	2pm	3pm	4pm	5pm	6pm	7pm	8pm
Avatar Flight of Passage	120	150	120	120	100	100	100	100	120	120	90	70
DINOSAUR	10	20	30	40	40	40	40	30	20	20	10	10
Expedition Everest	15	20	35	40	40	40	30	25	20	20	10	5
It's Tough to be a Bug	5	5	5	5	5	5	5	5	5	5	5	5
Kali River Rapids (hot)	15	20	50	60	60	60	60	50	40	30	20	5
Kali River Rapids (cool)	5	15	15	20	20	15	15	15	10	5	5	5
Kilimanjaro Safaris	20	30	40	50	50	50	40	30	30	40	30	10
Na'vi River Journey	70	80	80	80	70	60	60	60	70	70	60	50
Primeval Whirl	10	10	20	30	30	30	30	30	20	20	10	5
TriceraTop Spin	5	5	5	10	10	10	5	5	5	5	5	5

Moderate Crowds, 11pm Close

	9:30am	10am	11am	12pm	1pm	2pm	3pm	4pm	5pm	6pm	7pm	8pm	9pm	10pm	11pm
Avatar Flight of Passage	120	150	120	120	100	100	100	100	120	120	90	90	90	90	70
DINOSAUR	10	20	30	40	40	40	40	30	30	30	20	20	10	10	5
Expedition Everest	15	20	35	40	40	40	30	30	30	30	20	20	20	15	5
It's Tough to be a Bug	5	5	5	5	5	5	5	5	5	5	5	5	5	5	5
Kali River Rapids (hot)	15	20	50	60	60	60	60	50	40	30	20	15	10	5	5
Kali River Rapids (cool)	5	15	15	20	20	15	15	15	10	10	10	10	5	5	5
Kilimanjaro Safaris	20	30	40	50	50	50	40	30	30	30	30	30	30	30	10

Heavy Crowds, 8pm Close

	8:30am	9am	10am	11am	12pm	1pm	2pm	3pm	4pm	5pm	6pm	7pm	8pm
Avatar Flight of Passage	150	180	180	150	120	150	120	120	150	150	150	120	90
DINOSAUR	10	10	20	40	60	70	60	60	50	40	40	20	10
Expedition Everest	15	25	45	60	60	60	60	50	50	50	35	20	10
It's Tough to be a Bug	5	5	10	15	20	20	20	15	15	15	10	10	5
Kali River Rapids (hot)	15	20	35	70	80	90	90	90	80	70	60	30	20
Kali River Rapids (cool)	5	5	15	25	25	25	20	20	20	15	10	5	5
Kilimanjaro Safaris	10	20	60	70	80	90	90	80	70	60	50	40	20
Na'vi River Journey	90	100	100	100	90	80	80	80	90	90	80	80	70
Primeval Whirl	10	20	20	30	40	50	50	40	40	30	30	20	5
TriceraTop Spin	5	5	10	20	20	20	20	20	20	15	10	5	5

Heavy Crowds, 11pm Close

	8:30am	9am	10am	11am	12pm	1pm	2pm	3pm	4pm	5pm	6pm	7pm	8pm	9pm	10pm	11pm
Avatar Flight of Passage	150	180	180	150	120	150	120	120	150	150	150	150	150	150	120	90
DINOSAUR	10	10	20	40	60	70	60	60	50	40	40	20	20	15	10	5
Expedition Everest	15	25	45	60	60	60	60	50	50	50	35	30	25	25	15	5
It's Tough to be a Bug	5	5	10	15	20	20	20	15	15	15	10	10	5	5	5	5
Kali River Rapids (hot)	15	20	35	70	80	90	90	90	80	70	60	40	20	15	10	5
Kali River Rapids (cool)	5	5	15	25	25	25	20	20	20	15	10	10	5	5	5	5
Kilimanjaro Safaris	10	20	60	70	80	90	90	80	70	60	50	40	30	40	30	20
Na'vi River Journey	90	100	100	100	90	90	90	90	90	90	100	100	100	90	80	70
Primeval Whirl	10	20	20	30	40	50	50	40	40	30	30	20	20	15	10	5
TriceraTop Spin	5	5	10	20	20	20	20	20	20	15	10	5	5	5	5	5

Epcot Cheat Sheet

PARK MAP

TOURING AT EPCOT

GENERAL TOURING PHILOSOPHY Because of its massive size and the long duration of many of its attractions, Epcot is best experienced over two days, particularly now that Frozen Ever After is such a high priority.

Most visitors will want to use FastPass+ at Frozen on at least one day and otherwise keep mostly to one side of the park on each day. This way, you cut down on the amount of walking necessary and you won't run into waits longer than a few minutes all day. On one day, visit Future World East and the World Showcase pavilions from Mexico through the US, riding Frozen with FP+ in the early afternoon. On another day, hit Future World West and the pavilions from Canada through Japan, potentially adding Frozen with FP+ on the way out.

With just one day, things are more complicated if you want to try to do Soarin', Test Track, Frozen, and IllumiNations. The best way to accomplish that is to ride Test Track at rope drop, use FastPass+ at Frozen, ride Soarin' around 7pm, and then see IllumiNations after. If you're willing to forego seeing IllumiNations, Frozen typically has an actual wait under 30 minutes at the very end of the night, but the ride may not be operational. If you're willing to risk it, ride Test Track or Soarin' first thing, use FastPass+ at the other, and get in line for Frozen about five minutes before park close. Those skipping Frozen can instead enjoy IllumiNations. Test Track single rider is a viable option with actual waits typically under 20 minutes all day.

CHARACTERS Joy and Sadness inside Innoventions West are the highest priority and see waits of 30–60+ minutes. Visit first thing if possible or late at night. The princesses in World Showcase can see substantial waits. Mickey, Minnie, and Goofy at Character Spot can also see 30–50 minute waits. It's best to do Character Spot near park close or use FastPass+. Most other characters will have 5–20 minute waits. Random characters may also appear in between the Canada and United Kingdom pavilions and to the left of Liberty Inn in the US in the afternoon.

ROPE DROP Epcot has two entrances. Guests arriving via Disney bus, monorail, or their own vehicles will enter via the main entrance at the front of the park. The International Gateway entrance in between the France and UK Pavilions in World Showcase is used by those arriving from the BoardWalk, Beach Club, Yacht Club, Swan, and Dolphin resorts.

Disney will begin letting guests enter the park from both entrances at 20–40 minutes before open. If your group arrives at the main entrance later than you'd like, check to see if Disney is still letting in guests with breakfast reservations on the far right (sometimes left) side of the entrance. If yes, wait until these lines open to everyone and hurry over for a shorter wait.

Guests at the main entrance are then held at Spaceship Earth typically until 10 to 15 minutes before official open and then allowed to head to the attraction of their choice freely. Guest at the International Gateway are held at the top of the hill in front of Yorkshire Fish in the UK Pavilion until 10 to 15 minutes before official open and then allowed to head to the attraction of their choice freely.

The International Gateway entrance is typically better for Frozen, but will put you at a slight disadvantage at Soarin' or Test Track due to how far away it is. Those with pre-opening breakfast reservations at Akershus in Norway have an advantage if they are able to finish breakfast and be outside by 8:50am. On less crowded days, Disney may not use holding areas and allow guests to head to the attraction of their choice freely.

FASTPASS+ AT EPCOT

FASTPASS+ PRIORITY FastPass+ at Epcot is divided into two tiers. Guests may initially select only one Tier 1 experience. Frozen is the highest priority as it will save the most time and guarantee you will be able to ride should the attraction go down for technical difficulties. Soarin' and Test Track are more or less even as a second priority though Test Track gets the nod now that capacity at Soarin' has increased and waits are down. Test Track is typically more convenient to ride in standby first thing, so many guests may still elect to use FastPass+ at Soarin' instead. On the other hand, those willing to ride Test Track in single rider may favor using FP+ at Soarin'.

There are eight options for Tier 2 and you may initially select two of them. Most guests will want to initially select two of the top four choices. Note that Mission: SPACE does not require selecting Orange/Mars or Green/Earth in advance, but Orange/Mars waits are routinely longer and those that prefer the more intense Mars version will save more time using FP+ for it.

Tier One (choose one)
1. Frozen Ever After
2. Test Track
3.   Soarin'
4. IlluminNations

Tier Two (choose two)
1. Character Spot (only offered for the Mickey side; Joy/Sadness do not offer FastPass+)
2. Spaceship Earth
3. Mission: SPACE
4. Turtle Talk with Crush
5. Journey into Imagination with Figment

6. The Seas with Nemo and Friends

7. Living with the Land

8. Pixar Short Film Festival

4TH FASTPASS+ SELECTION AVAILABILITY Tier 1 selections will be limited by noon and only cancelations may be available. Refresh the app as often as possible for the most availability. Lower Tier 2 priorities will have plentiful availability for most of the day and may save a handful of minutes at each, though it's usually easy enough to see the attractions in standby during a recommend time.

NO FROZEN FASTPASS+ AVAILABILITY: If you cannot get FastPass+ for Frozen Ever After, the best time to ride Frozen in standby is getting in line just a couple of minutes before close when actual waits are typically under 30 minutes. You can ride first thing but it puts you a long ways away from Future World and you'll need to rush there first thing to experience a short wait. Otherwise, actual waits are typically shortest around 10:30am.

FASTPASS+ KIOSKS Add or change FastPass+ at the following locations, or over your phone:

- Future World West breezeway across from the entrance to Character Spot
- Future World East breezeway outside Mouse Gear and across from Electric Umbrella
- International Gateway in between UK and France pavilions near entrance/exit

TWO DAY EARLY ARRIVAL TOURING PLAN

Two Day Early Arrival Plan, Morning, Day 1

Use FastPass+ at Turtle Talk with Crush (10–11am), Character Spot (11am–12pm), and Soarin' or Frozen Ever After (12–1pm).

1. Ride Soarin': 9–9:25am.

2. Ride Living with the Land: 9:30–9:45am.

3. Ride Journey into Imagination with Figment: 9:55–10:15am.

4. Ride The Seas with Nemo and Friends: 10:20–10:40am.

5. See Turtle Talk with Crush with FP+ and look around the Seas: 10:45–11:30am.

6. Visit Character Spot with FastPass+: 11:35–11:50am.

7. Ride Soarin' or Frozen Ever After with FastPass+: 12–12:30pm

8. Have lunch at Sunshine Seasons in the Land or in World Showcase.

Two Day Early Arrival Plan, Afternoon and Evening, Day 1

You have a lot of options depending on what you want to do and where you'll have dinner. Consider heading up to World Showcase beginning with the Canada Pavilion. Even though there aren't waits at the attractions in Canada, France, etc., touring the area in low crowds means you'll have an easier time in the shops and fewer people in front of you at the various acts. Consider returning to Future World around 5pm. You'll be exiting World Showcase when crowds peak there and returning to Future World where waits will be short for everything other than Soarin' and Test Track. See IllumiNations tonight or on your second night.

Two-Day Early Arrival Plan, Morning, Day 2

Use FastPass+ at Test Track (9:30–10:30am), Spaceship Earth (10:30–11:30am), and a third attraction.

1. Ride Test Track: 8:55–9:20am.
2. Ride Mission: SPACE: 9:25–9:45am.
3. Ride Test Track with FastPass+: 9:50–10:15am.
4. Ride Spaceship Earth with FastPass+: 10:25–10:45am.
5. Experience a third attraction with FastPass+.

Two-Day Early Arrival Plan, Late Morning and Evening, Day 2

You have some options depending on what you plan to do in World Showcase and whether you're planning to head back to Future World. Consider heading up to World Showcase beginning with the Gran Fiesta Tour in the Mexico Pavilion. You can stay in World Showcase or take the boat in Germany back to Future World around 5pm when crowds thin. Standby waits will be short for anything other than Test Track, which has the single rider line, and Soarin'. See IllumiNations if you did not see it on Day 1.

ONE DAY TOURING PLAN

Use FastPass+ at Spaceship Earth (9:15–10:15am), Character Spot (10:15am–11:15am), and Frozen Ever After (whatever is available; ideally earlier in the day).

1. Ride Test Track: 8:55–9:20am.
2. Ride Mission: SPACE Green or Orange: 9:25–9:50am.
3. Ride Spaceship Earth with FastPass+: 9:55–10:15am.
4. Visit Character Spot with FastPass+: 10:25–10:40am.
5. Meet Baymax if desired across from Character Spot: 10:42–11am.
6. Tour World Showcase. Start on the Mexico/Norway side if you have an earlier Frozen FastPass+ time. Start with Canada/UK

if it's later. Have lunch and check for additional FastPass+ availability after riding Frozen: 11am–5pm.

7. Ride Journey into Imagination with Figment: 5:10–5:30pm.

8. Ride The Seas with Nemo and Friends: 5:35–5:50pm.

9. See Turtle Talk with Crush or look around The Seas: 5:55–6:30pm.

10. Ride Living with the Land: 6:35–7pm.

11. Ride Soarin' standby unless you have FastPass+: 7–8pm.

12. Have dinner at Sunshine Seasons or grab snacks in World Showcase: 8:05–8:45pm.

13. See IllumiNations: 8:50–9:15pm (IllumiNations is sometimes at 9:30pm or 10pm).

TWO DAY LATE ARRIVAL TOURING PLAN

Frozen Ever After complicates late arrivals on two days as there are now three high priority attractions that all see long waits and most guests will only be able to initially select two Tier 1 FastPass+ experiences. Try to book Soarin', Test Track, or Frozen as a 4th FastPass+ on both days and you'll have an easier time. Otherwise, ride one at park close to experience short waits.

Two Day Late Arrival Plan, Day 1

Use FastPass+ at Spaceship Earth (10:30–11:30am), Character Spot (11:30am–12:30pm), and Frozen Ever After (whenever available, ideally around 1pm).

1. Arrive between 10:30 and 11am.

2. Ride Spaceship Earth with FastPass+: 11–11:20am.

3. Visit Character Spot with FastPass+: 11:30–11:50am.

4. Explore Mexico through United States or Japan.

5. Ride Gran Fiesta Tour: 12–12:15pm.

6. Have lunch. There are lots of options in World Showcase.

7. Ride Frozen Ever After with FastPass+: 1–1:30pm.

8. Check FastPass+ availability for Mission: SPACE aiming for a return time around 8pm.

9. Meet Anna and Elsa at Royal Sommerhus if desired: 20 minutes whenever convenient.

10. Have dinner in World Showcase and walk back to Future World: 6:30pm or 7–8pm

11. Ride Mission: SPACE, ideally with FastPass+: 8:10–8:45pm.

12. Ride Test Track: 8:55–9:20pm.

Two Day Late Arrival Plan, Day 2

Use FastPass+ at The Seas with Nemo and Friends (10:15–11:15am), Turtle Talk with Crush (11:25am–12:15pm), and Soarin' (1:15–2:15pm).

1. Arrive between 10:30 and 11am.
2. Ride The Seas with Nemo and Friends with FastPass+: 11–11:15am.
3. See Turtle Talk with Crush with FastPass+ and look around The Seas Pavilion: 11:25am–12:30pm.
4. Have lunch at Sunshine Seasons: 12:40–1:30pm.
5. Ride Soarin' with FastPass+: 1:35–2pm.
6. Ride Living with the Land: 2:05–2:30pm.
7. Ride Journey into Imagination with Figment: 2:40–3pm.
8. See Disney Pixar Short Film Festival, if desired: 3:05–3:30pm.
9. Tour World Showcase from Canada to Japan.
10. Enjoy dinner in World Showcase or back in Future World.
11. See IllumiNations or get in line for Soarin', Test Track, or Frozen at 8:55pm.

ILLUMINATIONS

IllumiNations is the nightly entertainment at Epcot, scheduled at 9pm most nights. For the best spots, arrive 15–30 minutes before the show starts. The best spots are listed below, but plan a backup spot in case your first choice is booked for a private event or there is little front row space.

Best Spots

1. Base of the World Showcase directly across the lagoon from the United States Pavilion. This "front of house" view is elevated with a direct view of the globe and fireworks. Parts of this area are reserved for FastPass+.
2. The next best spot is the bridge connecting the UK and France. It can't be reserved and the IllumiNations cruisers will stop below you, enjoying a similar view.
3. The Italy Isola, or raised section across from Italy. Parts can be reserved, but the viewing location behind the seated guests is almost as good.
4. The stretch from Mexico to Norway is good. Areas closer to Norway have fewer people.
5. Other options: There's limited space outside Tokyo Dining on the second level in Japan. Limited viewing is available along Canada into the UK. There are areas to the right of the UK downstairs that are good locations, but they may be reserved for private events.

6. Rose & Crown has patio seating and a reserved platform for those dining inside prior to the show. La Hacienda de San Angel also has indoor viewing, but only some of the tables face the windows. It isn't a great choice if you're looking for a guaranteed view. Consider a meal that begins after 7:45pm.

After IllumiNations, hang out for 20–45 minutes and let others exit in front of you.

TYPICAL EPCOT WAIT TIMES IN MINUTES

Low Crowds

	9:30am	10am	11am	12pm	1pm	2pm	3pm	4pm	5pm	6pm	7pm	8pm	9pm
Character Spot	10	20	20	20	20	20	20	20	20	10	10	10	10
Frozen Ever After	45	45	45	60	75	75	75	75	90	90	75	60	30
Gran Fiesta Tour	n/a	n/a	5	5	5	5	5	5	5	5	5	5	5
Journey into Imagination	5	5	5	10	10	5	5	5	5	5	n/a	n/a	n/a
Living with the Land	5	5	5	5	5	5	5	5	5	5	n/a	n/a	n/a
Mission: Space Green	10	10	15	15	15	15	15	15	15	15	20	15	5
Mission: Space Orange	15	15	20	25	20	20	20	20	20	20	25	20	10
Royal Sommerhus Meet	5	10	15	15	10	10	10	10	10	10	10	10	10
Seas with Nemo	5	5	10	10	10	10	10	5	5	5	5	5	10
Soarin'	15	30	40	40	40	40	40	30	30	30	20	20	10
Spaceship Earth	5	10	20	20	15	10	10	10	5	5	5	5	5
Test Track	30	30	50	60	50	40	40	40	40	40	30	20	20

Moderate Crowds

	9:30am	10am	11am	12pm	1pm	2pm	3pm	4pm	5pm	6pm	7pm	8pm	9pm
Character Spot	25	30	35	30	30	30	30	30	20	20	20	15	10
Frozen Ever After	60	75	75	75	90	90	90	90	120	120	120	75	45
Gran Fiesta Tour	n/a	n/a	5	5	5	5	5	5	5	5	5	5	5
Journey into Imagination	5	10	20	30	30	30	30	30	20	10	n/a	n/a	n/a
Living with the Land	5	10	20	30	30	20	20	10	10	10	n/a	n/a	n/a
Mission: Space Green	10	25	35	35	30	30	25	25	20	15	25	25	10
Mission: Space Orange	15	30	40	40	40	35	30	30	25	20	30	30	15
Royal Sommerhus Meet	20	25	20	20	20	20	20	15	15	15	10	10	10
Seas with Nemo	5	10	35	30	20	10	10	10	10	10	5	5	5
Soarin'	30	45	60	60	60	60	60	60	45	45	45	40	20
Spaceship Earth	15	30	30	30	25	25	20	15	10	10	5	5	5
Test Track	45	60	70	80	80	70	60	60	60	60	50	40	30

Heavy Crowds

	9:30am	10am	11am	12pm	1pm	2pm	3pm	4pm	5pm	6pm	7pm	8pm	9pm
Character Spot	25	35	45	45	40	40	40	40	30	30	30	20	10
Frozen Ever After	75	120	120	120	120	120	120	120	150	150	120	75	75
Gran Fiesta Tour	n/a	n/a	5	5	10	10	10	10	10	10	5	5	5
Journey into Imagination	5	10	35	45	45	40	40	35	30	20	n/a	n/a	n/a
Living with the Land	5	15	30	40	40	40	30	30	20	10	n/a	n/a	n/a
Mission: Space Green	10	25	55	65	65	50	50	45	35	35	50	35	15
Mission: Space Orange	15	35	65	80	80	65	65	55	55	45	55	45	20
Royal Sommerhus Meet	20	30	25	25	25	25	25	25	20	15	15	15	10
Seas with Nemo	5	20	45	40	40	25	20	20	15	10	10	5	5
Soarin'	40	60	70	80	80	70	70	70	70	60	50	45	30
Spaceship Earth	15	35	45	45	35	30	25	25	20	15	15	10	5
Test Track	80	90	100	120	120	120	100	100	90	80	70	60	50

Hollywood Studios Cheat Sheet

PARK MAP

TOURING AT DISNEY'S HOLLYWOOD STUDIOS

GENERAL TOURING PHILOSOPHY Most guests arriving prior to park opening will want to ride Toy Story Mania or Rock 'n' Roller Coaster first. Until Toy Story Land opens on June 30, 2018, Toy Story Mania will be operating a reduced capacity and will see the highest waits in the park. Visit it absolutely first thing or use FastPass+ if available. Tower of Terror usually sees the third longest waits and Star Tours is the only other attraction that often has posted waits longer than 20 minutes. A typical problem is trying to see all the scheduled shows, which each take 40–60 minutes, and both of the evening entertainments, Fantasmic! and the Star Wars fireworks. With one day, you may need to prioritize several of the shows that appeal to your group while skipping others—there just isn't enough time. On nights with just one Fantasmic showing (the usual schedule), depending on schedules you may need to pick either it or the Star Works fireworks.

CHARACTERS The *Toy Story* characters across from Toy Story Mania are the highest priority and see 30–50 minute afternoon waits. Try to visit immediately after riding Toy Story Mania in the morning or as late in the evening as possible. Chewbacca and BB-8 in Star Wars Launch Bay typically sees 30-minute peak waits while Kylo Ren usually maxes out at 20. Visit during the heat of the day as all three are inside with air-conditioned queues. Mickey and Minnie meet across from Sci-Fi Dine-In to 25ish minutes waits. Other priorities include the Disney Jr. characters like Doc McStuffins and Sofia the First in Animation Courtyard outside Disney Jr. Olaf sees 10–20 minute waits across from Backlot Express and Star Tours.

JEDI TRAINING ACADEMY Kids between the ages of 4 and 12 have the opportunity to participate in this show held next to Star Tours. To sign them up, it's essential that you arrive at least 45 minutes before park open and bring the participating child to the Adventurers Outpost store to the right of 50's Prime Time Café as quickly as possible or you risk a 30+ minute wait in the sign-up line or finding all shows are full. Those with kids that don't necessarily have to participate on a certain day may check availability around 10:30am when waits to sign up are shorter but slots are not guaranteed. There are usually 12–15 shows scheduled throughout the day. Ask for a show in the late morning or afternoon so it doesn't interfere with early morning touring. Kids participating in the show are required to return to the sign-up location 30 minutes before the show to practice. Those with pre-opening reservations at the Hollywood & Vine character breakfast may be able to sign their kids up before breakfast without a wait, which is an added perk.

ROPE DROP The Studios typically lets guests into the park 15–30 minutes prior to open and guests signing up kids for Jedi Training will be able to immediately do so after entering the park. Everyone else will be held on Hollywood Boulevard just past Trolley Car Café Starbucks until official park open. For Rock 'n' Roller Coaster or Tower of Terror, keep to the far right. For Toy Story Mania, stay center and prepare to head straight and then to the right around Grauman's Chinese Theatre. There is much less of a hurry to any other attraction.

FASTPASS+ AT HOLLYWOOD STUDIOS

FASTPASS+ PRIORITY Guests may initially select one Tier One attraction, which makes it a struggle for those arriving late to ride both Toy Story Mania and Rock 'n' Roller Coaster. Most guests will want to arrive well before open, select either Toy Story Mania or Rock 'n' Roller Coaster as their FastPass+, and ride the other in standby first thing. Rock 'n' Roller Coaster offers a single rider line, though waits are usually in the 15–20 minute range due to the way the vehicles are loaded, and it's impossible to gauge how many people are in line until the final loading area.

Tier 1 (choose one)

1. Toy Story Mania (expected to be unavailable April 7 to May 7)
2. Rock 'n' Roller Coaster
3. Fantasmic! (first show); only use FP+ for the second show if you can get it as a 4th FP+
4. Beauty and the Beast Live on Stage

Tier 2 (choose two)

1. Tower of Terror
2. Star Tours
3. Voyage of the Little Mermaid
4. Frozen Sing-Along
5. Indiana Jones Epic Stunt Spectacular
6. Disney Jr. Live on Stage
7. Muppet Vision 3D

With average peak waits of 60+ minutes, Tower of Terror FastPass+ is a no-brainer. A second Tier 2 selection may be less obvious. FastPass+ is largely useless at the shows, as users must arrive early to enjoy any benefit and with the chance that the reserved seats will be worse than standby. Star Tours is the second-highest priority with peak waits that typically hit 30+ minutes and less availability than other attractions. Voyage of the Little Mermaid is another priority due to its small theater and the likelihood that guests arriving in the afternoon will have to wait through at least one complete show before entering the theater, resulting in actual waits of 15–30 minutes. FastPass+ allows you to walk right in to the specified show even as it nears being full, with less lead time. The Frozen Sing-Along is prioritized over the other shows because it's least likely to be available as a 4th FP+ and shows are most likely to be full, making FastPass+ more useful.

4TH FASTPASS+ SELECTION AVAILABILITY Toy Story Mania, Rock 'n' Roller Coaster, Tower of Terror, and Frozen Sing-Along will either have extremely limited or no availability come 12pm. Fantasmic! may or may not be available, but by selecting it early you won't be able to use FastPass+ elsewhere until after the show in the late evening. Using a 4th FP+ at Star Tours makes the most sense, but standby waits are reliably short after 6:30pm. If you're planning on Fantasmic, keep checking for FastPass+ throughout the evening even if it isn't initially available. Others cancelling should open up availability.

FASTPASS+ KIOSKS Add or change FastPass+ at the following locations or on your phone:

- Main tip board near the end of Hollywood Boulevard
- To the right of the entrance to Muppet Vision 3D
- Tower of Terror's old FASTPASS machines to the left of the attraction entrance
- Toy Story Midway Mania's old FASTPASS machines to the right of the attraction entrance

TOURING PLAN
••

Morning Plan: Toy Story Mania First
(Use this plan when FastPass+ for Toy Story Mania is unavailable.) Use FastPass+ at Tower of Terror (9:15–10:15am), Rock 'n' Roller Coaster (10:15–11:15am), and Star Tours (12:15–1:15pm).

1. Ride Toy Story Midway Mania: 9–9:20am.
2. See the 9:30am Voyage of the Little Mermaid: 9:22–9:45am.
3. Ride Tower of Terror with FastPass+: 9:55–10:20am.
4. Ride Rock 'n' Roller Coaster with FastPass+: 10:22–10:45am.
5. See 11am Beauty and the Beast Live on Stage: 10:50–11:30am.
6. Have lunch: Sunset Ranch Market/Backlot Express/PizzeRizzo are convenient: 11:35–12:20pm
7. Ride Star Tours with FastPass+: 12:30–12:50pm.
8. Schedule a 4th FastPass+ via the phone app or Muppet*Vision kiosk.

Afternoon and Evening Plan (Toy Story Mania First)

It's time for the Studios' other scheduled stage shows blended in with whatever additional FastPass+ experiences that you are able or willing to secure, and the Studio's evening entertainment (see below). Seeing Muppet Vision 3D followed by the 2pm Indiana Jones show might make sense as would meeting Olaf or another character, heading to Launch Bay or a Star Wars show, or back to your resort for a break.

Morning Plan (Rock 'n' Roller Coaster First)

Use FastPass+ at Tower of Terror (9:30–10:30am), Toy Story Mania (10:30–11:30am), and Star Tours (11:30am–12:30pm).

1. Ride Rock 'n' Roller Coaster: 9–9:20am.
2. Ride Tower of Terror: 9:22–9:45am.
3. Ride Tower of Terror with FastPass+: 9:47–10:05am.
4. See Voyage of the Little Mermaid or visit Star Wars Launch Bay: 10:15–10:40am.
5. Ride Toy Story Mania with FastPass+: 10:45–11:05am.
6. See Star Wars Movie Clip Show or Meet Olaf: 11:15–11:35am.
7. Ride Star Tours with FastPass+: 11:40am–12pm.
8. Book a 4th FastPass for around 1:30–2:30pm.
9. Have lunch. Backlot Express and PizzeRizzo are closest: 12–12:50pm.
10. See Indiana Jones Epic Stunt Spectacular (1:15pm show): 12:55–1:45pm.
11. See Muppet*Vision 3D: 1:45–2:15pm.
12. Use 4th FastPass+: 2:25–2:50pm.

Afternoon and Evening Plan (Rock 'n' Roller Coaster First)

It's time for the Studios' other scheduled stage shows blended in with whatever additional FastPass+ experiences that you are able or willing to secure, and the Studio's evening entertainment (see below). Meeting Olaf might make sense as would meeting another character, heading to Launch Bay or a Star Wars show, or back to your resort for a break.

CHARACTER-CENTRIC TOURING PLAN

Morning Plan

Use FP+ at Toy Story Midway Mania (9:15–10:15am), Frozen Sing-Along (11:05–11:20am), and Star Tours (1–2pm). When Toy Story FP+ is unavailable, use FastPass+ at a different Tier 1 and flip steps 2 and 3 so that Toy Story is experienced first.

1. If desired, sign the kids ages 4–12 up for Jedi Training Academy. If you're not doing this, you may be able to ride Toy Story Mania standby with a short wait before meeting the characters. Long waits may develop if you sign kids up for Jedi Training.

2. Visit Toy Story characters: 9–9:15am.

3. Ride Toy Story Mania with FastPass+: 9:17–9:35am.

4. Visit Disney Jr. characters in Animation Courtyard: 9:40–10:15am.

5. See the 10:30am Disney Jr. Live on Stage show: 10:20–10:55pm.

6. See the 11:30 Frozen Sing-Along with FastPass+: 11:10am–12pm.

7. Have lunch. Backlot Express and Min & Bill's are close: 12:10–1pm.

8. Ride Star Tours with FastPass+: 1:10–1:30pm.

9. Check phone app or kiosk for a 4th FastPass+. Voyage of the Little Mermaid is smart.

10. Meet Olaf across from Backlot Express: 1:35–2pm.

11. Meet the characters outside Sci-Fi Dine-In: 2:10–3pm.

12. Meet the character in the back of Walt Disney Presents if available: 3:10–3:40pm.

13. Meet Mickey and Minnie and/or visit Star Wars Launch Bay or take a break.

Afternoon Plan

The plan above covers most characters and kid-friendly rides and shows. If you are returning for an evening show (see below), consider putting Step 13 off for the evening when waits will be shorter. Both are air-conditioned, but waits are longer in the afternoon. Otherwise, blend in additional FastPass+ opportunities with scheduled shows and characters.

LATE-ARRIVAL TOURING WITH FASTPASS+

Use FastPass+ at Toy Story Mania or Rock 'n' Roller Coaster and for two of the attractions from Tier 2. Most people will want to select Tower of Terror and Little Mermaid or Star Tours. Visit the anytime attractions in the afternoon when crowds are heaviest, prioritizing the shows that run on a set schedule. Visit characters in the last 60–90 minutes they're scheduled to appear. End the evening with Fantasmic! or the Star Wars fireworks, or visit Tower of Terror, Rock 'n' Roller Coaster, and Toy Story Mania (in that order) in the final 90 minutes when waits are shorter. Disney will allow guests to enter the line and ride any operating attraction until one minute before official park close regardless of posted wait time. Posted waits at the end of the night are usually exaggerated.

STAR WARS SHOWS

Hollywood Studios is home to two Star Wars stage shows: Star Wars: A Galaxy Far, Far Away and March of the First Order. A Galaxy Far, Far Away is typically scheduled at 11:30am, 12:30pm, 1:30pm, 3:30pm, 4:30pm, and 5:30pm with the potential for one more show. It happens on the stage in front of Grauman's Chinese Theatre. To see it, arrive about 15 minutes before show time and find a spot further back on the far left or right hand sides of the stage. Because of the low height of the stage, it's difficult to see over people's heads from the center. For front row spots, arrive at least 30 minutes early. March of the First Order is a parade of Stormtroopers that begins on Hollywood Boulevard near the entrance and continues to the same stage. There is a brief show and then the Stormtroopers return the way they came. Arrive on Hollywood Boulevard about five minutes before a March starts then follow the Stormtroopers to the stage.

EVENING ENTERTAINMENT: FANTASMIC

Hollywood Studios' nighttime spectacular is scheduled at least once almost every night. During extremely busy times, a second show is scheduled 90 minutes after the start of the first, and the most crowded days of the year may see three shows. Shows can start as early as 6:30pm or as late as 10pm. If two shows are scheduled, the second will virtually always be less crowded, especially if it begins at 9pm or later, due to the number of families that opt for the earlier show. If you're headed to the first or only Fantasmic!, arrive 60–75 minutes early to secure good seats together. For the second show, arrive 20–30 minutes early. Seating is bleacher-style, uncomfortable, and without backs. The best seats are at least half-way up in the middle section. Any closer and you risk getting wet and won't be able to see what's happening on the water. The Fantasmic! Dining Package, a fixed price meal at Hollywood Brown Derby, Hollywood & Vine, or Mama Melrose, guarantees a seat for the show and a three-course meal. A Dessert Package with reserved seating is also available. Reserved seats for both are front and center. Those using either should arrive at least 20 minutes early. FastPass+ has a reserved section next to the Dining Package section. Because it's in Tier 1, most guests will want to use their pre-scheduled selection on Toy Story Midway Mania or Rock 'n' Roller Coaster and either see the second Fantasmic! or check to see if the show is available as an additional FastPass+ choice later in the day. While Fantasmic may not initially be available, thousands of spots are available and people consistently cancel. Keep refreshing the app and Fantasmic should show up.

EVENING ENTERTAINMENT: STAR WARS FIREWORKS

Star Wars: A Galactic Spectacular, predominantly a projection show on the façade of Grauman's Chinese Theatre with accompanying fireworks, is usually scheduled once per night shortly after sundown. Guests wishing to see the fireworks, which are almost exclusively shot off on the right side of the building, will need to arrive at least 35 minutes prior to the start of the show and position themselves in the Center Stage area about half way between the theater and the two tall projection towers near Hollywood Boulevard. There's typically room to fill in this area without much trouble. This is the ideal location for both the fireworks and the Disney Movie Magic projection show that precedes them.

EVENING ENTERTAINMENT: DISNEY MOVIE MAGIC

This 10-minute projection show on the Grauman's Chinese Theatre façade features movie clips and animation from Disney's vast catalog. The show is typically scheduled 20-30 minutes before the Star Wars fireworks. Those seeing the fireworks should arrive ten minutes before the start of Movie Magic to take in the show and then wait for the fireworks.

FANTASMIC AND STAR WARS
FIREWORKS ON THE SAME NIGHT

With the way the two nighttime shows are usually scheduled, it will be difficult or impossible to see both if only one Fantasmic is scheduled. Disney typically schedules the Star Wars Fireworks 15 or 30 minutes after the first Fantasmic. If it's 15 minutes, that makes it impossible to see both. If it's 30 minutes, you'll have to quickly exit Fantasmic and try to find spots as close to the recommended viewing area as possible. With two Fantasmic shows, see the Star Wars Fireworks first followed by the second Fantasmic.

JINGLE BELL, JINGLE BAM

Disney typically offers a holiday-inspired projection show with accompanying fireworks in place of the Star Wars show from the second week in November through December 31. The advice on seeing the show is the same as for Star Wars.

TYPICAL HOLLYWOOD STUDIOS WAIT TIMES IN MINUTES

Low Crowds, 8pm Close

	9:30am	10am	11am	12pm	1pm	2pm	3pm	4pm	5pm	6pm	7pm	8pm
Muppet Vision 3D	5	5	5	5	5	5	5	5	5	5	5	5
Rock 'n' Roller Coaster	20	30	40	40	40	40	30	30	30	30	20	20
Star Tours	5	10	20	20	20	20	20	20	10	10	5	5
Tower of Terror	10	20	30	30	30	30	30	30	30	20	10	10
Toy Story Mania	20	30	30	30	30	30	30	30	30	20	20	10
Voyage of the Mermaid	10	10	10	10	10	10	10	10	10	10	10	10

Moderate Crowds, 9pm Close

	9:30am	10am	11am	12pm	1pm	2pm	3pm	4pm	5pm	6pm	7pm	8pm	9pm
Muppet Vision 3D	5	5	5	5	5	5	5	5	5	5	5	5	5
Rock 'n' Roller Coaster	25	40	50	60	60	60	60	50	50	50	30	30	20
Star Tours	5	20	30	30	20	20	20	20	20	10	10	10	5
Tower of Terror	10	30	40	40	40	40	40	40	30	30	30	20	10
Toy Story Mania	20	30	40	40	40	30	30	30	30	30	30	20	20
Voyage of the Mermaid	10	10	10	10	10	10	10	10	10	10	10	10	10

Heavy Crowds, 9pm Close

	9:30am	10am	11am	12pm	1pm	2pm	3pm	4pm	5pm	6pm	7pm	8pm	9pm
Muppet Vision 3D	10	10	15	20	20	20	15	15	10	10	5	5	5
Rock 'n' Roller Coaster	50	60	75	90	100	100	90	90	80	75	75	60	30
Star Tours	30	40	50	60	60	60	50	40	40	30	30	20	10
Tower of Terror	40	50	70	80	90	90	80	70	60	50	50	30	20
Toy Story Mania	50	60	60	60	60	60	60	60	60	60	50	40	20
Voyage of the Mermaid	15	20	20	20	20	20	20	20	20	20	10	10	10

Magic Kingdom Cheat Sheet

PARK MAP

TOURING AT MAGIC KINGDOM

GENERAL TOURING PHILOSOPHY With 60+ attractions, Magic Kingdom is best toured over two or more days. The best plans compartmentalize the park by visiting two or three Lands each day. Visit the character and attraction priorities in one Land before moving on to the next. Have lunch and then head back to the same Lands visiting the "anytime attractions". This minimizes both waiting and walking. One-day touring will require more walking. You can still accomplish a lot in a day by touring intelligently, but some attractions will need to be skipped.

CHARACTERS Home to about 40 characters at any given time, the princesses are typically high priorities, whether it means meeting them early in the morning or with FastPass+ to avoid long waits. Check the My Disney Experience app or https://disneyworld.disney.go.com/entertainment/magic-kingdom/ for character meeting times and locations.

ROPE DROP With a 9am open, Disney lets guests enter the park around 7:45am. Most of Main Street is open, including Guest Relations, stroller/ECV rental, most stores, and Starbucks. Guests are held in the hub area in front of Cinderella Castle with ropes blocking access to the other lands. At 8:55am, a 4-minute opening show featuring Mickey Mouse welcomes guests and then the ropes are dropped and guests are free to visit the attraction of their choice. For Seven Dwarfs Mine Train, arrive no later than 8:15am and position yourself on the walkway to the right of Cinderella Castle heading toward Mad Tea Party. Get as close to the rope as possible. For Peter Pan's Flight or Princess Fairytale Hall, position yourself in front of the castle at the rope leading up through the castle. For other attractions, there is much less of a rush and you can enjoy the Welcome Show front and center in the hub. On morning Extra Magic Hour days, the Welcome Show still starts five minutes before regular park open. For regular 8am opens, guests are allowed inside Magic Kingdom at 7:45am with the Welcome Show at 7:55am.

FASTPASS+ AT MAGIC KINGDOM

FASTPASS+ PRIORITY There are far more FastPass+ opportunities at Magic Kingdom than any of the other theme parks, making the decision on which to pick difficult. Consider picking three high priority attractions in a Land that you don't plan to visit until the afternoon or evening. For example, if you plan to start your day with Jungle Cruise, Pirates of the Caribbean, Big Thunder Mountain, and Splash Mountain, then you may want to use FastPass+ in the afternoon in Fantasyland at Peter Pan's Flight, Enchanted Tales with Belle, and the Mine Train, or in Tomorrowland at Space Mountain, Tomorrowland Speedway, and Buzz Lightyear.

1. Seven Dwarfs Mine Train
2. Peter Pan's Flight
3. Space Mountain
4. Splash Mountain (when high temperatures are 80+ degrees)
5. Meet Mickey at Town Square Theater
6. Big Thunder Mountain Railroad
7. Meet Cinderella and a Visiting Princess
8. Meet Rapunzel and a Visiting Princess
9. Enchanted Tales with Belle

10. Meet Ariel at Ariel's Grotto

11. Buzz Lightyear's Space Ranger Spin

12. Tomorrowland Speedway

13. Jungle Cruise

14. Haunted Mansion

15. Pirates of the Caribbean

16. The Many Adventures of Winnie the Pooh

17. Splash Mountain (when high temps are less than 80 degrees)

18. Meet Tinker Bell at Town Square Theater

19. Magic Carpets of Aladdin

20. "it's a small world"

21. Barnstormer

22. Under the Sea ~ Journey of the Little Mermaid

23. Dumbo the Flying Elephant

24. Mad Tea Party

25. Monsters Inc. Laugh Floor

26. Mickey's PhilharMagic

4TH FASTPASS+ SELECTION AVAILABILITY Unlike the other parks, Magic Kingdom has plenty of FP+ enabled attractions and 10 or more will still have availability even around 2pm. Schedule a high priority attraction with limited availability for after a break or schedule several lower priority experiences back-to-back if you plan to stay in the park. Continue refreshing the app checking for other people's canceled Fast-Pass+ selections as they will become available for anyone else to book.

FASTPASS+ KIOSKS Add or change FastPass+ at the following locations or on your phone:

- *Adventureland*—Jungle Cruise's old FASTPASS machines to the left of the entrance
- *Adventureland*—Breezeway to the right of Diamond Horseshoe across from Swiss Treehouse
- *Fantasyland*—To the right of Mickey's PhilharMagic
- *Tomorrowland*—To the left of Stitch's Great Escape entrance

TWO DAY TOURING PLAN

Two-Day Plan, Morning, Day 1
Use FastPass+ at Many Adventures of Winnie the Pooh (9:30–10:30am), Seven Dwarfs Mine Train (11:45am–12:45pm), and Enchanted Tales with Belle (12:45–1:45pm).

1. Ride Space Mountain: 9–9:20am.
2. Ride Buzz Lightyear's Space Ranger Spin: 9:25–9:35am.
3. Ride Tomorrowland Speedway (if desired): 9:40–10am.
4. Ride The Many Adventures of Winnie the Pooh with FastPass+: 10:05–10:20am.
5. Ride Barnstormer: 10:25–10:40am.
6. Ride Dumbo: 10:42–11:05am.
7. Ride Journey of the Little Mermaid: 11:10–11:30am.
8. Ride Seven Dwarfs Mine Train with FastPass+: 11:35–11:50am.
9. Have lunch. Be Our Guest and Pinocchio Village Haus are closest: 12–12:45pm.
10. Visit Enchanted Tales with Belle with FastPass+: 12:50–1:30pm.
11. Select a nearby 4th FastPass+ via the phone app or the kiosk near Mickey's PhilharMagic.
12. Visit Mickey's PhilharMagic or Prince Regal Carrousel: 1:35–2:35pm.
13. Find spots for Festival of Fantasy and watch parade: 2:40–3:15pm.
14. Use 4th FastPass+, shop, grab snacks, or look around.

Two Day Plan, Afternoon and Evening, Day 1

Consider an afternoon break or visit the anytime attractions in Fantasyland and Tomorrowland like Mickey's PhilharMagic, Prince Charming's Regal Carrousel, Monsters Inc. Laugh Floor, Tomorrowland PeopleMover, and Carousel of Progress. Blend these with additional FastPass+ selections as they become available. Visit priority attractions like Astro Orbiter in the two hours prior to park close when wait times are shorter than the afternoon, ending with a re-visit to a high priority ride like Seven Dwarfs Mine Train or Peter Pan's Flight right before close. See the evening entertainment tonight or the night of Day 2.

Two-Day Plan, Morning, Day 2

Use FastPass+ at Peter Pan's Flight (10–11am), Jungle Cruise (11am–12pm), and Pirates of the Caribbean (12–1pm).

1. Ride Big Thunder Mountain Railroad: 9–9:15am.
2. Ride Splash Mountain: 9:18–9:45am.
3. Ride Haunted Mansion: 9:55–10:15am.
4. Ride "it's a small world": 10:17–10:40am.
5. Ride Peter Pan's Flight with FastPass+: 10:42–11am.
6. Ride Jungle Cruise with FastPass+: 11:10–11:30am.
7. Have lunch. Tortuga Tavern, Pecos Bill, and Skipper Canteen

are closest. Columbia Harbour House, Liberty Tree Tavern, and Casey's Corner are relatively close. 11:30am–12:30pm.

8. Ride Pirates of the Caribbean with FastPass+: 12:30–12:50pm.
9. Check app or Jungle Cruise kiosk for more FastPass+ selections.

Two Day Plan, Afternoon and Evening Day 2

Consider an afternoon break or visit the anytime attractions like Tom Sawyer Island, Hall of Presidents, Liberty Square Riverboat, Country Bear Jamboree, Enchanted Tiki Room, and Swiss Family Treehouse. Schedule nearby FastPass+ experiences as they become available. See the evening entertainment if you did not see it on Day 1.

CHARACTER-CENTRIC TWO DAY TOURING PLAN

Two Day Character-Centric Plan, Morning, Day 1

Use FastPass+ at Seven Dwarfs Mine Train (11:15am–12:15pm) Enchanted Tales with Belle (1–2pm), and Rapunzel at Fairytale Hall (2–3pm).

1. Ride Peter Pan's Flight: 9–9:15am.
2. Ride The Many Adventures of Winnie the Pooh: 9:20–9:30am.
3. Meet Ariel at Ariel's Grotto: 9:35–9:50am.
4. Meet Gaston outside Gaston's Tavern in New Fantasyland: 9:55–10:10am.
5. Meet Daisy and Minnie at Pete's Silly Sideshow: 10:15–10:30am.
6. Meet Donald and Goofy at Pete's Silly Sideshow: 10:31–10:45am.
7. Ride Barnstormer: 10:47–11am.
8. Ride Dumbo the Flying Elephant: 11:03–11:30am.
9. Ride Journey of the Little Mermaid: 11:35am–12pm.
10. Ride Seven Dwarfs Mine Train with FastPass+: 12:05–12:20pm.
11. Have lunch. Be Our Guest Restaurant and Pinocchio Village Haus are closest. Cosmic Ray's is nearby: 12:30–1:20pm.
12. Visit Enchanted Tales with Belle with FastPass+: 1:25–2pm.
13. Meet Rapunzel at Princess Fairytale Hall with FastPass+: 2:05–2:20pm.
14. Check the app or Mickey's PhilharMagic FastPass+ kiosk for a 4th FastPass+.
15. Meet Tinker Bell at Town Square: 2:30–2:50pm.
16. Meet Mickey Mouse at Town Square: 2:50–3:20pm.

Two Day Character-Centric Plan, Afternoon and Evening, Day 1

Consider a lengthy afternoon break in preparation of returning for dinner, some late night rides when waits drop, and the nighttime shows.

Alternatively, continue scheduling available FastPass+ experiences and work in anytime attractions while waiting for the return windows to open.

Two Day Character-Centric Plan, Morning, Day 2
Use FastPass+ for Cinderella at Fairytale Hall (11am–12pm), Jungle Cruise (1–2pm), and Pirates of the Caribbean (2–3pm).

1. Ride Buzz Lightyear's Space Ranger Spin: 9–9:10am.
2. Ride Space Mountain or Astro Orbiter: 9:15–9:35am.
3. Ride Tomorrowland Speedway: 9:40–10am.
4. Meet Buzz Lightyear: 10:05–10:20am.
5. Meet Stitch: 10:25–10:40am.
6. See Move It! Shake It! Parade in front of the Castle: 10:45–11:30am.
7. Meet Cinderella at Princess Fairytale Hall with FastPass+: 11:35 –11:55am.
8. Lunch. Be Our Guest/Pinocchio Village/Columbia Harbour are nearby: 12–12:50pm.
9. See the 1pm Mickey's Royal Friendship Faire show in front of the castle: 1–1:30pm.
10. Ride Jungle Cruise with FastPass+: 1:40–2pm.
11. Ride Pirates of the Caribbean with FastPass+: 2:05–2:30pm.
12. See Festival of Fantasy Parade in Frontierland or Liberty Square: 2:40–3:20pm.
13. Meet Merida, Aladdin/Jasmine, or other skipped characters.

4th FastPass+ Selection: "it's a small world" or Haunted Mansion are good choices.

Two Day Character-Centric Plan, Afternoon and Evening, Day 2:
Consider an afternoon break or visit the anytime attractions like Tom Sawyer Island, Hall of Presidents, Liberty Square Riverboat, Country Bear Jamboree, Enchanted Tiki Room, and Swiss Family Treehouse. Visit it's a small world, Haunted Mansion, Big Thunder Mountain, Splash Mountain and any other skipped attractions late in the evening or with FP+. Check your Times Guide or app for missed characters and visit them in the last hour they're scheduled to appear. See the evening entertainment if you did not see it on Day One.

ONE DAY TOURING PLAN
....

One Day Plan, Morning and Afternoon:
Use FastPass+ at Seven Dwarfs Mine Train (11am–12pm), Big Thunder Mountain (12:15–1:15pm), and Splash Mountain (1:15–2:15pm).

1. Ride Peter Pan's Flight: 9–9:10am.
2. Ride The Many Adventures of Winnie the Pooh: 9:15–9:25am.
3. Ride Space Mountain: 9:35–9:55am.
4. Ride Buzz Lightyear's Space Ranger Spin: 10–10:15am.
5. Ride The Barnstormer: 10:20–10:35am.
6. Ride Dumbo: 10:37–11am.
7. Ride Under the Sea ~ Journey of the Little Mermaid: 11:05–11:30am.
8. Ride Seven Dwarfs Mine Train with FastPass+: 11:35–11:55am.
9. Have lunch. Be Our Guest and Pinocchio Village Haus are close: 12–12:45pm.
10. Ride Big Thunder Mountain with FastPass+: 1–1:20pm.
11. Ride Splash Mountain with FastPass+: 1:22-2pm.

One Day Plan, Afternoon and Evening

Continually check the phone app for FastPass+ availability for the best Jungle Cruise, Haunted Mansion, Pirates of the Caribbean, and "it's a small world" return times throughout the day, in addition to whatever other FastPass+ enabled attractions that you would like to experience. Mix in nearby anytime attractions in between FastPass+ windows, and see the evening entertainment if scheduled for your visit.

LATE ARRIVAL

Crowds only diminish most nights after 9pm as families with small children leave early. The later it gets, the lower wait times will be, particularly if close is 11pm or later. Use FastPass+ when you arrive when wait times are longest. Visit the anytime attractions colored light gray on the map until two to three hours before close. Then move on to the medium gray attractions like Buzz Lightyear and Big Thunder Mountain and finish the night with the highest priority attractions like Peter Pan's Flight, Seven Dwarfs Mine Train, and Space Mountain.

PARADES, SHOWS, EVENING ENTERTAINMENT, AND EXIT

FESTIVAL OF FANTASY PARADE is usually scheduled at 3pm and runs from Frontierland to the left of Splash Mountain, through Liberty Square, and then through Main Street, exiting in between the firehouse and the Emporium. The best/lowest wait viewing locations are in Frontierland in the Pecos Bill area through Liberty Square in front of Hall of Presidents. For Main Street viewing, see the show in front of the Confectionery or Town Square Theater where crowds are thinner. The parade may be scheduled at 2pm during the fall months. If that happens, modify the touring plans above by finding spots for Festival of Fantasy one hour earlier and move the attractions visited between 2pm and 3pm to between 3pm and 4pm.

MOVE IT, SHAKE IT, DANCE AND PLAY IT street party is usually scheduled three times daily and runs from Main Street in between the firehouse and Emporium up to Cinderella Castle, where it stops for about 20 minutes, before returning the same way that it came. Arriving more than five minutes before it steps off is not necessary. Meet the parade on Main Street and follow it to Cinderella Castle or wait at the castle for it to arrive.

MICKEY'S ROYAL FRIENDSHIP FARE is usually scheduled five times per day at the stage in front of Cinderella Castle. Try to arrive ten to fifteen minutes before one of the shows. Earlier shows are typically less crowded. Consider watching from the very back of the area near the statue of Walt and Mickey as it's elevated and easier to see over the heads of people standing closer to the stage.

HAPPILY EVER AFTER This fireworks and projection show replaced Wishes on May 12, 2017. Fortunately, it actually increases the amount of pyro, in addition to adding impactful projections on Cinderella Castle. The best place to see it is between Casey's Corner on Main Street and the Partners statue in the center of the Hub. Arrive 30-45 minutes before the show begins.

ONCE UPON A TIME A projection show visible on the front of Cinderella Castle, Once Upon a Time usually begins 45 minutes after the fireworks. See it either from the same spot as the fireworks or a little closer to the castle for the best views.

LAST MINUTE RIDES AND EXIT Consider getting in line for Seven Dwarfs Mine Train, Peter Pan's Flight, or another attraction with a few minutes until close. Disney will let you ride any operating attraction as long as you get in line at least a minute before close, even if the posted wait is long. Main Street stores will remain open for about an hour after park close. Linger a bit while others exit in front of you. The express monorail is the fastest way to the Transportation and Ticket Center (parking lot) unless the line is significantly backed up. The ferry is often a more comfortable ride with more room to spread out, particularly up the stairs on the second level.

TYPICAL MAGIC KINGDOM WAIT TIMES IN MINUTES

Low Crowds, 8pm Close

	9:30am	10am	11am	12pm	1pm	2pm	3pm	4pm	5pm	6pm	7pm	8pm
Ariel's Grotto	10	15	30	30	30	30	30	30	30	20	15	10
Astro Orbiter	10	15	20	30	30	30	30	20	20	20	15	10
Barnstormer	5	5	10	20	20	20	15	15	15	10	10	5
Big Thunder Mountain	10	20	30	35	45	40	40	40	30	20	20	10
Buzz Lightyear Spin	5	15	30	30	40	40	30	30	25	20	15	10
Dumbo	10	15	15	20	20	20	20	20	20	15	10	5
Enchanted Tales w/ Belle	15	20	30	40	30	30	30	30	30	20	20	10
Haunted Mansion	10	20	30	35	40	30	30	30	25	20	10	5
it's a small world	5	10	15	20	25	25	20	20	20	15	10	5
Jungle Cruise	10	30	40	40	50	40	40	30	30	30	20	10
Mad Tea Party	5	5	5	10	10	10	10	10	5	5	5	5
Magic Carpets of Aladdin	5	10	15	20	20	20	20	20	15	15	10	5
Many Adventures of Pooh	10	20	30	40	40	30	30	30	20	20	10	5
Monster's Inc Laugh Floor	10	10	10	10	10	10	10	10	10	10	10	10
Peter Pan's Flight	60	60	70	70	70	70	60	60	60	45	30	20
Pirates of the Caribbean	5	10	20	30	35	30	30	30	20	15	10	5
Prince Regal Carrousel	5	5	5	5	5	5	5	5	5	5	5	5
Princess Fairytale Cinderella	20	30	40	50	50	40	30	30	30	30	20	10
Princess Fairytale Rapunzel	20	30	40	50	50	40	30	30	30	30	20	10
Seven Dwarfs Mine Train	60	60	70	80	80	80	70	60	60	50	50	40
Space Mountain	10	20	30	40	50	50	40	40	35	25	15	10
Splash Mountain (Hot)	10	30	40	50	50	40	35	30	30	25	20	10
Splash Mountain (Cold)	5	5	10	15	20	20	20	15	10	10	5	5
Stitch's Great Escape	5	5	5	5	5	5	5	5	5	5	5	5
Swiss Family Treehouse	0	0	0	0	0	0	0	0	0	0	0	0
Tomorrowland Speedway	10	20	20	30	30	30	20	20	20	20	10	10
Tomorrowland PeopleMover	0	0	0	0	0	0	0	0	0	0	0	0
Town Square Mickey	20	30	50	40	30	30	15	30	30	20	10	10
Under the Sea ~ Little Mermaid	10	15	20	20	20	20	15	10	10	10	10	10

Moderate Crowds, 11pm Close

	9:30am	10am	11am	12pm	1pm	2pm	3pm	4pm	5pm	6pm	7pm	8pm	9pm	10pm	11pm
Ariel's Grotto	15	20	35	50	45	45	40	40	40	40	30	20	20	15	10
Astro Orbiter	10	20	20	30	40	30	30	30	30	20	20	20	20	15	10
Barnstormer	5	10	20,	20	30	20	20	20	20	20	15	15	15	10	5
Big Thunder Mountain	10	20	40	50	60	60	40	40	40	40	35	30	20	15	10
Buzz Lightyear Spin	5	25	40	45	50	50	40	40	40	30	30	20	20	15	10
Dumbo	10	15	25	30	40	30	30	30	25	20	15	15	15	10	5
Enchanted Tales w/ Belle	20	30	40	40	40	40	40	40	40	30	30	30	20	20	10
Haunted Mansion	10	20	30	40	50	45	40	40	40	30	25	20	15	10	10
it's a small world	10	15	20	30	30	35	30	30	30	20	15	10	10	10	10
Jungle Cruise	10	20	35	45	50	50	40	40	40	40	35	30	25	20	10
Mad Tea Party	5	5	10	15	15	15	15	15	10	10	10	10	5	5	5
Magic Carpets of Aladdin	5	10	20	30	30	30	20	20	20	15	20	10	10	5	5
Many Adventures of Pooh	20	35	45	50	50	40	40	40	30	30	20	20	15	10	5
Monster's Inc Laugh Floor	10	10	10	20	20	20	20	10	10	10	10	10	10	10	10
Peter Pan's Flight	60	60	70	80	90	90	80	70	70	70	60	60	50	40	20
Pirates of the Caribbean	5	15	30	40	45	40	40	30	30	30	20	20	15	5	5
Prince Regal Carrousel	5	5	5	5	5	5	5	5	5	5	5	5	5	5	5
Princess Fairytale Cinderella	20	30	40	50	50	50	30	40	40	40	30	30	20	20	10
Princess Fairytale Rapunzel	20	30	40	50	50	50	30	40	40	40	30	30	20	20	20
Seven Dwarfs Mine Train	60	70	80	90	80	80	80	70	70	60	60	60	50	50	30
Space Mountain	10	35	50	60	70	80	60	60	60	50	45	40	30	20	10
Splash Mountain (Hot)	15	30	60	70	70	60	60	60	60	60	50	40	30	15	10
Splash Mountain (Cold)	5	10	20	25	25	20	20	20	20	20	15	10	5	5	5
Stitch's Great Escape	5	5	5	5	5	5	5	5	5	5	5	5	5	5	5
Swiss Family Treehouse	0	0	0	0	0	0	0	0	0	0	0	0	0	0	0
Tomorrowland Speedway	10	20	25	40	40	30	30	30	30	30	20	20	15	10	10
Tomorrowland PeopleMover	0	0	0	5	5	5	5	5	5	5	5	0	0	0	0
Town Square Mickey	20	40	50	60	50	50	25	40	40	30	20	20	20	15	10
Under the Sea ~ Little Mermaid	10	15	20	30	30	30	30	20	20	20	20	10	10	10	5

Heavy Crowds, Midnight Close

	9:30am	10am	11am	12pm	1pm	2pm	3pm	4pm	5pm	6pm	7pm	8pm	9pm	10pm	11pm	12am
Ariel's Grotto	15	20	50	60	60	60	50	50	50	40	35	25	20	15	10	5
Astro Orbiter	15	20	40	50	50	50	40	30	30	30	30	25	20	15	10	10
Barnstormer	5	10	25	30	40	40	35	35	30	30	30	20	20	10	5	5
Big Thunder Mountain	25	35	50	60	70	70	70	70	60	60	50	40	30	25	20	10
Buzz Lightyear Spin	10	15	50	60	60	60	60	60	50	50	40	30	25	15	10	10
Dumbo	15	20	30	40	50	60	50	50	50	45	30	25	15	10	5	5
Enchanted Tales w/ Belle	25	30	40	50	40	40	40	40	40	30	30	30	15	15	10	10
Haunted Mansion	15	25	50	60	60	60	50	50	45	45	40	30	20	10	10	5
it's a small world	15	20	30	40	40	40	40	30	30	30	30	25	20	15	10	5
Jungle Cruise	25	40	60	75	75	75	60	60	60	60	45	40	30	20	15	10
Mad Tea Party	5	5	10	30	30	30	20	20	20	20	15	10	10	5	5	5
Magic Carpets of Aladdin	10	15	20	30	30	30	25	25	25	25	20	20	15	10	5	5
Many Adventures of Pooh	45	60	60	60	60	50	45	40	40	40	40	25	20	15	10	
Monster's Inc Laugh Floor	10	10	20	30	30	20	20	20	20	20	20	10	10	10	10	
Peter Pan's Flight	65	75	80	90	100	100	90	90	80	80	80	70	60	50	35	25
Pirates of the Caribbean	10	15	45	60	70	60	60	50	50	40	40	30	20	15	15	10
Prince Regal Carrousel	5	5	10	10	10	10	10	10	10	10	10	5	5	5	5	5
Princess Fairytale Cinderella	30	40	60	60	70	60	40	60	60	50	40	30	20	20	20	10
Princess Fairytale Rapunzel	30	40	60	60	70	60	40	60	60	50	40	30	20	20	20	10
Seven Dwarfs Mine Train	80	90	100	120	120	120	120	120	120	100	90	90	70	70	60	40
Space Mountain	50	60	90	120	120	120	90	90	90	80	80	70	70	60	40	20
Splash Mountain (Hot)	45	60	80	100	100	100	90	90	80	80	70	60	40	30	20	15
Splash Mountain (Cold)	10	15	25	30	30	30	30	30	30	30	25	10	10	5	5	5
Stitch's Great Escape	5	10	10	20	20	20	20	20	20	20	10	10	10	5	5	5
Swiss Family Treehouse	0	0	0	5	5	5	5	5	0	0	0	0	0	0	0	0
Tomorrowland Speedway	25	30	30	40	50	40	40	30	30	30	30	25	20	15	10	5
Tomorrowland PeopleMover	0	0	5	5	5	5	5	5	5	5	5	5	0	0	0	
Town Square Mickey	25	30	30	40	50	50	30	45	40	30	30	25	20	20	20	10
Under the Sea ~ Little Mermaid	20	20	30	30	40	40	40	40	30	30	30	20	20	10	10	10

Party Night, 7pm Close

	9:30am	10am	11am	12pm	1pm	2pm	3pm	4pm	5pm	6pm	7pm
Ariel's Grotto	10	15	30	30	30	30	30	30	30	20	10
Astro Orbiter	10	15	20	30	30	30	30	20	20	20	15
Barnstormer	5	5	10	20	20	20	15	15	15	10	10
Big Thunder Mountain	10	20	30	35	45	40	40	40	30	20	15
Buzz Lightyear Spin	5	15	30	30	40	40	30	30	25	20	10
Dumbo	10	15	15	20	20	20	20	20	20	15	10
Enchanted Tales w/ Belle	15	20	30	40	30	30	30	30	30	20	20
Haunted Mansion	10	20	30	35	40	30	30	30	25	20	10
it's a small world	5	10	15	20	25	25	20	20	20	15	10
Jungle Cruise	10	30	40	40	50	40	40	30	30	30	20
Mad Tea Party	5	5	5	10	10	10	10	10	5	5	5
Magic Carpets of Aladdin	5	10	15	20	20	20	20	20	15	15	10
Many Adventures of Pooh	10	20	30	40	40	30	30	30	20	20	10
Monster's Inc Laugh Floor	10	10	10	10	10	10	10	10	10	10	10
Peter Pan's Flight	60	60	70	70	70	70	60	60	60	45	30
Pirates of the Caribbean	5	10	20	30	35	30	30	30	20	15	10
Prince Regal Carrousel	5	5	5	5	5	5	5	5	5	5	5
Princess Fairytale Cinderella	20	30	40	50	50	40	30	30	30	20	20
Princess Fairytale Rapunzel	20	30	40	50	50	40	30	30	30	20	20
Seven Dwarfs Mine Train	60	60	70	80	80	80	70	60	60	50	50
Space Mountain	10	20	30	40	50	50	40	40	35	25	10
Splash Mountain (Hot)	10	30	40	50	50	40	35	30	30	25	10
Splash Mountain (Cold)	5	5	10	15	20	20	20	15	10	10	5
Stitch's Great Escape	5	5	5	5	5	5	5	5	5	5	5
Swiss Family Treehouse	0	0	0	0	0	0	0	0	0	0	0
Tomorrowland Speedway	10	20	20	30	30	30	20	20	20	20	10
Tomorrowland PeopleMover	0	0	0	0	0	0	0	0	0	0	0
Town Square Mickey	20	30	50	40	30	30	15	30	30	20	10
Under the Sea ~ Little Mermaid	10	15	20	20	20	20	15	10	10	10	10

Where to Eat

There are three keys to successfully navigating Walt Disney World dining:

- Several dining venues are among the most memorable and delightful experiences Walt Disney Word has to offer. Options range from dining in the banquet hall inside Cinderella Castle with the Disney Princesses to sharing sushi and filet mignon on the 15th floor of the Contemporary to joining Mickey and the Gang for lunch in an exotic African marketplace.

- Table service reservations open 180 days in advance, and availability at the most sought-after restaurants is gobbled up almost immediately. A list of the hardest restaurants to reserve follows later.

- Disney World dining is expensive. Expect to pay 25–40% more on-property than you would for comparable meals off-property, whether we're talking about a fast food hamburger at Cosmic Ray's or a 28-ounce Porterhouse at Yachtsman Steakhouse. In effect, most of the upcharge is a convenience fee, but the Disney restaurants offer a reliably consistent experience, many times in unique settings.

The rest of this chapter:

- Offers suggestions on where to eat
- Explains how to reserve meals at Disney World—and why starting to do so 180 days before your visit is crucial
- Introduces and compares the various Disney Dining Plans
- Shares some thoughts on saving money

The chapter ends with overviews of dining at the parks and brief reviews of all the Disney World table service dining options.

Where to Eat at Walt Disney World

Service, food quality, and atmosphere vary immensely among the Disney World restaurants, even those inside the same park with similar price points. The information and reviews that follow will help identify restaurants that are the perfect fit for your group's budget and preferences. Disney World dining locations come in several shapes and sizes:

QUICK OR COUNTER SERVICE Basically a fancy name for fast food, quick service locations don't accept reservations and food is usually ordered at a register and then available for pickup several minutes later. (Be Our Guest is the one exception. It accepts and usually requires a reservation for quick service breakfast and lunch.) An increasing number of outlets are also introducing mobile order as an option. At participating locations, guests have the opportunity to use the My Disney Experience app to create their order and then pay for it using an attached credit card, or when applicable, the Disney Dining Plan. When it's time to eat, simply click the "I'm here" button and the order will be prepared fresh for retrieval. That gives users the ability to discuss orders and look over menus well ahead of meal time rather than having to rush to judgment in a crowded ordering area while looking at a distant menu board. A separate counter is used for mobile order pickup, so no waiting in line is usually necessary. It's incredibly useful during peak meal times when waits are long. Quick service is usually cheaper and faster than table service. Menus, food quality, and atmosphere vary wildly among the various options, making your choices more important than you might expect.

TABLE SERVICE These venues are typical restaurant experiences, where a host will seat your party and a server will take your order and deliver the food to the table. Most require reservations, particularly for dinner. Prices range from $15 sandwiches at The Plaza Restaurant in Magic Kingdom to $185+ for a seven-course meal at Victoria & Albert's. Buffets are generally lumped into this category, even when guests typically serve themselves.

DINNER SHOWS Spirit of Aloha at the Polynesian and Hoop-Dee-Doo Revue at Fort Wilderness offer all-you-care-to-enjoy family-style dining accompanied by two-hour shows. Mickey's Backyard Barbecue, also located at Ft. Wilderness, is an all-you-care-to-enjoy buffet amidst fun line dancing and live music.

FAVORITE FAMILY DINING

In addition to the food, the most fun and best-loved family dining contains some or all of the following:

- A fun setting
- Some kind of show and/or interactive play-along elements
- Visits by Disney characters like Mickey, Tigger, or the Disney Princesses.

On almost every family's list of the best among these are:

- The Hoop-Dee-Doo Musical Revue, a silly, energetic dinner show with interactive elements and plenty of audience participation at Disney's Fort Wilderness Resort.
- The Princess meals: Cinderella's Royal Table in the Magic Kingdom and Akershus Royal Banquet Hall in Epcot. The first has the better setting, the second is much less expensive.
- Dining with Tigger, Pooh, and friends at the Crystal Palace in the Magic Kingdom.
- Dining with Mickey and friends at Chef Mickey's at Disney's Contemporary Resort and 'Ohana breakfast at Disney's Polynesian Resort.
- Dining in the Beast's Castle at Be Our Guest Restaurant in the Magic Kingdom.
- Various degrees of wait-staff induced silliness at 50's Prime Time Café in Disney's Hollywood Studios and Whispering Canyon Café at Disney's Wilderness Lodge.
- Exotic settings in the local versions of national chain restaurants like the Rainforest Café, in both Disney's Animal Kingdom and Disney Springs, and T-REX in Disney Springs.

SELECTING CHARACTER MEALS

Character meals are table service meals or dinner shows where the group has the opportunity to interact and take pictures with the characters during the dining experience. There are several benefits to these meals. First, they replace the lengthy waits to meet the characters inside the theme parks. At Magic Kingdom, meeting Mickey, Minnie, Goofy, Donald, and Pluto might take 90 or more minutes standing in line, often outdoors and unprotected from the heat and rain. At Chef Mickey's, you can enjoy your ice cream sundae while they all come to you. In addition, several characters don't ordinarily meet outside of character meals, including Piglet, Beast, and Prince Charming.

When deciding on a character meal, first identify which characters you'd like to meet. Then narrow down the potential choices by cost, setting, and convenience via the reviews that follow.

Character meal options include:

Animal Kingdom:
- Tusker House: Mickey, Donald, Daisy, Goofy in safari gear.

Epcot:
- Garden Grill: Mickey, Pluto, Chip, Dale in farming apparel.
- Akershus Royal Banquet Hall: Belle, in her yellow gown, joins diners for a picture before they're seated. Ariel, Aurora, Jasmine, and Snow White usually greet tableside.

Hollywood Studios:
- Hollywood & Vine (breakfast only): Sofia, Doc McStuffins, Jake, Handy Manny.
- Hollywood & Vine (lunch and dinner): Minnie, Mickey, Donald, Daisy, and Goofy in seasonal costumes

Magic Kingdom:
- Be Our Guest Restaurant (dinner only): While not a "character meal" per se, guests have the opportunity to meet and take pictures with Beast after the meal.
- Cinderella's Royal Table: Pictures with Cinderella before the meal, with Ariel, Aurora, Jasmine, and Snow White usually meeting tableside.
- Crystal Palace: Pooh, Tigger, Eeyore, and Piglet.

Resorts:
- 1900 Park Fare Breakfast at Grand Floridian: Mary Poppins, Alice, the Mad Hatter, Tigger, and Winnie the Pooh.
- 1900 Park Fare Dinner at Grand Floridian: Cinderella and Prince Charming, Lady Tremaine, Anastasia, Drizella, Fairy Godmother.
- Cape May Café at Beach Club Resort (breakfast only): Goofy, Minnie, and Donald in ridiculous beach outfits.
- Chef Mickey's at the Contemporary Resort: Mickey, Minnie, Donald, Pluto, and Goofy in culinary outfits.
- 'Ohana (breakfast only): Mickey, Pluto, Lilo, and Stitch in Hawaiian outfits.
- Mickey's Backyard Barbecue at Fort Wilderness: Mickey, Minnie, and "friends"—typically Goofy, Chip, Dale—in cowboy outfits.
- Trattoria al Forno at the BoardWalk: Rapunzel, Flynn, Ariel, Eric (breakfast only)

For the princesses, we prefer Cinderella's Royal Table, which is also the only opportunity to see inside the beautiful castle. Absurdly expensive? Yes, but it's a special experience that can't be duplicated elsewhere.

For Mickey, we like Garden Grill at Epcot and Tusker House lunch at Animal Kingdom. Both are conveniently located inside the theme parks, making them easy to access while you're visiting those parks. For Mickey at the resorts, Chef Mickey's is a family favorite, as is breakfast at 'Ohana.

DINING FOR COUPLES

For couples looking for the most romantic atmosphere and the best food, we suggest:

- **California Grill**: Located on the 15th floor of the Contemporary Resort, California Grill offers breathtaking views of Magic Kingdom during the evening fireworks, in addition to a great menu focused on fresh ingredients, sushi, and contemporary cocktails.
- **Artist Point**: Nestled inside Wilderness Lodge, this romantic rendezvous is themed to the restaurants found in the great National Park lodges of the west. Buffalo, salmon, and a terrific mushroom soup and berry cobbler are menu mainstays.
- **Victoria & Albert's**: For a truly special occasion; astonishing dining.

WHAT ABOUT EARLY BREAKFAST AT THE PARKS?

Tusker House at Animal Kingdom, Akershus Royal Banquet Hall and Garden Grill at Epcot, Hollywood & Vine at Hollywood Studios, and Cinderella's Royal Table, Crystal Palace, and Be Our Guest Restaurant at Magic Kingdom all routinely open at 8am for breakfast, which is often a full hour before the rest of the park. Many people recommend these 8am breakfasts because they afford an opportunity to get pictures in the park "when nobody else is around". Unfortunately, and particularly at Magic Kingdom and Hollywood Studios, this is not usually the case because hundreds of other people have the same idea. 8am reservations are also awfully early and awfully expensive. Transportation from the resorts is also dodgier and less consistent so early. With the parks routinely opening as much as an hour prior to the officially stated time, an 8am reservation either means rushing through the meal and hoping the characters arrive in time for a hasty exit, or wasting precious morning touring time eating. Instead, we recommend a late breakfast or early lunch, which allows you to sleep in an extra hour and hit the priority attractions when crowds are lowest before taking a restful, air-conditioned break with the characters.

There are two possible exceptions, the first of which is Be Our Guest, which currently serves quick service breakfast without characters for $25 for adults and $14 for kids. It includes choice of entrée, beverage, and a pastry platter for the table to share. With a 9am open, everyone with a reservation before then will be allowed to enter Magic Kingdom around 7:45am, even if your reservation is for 8:30am or 8:45am. With a pre-opening reservation, do your best to arrive by 7:30am and be done with breakfast and back outside the restaurant no later than 8:45am. This offers a great advantage for those planning to visit Seven Dwarfs Mine Train or Princess Fairytale Hall first thing because diners have the ability to arrive before anyone entering from the main entrance.

The second exception is Akershus Royal Banquet Hall in Norway at Epcot, where a reservation before 9am offers a substantial advantage in getting to the Frozen Ever After ride. Guests with pre-opening

Guide to Disney World Dining

Bold=Character Meal; <u>Underline</u>=Requires 2 Dining Plan Credits; (paren)=which meal, if ratings differ; *Italic*=Resort Casual Dress Code; CAPS=Location (see key below)

				ADULT APPEAL
K I D A P P E A L	High	Chef **Mickey's** C, 50's Prime Time Café HS	**Akershus** E, Beaches & Cream BC, Biergarten E, **<u>Cinderella's Royal Table</u>** MK, **Crystal Palace** MK, Hollywood & Vine HS (l,d), <u>Hoop-dee-Doo</u> <u>Revue</u> FW, **Mickey's** <u>**Backyard**</u> <u>**Barbecue**</u> FW, **'Ohana** P (b), Rainforest Café AK DS, San Angel Inn E, Sci-Fi Dine-in Theater HS, Trattoria al Forno BW (b), **Tusker House** AK, Whispering Canyon Café WL	
	Medium	**Hollywood and Vine*** HS (b)	Cape May Café BC (b), Cape May Café BC (d), Coral Reef E, ESPN Club BW, **Garden Grill** E, La Hacienda de San Angel E, Liberty Tree Tavern MK, Mama Melrose's HS, Nine Dragons E, **1900 Park Fare** GF (b,d), 'Ohana P (d), Olivia's OKW, Plaza MK, Restaurant Marrakesh E, Rose & Crown E, Jungle Skipper Canteen MK, Tony's Town Square MK, Turf Club SS, Tutto Italia E, Via Napoli E, Yak & Yeti AK	Be Our Guest MK (d), *California Grill* C, Boma AKL, <u>Hollywood Brown Derby</u> HS, <u>Le Cellier</u> E, Sanaa KAKL (l,d),Teppan Edo E
	Low	<u>Spirit of Aloha Polynesian Luau</u> P	Big River Grille BW, Ale & Compass YC, Grand Floridian Café GF, Kona Café P, Les Chefs de France E, Spice Road Table E, Trattoria al Forno BW (l,d)	*Artist Point* WI, *Monsieur Paul's* E, *Citricos* GF, *Flying Fish Café* BW, *Jiko* AKL, *Narcoossee's* GF, Queen Victoria's Room** GF, <u>Tiffins</u> AK, Tokyo Dining E, Victoria & Albert** GF, The Wave C, *Yachtsman Steakhouse* YC
		Low	Medium	High

ADULT APPEAL

Locations: AK=Animal Kingdom, AKL=Animal Kingdom Lodge, BC=Beach Club, BW=BoardWalk, C=Contemporary, DS=Disney Springs, E=Epcot, FW=Fort Wilderness, GF=Grand Floridian, HS=Hollywood Studios, KAKL=Kidani Village at AKL, MK=Magic Kingdom, OKW=Old Key West, SS=Saratoga Springs, WL=Wilderness Lodge, YC=Yacht Club

* Though a character meal, low kid appeal except for fans of Playhouse Disney
** Not on Dining Plan; jacket required; no kids under 10

reservations will be allowed to enter the park just before 8am regardless of whether their reservation is for 8:15am or 8:45am. Hurry to the restaurant, eat quickly, and be out in front of the attraction entrance by 8:45am in order to basically walk on Disney's most popular new ride.

Note that this advantage is moot on days with morning extra magic hours or with regular 8am opens and those with reservations will likely want to cancel them or schedule a reservation for later on these days.

RECOMMENDED DINING

Families using the 9-day itineraries introduced in Chapter 6 will find recommended dining at the top of each day in the graphic of the itinerary. The associated To-Do Lists for these itineraries have instructions on when and how to book the reservable table service meals, in addition to walking you through each step of the planning process. Each of the park "Cheat Sheets" in the previous chapter has recommended counter-service options.

Our recommendations are not set in stone. Families with much younger kids may wish to cut some of the non-character meals and replace them with character meals. Families with teens might want to do the opposite. Substitutions can be based on the "Guide to Disney Dining" graphic—which ranks the Disney World theme park and resort table service options based on kid and adult appeal—or on the capsule reviews that follow at the end of this chapter.

In the graphic, high adult appeal is based on "date night" criteria: a restaurant having fine dining, fine service, and a lovely setting. High kid appeal means that a restaurant has the elements that make the rest of Disney World a joy for kids—playful action, characters, and a fun setting—and also has a menu suited to picky eaters. By these criteria, it's hard for a restaurant to appeal to both. Be Our Guest in the Magic Kingdom comes closest, and if it had a better kids menu for picky eaters, would be ranked with high appeal for both groups.

Because kids and adults vary, it's best to use the chart and the reviews at the end of this chapter together.

Advance Dining Reservations

Make Advance Dining Reservations (ADRs) beginning 180 days before your arrival date.

The best Disney World dining options have limited capacity and are wildly popular. Because of this, these restaurants can be filled almost as soon as reservations open for them.

One topic that surprises first-time visitors is the importance and fun of dining experiences. Because quality and price vary so much between restaurants in the same vicinity, researching your options and booking the best restaurants far in advance puts you in the best possible position to have a fun, stress-free vacation. Identify your table service dining favorites as soon as possible and then make your ADRs as soon as reservations open.

Note that ADRs are not "reservations" in the traditional sense. With the exception of Victoria & Albert's and the dinner shows, the restaurant does not actually reserve a table. Instead, your party will receive the next available table that opens up. This can lead to the occasional long wait, particularly at the popular buffets that are often overbooked. To help mitigate this, book a meal right after the restaurant starts service or near the end of service when empty tables are more common.

MAKING YOUR RESERVATIONS

Reservations currently open 180 days before the date of dining—online at 6 a.m. and over the phone at 7 a.m. Moreover, if you are staying at a Disney World hotel, once 180 days from your hotel arrival date rolls around, you can make ADRs for not just that day, but also for the first ten days of your visit. You'll sometimes see this referred to as 180+10. Input your arrival date into HTTP://PSCALCULATOR.NET/PSCALC.PHP to identify the first day you can make reservations. As an example, let's say you're visiting from December 1–8 and staying on property at Art of Animation. According to the calculator, the first day you can make reservations is June 4. Not only could you make reservations for December 1, the first day of our hypothetical vacation, but you can also make reservations for up to ten additional days because you're staying at a Disney-owned resort. Off-site guests visiting on the same dates would also be able to make their reservations for December 1 on June 4, but they would need to call or go online again on June 5 to book December 2, June 6 to book December 3, and so forth.

Most table service reservations require prospective diners to put a credit card on file. A $10 per person fee will be assessed if the group does not show up within 15 minutes of the reservation time. To avoid this fee, cancel the reservation no later than the day before. Same-day cancellations will be charged the no-show fee. Note that only one person needs to show up regardless of how many people are on the reservation. So if you have a reservation for six and only three show up, your party will not be assessed any fees. If weather, transportation delays, or some-thing else causes you to miss your reservation, visit Guest Services and explain your case. Disney will likely waive the charge for worthy stories.

The hardest reservations to get, and which you should book as soon as you can, are:

- Be Our Guest Restaurant [Magic Kingdom]
- Trattoria al Forno breakfast [Boardwalk]
- Cinderella's Royal Table [Magic Kingdom]
- Chef Mickey's [Contemporary Resort]
- 'Ohana [Polynesian Resort]
- Akershus Royal Banquet Hall [Epcot]
- 1900 Park Fare Dinner [Grand Floridian Resort]
- California Grill [Contemporary Resort]
- Crystal Palace [Magic Kingdom]

Typically, over 40 restaurants will have same-day reservations available at some point during the day. It's always best to secure reservations via 407-WDW-Dine, DISNEYWORLD.COM, the My Disney Experience mobile app, or in person at Guest Services or the restaurant itself. It's not uncommon for a restaurant to entirely turn guests away without reservations, particularly at peak dinner times. Make reservations as soon as you know where you want to eat.

If there is a reservation that you would like but were unable to initially secure, refresh availability on the day before as many people cancel their reservations, which are subsequently offered to other guests.

The Disney Dining Plan

Disney World dining is expensive. For some guests, it may even be the priciest component of the vacation, eclipsing the cost of lodging and theme park tickets. The three versions of the Disney Dining Plan (Quick Service, Regular, and Deluxe) are a way to prepay some of these dining expenses.

Years ago, when the Regular Dining Plan included appetizer and tip at sit-down restaurants, you could actually save some money by using these plans. These days it's hard for us to recommend them, although the new-for-2018 inclusion of a single alcoholic drink per meal will improve the value payoff of these plans for some, and for others make the cost of the plans easier to forget.

Ignoring alcohol:

- The Quick Service Dining Plan is priced so high that it's only possible to break even or come out ahead if you use the credits solely for lunch and dinner. From there, you'll need to order only the most expensive items to eke out a potential savings of a dollar or two per day.
- At a cost just over $75 per adult per night, the Regular Dining Plan is expensive and saving money with it requires planning only the most expensive meals.

- The Deluxe Dining Plan comes with three quick or table service meals per day at a cost of about $116 per night per adult. Users either spend three or more hours per day eating table service meals or use their credits on faster quick service meals, in turn reducing the value of each credit.

The addition of one alcoholic drink for each quick and table service credit will change the value equation of these plans for some. The Dining Plan includes most beers, wines, cocktails, and other drinks up to around $17. Certain pricier pours, particularly at Disney signature restaurants, are excluded. At press time, no quick service venues at Magic Kingdom offer alcohol, although that may quickly change. But those who would otherwise have paid cash for at least one less-expensive alcoholic drink at most of their meals anyway will see an additional value of around $15–30 per night for the Quick Service and Regular Plans, and even more for the Deluxe Plan. This additional value may well turn the plans into more reasonable economic choices for those who imbibe in the ways that they reward.

(Also new in 2018 is the option of a single non-alcoholic specialty drink per quick service and table credit for those over and under 21—think milkshakes, smoothies, and such. Those 21 and over can do only one drink or the other. Those who would have paid cash for these anyway will also see value to the change.)

We suggest skipping the dining plans, with these exceptions:

- If you take comfort in pre-paying some of your dining expenses as a budgeting tool (even if this means you spend more money), the Quick Service or Regular plans may make sense for you—the cash loss may be worth the budget comfort. It's nice knowing that food is pre-paid and users are free to order whatever entrees and desserts that they like, even if those prices are higher than they're accustomed to paying. As an alternative, consider loading a Disney gift card with the amount of money you plan to pay for meals.
- Pricing on the Regular Plan is advantageous for groups with kids under the age of ten that plan multiple buffets and character meals. The cost of a child buffet at many character meals exceeds their cost of the Regular Dining Plan for that day.
- Those 21 and over who would have had an eligible alcoholic drink at most of their quick and table service meals anyway may come out ahead, especially on the Quick Service Plan, which gives you just as many free drinks per night as the Regular Plan but costs about $23 per night less.

With or without a dining plan, the typical family eating their meals on property should budget $40–$75+ per adult per day, and between $20 and $40/day for the kids—depending on their ages and appetites.

DINING PLAN CREDITS AND WHAT THEY COVER

The Dining Plans are only available to guests staying at Disney owned and operated resorts. All guests on a single reservation (except children under three—not covered on any plan) must opt for the same Dining Plan if you elect to purchase it. There's no such thing as having four people on a room reservation and only three people on the Deluxe Plan. And it isn't possible for one person to purchase Deluxe, while the other chooses Regular. The plan must be purchased for each night of the booked stay. Everyone over the age of nine must pay the adult rate, regardless of how much they plan to eat. And kids 3–9 might be required to order from the Kids' Menu if the dining location has one.

Those on the Dining Plan receive credits based on the number of nights they're staying. The Dining Plan and credits are not connected to theme park tickets—just the number of nights on the reservation. Credits are usable from check-in day through midnight on checkout day, and can be used in any order on any of these days. On a three-night stay, a guest could use all their credits on the first day, the last day, or space them out.

Quick service meals generally consist of one entrée or combo meal, and one beverage—for 2018 plans, as noted above, this beverage can be a "regular" beverage (think milk or Coke), "specialty" non-alcoholic beverage (think milkshake or smoothie), or for those over 21 an alcoholic beverage. In 2017, Disney eliminated the former dessert entitlement and added in its place an additional snack credit per day, which can be used either on dessert or on something else at any time, making these plans much more flexible. Virtually every quick service on property participates in the Dining Plan, although not all of them—especially at Magic Kingdom—offer alcohol or specialty drinks. All quick service meals cost one credit.

In 2018, table service meals include one entrée, one dessert, and one regular, specialty, or alcoholic beverage, and cost one or two credits. Two credit meals are signature experiences at the most expensive dinner shows, buffets, and restaurants like Hoop-Dee-Doo Revue, Cinderella's Royal Table, and California Grill. The Deluxe Dining Plan credits also include an appetizer, in addition to the entrée, dessert, and the three beverage options. Snack credits can be used on small food items like candy apples, ice cream bars, pastries, and bottles of water and soda. Look for the Dining Plan symbol on any menu to see what qualifies as a snack credit.

The credits don't always cover everything you might want at a meal and most don't cover tips. Most guests have some additional dining expenses, in addition to the cost of the Dining Plan.

THE QUICK SERVICE DINING PLAN

The 2018 Quick Service Dining Plan includes per person, per night:

- Two quick service meals (entrée/beverage)
- Two snacks

In addition, each guest receives a refillable mug for use at their resort's quick service, and, if available, pools.

So a family of four staying for five nights would receive ten quick service meals, ten snacks, and a refillable mug each. For 2018, after-tax pricing is:

- $52.49 per night for those ten and older
- $21.75 per night for kids ages three to nine

Ignoring alcohol, adult quick service entrees are typically $10–$14 in the theme parks. Add a $3 fountain beverage and your average meal comes to around $15. Eat two of those, in addition to a $4 Mickey Ice Cream Bar and $5 pretzel, and add about $2.50 for a day's worth of the refillable mug, and you're about eight dollars away from breaking even, after adding tax. Substitute an $8 beer or $10 mixed drink for the soda and you're closer. Kids' Picks generally come in around $7 each. Eat two and add a $3 popsicle and $4 popcorn and the use of the refillable mug, and you've covered the day's cost.

While technically possible to eke out a savings of a dollar or two per day, those savings evaporate whenever you eat breakfast, when prices are usually lower, or whenever someone is forced to order something they ordinarily wouldn't. It also makes it difficult to schedule a table service meal or character buffet since they aren't included on the Plan. You can pay cash for such meals, but if doing so pushes you to using a credit for breakfast—or worse, ending your vacation with unused credits—the Quick Service plan will cost you money. On the other hand, as noted, the value of an alcoholic drink at each meal may well put those 21 and older ahead of the cost of this plan.

THE "REGULAR" DINING PLAN

The 2018 "Regular" Dining Plan—often known simply as the Disney Dining Plan—includes per person, per night:

- One quick service meal (entrée/beverage)
- One table service meal (entrée/dessert or select side/beverage)
- Two snacks

In addition, each guest receives a refillable mug for the duration of the stay. For 2018, after-tax pricing is:

- $75.49 per night for those ten and older
- $25.80 per night for kids ages three to nine

Child pricing is advantageous with a cost just about $4 more than the Quick Service Plan. With several character buffets priced over $20, it's easy for kids to come out ten dollars or more ahead each day they dine at such a venue. For those older than 9, the price of $23/per day more than the Quick Service is harder to justify. There are meals where you do well—Akershus for lunch or dinner, after tax, is over $55. Over the course of a day, an adult ordering a typical quick service lunch alongside a beer, a snack, and dinner at Akershus will pay less under the Dining Plan than with cash. Dinner at Crystal Palace approaches this cost, as does Chef Mickey's.

Outside of buffets and ignoring alcohol, it's difficult to find restaurants with average entrée and dessert prices high enough to cover the cost of the plan. Let's assume you're spending the day at Hollywood Studios and select 50's Prime Time Café for dinner. You select the second most expensive entrée, the $23 Sampling of Mom's Favorite Recipes, and the most expensive dessert (Traditional Warm Apple Crisp a la Mode for $8) with a $6 milkshake as your beverage. With tax, the meal comes out to $39.41, which is $36 away from covering the cost of the Dining Plan with just a quick service meal and two snacks to go. At the costliest quick service, ABC Commissary, the most expensive quick service meal you could put together is $24 with tax. That's about $6 higher than average. Even so, add a $4 Mickey Ice Cream Bar and $5 pretzel as snacks and you've only "saved" $10 compared to the price of one day on the Dining Plan after going out of your way to order the most expensive items at the park. If you had simply ordered the fried chicken instead of the sampler at 50's Prime Time, and the burger instead of the Ribs/ Chicken Combo at ABC Commissary, you would come out behind the cost of one day on the Dining Plan. On the other hand, the value of an alcoholic drink at each meal may well put those 21 and older ahead of the cost of this plan even for more "typical" meals.

The economics of two-credit meals are even worse. Signature restaurant cash prices generally are about 1.5x the cash cost of regular restaurants, but cost twice the number of credits, resulting in a lower per-credit value. For example, the most expensive meal you could put together on the Dining Plan at California Grill is a $49 filet mignon, $14 chocolate cake, and $12 cocktail. That's $80 after tax, or just $40 per credit for the most expensive meal at one of the most expensive restaurants on property. To compare, the most expensive meal you could put together at Teppan Edo at Epcot, a single credit restaurant, is $37 Steak and Shrimp, $7 cake, and $12 cocktail. The value of that credit with tax is $59.64, or almost 50% more value than you'd find at California Grill.

THE DELUXE DINING PLAN

The 2018 Deluxe Dining Plan includes per person, per night:

- Three meals per day—either quick service or table service. Table service meals include an appetizer where applicable, and all meals include the specialty and alcoholic beverage credit
- Two snacks

In addition, each guest receives a refillable mug for the duration of the stay. For 2018, after-tax pricing is:

- $116.24 per night for adults
- $39.90 per night for kids ages three to nine

On paper, there is a lot of value potential here, particularly for kids under the age of ten and those over 21 who drink at every meal. To maximize that value, however, you could be spending more than three hours a day dining—even more if you avoid two-credit meals—and building an itinerary largely around being at specific restaurants at specific times. And let's not forget the actual cost. A family of two adults, a 15-year old, and a 7-year old would cost a whopping $389 per night. For that, Josh and Dave will cook and serve your family of four both lunch and dinner, and offer all the Bud Light you can handle, while intermittently breaking out into song and dance. (A word to the wise though: Josh's specialty is Hot Pockets and Dave's favorite ingredient is Sriracha.)

Saving Money on Dining

Purchasing ingredients and preparing meals where you're staying is the easiest way to slash a food budget. This works best for quick breakfasts in the room. Pack or purchase a dozen bagels or donuts, fruit, cereal and milk, and some protein bars and you can easily eliminate busy breakfasts at the resort food court, in addition to cutting meal time down to a few minutes from 30+.

Unfortunately, Disney doesn't make purchasing these items economical at its resort gift shops, for reasons you might be able to guess. Other than Fort Wilderness and the Disney Vacation Club properties, pickings can be slim and prices are high. On top of that, only Ft. Wilderness cabins and the villas in the DVC resorts have kitchens, making even simple prep work difficult in most situations. If you have a car and the time to shop, we recommend the Speedway stores on property for convenience. One is located across the street from the BoardWalk Inn near Epcot, another after the exit to Magic Kingdom parking, and the third is across the street from the Marketplace section of Disney Springs. For a better selection, visit the Winn-Dixie (and nearby liquor store) at 1957 S Apopka Vineland Rd, in Orlando, or the Publix (and nearby liquor store) at 29 Blake Boulevard, in Kissimmee. The nearest to your hotel will be about a 10–15 minute drive.

Without transportation or the ability to venture out to a supermarket on vacation, consider a grocery delivery service. We like GARDENGROCER. COM and WEGOSHOP.COM. Garden Grocer is the most popular, but you're limited to what you can order based on their web store. We Go Shop will visit whatever area store you specify for whatever specific products you want, but the delivery fee is higher. Both deliver beer and wine. Amazon Pantry and Prime Now will deliver directly to your resort.

Dining Reviews: Introduction

Brief reviews of the table service restaurants in the parks, Disney Springs, and the Disney resorts follow.

First, you'll find reviews of the restaurants inside each theme park, in alphabetical order. Next, you'll find an alphabetized list of the resorts, with reviews of all restaurants located at that resort.

We start with the venue name and location within its area, indicating also whether a meal is a character meal or a dinner show. We then note cuisine, operating hours, and whether or not it is on the Disney Dining Plan (abbreviated as DDP)—note that some DDP meals require two credits and are so indicated. Next, we note current price ranges for adult appetizers and entrees, in addition to kids' meals. Buffet prices with tax included are also noted where applicable. We then get into the food and ambiance of the restaurants themselves. This material is necessarily brief—for more, see Josh's EASYWDW.COM. Prices, menus, hours, required credits, discounts etc., are all subject to change.

We also throw some Disney jargon around:

- Signature Restaurant: two credit venues usually aimed at adults—that is, thin on kid appeal, but with finer and more elegant dining. Most have a mild dress code, e.g., on men, pants are preferred, nice shorts are OK, but no tank tops.
- Family Style: food for the entire table is served on platters and shared amongst the table.
- Walk-up: trying to get a seating without having a reservation.

Note also that some venues will require full pre-payment—at press time, Hoop-Dee-Doo, Spirit of Aloha, Mickey's Backyard Barbecue, and

Cinderella's Royal Table—and most others will require a credit card so that a no-show fee can be charged. To avoid no-show fees, cancel no later than 11:59pm on the day before the reservation.

Dining Reviews: The Theme Parks

DINING AT DISNEY'S ANIMAL KINGDOM

Disney's Animal Kingdom offers a nice variety of consistently high-quality restaurants and quick services, and we like each for different reasons. The Rainforest Café at the front of the park is much less crowded than the Disney Springs iteration, and offers the same fun atmosphere fueled by Animatronics and a vast menu. Theme park admission is not required to dine there. Tusker House in Africa is a low-key character meal featuring Donald and Mickey for all three meals. The expansive buffet area makes sampling the 30+ items easy, and the characters have more time to spend with guests than at the more crowded resort character meals. Yak & Yeti serves up fantastic Pan-Asian food in a restaurant full of authentic artifacts from India, China, and elsewhere. Tiffins is a new signature restaurant featuring African, Asian, and South American flavors that's quickly become one of Disney's best overall dining experiences. Food might seem adventurous at first blush, but flavors should be more accessible than you might expect. Diners also have the opportunity to visit Nomad Lounge with a menu featuring carefully crafted cocktails along with wines and beers from around the world.

Like the other theme parks, Animal Kingdom quick service is largely hit or miss. Pizzafari serves up flatbread pizzas that are edible, but unlikely to wow. Restaurantosaurus in DinoLand USA is your burger and nugget option. You'll find plenty of air-conditioned seating, in addition to out-door patio tables. Better is Yak & Yeti Local Food Cafes, which serves up Asian specialties like Teriyaki Beef and Honey Chicken. Unfortunately, all seating is outdoors, and it can be uncomfortably hot and wet in the summer. Harambe Market in the Africa section opened in May 2015 near the entrance to the Wildlife Express train that transports guests to Rafiki's Planet Watch. It adds another open-air quick service option with outdoor seating and a unique menu. It's an excellent choice if the weather cooperates, but with all seating outdoors, it can be unpleasant in the rain or heat. Better is Flame Tree Barbecue, where you'll find Disney's best quick service ribs, pork sandwiches, and half chickens. While seating is outdoors, it's better covered with fans overhead. Walk all the way down to the water for expansive views of Asia and Expedition Everest. Satu'li Canteen in Pandora is the new kid on the block, offering some surprisingly unique flavors in their various bowl entrees that feature grilled beef, chicken, fish, or tofu on top of bases that include romaine and kale salad or mixed whole grain and rice. Air-conditioned seating is available, in addition to patio seating outside.

Rainforest Café

Front of park; theme park admission not required to dine

CUISINE American. **HOURS** 8:30am–late. **DDP** Yes.

PRICES Breakfast: $9–$17. Lunch/Dinner Appetizers: $8–$20. Entrées: $15–$36. Kids: $9.

OVERVIEW Part of a chain of 25+ restaurants around the world, Rainforest Cafe blends an immersive environment with a laundry list menu. Dine on steaks, pastas, salads, burgers, or one of 50+ other items, while Animatronic gorillas pound their chests, birds sing, and thunder booms from the starry night sky. The food won't impress, but it's all serviceable and portions are huge. The restaurant is extremely loud and the atmosphere may startle young children apprehensive about rides like DINOSAUR and Haunted Mansion, although older children love the atmosphere. Because it's located at the front of the park, plan to eat when you're near the entrance/exit.

Tiffins

Attached to the back of Pizzafari, on Discovery Island

CUISINE Global, but mostly Asian, African, and South American. **HOURS** 11:30am–late. **DDP** 2 credits.

PRICES Lunch/Dinner Appetizers: $10–$16. Lunch Special: $28. Entrées: $29–$53. Kids: $9–$15.

OVERVIEW Tiffins extends Animal Kingdom's keen eye for detail at a restaurant that celebrates the bold globetrotting spirit of Disney's Imagineers as they explored the world to create Disney's Animal Kingdom. Of the three elegant dining rooms, we recommend requesting the Grand Gallery, where concept art for Rivers of Light lines the walls, or the Safari Gallery, where guests dine amidst authentic artifacts and actual field notes from the Imagineers' adventures in Africa. The menu skews toward the foreign for most people, but flavors should be more accessible than you might expect with the usual beef, chicken, lamb, and vegetables making up the majority of most dishes. The Wagyu Strip Loin is a crowd favorite as is the Chocolate Ganache dessert. The atmosphere is casual and inviting with service that should exceed expectations. It's our favorite new restaurant.

Nomad Lounge is located to the left of the main lobby area and enjoys its own menu of small plates and an expanded drink menu. We love stopping by for a cocktail or draft beer, the exclusive Kungaloosh Excursion Spiced Ale being our favorite, but portions are small for the money. Consider noshing on a couple of appetizers, but most people will need to spend $40 or $50 in the lounge to truly fill up. Tiffins presents more value for a full meal.

Tusker House

Character meal, in Africa

CUISINE African-inspired. **DDP** Yes.

HOURS AND PRICES *Breakfast* (8–10:55am): $34 adults, $21 kids. *Lunch* (11am–3:30pm; may extend later): $48 adults, $29 kids. *Dinner* (4:30pm– late): $48 adults, $29 kids. Pricing may vary depending on the season.

OVERVIEW Donald, Daisy, Mickey, and Goofy greet guests tableside inside this vibrant African marketplace. Some of the 30+ items at each meal retain touches of African flair and spice, but Disney is careful to cater to the typical American palate. Character interaction is among the best, with the characters leading parades around the restaurant and playing games with guests.

Yak & Yeti

Asia, between Flights of Wonder and Kali River Rapids

CUISINE Asian. **HOURS** 11am–late. **DDP** Yes.

PRICES Lunch/Dinner Appetizers: $6–$17. Entrées: $17–$35. Kids: $9.

OVERVIEW Located in Asia, this air-conditioned respite is appropriately themed to a rural countryside sanctuary set in the heart of the Himalayan Mountains. The menu is reminiscent of P.F. Chang's and features such favorites as Lettuce Cups, Crispy Honey Chicken, and Sweet-and-Sour Pork, in addition to a Kobe Beef Burger or Steak. Portions are large and service is friendly as guests dine amongst hundreds of authentic artifacts from all over Asia. Request a window table upstairs for a great view.

DINING AT EPCOT
....

Epcot offers an overwhelming number of dining options, mostly in World Showcase with national cuisines tied into the respective pavilions. You could visit Epcot every day for a month and dine in a different venue each day. We present reviews of all the table service options below, but our recommended restaurants are Biergarten in Germany, Via Napoli in Italy, Akershus Banquet Hall in Norway, and San Angel Inn in Mexico.

Biergarten is a richly themed buffet restaurant with authentic German items like beer cheese soup, sauerbraten, spaetzle, veal sausage, mini frankfurters, and a whole lot more. A live oompah band plays intermittently, with guests invited up to the dance floor to sing and dance along.

Via Napoli is an authentic Neapolitan pizzeria serving some of the best pizza on property. A large mezzo-metro pizza is plenty to feed a family of four for about $11 per person, making it a great value. Stay conservative with a signature pepperoni pie or try something like the Prosciutto e Melone Signature Pie (fontina, mozzarella, prosciutto, and cantaloupe).

Akershus is the part-buffet, part-table service character meal in Norway. While pricey, it's significantly less expensive than Cinderella's Royal Table at the Magic Kingdom, and the price includes a digital picture with Belle in her yellow gown, along with four other princesses meeting tableside. The cold buffet guarantees everyone will have plenty to eat, and the entrees are varied and above average as well.

At San Angel Inn, guests dine underneath perpetual twilight as the boats from the Gran Fiesta Tour next door glide by. Food quality is a bit lower than at our other three picks, but the unique atmosphere can't be replicated elsewhere.

Quick service options at Epcot are even more abundant.

Of the Future World options, Sunshine Seasons near Soarin' in the Land Pavilion receives nearly universal acclaim. Serving freshly grilled pork chops, rotisserie chicken, salmon, salads, sandwiches, Asian entrees, and more, with plentiful air-conditioned seating, it's a great choice for a convenient Future World lunch. Electric Umbrella is your Future World spot for the usual Disney hamburgers and chicken nuggets.

In World Showcase, you may pick a quick service based on the mood—or location—of the group at the time. We both highly recommend Tangierine Café in Morocco. While the menu of shawarma, falafel, kefta, and tabouleh might initially seem exotic, the typical Mediterranean flavors are more familiar than you might expect. Food is also higher quality and portions are larger than at just about any other quick service. Josh likes the U.K.'s Fish and Chips, particularly when a table overlooking the lagoon is available. Liberty Inn in the U.S. serves a surprisingly decent New York Strip Steak with fried Shrimp for around $15, in addition to Disney quick-service mainstays. With plenty of air-conditioned and outdoor seating, the only thing keeping it from being highly recommended is the fact that it's all American, and it seems like World Showcase should be an opportunity to try something a little different. Dave wishes that Liberty Inn would shift to an all-barbecue theme, highlighting all the different U.S. barbecue variants and their regional fixin's. Sommerfest in Germany is quite good, but the seating section consists of only a handful of tables, and there's rarely anywhere comfortable to sit.

La Cantina de San Angel in Mexico and Lotus Blossom Café in China both offer menus that should be familiar to most guests and for that reason, we don't necessarily recommend stopping over more interesting options. But the nachos in Mexico are a very shareable snack and the chicken and beef entrees in China should satisfy most appetites for less money than other options. Katsura Grill in Japan doesn't live up to its potential, but the udon and chicken cutlet curry are good and the outdoor garden seating area is among the most peaceful you'll find. The sushi largely disappoints. Boulangerie Patisserie in France offers some unique quiche, sandwich, and salad fare, but the ordering process is confusing and the seating section is small, loud, and chaotic.

Overall, visiting Tangierine Café or Sunshine Seasons for lunch and one of our recommended table service restaurants for dinner is your best bet. But most guests are satisfied no matter where they choose to dine.

Akershus Royal Banquet Hall

Princess character meal, in Norway Pavilion

CUISINE Norwegian/American. **DDP** Yes.

HOURS AND PRICES *Breakfast* (8–11:10am): $52 adults, $31 kids. *Lunch* (11:55am–3:30pm): $61 adults, $36 kids. *Dinner* (4:55pm–park close): $61 adults, $36 kids.

OVERVIEW Themed to a 14th century Scandinavian castle, Akershus is Epcot's much less expensive version of Cinderella's Royal Table. A picture with Belle begins the adventure and will be available on PhotoPass, and four other princesses meet tableside—usually Ariel, Aurora, Cinderella, and Snow White. For breakfast, guests are brought platters of hot breakfast foods like scrambled eggs, potato casserole, sausage, and bacon. Lunch and dinner feature a set menu of Norwegian and American favorites like Norwegian Meatballs with Lingonberry Sauce, Salmon, and Chicken Breast. All meals include unlimited access to the cold bar, which includes bread, salads, sliced meats, cheeses, fish, and a variety of other chilled foods, including traditional Scandinavian items. Kids' meals include pizza, salmon, pasta, and meatballs. Breakfast is the most consistent and least expensive meal.

Biergarten

Germany Pavilion

CUISINE German. **DDP** Yes.

HOURS AND PRICES *Lunch* (12–3:10pm): $35 adults, $20 kids. *Dinner* (4pm–park close): $43 adults, $24 kids.

OVERVIEW Be transported to a quaint Bavarian village in the heart of Oktoberfest at this German buffet that features live oompah music throughout the day. Selections include bratwurst, rotisserie chicken, pork schnitzel, and a variety of seasonal salads. Dessert includes Apple Strudel and Black Forest Cake. The selection and food quality are both outstanding. Service is genuinely friendly and the music is a lot of fun. Tables seat eight and smaller parties will be seated with others. There is no dedicated buffet section for kids, though most will be happy loading up on macaroni and cheese, chicken, pretzel rolls, and dessert. The liters of beer are a lot of fun and a good value.

Chefs de France

France Pavilion, ground level

CUISINE French. **HOURS** 12pm–park close. **DDP** Yes.

PRICES (One all-day menu) Appetizers: $9–$17. Entrées: $20–$36. Kids: $8–$10.

OVERVIEW This family-friendly Parisian café provides a casual atmosphere for guests to sample French cuisine llike Casserole of Burgundian Escargots, French Onion Soup, and Duck Breast and Leg Confit. Steaks, roasted chicken, and broiled salmon are also available. The charming French service is perhaps a bit too authentic at times, but meals at this busy brasserie are a lot of fun. The kids' menu may be limiting, with just Chicken Strips, Ground Beef Steak on a Brioche Bun, Pasta, and Grilled Fish typically available.

Coral Reef

To the right of The Seas with Nemo and Friends

CUISINE American. **HOURS** 11:30am–park close. **DDP** Yes.

PRICES Lunch/Dinner Appetizers: $10–$15. Entrées: $24–$35. Kids: $10–$13.

OVERVIEW More than 4,000 creatures, including sharks, rays, and turtles, join diners seated in front of the 5.7 million gallon aquarium glass. Food is average table service quality and the menu skews towards fish and beef with the salmon and shrimp & grits standing out as excellent. Kids love the aquarium view and their menu features steak, cheesy shells, and fish & chips. Request a lower-level aquarium view at check-in.

Garden Grill

Character meal, upper floor of the Land Pavilion

CUISINE American. **DDP** Yes.

HOURS AND PRICES *Breakfast* (8–10:30am): $34 adults, $20 kids. *Lunch* (11:30am–3pm): $48 adults, $29 kids. *Dinner* (4–8:30pm): $48 adults, $29 kids.

OVERVIEW Join Chip, Dale, Mickey, and Pluto at this fun restaurant featuring views of the Living with the Land ride below. All three meals are served family-style with the usual assortment of eggs, bacon, and other favorites at breakfast, though the accompanying warm chocolate-hazelnut sauce helps elevate the Mickey waffles and the cinnamon roll is quite good. Lunch and dinner include turkey breast, carved pork, pot roast, vegetables, mashed potatoes, and non-alcoholic beverages (alcohol is available for an additional cost). Kids receive chicken drumsticks, macaroni-and-cheese, broccoli, and fries. For dessert, expect cupcakes for the kids and short cake for the adults. Food is quite good, and this is one of the more laid-back character meals, with excellent character interaction.

La Hacienda de San Angel

Mexico Pavilion, outside on the water

CUISINE Mexican. **HOURS** 4pm–park close. **DDP** Yes.

PRICES Dinner Appetizers: $9–$14. Entrées: $26–$32. Kids: $9–$10.

OVERVIEW This restaurant on the Lagoon features floor-to-ceiling windows with the potential for grand views of World Showcase Lagoon. The limited menu (seven entrée choices averaging $27) skews away from typical Tex-Mex and towards grilled and marinated meats and seafood. Parties of two or more should stick to one of the two combination skillets for $59 each; plenty of food for up to three to share. Kids' meals include cheese quesadillas, steak or chicken tacos, and grilled chicken. Food quality and service range from below average to average. The nearby San Angel Inn is more charming.

Le Cellier Steakhouse

Canada Pavilion (look for the walkway down to the O Canada! show)

CUISINE Steak and fish, mostly. **HOURS** 12:30pm–park close. **DDP** 2 credits.

PRICES Lunch/Dinner Appetizers: $11–$24. Entrées: $29–$54. Kids: $9–$17.

OVERVIEW Now a two-credit signature meal on the Dining Plan, this dark, wine-cellar-themed restaurant that focuses on Canadian beef is an expensive proposition. No steak currently comes in under $49. While cozy, tables are virtually on top of each other, creating a less-than-intimate atmosphere. Food quality is high and service is typically above average, but it's hard to justify these prices. On the plus side, the $11 cheese soup is excellent, the complimentary pretzel bread is out of this world, and the Unibroue beer is world-class. Kids, who are unlikely to be enthralled by the restaurant, can get in on the action with a grilled sirloin steak, seared salmon, and a kids' portion of the cheese soup.

Monsieur Paul

France Pavilion, above Les Chefs de France

CUISINE French. **HOURS** 5:30pm–park close. **DDP** 2 credits.

PRICES Dinner Appetizers: $15-$29. Entrées: $39–$44. Kids: $13–$16.

OVERVIEW This upscale gourmet French restaurant replaced Bistro de Paris above Chefs de France in December 2012. Couples looking for the most intimate experience inside Epcot should look no further, but the formal atmosphere is not particularly kid friendly. Luckily, the restaurant introduced a kids' menu that includes seared chicken, roasted salmon, or beef tenderloin with choice of side to cater better to younger clientele. The very French staff may struggle to communicate in English, but they are among the most attentive property wide. Food impresses in quality and presentation and is not much more expensive than the pricier entrees downstairs.

Nine Dragons

China Pavilion

CUISINE Chinese. **HOURS** 12pm–park close. **DDP** Yes.

PRICES Lunch/Dinner Appetizers: $4–$13. Lunch Entrées: $16–$23. Dinner Entrées: $16–$39. Kids: $8–$11.

OVERVIEW Featuring a beautiful glass mural of two dragons chasing a glowing pearl, rosewood wall panels, and Chinese lantern lighting, Nine Dragons is not your typical neighborhood dive. The menu offers familiar favorites like Kung Pao Chicken and Honey-Sesame Chicken along with traditional dishes like the Fragrant Five-Spiced Fish, all for $25 or less. Kids can get in on the action with interesting items like Pot Stickers, Sweet-and-Sour Chicken, and Ginger Ice Cream. Portions are huge and the kitchen consistently executes food that is less expensive than other restaurants. Service is friendly but tends to be abrupt. While Nine Dragons suffers from a poor reputation, we think it's improved handily in recent memory and don't have any qualms about recommending it, particularly as a last-minute walk-up.

Restaurant Marrakesh

Morocco Pavilion, in the very back

CUISINE Moroccan/Mediterranean. **HOURS** 11:30am–park close. **DDP** Yes.

PRICES Lunch/Dinner Appetizers: $8–$18. Lunch Entrées $17–$25. Dinner Entrées $22–$30. Kids: $8.

OVERVIEW This hard-to-find restaurant in the back of the Morocco Pavilion is unique and under-rated. Themed to an ornate Moroccan palace, stained-glass chandeliers provide the only light for the visiting band and belly dancer that perform throughout the day. Lunch is a better value with the same entrees as dinner at reduced prices, including a three-course chicken kebab lunch under $25. Kids' entrees may disappoint, offering only chicken tenders, a hamburger, or Moroccan-style Pasta. Consider letting adventuresome kids sample some items from one of the adult feast samplers. Rarely busy, this is the easiest walk-up at Epcot and the easiest reservation to snag same-day.

Rose & Crown Dining Room

United Kingdom Pavilion

CUISINE British. **HOURS** 12pm–park close. **DDP** Yes.

PRICES Lunch/Dinner Appetizers: $8–$14. Entrées: $20–$34. Kids: $9–$12.

OVERVIEW Situated along World Showcase Lagoon, Rose & Crown provides the only guaranteed IllumiNations viewing from a restaurant. Views are best outside on the patio, but guests seated inside the family-friendly pub, heavy on wooden furniture, will be invited outside shortly before the show. Food quality has fallen in recent years as chefs seem to push out a new menu every couple months. Stick with long-standing favorites like Bangers & Mash, Fish & Chips, and Shepherd's Pie. Kids choose from a menu that includes steak and fish & chips.

Rose & Crown Pub

United Kingdom Pavilion

CUISINE Mostly beer. **HOURS** 11:30am–park close. **DDP** No.

PRICES Limited food menu with prices ranging from $4–$13.

OVERVIEW Frosted windows protect the privacy of those imbibing inside this cozy pub, which is virtually always hopping. The entrance is separate from the restaurant and reservations are not accepted here. Draft beer includes Bass, Bodington's, Guinness, Stella, and Harp. Scotch flights, mixed drinks like the Pimm's Cup, and wine are other options.

San Angel Inn

Mexico Pavilion, inside the pyramid

CUISINE Mexican. **HOURS** 11:30am–park close. **DDP** Yes.

PRICES Lunch/Dinner Appetizers: $8–$14. Entrées $22–$34. Kids: $9–$10.

OVERVIEW San Angel Inn sits inside the Mesoamerican pyramid, and is themed as a Mexican village square at twilight. The evening theming makes the restaurant dark, to the point where reading the menu is nearly impossible without the help of tabletop candles. Like La Hacienda outside, the limited menu focuses on grilled meats rather than burritos and enchiladas. Unfortunately, tables are so close together that diners a table over might as well be on your reservation, eliminating any sense of intimacy. A good family choice as parents will find the setting romantic, and kids will find it fun. Request a table on the water for a delightful view of the Gran Fiesta Tour boats gliding by below. Kids' menu items include beef or chicken tacos, cheese quesadillas, and grilled chicken or tilapia.

Spice Road Table

Morocco Pavilion, along the Lagoon

CUISINE Moroccan/Mediterranean. **HOURS** 11am–park close. **DDP** Yes.

PRICES Small Plates: $8–$13. Entrees: $23-35. Kids: $9.

OVERVIEW This water-side eatery offers small-plate Mediterranean specialties like lamb sausage, fried calamari, and harissa chicken rolls. Additional emphasis is placed on mixed drinks, Moroccan wine, and Mediterranean beer. Spice Road accepts reservations, but walk-ups are nearly always available without a wait. Since opening, menu variety and portion size have improved, and we like making a stop here in the middle of the afternoon to cool off, pass around shared appetizers, and try a couple of fruity drinks. More expensive entrees are probably done better elsewhere, as the menu unsuccessfully tries to marry mainstream-sounding dishes with more-interesting spices. Kids can pick from a Beef Slider or Chicken Kebab for $8 each. The view of IllumiNations is largely blocked by islands and trees, but it's a suitable spot for casual viewing and to enjoy the lovely music.

Teppan Edo

Japan Pavilion, above Mitsukoshi Department Store

CUISINE Japanese steakhouse. **HOURS** 12pm–park close. **DDP** Yes.

PRICES Lunch/Dinner Appetizers: $4–$15. Sushi: $15–$18. Entrées: $24–$37. Kids: $14–$15.

OVERVIEW This Japanese steakhouse seats eight guests around each of the many hibachi grills in one of six contemporary, windowless dining rooms. Parties with fewer than eight will most likely be seated with other parties. Food is prepared at each grill by Japanese chefs who interact with guests and put on a small show while cooking. Steak, chicken, shrimp, swordfish, vegetables, and other entrees are consistently under-seasoned, but the accompanying dips aid flavor. All meals arrive alongside rice and yakisoba. Kids are usually enamored by the friendly chefs as meals are created before their eyes. Service is sweet and attentive. We would rate this restaurant higher if it weren't so similar to the Benihana chain.

Tokyo Dining

Japan Pavilion, above Mitsukoshi Department Store

CUISINE Japanese, mostly tempura and sushi. **HOURS** 12pm–park close. **DDP** Yes.

PRICES Lunch/Dinner Appetizers: $5–$10. Sushi: $12–$18. Entrées: $20–$34. Kids: $14–$15.

OVERVIEW Tokyo Dining is a sleek, traditional Japanese restaurant with floor-to-ceiling windows looking out at World Showcase Lagoon on one side. It is much quieter and calmer than sister restaurant Teppan Edo, and, without the hibachi grills, is a more traditional dining experience. The menu focuses on sushi, steak, and tempura, with over two dozen selections. Kids' options have been dumbed down in recent memory and include just Chicken Tempura Nuggets or a California Roll.

Tutto Italia

Italy Pavilion, on the left

CUISINE Italian. **HOURS** 11:30am–park close. **DDP** Yes.

PRICES Lunch/Dinner Appetizers: $9–$32. Lunch Entrées: $19–$31. Dinner Entrées: $25–$35. Kids: $10+.

OVERVIEW Featuring murals of ancient Rome amid shimmering chandeliers, Tutto Italia evokes Old World charm inside this traditional, formal Italian restaurant. Your omnipresent server will cater to your every need as you peruse a menu heavy on pasta, prosciutto, and lean protein. Lunch is less expensive than dinner, with several sandwiches and entrees around $20. Unlike most restaurants that offer "Kids Complete Meals" for $9–$12, Italia offers only a la carte options with $6 appetizers, $10 entrees (pizza, spaghetti, mozzarella sticks, chicken tenders), and $6 desserts. The venue is not unique, but service is splendid with high-quality food and a keen eye for detail.

Via Napoli

Italy Pavilion, in the back

CUISINE Pizza (predominantly). **HOURS** 11:30am–park close. **DDP** Yes.

PRICES Lunch/Dinner Appetizers: $8–$28. Salad Entrées: $18–$27. Pasta Entrées: $22–$32. Pizzas: $18–$48+. Kids: $10+.

OVERVIEW Themed to a rustic Neapolitan pizzeria, Via Napoli takes its pizza, which is cooked at 900 degrees in one of three wood-fired ovens, very seriously. So seriously that they import their flour and tomatoes from Italy and source water from a secret spring in Pennsylvania that has the same unique properties as water from the homeland. Prices may seem high at first glance, but a $45 specialty mezzo metro pizza is plenty to feed four to five hungry adults, bringing per-person costs lower than most other Disney restaurants. Napoli is loud and service is frequently impersonal, but stick to the big pizzas and you'll leave satisfied for not much more money than quick service.

DINING AT DISNEY'S HOLLYWOOD STUDIOS

Disney's Hollywood Studios runs the food quality gamut more than any of the other theme parks. Our recommendations are Sci-Fi Dine-In Theater and 50's Prime Time Café, both of which offer richly themed atmospheres and relatively inexpensive fare. Dave prefers the comfort food favorites at 50's Prime Time, while Josh gives the nod to Sci-Fi, with its fun mockup of a drive-in theater and a menu that focuses on inexpensive sandwiches and hamburgers, in addition to steak and ribs. Much more expensive—and with much finer food—is Hollywood Brown Derby, a signature restaurant (two credits on the Dining Plan) where the servers wear tuxedos and the fancy dinner entrées average $39. Lunch offers tremendous value with several sandwiches and other entrees under $25. If you're paying cash, consider an afternoon reservation before 3pm to take advantage of less expensive options. Mama Melrose serves relatively inexpensive basic Italian favorites alongside flatbread pizzas that are higher quality than the nearby quick service pizzeria for only a couple dollars more. Hollywood & Vine is a fun character buffet hosted by singing and dancing Disney Jr. characters for breakfast followed by a seasonally themed lunch and dinner hosted by Minnie and friends.

Quick service options are limited at the Studios with the closures of several eateries in early April 2016 to make way for Star Wars Land. Starring Rolls also closed in February 2017. For the most options, visit Sunset Ranch Market on Sunset Boulevard in front of Tower of Terror, where you'll find everything from burgers to pizza to barbecue to salads to hot dogs to ice cream sundaes. On the downside, the market is made up of five or six individual kiosks that all offer different menu items and seating is all outside.

We're less enthusiastic about most of the other options. Backlot Express is your spot for typical Disney burgers and chicken nuggets, now spiced up a bit with some *Star Wars*-themed entrees. It's richly themed with a lot of covered outdoor seating, but the food is decidedly below average even if the names of some of the items are cute. Dockside Diner is located on Echo Lake and offers a revolving menu of entrees that currently includes hot dogs, sliders, and snacks. Finally, ABC Commissary offers the most air-conditioning, but only a handful of entrees are available at any given time. The popular Chicken & Ribs combo that was once at Cosmic Ray's is available here though, in addition to burgers and chicken nuggets. After 4pm, a fast casual concept takes over where diners order at the register and food is delivered to the table. Entrees are more expensive with a chimichurri steak leading the way at $17.49. Overall, we recommend Starring Rolls and Sunset Ranch Market first, with Backlot Express and ABC Commissary as air-conditioned backups for simpler food.

In addition to the current lineup, Toy Story Land will bring Woody's Lunch Box, a new quick service serving breakfast, lunch, and dinner, when the land opens on June 30, 2018. "Classic American Fare" is promised alongside old-fashioned soda floats and other Toy Story-themed specialties. We expect it to be an instant hit whether or not the food is anything to alert the ranch about.

50's Prime Time Café

Echo Lake, near Hollywood & Vine

CUISINE American comfort food. **HOURS** 11am–park close. **DDP** Yes.

PRICES Lunch/Dinner Appetizers: $8–$12. Entrees: $16–$26. Kids: $9–$11.

OVERVIEW This nostalgic throwback to a simpler time features a number of period piece knick-knacks as well as televisions that show clips from 1950s-era shows. Themed to Mom's kitchen, your servers will take responsibility for raising you right and dole out punishment as required. The kids are sure to get a kick out of your server chastising Dad for wearing his Mickey Ears to the table. A good sense of humor is needed to enjoy the fried chicken, pot roast, meatloaf, and Mom's other comfort foods. Fried chicken, the fresh fish, and the chicken pot pie are your best bets. Request a table with a TV.

Hollywood Brown Derby

End of Hollywood Boulevard, on the right

CUISINE Contemporary American fine dining. **HOURS** 12pm–park close. **DDP** 2 credits.

PRICES Lunch/Dinner Appetizers: $9–$16. Lunch Entrees: $18–$49. Dinner Entrees: $32–$49. Kids: $7–$15.

OVERVIEW Serving up the best food at Hollywood Studios, this signature restaurant focuses on filets of beef and crab cakes rather than burgers and chicken nuggets. A replica of the original Brown Derby, it retains much of the glamour of the 1930s original, with white linen tablecloths, tuxedo-clad servers, and an exquisite eye for detail—if it weren't for all the guests wearing cargo shorts, WDW t-shirts, and Goofy hats. Kids are unlikely to connect here, but they are welcome, with a kids' menu that includes hot dogs, fish sticks, grilled black grouper, and penne pasta. We prefer lunch when a couple of sandwiches in the $18-$25 range are typically offered through 3pm.

When the weather is nice, the outdoor patio area works as a walk-up lounge that offers a menu of tapas and drinks, in addition to the full Brown Derby menu. If there's space, it's a great way to indulge on a margarita flight or glass of wine alongside a famous Cobb Salad or innovative sliders.

Hollywood & Vine

Character meal (Disney Junior favorites at breakfast; Minnie, Mickey, Goofy, Donald, and Daisy at lunch and dinner), at Echo Lake near 50's Prime Time Café

CUISINE American. **DDP** Yes.

HOURS AND PRICES *Breakfast* (8–10:20am): $34 adults, $20 kids. *Lunch* (11:20am–3pm): $54 adults, $32 kids. *Dinner* (3:30pm–late): $54 adults, $32 kids. Pricing may vary by season.

OVERVIEW Featuring Doc McStuffins, Sofia the First, Jake from *Jake and the Neverland Pirates*, and Handy Manny for Play 'n Dine breakfast, this character meal is squarely aimed at kids who are invited to join the characters for singing, dancing, and parading throughout the meal. Food is best at breakfast, which includes all the usual suspects like Mickey waffles, bacon, and made-to-order omelets. Minnie hosts a character meal for lunch and dinner alongside Mickey, Goofy, Donald, and Daisy featuring seasonal specialties that may include items like Pastrami Rubbed Porkloin, Beer Braised Boneless Beef Short Ribs, and Lobster & Shrimp Mac n' Cheese with quality that has steadily improved.

Mama Melrose's Ristorante Italiano

Streets of America, across from the exit to Muppet Vision 3D

CUISINE Americanized Italian. **HOURS** 11:30am–park close. **DDP** Yes.

PRICES Lunch/Dinner Appetizers: $8–$17. Entrees: $18–$33; Kids: $10–$11.

OVERVIEW Mama Melrose herself (not really) serves up Americanized Italian food in this backlot warehouse that's been repurposed (not really) into an eclectic neighborhood eatery. Mama does pizzas ($17 or less), spaghetti ($21), and Chicken alla Parmigiana ($23) better than the more expensive steaks ($33) and Pork Tenderloin ($28). With one menu served all day, Mama is best at dinner. While not as richly themed as Sci-Fi or 50's, Mama's checked curtains, overhead Christmas lights, and old-time photographs of Disney characters create a fun and casual atmosphere. Kids' menu includes cheese pizzas, chicken parmesan, spaghetti, and grilled chicken.

Sci-Fi Dine-In Theater

Streets of America, near ABC Commissary

CUISINE American. **HOURS** 11am–park close. **DDP** Yes.

PRICES Lunch/Dinner: Appetizers: $8–$19. Entrees: $14–$33. Kids: $10–$12.

OVERVIEW Diners sit inside classic car-shaped booths at this indoor "drive-in theater" while old black-and-white movie clips, trailers, and commercials play on a large movie screen ahead. Above, the ceiling is lit up like the night sky, complete with twinkling stars. The menu offers several sandwiches and burgers under $20 all day, making this a great value out-of-pocket at dinner. The more expensive steak ($33) and chicken pasta ($24) don't offer as much value. The restaurant is dark, but kids usually love the carhop shtick and campy clips on screen. Kids' meal choices include grilled salmon, cheeseburgers, popcorn chicken, and pasta.

DINING AT MAGIC KINGDOM

Three of the most popular restaurants in all of Walt Disney World are in Magic Kingdom. The most popular, Be Our Guest, not only serves upscale, French-inspired fare at (relatively) reasonable prices, but it was also the first place in the Magic Kingdom to offer wine or beer with dinner. It operates as a quick service for breakfast from 8–10am and then serves lunch from 10:30am to 2:30pm daily. It's currently the only quick service that not only accepts reservations for breakfast and lunch up to 180 days in advance, but largely requires them if you'd like to dine. They do accept a limited number of walkups if you're unable to secure a reservation, particularly after 2pm. If you're interested in reserving breakfast or lunch, do so as early as possible. Beginning on July 27, 2018, the restaurant will begin exclusively serving a prix-fixe dinner that includes choice of appetizer and entrée along with a dessert platter. A la carte ordering is expected to be unavailable beginning at that time.

Magic Kingdom is also home to two of the most popular character meals: Crystal Palace and Cinderella's Royal Table. The Crystal Palace buffet features Winnie the Pooh, Tigger, Piglet, and Eeyore in a Victorian solarium setting. Royal Table is located inside Cinderella Castle and includes a picture with Cinderella, in addition to four princesses meeting diners tableside. Both are excellent overall experiences for the target audience, but neither is likely to impress on food quality alone.

Liberty Tree Tavern specializes in an all-you-care-to-enjoy platter featuring turkey, pot roast, sliced pork loin, and all the accompaniments for both lunch and dinner. A couple of a la carte entrees are also available for lunch, including a hamburger, fish and chips, pasta, entrée salad, and pot roast, but the turkey is only available as part of the platter. Plaza Restaurant and Tony's Town Square serve one menu all day. We prefer Plaza, where most sandwiches come in under $20 and the quaint Victorian theming charms. We're less enthusiastic about Tony's Town Square after it went to just one menu served all day in June 2015. Many of the less expensive options were eliminated and what's left is generally overpriced and lower quality than most other restaurants, though the remaining pizzas in the $19-$21 range are much better than their quick service counterparts.

Jungle Skipper Canteen is the new kid on the block, having opened in December 2015 in the old Adventureland Veranda space across from Swiss Family Robinson Treehouse. The theming and details in each of the three main dining rooms are a lot of fun and while the food might initially seem exotic, the flavors are more familiar than you might be expecting. Entrée prices are between $17 and $35, so those who enjoy things like whole fried fish and seafood stew may want to give it a closer look. It's definitely a change of pace from other more straightforward options.

The character meals are excellent if you can swing the cost and have members of the group that want to meet the characters. Otherwise, for table service lunch with cash, we like Skipper Canteen and Plaza Restaurant. Dinner is best at Be Our Guest and Plaza Restaurant.

Magic Kingdom quick service is mostly burgers, hot dogs, and chicken nuggets, but variety has improved in recent memory. Josh's recommendation is Columbia Harbour House, where you'll find grilled salmon, lobster rolls, fried shrimp platters, a tuna fish sandwich, and great soups and fresh salads. The second floor seating area is usually quiet because there's no elevator access for strollers and the view of the Rapunzel area is more scenic than most. We also like Pecos Bill in Frontierland, where you'll find a variety of southwestern hits like burritos and tacos, in addition to burgers and nachos. The extensive toppings bar allows diners to load up their food with as much guacamole, sour cream, cheese, salsa, and more as they like.

Cosmic Ray's in Tomorrowland usually consolidates its menu into about ten different entrees that are now available at all three bays, which is a departure from how it used to operate with different offerings at each set of registers. Air-conditioning is plentiful, but this is decidedly average Disney fast food with few exceptions though the falafel burger and Greek salad with chicken are quite good. Pinocchio Village Haus in Fantasyland serves interesting flatbread pizzas, salads, and a chicken parmesan in a sandwich or with pasta for lunch. As of early 2018, the quick service is also testing a buffet with a selection of similar items during dinner. Casey's Corner, serving up a few variations of the usual hot dog, is the last major quick service. About $12 buys you a foot-long all-beef hot dog with your choice of chili/cheese or macaroni & cheese/bacon with fries or apple slices. A plain hot dog and corn dog nuggets are also available.

Several quick service outlets are seasonal, based on expected crowds, or operate with limited hours or menus. Tortuga Tavern across from Pirates of the Caribbean serves hot dogs and barbecue sandwiches. Sleepy Hollow Refreshments serves a fantastic Fruit and Nutella Waffle Sandwich, in addition to a Spicy Chicken Sandwich, waffles, funnel cakes, and more. Gaston's Tavern no longer serves the popular pork shank, instead opting for less-than-stellar temporary fillers. Friar's Nook serves tater tots with a variety of different flavor combinations including Greek, Fiesta, and Chili Cheese. When it's open, Tomorrowland Terrace provides a pretty setting and an ever-changing menu that's often inconsistent. But if it is operating, it's a quick, no-nonsense experience. Other kiosks serve a variety of turkey legs and other snacks.

Overall, we suggest Columbia Harbour House, Be Our Guest, and Pecos Bill for quick service lunch.

Be Our Guest Restaurant

Fantasyland, near Belle's Village

CUISINE French/American. **HOURS** 4pm–late. **DDP** Yes. Beginning July 27, 2018, requires two credits.

PRICES Through July 26, 2018: Dinner Appetizers: $10–$17. Entrées: $22–$36. Kids: $10-$13. (Lunch and breakfast are available as reservable quick service meals. Make a reservation as early as you can because they're severely limited.) Beginning July 27, 2018: Prix fixe: $59 adults, $38 kids (includes tax).

OVERVIEW Set inside Beast's enchanted castle, Be Our Guest is one of Disney's most lavishly themed restaurant and the hardest reservation to snag. With three elaborately themed rooms, you may find yourself in the dark and mysterious West Wing, the expansive two-story Grand Ballroom, or the bright Rose Gallery complete with a spinning Belle and Beast music box. The menu is French-inspired and, through July 26, 2018, includes items like Grilled Pork Chops, Sautéed Shrimp and Scallops with Lobster, Strip Steak, and a Roasted Lamb Chop, all under $40 each. The kids' menu may be too refined for the picky eater and includes Grilled Cheese and Turkey Noodle Soup, Beast Casserole, Grilled Steak, Chicken Brochette, and Grilled Fish of the Day. Beginning July 27, 2018, a 3-course fixed-price menu will take over offering upscale cuisine with a French twist. Appetizer choices will include Escargots or Charred Octopus, in addition to French Onion Soup. Entrée selections include Center Cut Filet Mignon, Poulet Rouge Chicken, Saffron-Infused Seafood Bouillabaisse, Roasted Lamb Chops and Kurobuta Pork Tenderloins. Dessert is a sampler platter. Food and service should remain as good or better than other Magic Kingdom restaurants and it's worth going out of your way to book at 180 days if possible.

Cinderella's Royal Table

Princess character meal, in Cinderella Castle with check-in at rear of castle

CUISINE American. **DDP** Yes (2 credits).

HOURS AND PRICES *Breakfast* (8–10:15am): $63 adults, $39 kids. *Lunch*

(11:40am–2:50pm): $79 adults, $47 kids. *Dinner* (4pm–late): $79 adults, $47 kids.

OVERVIEW By far the most popular character meal, dining here is ordinarily the only way for guests to see the inside of Cinderella Castle. The pricey affair begins in the Grand Hall waiting area and continues through a personal meet and greet with Cinderella on the ground floor. Continue up the red-carpeted spiraling staircase and enter the banquet hall fit for kings and queens. Four princesses greet tableside–usually Ariel, Aurora, Jasmine, and Snow White, and a picture package with Cinderella is available on PhotoPass. Diners select items from a set menu featuring upscale fare. Breakfast choices include the standard plate of bacon, eggs, and sausage, or the more lavish shrimp and grits or grilled beef tenderloin. Lunch and dinner bring items like pork tenderloin or a seasonal vegetarian dish, in addition to the grilled beef tenderloin and shrimp. Food quality and service are decent, but you're paying for the magical atmosphere, princess interaction, and photos. For cash, breakfast is the best and cheapest meal; on the DDP, all meals are two credits. Lunch is the easiest reservation to secure.

The Crystal Palace

Character meal, at end of Main Street on the left, past Casey's Corner

CUISINE American. **DDP** Yes.

HOURS AND PRICES *Breakfast* (8–10:45am): $34 adults, $20 kids. *Lunch* (11:30am–2:45pm): $48 adults, $29 kids. *Dinner* (3pm–late): $48 adults, $29 kids.

OVERVIEW Join Winnie the Pooh, Tigger, Eeyore, and Piglet at this all-you-care-to-enjoy buffet. The bright, airy restaurant is inspired by Victorian greenhouses of the late 1800s, complete with high ceilings, character topiaries, and plenty of natural sunlight. Character interaction is above average, as is the food, which includes Spit-roasted Carved meats, Spice Boiled Shrimp, 20+ salads, and over a dozen desserts. Crystal Palace is often the most over-booked restaurant on property. Even with a reservation, plan to wait 15–30 minutes for your table. For guests paying cash, a late breakfast is the best choice—cheaper than lunch or dinner, shorter waits, and no rush to get through the meal.

Jungle Navigation Co., Ltd. Skipper Canteen

Adventureland near Sunshine Tree Terrace and Swiss Family Robinson Treehouse

CUISINE Primarily Asia, South America, and Africa. **HOURS** 11:30am–late. **DDP** Yes.

PRICES Lunch/Dinner Appetizers: $9–11. Entrees: $18–35. Kids: $10–13.

OVERVIEW Skipper Canteen marries innovative design details with a menu of authentic flavors born from the adventures of the punny Jungle Cruise skippers just down the road. With several unique dining rooms, from the bright and airy colonial-era mess hall to the mysterious secret meeting room used by the famous Society of Explorers and Adventurers, the Canteen may just be Disney's most immersive restaurant yet. Food choices breathe a bit of fresh air into Magic Kingdom's culinary landscape, but the menu may not initially appeal to those uninterested in trying something a little different. But never fear, the flavors are more familiar than you might expect, with the usual chicken, steak, pork, and lamb gussied up with some unique spices and sauces. Kids' choices include flank steak, grilled fish, chicken noodle soup, and macaroni and cheese. Overall, Skipper Canteen is a unique opportunity to try something completely unlike anything else at Magic Kingdom. We recommend giving it a try.

Liberty Tree Tavern

Liberty Square, near Diamond Horseshoe

CUISINE American. **DDP** Yes.

HOURS AND PRICES *Table-service Lunch* (11am–3pm): Appetizers: $7–$15. Entrees: $16–$33. Kids: $9. *Family-style Lunch and Dinner* (11am–close): $38 adults, $21 kids.

OVERVIEW Liberty Tree is a Colonial-themed tavern featuring candelabra chandeliers, brick fireplaces, and rooms filled with artifacts from some of America's most famous patriots. The Patriot's Platter is the featured item for both lunch and dinner and includes turkey, pot roast, and pork loin, with sides of macaroni & cheese, mashed potatoes, and stuffing. The meal begins with salad and ends with a warm dessert. While the Patriot's Platter is the only dinner item, lunch offers a few a la carte entrée options, like pot roast, fish & chips, and a hamburger. These less expensive options are plenty to fill most appetites and may be preferable over the fixed price dinner for those paying cash. Platter food quality varies between average and above average, making other options more appealing in most situations.

The Plaza Restaurant

End of Main Street, on the right

CUISINE American. **HOURS** 11am–late. **DDP** Yes.

PRICES Lunch/Dinner Appetizers: $7–$8. Entrees: $15–$21. Kids: $9–$11.

OVERVIEW The Plaza features Art Nouveau touches inside a turn-of-the-century ice cream parlor. As one of the least expensive theme park sit-down restaurants, Plaza is an excellent choice for cash guests on a budget, particularly at dinner, when sandwiches average $17 and only a couple of entrees come in a touch over $20. Kids' options include a cheese sandwich, burger, chicken strips, turkey sandwich, and PB&J. Food and service are great for the money, but we are not talking highfalutin' dining at this casual eatery.

Tony's Town Square Restaurant

Entry Plaza, on the right

CUISINE Americanized Italian. **HOURS** 11:30am–late. **DDP** Yes.

PRICES Lunch/Dinner Appetizers: $9–$16. Entrees: $20–$32. Kids: $10–11.

OVERVIEW Modeled after Tony's from *Lady and the Tramp*, guests have an opportunity to relive the romance at this casual family trattoria that serves Olive-Garden-quality Italian food in a relaxing atmosphere. Since moving to one menu all day, Tony's has eliminated many of the less expensive lunch entrées that presented a good value to diners. Quality on the higher-end items doesn't justify the prices, and we usually recommend that people head elsewhere. Kids' choices include spaghetti, pizzas, and pasta. Service is conspicuously fast, with most meals complete within an hour.

Dining Reviews: Disney Springs

Formerly known as Downtown Disney, the Disney Springs ("DS" or occasionally "Springs") shopping and entertainment complex includes more than three dozen table service restaurants and quick services, most on the Dining Plan and reservable on My Disney Experience. Some, like The BOATHOUSE, Paradiso 37, Morimoto Asia, House of Blues, STK, Frontera Cocina, Bongos, and Raglan Road, have additional capacity that can be reserved directly with the restaurant over the phone or via OpenTable.com. In addition to restaurants, you'll find many stores, some Disney and others of the variety you'd find at the local mall. There's also the AMC movie theater, Splitsville upscale bowling alley, and House of Blues concert venue. Note that DisneyQuest permanently closed in July 2017 to make way for a new NBA concept and Cirque du Soleil's final performance of La Nouba was December 31, 2017.

Disney Springs features four distinct neighborhoods: The Landing, Marketplace, West Side, and Town Center. The bulk of the new venues are in The Landing and Town Center, while The West Side and Marketplace remain relatively untouched from their former Downtown Disney days.

The West Side. West Side quick service options are diverse, though relatively limited. Bongos Cuban Café includes a small takeout window offering mostly sandwiches with a few traditional Cuban entrees from the kitchen available to-go. With drab outdoor seating as the only option, most guests will bypass it for something more comfortable. House of Blues opened a very good barbecue joint in late 2013 —seating is also outside, but live music permeates the area beginning daily around 4pm and happy hour offers some drink specials from 3pm to 5pm daily. The larger of the two Starbucks locations is here, reliably offering the company's usual beverage and food lineup for about the same cost as your local shop. Finally, Disney has gotten into the food truck game with an area dedicated to food trucks to the right of Bongos. The trucks serve an ever-changing selection of items, some of which are inspired by classic theme park offerings and others designed exclusively for Disney Springs. Closer to Planet Hollywood, you'll find a collection of quick service kiosks that include Haagen-Dazs, Wetzel's Pretzels, Italian Ice, and a kiosk that serves build your own wraps/rice bowls/noodle bowls, beer, and drinks called YeSake. Each offers quick, no-nonsense snacks mostly between three and ten dollars.

On the table service front, Splitsville often has last-minute availability and is an easy walk-up when other restaurants are quoting 45+ minute waits without a reservation, as they often are after 6pm. Its pizza, burgers, and sushi are surprisingly good. House of Blues is economically priced and extremely casual for a nice, no-fuss lunch or dinner. It may be busier if a popular act is scheduled to perform in the club next door. Bongos Cuban Café's menu favors quantity over quality, where you'll find over 50 entrée choices. Grab a mojito from the outdoor bar and look for dinner elsewhere. All of West Side's Wolfgang Puck outlets closed in August 2017 to make way for a Spanish restaurant from Chef José Andrés called Jaleo. A new concept called Wolfgang Puck Bar & Grill will open in the Town Center section sometime in 2018.

The Landing. Once home to Pleasure Island, The Landing shifts focus away from the clubs and dance halls that used to permeate the area and replaces them with restaurants, bars, and outdoor music in the evenings. There are just two holdovers from the previous era: Paradiso 37 and Raglan Road. Portobello survived for a while, but will convert to a new family-style concept called Terralina Crafted Italian in early-to-mid 2018. Raglan Road Irish Pub is best at dinner. While prices are a couple dollars higher here and there, the live music and dancing are worth the extra cost. Paradiso is great for appetizers and margaritas, but the south-of-the-border entrees are overpriced and the atmosphere is lackluster considering the other options. Fulton's Crab House reopened as Paddlefish in February 2017 with a similar focus on steak and seafood. Our favorite meal is the weekend brunch, when items like the Crab Benedict and Monte Cristo are added to the reasonably priced lunch menu.

The BOATHOUSE (the capitalization is part of the name), offering upscale seafood and steaks, in addition to less expensive salads and sandwiches, opened in May 2015 as the first of the major new restaurants. Operated by Gibsons out of Chicago, we like that the menu offers a wide range of prices in a casual atmosphere. Morimoto Asia, brought to you by Chef Masaharu Morimoto of *Iron Chef* fame, opened in September 2015, serving high-end seafood, sushi, and Asian cuisine in an upscale atmosphere. Jock Lindsey's Hangar Bar might be the best themed dining venue on property, which is saying something when it's going up against the likes of T-Rex and Trader Sam's Grog Grotto. Visit for a fun cocktail served in one of their souvenir glasses or a casual bite to eat. All three offer expansive, walk-up bar areas. STK Orlando joined the field in late May 2016, blending expensive a la carte steaks and seafood in a kind of strange, club atmosphere that seems too loud and contemporary to fit in with most of what Disney Springs offers. It may yet find its intended audience. Helmed by celebrity chef Art Smith, Homecomin' Florida followed in mid-July with a menu emphasizing Southern cooking with specialties like fried chicken & doughnuts, cheddar cheese drop biscuits, and fried catfish. Drinks are particularly inspired.

Patina Group, the same parent company that operates the Italian eateries in Epcot and Morimoto Asia in Disney Springs, opened a trifecta of restaurants in late 2017. The Edison is an interesting venue with an industrial gothic-style theme designed to look like a 1920s electric company. Before 9:30pm, it operates like most restaurants offering table service lunch and dinner with plenty of bar and lounge areas spread out on two large floors. After 9:30pm, a night-club atmosphere takes over with live music and entertainment that includes contortionists, jugglers, aerialists, and more. We typically recommend dining elsewhere with those interested in a drink and a show arriving later in the evening.

Two Italian restaurants also join the scene. Better is Maria & Enzo's Ristorante, themed to an elegant eatery inside of an old airline terminal from the 1930s. The cocktail menu is diverse and the lunch menu in particular offers large portions of inspired food at reasonable prices. The atmosphere is a lot of fun. Enzo's Hideaway Bar is less impressive with the speakeasy theme falling flat along with an over-priced menu with food that doesn't match the restaurant next door. We don't recommend much more than a stop for a drink and perhaps a shareable appetizer.

Quick service options at The Landing are slimmer with three main options, each operated by its attached restaurant. Cookes of Dublin is operated by Raglan Road—we like their fish & chips, sandwiches, and other Irish fare a lot for lunch and early dinners, but it gets backed up in the evenings and there's rarely anywhere to sit. Morimoto Asia Street Food, which shares part of its kitchen with Morimoto Asia, serves several of the restaurant's specialties, in addition to bao tacos and lo mein. Seating for both is all outdoors. Pizza Ponte resides next to Maria & Enzo's and serves pizza similar to Via Napoli for around $7 per slice, in addition to sandwiches and desserts. It's a good choice for a quick bite when lines are short, but Blaze Pizza offers more customizability and larger portions. You'll also find a great stop for a cold treat in Vivoli il Gelato and at Tea Traders Café by Joffrey's, which offers a variety of inexpensive snacks and a full menu of teas and other drinks. There's also Erin McKenna's Bakery, specializing in vegan/allergy-friendly sweets, and The Ganachery, serving high-end ganache and chocolate.

Retail in The Landing is largely an after-thought, but some guests may enjoy perusing the footwear at Havaianas or Sanuk, the headwear at Chapel Hats, or the jewelry at Erwin Pearl, among a couple of other largely forgettable outlets.

The Marketplace. The Marketplace section is predominantly retail with a few restaurants and quick services mixed in. Shoppers looking for Disney items should pay special attention to World of Disney, Tren-D, Once Upon A Toy, The Art of Disney, and the Marketplace Co-Op. You'll find just about every imaginable theme park item in one of these stores. The LEGO Store is one of the most popular shops in all of WDW, with a huge variety of sets available for purchase, in addition to some interactive opportunities for kids to put together their own LEGO creations. The Bibbidi Bobbidi Boutique, a salon that specializes in magical makeovers for kids between the ages of 3 and 12, is attached to Once Upon A Toy. Consider booking a reservation if you can't find availability at its sister location inside Cinderella Castle.

The Marketplace is home to two of our favorite Springs' quick services from the Downtown Disney days: Earl of Sandwich and Wolfgang Puck Express. Earl of Sandwich serves excellent hot sandwiches for around eight dollars each, in addition to great tasting sides and desserts. Lines can appear long, but service is surprisingly fast. Wolfgang Puck Express is more expensive than most quick services, but its food is table service quality and a server will deliver your meal and take care of drink refills and other needs. Ghirardelli Ice Cream and Chocolate Shop is one of the best places on property to indulge. Decadent sundaes are $9–$10 and, for those looking to be able to walk out after without assistance, best shared. A walk-up Starbucks is located in front of World of Disney and serves the full drink menu to-go, in addition to select food items. Two quick service kiosks are located on the bridge that connects the LEGO Store area with the Rainforest Café area. B.B. Wolf's Sausage Co. specializes in what you might expect, offering a variety of sausage entrees to-go. Aristocrepes, offering sweet and savory crepes, is another option. But with few tables nearby, none of which are air-conditioned, most guests will likely want to seek out more of a destination eatery.

Two kid favorites operated by the same parent company are located in the Marketplace: Rainforest Café and T-REX. Rainforest is best known for providing dining in a tropical setting complete with Animatronic animals that rival some of Disney's best. T-REX is similar, but with a dinosaur theme. We give the nod to T-REX, partly because it's more likely to be new to a visitor (there are only two locations worldwide) but also because the food and drinks are slightly more inspired. Rainforest, however, is fun and less intimidating for some youngsters than T-REX.

Town Center. The majority of Town Center is new construction built on top of what used to be a parking lot and in essence more than doubles the amount of retail available to those visiting the Springs. It's virtually all mall brands from the likes of UGG, Vera Bradley, Under Armour, Sephora, Pandora, Anthropologie, UNIQLO, Zara, and about 35 more. Many are quick to point out that the aesthetic doesn't do much to differentiate itself from the outlet mall up the street, but that isn't necessarily a bad thing as walkways are wide and vibrant and the overall look is quaint and charming. A full listing of stores is available at DisneySprings.com.

Town Center is also home to Planet Hollywood, which reopened in February 2017 with a new planetary theme and Guy Fieri helming the burger menu. Relatively speaking, pricing is reasonable and many of the sandwiches and burgers are quite good. Still, the interior offers a hodgepodge of thematic elements and less memorabilia. It's a safe bet for anyone with limited tastes.

It also adds Frontera Cocina, a modern Mexican restaurant brought by celebrity chef Rick Bayless and operated by the same company that takes care of dining in the Mexico Pavilion at Epcot and at Coronado Springs. We like to visit the bar area for margaritas and appetizers, but anyone looking for enchiladas, tacos, or other Mexican specialties for lunch or dinner should give it strong consideration.

In addition, three new quick services join the lineup. Blaze Fast-Fire'd Pizza serves up their own creations or with any toppings you like for under $10. The "fast" in the name comes from the fact that it takes less than three minutes to cook your selection. D-Luxe Burger serves up the best quick service hamburgers on property, but a single burger and fry will run you anywhere from $15 to $18, though most people will find an $8 large fry is enough to share between three or more people. The Polite Pig, brought by popular local chefs James and Julie Petrakis, doesn't quite deliver on its potential. We prefer Homecomin', which offers similarly priced food that's more consistent in a more relaxing atmosphere. Amorette's Patisserie next to the Levi's store serves exquisite, handmade desserts and is a must-visit for anyone looking for something sweet that isn't served on a stick. Finally, The Daily Poutine is located near World of Disney and offers a menu of french fries topped with things like gravy & cheese curds or fried yucca, black beans, pulled pork, & queso fresco. Each bowl makes for a very shareable snack, but we're not sure we'd make one into a full meal for one.

Finally, the Coca-Cola Store is mostly retail inside of a large building, but does offer a rooftop bar that offers a variety of cocktails, in addition to fun trays full of Coca Cola soda samples from around the world. For around $15, you can sample sixteen different sodas and eight different ice cream floats with great views of the rest of Disney Springs. Visit for a taste of something different. Literally.

Visiting Disney Springs. A visit to Disney Springs is not necessarily an essential part of a vacation, particularly if it's your first visit. But now that construction has largely concluded and so much is new, many potential guests will want to eye at least one visit, particularly if you're looking to enjoy some of Disney's best restaurants. Our preference is to visit in the late morning through the afternoon when crowds are much lower than the evening, making it easy to visit just about any restaurant without a reservation and enjoy the various shops with few other people around. Take a break at your resort and then consider heading out to enjoy the nighttime entertainment at the theme parks and enjoy crowds as they thin the later it gets.

Disney Springs is served by buses to and from the Disney resort hotels. These buses are slow and can have many stops, so allow more time than you'd think. DS is also served by slow, low-capacity boats from the Port Orleans resorts, Old Key West, and Saratoga Springs, and there's a walking path from Saratoga Springs. After 4pm, Disney offers bus service from the theme parks to Disney Springs. These buses can be incredibly popular around park close, but should prove more convenient than trying to take a bus to a resort and then getting on a Disney Springs bus there. Bus service from Disney Springs to the theme parks is not offered at any time.

Getting to Disney Springs is much easier with Buena Vista Drive expanded to ten lanes and the addition of two parking garages, each of which is relatively easy to access from I-4 or on-property locations. Parking remains complimentary. Still, most Friday and Saturday nights see an influx of visitors beginning around 7pm and continuing for a couple of hours. Avoid these times if possible. Bus transportation has improved with the addition of dedicated lanes and less congestion on the roadways immediately surrounding the Springs, but routes remain convoluted and may still include a lengthy trip over to pick up/drop off at Typhoon Lagoon across the street. For those with watercraft access, we recommend taking advantage of it. Those deciding between their own vehicles or Disney buses will strongly want to consider driving themselves for the quickest trip. But those grabbing cocktails or otherwise not in much of a hurry may still prefer Disney buses. Note that there is only one bus stop now behind the Coca-Cola Store and Planet Hollywood in the Town Center section.

The BOATHOUSE

In between Paradiso 37 and Raglan Road

CUISINE Seafood and steaks. **HOURS** 11am–11pm. **DDP** Yes (2 credits).

PRICES Lunch/Dinner Appetizers: $8–$19. Entrées: $16–$65. Kids: $10.

OVERVIEW Offering picturesque waterfront dining, multiple bars inside and out, and a number of diversely themed dining areas, The BOATHOUSE brings upscale cuisine wrapped up in a casual atmosphere to Disney Springs. Entrees vary wildly in price, from the $20 hamburger and $30 lobster roll all the way up to $65 for a 12-ounce filet mignon or well over $100 for the dry-aged tomahawk steak and lobster for two, neither of which include a side. Fortunately, the kitchen reliably executes the pricier steak and seafood options perfectly, and the quality is a step above just about any Disney-operated restaurant. Those who want to spend considerably less can stick with sandwiches, salads, hamburgers, fried shrimp, fish & chips, and more, most of which are under $20. Despite the high price point on some entrées, the atmosphere is decidedly casual and service is largely unrefined. If you're looking for a quiet, intimate steak dinner, this isn't it, but some people may prefer the lack of pretention.

Bongos

West Side, across from Splitsville

CUISINE Cuban. **HOURS** 11am–11pm or Midnight. **DDP** Yes.

PRICES Lunch/Dinner Appetizers: $5–$24. Entrées: $22–$45. Kids: $6–$9.

OVERVIEW Enter this two-story 1950s-era Havana nightclub and dine on one of over 50 Cuban specialties, including Cuban Churrasco, Mojo Roasted Chicken, Seafood Paella, and Criollo Seafood. Or pull up a seat at one of three bars, including one housed inside of a 75-foot tall pineapple sculpture, and select from a cocktail list including everything from Bongos Original Mojito to a 45-ounce Cuban Rum Runner. Kids are welcome all day, but it's a loud and boisterous crowd on weekends and late nights when live music is prevalent and dancing encouraged. Service is spotty, but food is prepared well and drinks are excellent.

Crossroads at House of Blues

West Side, across from DisneyQuest

CUISINE Southern American. **HOURS** 11am–11pm on weekdays, 1am on weekends. **DDP** Yes.

PRICES Lunch/Dinner Appetizers: $7–$16. Entrées: $13–$26. Kids: $9. Sunday Gospel Brunch: $46 adults, $27 kids.

OVERVIEW Celebrity Chef Aaron Sanchez took over the menu in July 2011, "incorporating flavors from around the world" in the process. The menu still favors southern favorites like jambalaya, voodoo shrimp, and buttermilk fried chicken, but you'll find inexpensive flatbread pizzas, sandwiches, and pastas, too. Heavy on edgy religious artwork that may appeal to some more than others, Blues is supposed to be themed to a shack on the side of a road down in the New Orleans bayou. Free live music inside the restaurant on weekends after 10pm. Calmer and kid friendly until then.

The Edison

The Landing, across from STK Orlando

CUISINE American. **HOURS** 11:30am–1am or 2am. **DDP** Yes.

PRICES Lunch/Dinner Appetizers: $12–$17. Lunch Entrées: $17–$20. Dinner Entrées: $22–$38. Kids: $15.

OVERVIEW Themed to a 1920s electric company with an aesthetic somewhere between steampunk and industrial-gothic, The Edison serves up American comfort food favorites like meatloaf, steak, burgers, and fried chicken in an imaginative atmosphere. We think couples and adults 21+ will prefer the late night vibe when live music and unique acts like caberet dancers and contortionists entertain those nibbling on appetizers and enjoying cocktails from the extensive menu. Dinner food is overpriced if you're not visiting in the evening when the entertainment takes hold, but the lunch menu features several salads and sandwiches under $20 if you'd like to check the space out but aren't as comfortable with the nighttime energy. We were initially hesitant about the after-10pm crowd ourselves, but found a fun, welcoming atmosphere just like everywhere else in Disney Springs not-named-STK. Consider stopping for a bite and a drink, but it may not be the best place to plunk down $35+ on a steak.

Enzo's Hideaway

The Landing, across from Planet Hollywood and underneath Maria & Enzo's

CUISINE Italian. **HOURS** 11:30am–11pm. **DDP** Yes.

PRICES Lunch/Dinner Appetizers: $8–$19. Lunch Entrées: $21–$27. Dinner Entrées: $24–$37. Kids: $15.

OVERVIEW Enzo's Hideaway is supposed to be themed to Prohibition-era rum-running tunnels, but the space ends up being much more cavernous and much less interesting than one might hope to see. Instead of going all-in on the speakeasy vibe, the restaurant is large, open, and boring, and the food is overpriced and unimaginative. We could see stopping for a drink when other venues are crowded, but food is better elsewhere and the atmosphere is forgettable.

Frontera Cocina

Town Center, across the water from Morimoto Asia and across from Sprinkles

CUISINE Mexican. **HOURS** 11am–11pm. **DDP** Yes.

PRICES Lunch/Dinner Appetizers: $4–$14. Entrées: $14–$45. Kids: $9.

OVERVIEW Celebrity Chef Rick Bayless, who operates around ten Mexican restaurants mostly in the Chicago area, brings what is easily Disney's best Mexican restaurant to Disney Springs. The menu is relatively diverse, offering three different guacamoles in addition to ceviche and tostadas to start. Entrees like the Pepito Torta (slow-cooked shortribs, artisan jack cheese, black beans, pickled jalapeños, arugula, cilantro cream, chipotle salsa, taqueria salad) and Chicken Tacos both impress for under $20 as do the Carnitas and Carne Asada for a few dollars more. The food is much more vibrant than the restaurant, but you might care about that less after a couple margaritas, which are priced on the high side at $15–$19. Consider drinks and appetizers or split an entrée at the bar for the best value. Frontera is very good, but perhaps not unique enough to demand a visit if you're just stopping at Disney Springs for a single meal.

Homecomin'—Florida Kitchen and Shine Bar

The Landing, across from Morimoto Asia

CUISINE Southern American. **HOURS** 11am–11pm. **DDP** Yes.

PRICES Lunch/Dinner Appetizers: $10–$20. Entrées: $16–$32. Kids: $9.

OVERVIEW Chef Art Smith is perhaps best known as the personal chef of Oprah Winfrey, but those that appreciate his history with Disney will remind you that he completed an internship with their College Program as well. Homecomin' Florida showcases the state's fresh flavors with appetizers like house-made pimento cheese hushpuppies served with red jalapeño jelly. The deviled eggs, which arrive in a precious carton of six, taste as good as they are cute. But many will want to go straight for the signature fried chicken served in a sandwich for $17 or with doughnuts for $26 or creamy mashed potatoes and a cheddar drop biscuit for $28. Draft beer offers a nice variety of local choices and the cocktail list is inspired and reasonably priced. While the restaurant is homely and rustic, service is impeccable with a keen eye for detail and a friendly smile. It's one of our favorite new restaurants.

Jock Lindsey's Hangar Bar

The Landing in between The BOATHOUSE and Paradiso 37

CUISINE Small plate bar food. **HOURS** 12pm–1am. **DDP** No.

PRICES Lunch/Dinner Appetizers: $9–$16.

OVERVIEW As you may or may not be aware, Jock Lindsey is Indiana Jones' longtime pilot and the bar is ornately themed to his hangar which was recently converted into a bar for the enjoyment of his fellow members of the Society of Explorers and Adventurers. The atmosphere inside is rich and worth a stop for those with even a passing interest in Indiana Jones, though we think the food and drink options are better at nearby Morimoto Asia and The BOATHOUSE. Still, for $10–$12 you can order a round of easily-shareable appetizers like popcorn chicken, queso fundido, sliders, and a whole lot more. The diverse specialty drinks are a little less expensive than other locations, but they rarely pack a punch. Consider a draft beer.

Maria & Enzo's Ristorante

The Landing, across from STK and next to The Edison

CUISINE Italian. **HOURS** 11:30am–11pm. **DDP** Yes.

PRICES Lunch/Dinner Appetizers: $9–$18. Lunch Entrées: $18–$36. Dinner Entrées: $24–$42. Kids: $15.

OVERVIEW As the story goes, Maria & Enzo opened their elegant trattoria inside of this 1930s airline terminal, retrofitting it with floor-to-ceiling windows and a grand staircase for good measure. The atmosphere is slightly upscale, but still perfectly welcoming and it's fun to look around the restaurant and take in the bright posters and elegant details. The menu is executed well with a focus on pasta and parmigiana, in addition to steak, fish, and seafood. The Veal Parmigiana is excellent, as is the Busiate con Granchio with Spiral-shaped Pasta, Lump Crab, Yellow Cherry Tomato, and Parsley in a light citrus sauce. Start with the Calamari or Fried Sicilian Cheese and you're in for a treat. There are a lot of opportunities to eat Italian at Walt Disney World, but this is a safe bet if you're in the mood for good, familiar food and large portions in a pleasant atmosphere.

Morimoto Asia

The Landing across from Raglan Road and The BOATHOUSE

CUISINE Pan-Asian. **HOURS** 11:30am–1am. **DDP** Yes, two credits.

PRICES Lunch/Dinner Appetizers: $6–$17. Entrées: $16–$48. Sushi: $8–$14. Kids: $12.

OVERVIEW Officially helmed by Iron Chef Masaharu Morimoto and operated by Patina Group, the same company behind the restaurants in the Italy Pavilion at Epcot, Morimoto Asia opened in October 2015 to great fanfare. The restaurant is sleek and stylish, with impressive chandeliers said to resemble jellyfish. We prefer the restaurant's less expensive noodle and rice options with the Singapore laksa noodles and chatsu pork ramen leading the way. Sushi is on point, but the eight choices available in the main dining room all play it safe. Beer and cocktails are above average in price and quality. Consider a more casual meal in one of the two expansive bar areas.

Paddlefish

The Landing, between Portobello and T-Rex

CUISINE Steak and seafood. **HOURS** 11:30am–11pm. **DDP** Yes, two credits.

PRICES Lunch/Dinner Appetizers: $6–$20. Lunch Entrées: $12–$47+. Dinner Entrées: $25–$49+. Weekend Brunch Entrees: $16–$23. Kids: $9–$15.

OVERVIEW Paddlefish opened in February 2017 in place of Fulton's Crab House in a refurbished steamboat on the water. Still operated by Levy Restaurants, the problems with uneven service and questionable menu execution that plagued Fulton's seem to linger. On the plus side, the seafood is among the freshest on property and should impress. We like to visit the outdoor lounge on the third floor after it opens at 5pm for the most panoramic views and to share a couple of appetizers and drinks. Best are the Lobster Corn Dogs, Crab Fries (hand-cut potatoes, lump blue crab, Louie dressing), and Beef Skewers. Also a great weekend brunch stop, the Bloody Mary is out of this world and the Monte Cristo and Breakfast Burger (9 ounce proprietary blend, fried egg, hash browns, candied bacon, cheddar cheese, sweet onion jam, shredded lettuce, and tomato, served on brioche) impress on size and quality. Unfortunately, inconsistent food quality and service make it difficult to recommend given the high price point for that one "date night" style meal.

Paradiso 37

Old Pleasure Island, between Portobello and West Side

CUISINE North/South American. **HOURS** 11am–midnight on weekdays, 1am on weekends. **DDP** Yes.

PRICES Lunch/Dinner Appetizers: $5–$18. Entrées: $16–$40. Kids: $8.

OVERVIEW The appetizers and margaritas are better than the entrées at this waterfront restaurant that focuses on cuisine of the Americas. Much busier after 6pm when the live music starts outside, Paradiso is best experienced without kids, who are unlikely to be impressed by the Latin flair or tequila tower stacked with 37 varieties. Walk-up tables are usually available, as are seats at one of the three bars.

Planet Hollywood Observatory

West Side, across from entrance to AMC Fork-and-Screen Theater

CUISINE American; lots of burgers and sandwiches. **HOURS** 11am–11:45pm. **DDP** Yes.

PRICES Lunch/Dinner Appetizers: $11–$18. Entrées: $15–$30. Kids: $10.

OVERVIEW Planet Hollywood reopened with more of a planetarium theme in February 2017 after a lengthy refurbishment that brought many changes, including a burger menu helmed by celebrity chef Guy Fieri and the addition of an expansive outdoor bar. All under $20 each, the burgers and sandwiches should satisfy any appetite. We like the gigantic $15 Pimento Grilled Cheese best, followed by the $18 Bird is the Word fried chicken sandwich and $19 Mayor of Flavortown burger (with grilled pastrami, Swiss cheese, caraway slaw, pickles, Dijon mustard, and the restaurant's signature donkey sauce on a garlic-buttered pretzel bun). While miles away from high class dining, Planet Hollywood delivers on what it sets out to accomplish and those looking for a wide variety of comfort food favorites may prefer its atmosphere as one of the most casual restaurants on property. Inside, it's quite loud with top 40 hits playing nonstop and music videos projected onto the walls. Consider requesting an outdoor table offering a scenic views of Disney Springs and look at the various pieces of memorabilia on the way out. You'll need to walk around to see much of anything anyway.

Portobello

The Landing, to the left of The BOATHOUSE

Portobello closed in April 2017 to make way for Terralina Italian Crafted, a new restaurant that will still be helmed by "Top Chef Master" Tony Mantuano and operated by Levy Restaurant Group. Expected to have more of a focus on traditional flavors served family-style, we expect food to taste a little fresher with a bit more nuance than its straightforward predecessor. Look for it to open in spring 2018.

Raglan Road

The Landing, near Fulton's and Portobello

CUISINE Irish. **HOURS** 11am–1am. **DDP** Yes.

PRICES Lunch Appetizers: $13–$27. Lunch Entrées: $15–$24. Dinner Appetizers: $7–$27. Dinner Entrées: $17–$30. Kids: $8–$12.

OVERVIEW The restaurant features a live band playing Irish songs, popular ballads, and pub classics alongside traditional Irish jigs beginning at 6pm nightly (except for Sunday, when the live band plays only during brunch). Each of the four bars, some over 130 years old, were imported directly from Ireland. Celebrity Chef Kevin Dundon is no longer attached to the restaurant, but the menu still includes many of his recipes including Shepherd's

Pie, Guinness & Onion Bangers on Mash, and Roasted Chicken all under $25 each for lunch or dinner. Add Guinness, Smithwick's, and a dozen more beers on draft, and you have yourself an authentically Irish good time. Kids' entrees at this family-friendly, highly-recommended restaurant include steak, shepherd's pie, burgers, and macaroni-and-cheese. Nearly everything, from the food to the service to the beer, is excellent. A cult favorite among Disney World guidebook authors.

Rainforest Café

Marketplace, near Earl of Sandwich

CUISINE American. **HOURS** 11am–11pm or 12am. **DDP** Yes.

PRICES Lunch/Dinner Appetizers: $8–$20. Entrées: $15–$36. Kids: $9.

OVERVIEW See the Animal Kingdom table service reviews for background info on this raucous chain restaurant. The Disney Springs location is extremely popular with kids and online reservations are hard to come by because only part of the inventory is released to Disney. Call the restaurant directly at 407-827-8500 to book, or visit before 4pm when walk-ups don't require 60+ minute waits. The Lava Lounge next door offers the same menu without any of the restaurant's antics. The water view at the lounge is pleasant for couples, but most families will want to eat inside where the action is.

Splitsville Luxury Lanes

West Side, across from Bongos

CUISINE American, Sushi, Pizza. **HOURS** 11:30am–11pm or later. **DDP** Yes.

PRICES Lunch/Dinner Appetizers: $7–$16. Sushi: $11–$18. Entrées: $15–$27. Kids: $7–$8.

OVERVIEW The food at Splitsville is not quite as luxurious as the bowling setup (your've never read a sentence like that before, we bet), but it does offer a bevy of options, including a dozen freshly made sushi rolls, a half-dozen pizzas, a dozen sandwiches and salads, rice bowls, and more. The pricier entrées are best skipped in favor of sushi and pizza, which are executed quite well. The nicest part of dining in this 50,000 square foot complex loosely themed to 1960s kitsch is the lack of a wait for a table when Disney Springs is crawling with people. Eat outside to get away from the bowling noise and stick to beer—the cocktails are overpriced and watered down.

STK Orlando

The Landing, across from Paradiso 37

CUISINE Steak and seafood. **HOURS** 11:30am–11:55pm. **DDP** 2 credits.

PRICES Brunch Entrées: $12–$27. Dinner Appetizers: $10–$19. Dinner Entrées: $19–$63+. Kids: $10.

OVERVIEW STK is a significant departure away from anything else at Walt Disney World, blending an ultra-modern steakhouse aesthetic with an atmosphere that resembles more of a Las Vegas club than a traditional steakhouse. With a live DJ appearing at 8pm nightly in the main dining room, meals are often loud and bustling as partiers mingle about at the same time families with young kids are trying to enjoy a meal. But STK does steak very well, offering a wide variety of cuts cooked to your specifications, in addition to some seafood entrees. Recent additions include less expensive options like a Fried Chicken Sandwich for $19 and a Wagyu Beef Burger for $24. Unlike most other steakhouses, side dish portions are incredibly small for around $10 each. We prefer The BOATHOUSE for higher quality beef at a restaurant where we can hear ourselves think, but STK in the company of friends is a unique venue that some people much cooler than these Disney World book authors may prefer. Just be aware of what you're getting into at these prices.

T-REX Café

Marketplace, near the Lego Store

CUISINE American. **HOURS** 11am–11pm or 12am. **DDP** Yes.

PRICES Lunch/Dinner Appetizers: $8–$20. Entrées: $17–$35. Kids: $9.

OVERVIEW Operated by the same parent company as Rainforest Café, T-REX replaces Rainforest's drizzle with thundering meteor showers and singing birds with a massive undulating octopus and life-sized Animatronic dinosaurs. The T-REX menu offers a staggering number of items, mostly of decent quality and universally in large amounts. Stick with the lower-priced fare or chance a regrettable $35 steak. Younger kids may be scared of the dinosaurs, noise, fire, and occasional darkness, but most kids between the ages of six and twelve love the atmosphere. With apprehensive kids, consider a walk through the restaurant before committing to a meal, or request a table near the entrance. Call the restaurant directly at 407-828-8739 to book because few slots are offered to Disney Reservations.

Wine Bar George

Across from Jock Lindsay's Hangar Bar and next to Raglan Road

Master Sommelier George Miliotes, who helped open California Grill back in 1995, opens a new 2-story wine bar in spring 2018. We expect one of the best wine lists at Walt Disney World, in addition to some tasty, shareable appetizers and small plates, probably at prices higher than we'd like to pay.

Dining Reviews: The Disney Resorts

Disney's resorts offer the majority of the best restaurants on property, whether we're discussing five-star dining at Victoria & Albert's at the Grand Floridian or the rootin' tootin' good time that is hollering along to Hoop-Dee-Doo Revue at Fort Wilderness. We provide reviews of all these meals in the material that follows.

Unfortunately, resort-to-resort travel is often inconvenient because Disney does not offer resort-to-resort buses. Guests relying on Disney transportation from the values and moderates in particular will need to wait for a bus to a theme park or Disney Springs, then wait for a bus for the resort they're headed to, and then take the time to ride the bus over to the resort and find the restaurant. Disney recommends allowing 90 minutes each way for such travel. And they're not wrong. Travel is particularly taxing for early morning breakfasts when buses run less frequently (check with your concierge for the schedule) and for late night dinners when the theme parks may already be closed, limiting transfer options.

There are some alternatives. Taxis are usually stationed outside the resort or bell services will be glad to call, but they add $15-$40 roundtrip to the cost of the meal. Better potentially is Disney's Minnie Van service, which offers on-demand pickup service from the resorts and theme parks. For a flat $25 fee, service is available to and from anywhere that Disney buses operate on-property. We prefer Uber and Lyft, both of which offer on-demand transportation. A ride that would cost $30 in a Mears taxi would cost around $11 with Uber. Guests already renting cars have it easiest and can drive directly to the resort with the help of signs and GPS.

We have some tips on reducing the hassle using Disney transportation.

- Guests staying at the monorail resorts—Contemporary, Polynesian, and Grand Floridian—are connected by the resort monorail and visiting any of the monorail resorts from any other will only take about 15 minutes each way.
- Guests staying at the Contemporary, Wilderness Lodge, or Fort Wilderness are connected by boat and visiting any of the resorts from any other will only take about 15-30 minutes each way.
- Guests staying at the Epcot resorts—Beach Club, Yacht Club, BoardWalk Inn, Swan, and Dolphin—are all within a 15-minute walk from each other and watercraft transportation is also available between the resorts.
- If you find yourself at Magic Kingdom, you can take the resort monorail to any of the monorail resorts, or watercraft to Fort Wilderness or Wilderness Lodge.

- If you find yourself at Epcot, you can exit the park via the International Gateway between the United Kingdom and France Pavilions and either walk or take the boat to any Epcot resorts.

Particularly for first-time visitors relying on Disney transportation away from the monorail or Epcot area, our strong advice is eat where you otherwise plan to be in order to reduce the time commitment of transferring from one place to another. If you simply can't resist a breakfast with Mickey at the Contemporary or a romantic dinner at the Grand Floridian, that's fine, too. But take a Minnie Van or Uber/Lyft and consider it the low cost of doing business versus the high cost of your time.

DINING AT DISNEY'S ANIMAL KINGDOM LODGE

Boma - Flavors of Africa

Take the elevator to the first floor

CUISINE African-inspired. **DDP** Yes.

HOURS AND PRICES *Breakfast* (7:30–11:00am): $29 adults, $16 kids. *Dinner* (5-9:30pm): $46 adults, $26 kids.

OVERVIEW Featuring a robust dinner menu of over 50 African-inspired specialties, Boma is a favorite of many for its wide selection and high quality, unique options. Best are the soups and roasted meats, but just about everything from the seasonal salads to the zebra dome desserts are excellent. Kids enjoy the full buffet in addition to items like macaroni-and-cheese, mashed potatoes, pasta, and baked chicken legs. Breakfast is more pedestrian with the usual selection of French toast, Mickey waffles, bacon, sausage, and the like. The only downside is that very few tables in the African-marketplace-themed dining room have views of the savannas outside.

Jiko - The Cooking Place

Take the elevator to the first floor

CUISINE African. **HOURS** 5:30–10pm. **DDP** 2 credits.

PRICES Appetizers: $12–$22. Dinner Entrées: $30–$49. Kids: $9–$17.

OVERVIEW Jiko isn't afraid to use a liberal amount of exotic spices on many of its constantly changing menu items. Flatbreads, which are typically topped with things like duck confit or shrimp, virtually always impress. Filet mignon, fresh fish, and short ribs are menu mainstays. Kids have a wide range of options from macaroni-and-cheese or cheese pizza to fresh grilled fish and grilled steak. The main dining room, themed to the opening scenes from *The Lion King*, is elegant and reserved. This is one of the best date-night restaurants on property. Request a window table deep inside the restaurant to get away from the lobby noise.

Sanaa

In the Kidani Village wing (at Kidani, take the elevator to the first floor)

CUISINE African/Indian. **HOURS** *Lunch* 11:30am-3pm; *Dinner* 5–9:30pm. **DDP** Yes.

PRICES Lunch/Dinner Appetizers: $8–$15. Lunch Entrées: $16–$26. Dinner Entrées: $19–$33. Kids: $10–$12.

OVERVIEW Sanaa features expansive savanna views in a fun, low-key dining room themed to an African spice market. The Indian Bread Service with nine accompaniments is not to be missed. Excellent Tandoori options reliably come in under $20, in addition to slightly more expensive chicken and steak. Kids' options are a little out there and include items like Butter Chicken and Shrimp with Quinoa. The lounge is open until midnight. Request a window table during daylight for the best views.

Note: In late 2016 Sanaa began serving a simple fast-casual style quick service breakfast from 7–10am. While some interesting African flavors are available, it is a convenience to Kidani Village guests (who otherwise would have to go to the main Animal Kingdom Lodge to find breakfast) rather than a destination meal like lunch and dinner here are.

DINING AT DISNEY'S BEACH CLUB RESORT

Beaches and Cream Soda Shop

Behind Stormalong Bay

CUISINE American burgers, sandwiches, and ice cream. **HOURS** 11am–11pm. **DDP** Yes.

PRICES Lunch/Dinner Entrées: $12–$16. Kids: $9–$10.

OVERVIEW Themed to a boardwalk-style ice cream shop, Disney's smallest table service restaurant offers inexpensive burger and sandwich fare in a fun, bright setting. Most people eating here visit for the giant ice cream sundaes, which arrive with a ton of fun toppings. The restaurant began accepting reservations in late 2013, cutting down waits from as much as two hours to just a few minutes. The $32 Kitchen Sink Dessert, featuring eight scoops of ice cream and an entire bottle of whipped cream, is a favorite tradition of many returning visitors. An ice-cream to-go window is also available.

Cape May Café

Character meal (breakfast only); inside the lobby to the left of check-in

CUISINE American character breakfast with Minnie, Goofy, Donald in beach outfits. Dinner buffet is heavy on seafood. **DDP** Yes.

HOURS AND PRICES *Breakfast* (7:30–11:00am): $34 adults, $20 kids. *Dinner* (5–9pm): $49 adults, $26 kids.

OVERVIEW Like the rest of the resort, Cape May Café is themed to a comfortable beachside setting with inviting pastel colors. Breakfast is a character affair with the usual suspects like waffles and pancakes, in addition to elevated offerings like smoked salmon, creamy cheddar grits, and sliced capicola. Dinner is more expensive and characterless, with an emphasis on seafood paella, peel-and-eat shrimp, snow crab legs, salmon, clams, and mussels, in addition to salads and roasted meats. Kid options include chicken nuggets and macaroni. Both meals are above average, though the lack of Mickey at breakfast is disappointing.

DINING AT DISNEY'S BOARDWALK

Big River Grille and Brewing Works

On the end, near Jellyrolls

CUISINE American. **HOURS** 11am–11pm. **DDP** Yes.

PRICES Lunch/Dinner Appetizers: $5–$15. Entrées: $12–$27. Kids: $9.

OVERVIEW Big River is the only working brewpub on property, offering five beers brewed on-site, in addition to a robust menu featuring less expensive sandwich fare along with more expensive steaks and ribs. The less expensive burgers and sandwiches are more reliable than the more expensive items. Beer is unique and decent, but not up to snuff compared to some of the better bottled craft brews available at other restaurants. Diners can sit inside the family-friendly restaurant or outside on the boardwalk overlooking Crescent Lake. Most sports and beer fans will want to take a look at ESPN Club a few hundred feet away. The restaurant otherwise has very little kid appeal, though its menu includes similar burgers and sandwiches.

ESPN Club

Closest to Epcot

CUISINE American. **HOURS** 11am or 12pm–11pm. **DDP** Yes.

PRICES Lunch/Dinner Appetizers: $8–$24. Entrées: $15–$25. Kids: $8–$11.

OVERVIEW With around 100 video monitors showing every televised sporting event imaginable, ESPN is heaven for anyone looking to catch a game while on vacation. Food and drink are better and more varied than you might expect, though the entrées are primarily burgers and sandwiches. ESPN Club is popular during major sporting events and all day Saturday and Sunday during football season. Arrive early or take advantage of the $50+ reserved seats, which includes $50+ toward food and drink.

Flying Fish

To the right of Trattoria al Forno.

CUISINE Steak and Seafood. **HOURS** 5–9:30pm. **DDP** 2 Credits.

PRICES Appetizers: $10–$22. Entrées: $34–$60. Kids: $13–$17.

OVERVIEW Flying Fish reopened in August 2016 in the same location on the BoardWalk. The focus is still on fresh seasonal flavors, locally sourced ingredients, and sustainable seafood, but the interior replaces the whimsy of its predecessor with a more luxurious, sophisticated look. Because Flying Fish can't rely on fireworks views or some other gimmick, the focus is entirely on the food, which elevates it above most Disney signature restaurants on quality and presentation. The luxurious touches inside and expansion of the cocktail list also make this a great date night restaurant, but kids may not connect with the subtle details.

Trattoria al Forno

In between Flying Fish and ESPN Club

CUISINE Italian. **HOURS** *Breakfast* 7:30–12:05pm; *Dinner* 5–10pm. **DDP** Yes.

PRICES Character Breakfast: $36 adults, $21 kids. Dinner Appetizers: $8–$14. Personal Pizzas: $17–$19. Dinner Entrées: $20–$41. Kids: $10–$13.

OVERVIEW Trattoria al Forno replaced Kouzzina by Cat Cora in December 2014, bringing the number of Italian restaurants in the area to four. The dinner menu focuses on Italian classics like fried calamari, shaved Italian carved meats, baked lasagna, and chicken breast alla parmigiana, in addition to wood-grilled steak and innovative pizzas. On April 2, 2017, Rapunzel, Flynn, Ariel, and Eric began hosting a character breakfast with some Italian touches. The meal begins with a fresh fruit salad or mixed berry parfait to accompany a "frying pan of pastries including braided bread." That's followed by choice of entrée including a Calzone with scrambled Eggs, Soppressata, Bacon, Sausage, Blend of Cheeses and Sunday Gravy or Oak-Grilled Steak with Cheesy Egg Torte, Asparagus, Crispy Onions and Roasted Potatoes. This is the only location where Flynn and Eric typically greet guests and it's proving to be one of the most difficult reservations to secure.

DINING AT DISNEY'S CARIBBEAN BEACH RESORT

Shutters

Old Port Royale, on the far end of the food court

The table service restaurant at Caribbean Beach, Shutters, closed (as did the quick service offerings and shops here) in May 2017. These facilities will be replaced by extensive new waterfront dining expected to open in mid to late 2018. Until then, the temporary dining facilities in place do not include any table service options. See the Caribbean Beach review in chapter 5 for more details on dining at Caribbean Beach.

DINING AT DISNEY'S CONTEMPORARY RESORT

California Grill

Check in on 2nd floor, ride designated elevator to the restaurant on the 15th floor

CUISINE American, Sushi. **HOURS** 5–10pm. **DDP** 2 credits.

PRICES Appetizers: $14–$21. Sushi: $22–$26. Dinner Entrées: $37–$49. Kids: $9–$18.

OVERVIEW Best known for its wide-angle views of Magic Kingdom from the 15th floor of the Contemporary, California Grill underwent renovations throughout much of 2013. The restaurant retains its emphasis on $50 steaks, in addition to many of the same excellent, albeit pricey, sushi dishes. Schedule a meal about an hour before the fireworks begin. Guests may watch the show from their table or head outside to the balcony. It's first come, first served at the large bar and lounge area in the middle of the restaurant, making it perfect for drinks and appetizers closer to when the restaurant opens. Check on the second floor for availability. California Grill is great for a date night, but kids are more common than at other signature restaurants due to the excellent fireworks view. Kids may choose between cheese pizza, pasta, chicken, or grilled beef tenderloin.

Disney introduced a weekly Sunday brunch in early 2016 at a cost of $80 for adults and $48 for those between the ages of 3 and 11. Diners have an opportunity to interact with chefs during the meal as they prepare dishes in the open kitchen. Arrive hungry as there is an all-you-care-to-enjoy component with small bites and sushi, in addition to a plated entrée that includes the likes of Grilled Hanger Steak or Eggs Benedict with Butter-poached Maine Lobster. A complimentary sparkling wine cocktail will be served as the host walks you to your table and they are bottomless throughout the meal. It's going to be a splurge for most, but the experience can't be replicated anywhere else.

Chef Mickey's

Character meal, 4th floor Concourse

CUISINE American. Character meal with Mickey, Minnie, Goofy, Donald, and Pluto in chef gear. **DDP** Yes.

HOURS AND PRICES *Breakfast* (7–11:30am): $43 adults, $26 kids. *Brunch* (11:30am–2:30pm): $43 adults, $26 kids. *Dinner* (5–9:30pm): $53 adults, $32 kids.

OVERVIEW Consistently the most popular and one of the most expensive single-credit character meals on property, this is the only place you'll find Mickey, Minnie, Donald, Goofy, and Pluto together greeting diners tableside. Meals are a crowded, raucous affair with the monorail whizzing by just one floor up, but kids don't seem to mind and parents are happy to take pictures of the Fab Five without having to wait an hour in the sun. Breakfast is the strongest and least expensive meal with all of the usual suspects, in addition to Pixie-Dusted Challah French Toast, Minnie's Breakfast Pizza, and Pluto's Cheese Blintz. Brunch swaps things like oatmeal for peel-and-eat shrimp and salads in place of cereals, in addition to carved ham instead of bacon and ribs and salmon instead of biscuits and pancakes. Dinner food quality is below average, but there's a wide variety of roasted meats, soups, and salads, in addition to an all-you-can-eat ice cream bar. Brunch may be a good option for those looking to take some time away from the parks during the busy afternoons and also makes securing a reservation easier. Visit only if the characters are important.

The Wave of American Flavors

First floor on the left, past the check-in area

CUISINE American. **HOURS** Breakfast 7:30–11am; Lunch 11:30am–2pm; Dinner 5–9:30pm. **DDP** Yes.

PRICES Breakfast Entrées: $10–$17. Breakfast Buffet: $25 adult, $14 kid. Lunch/Dinner Appetizers: $9–$15. Lunch Entrées: $14–$20. Dinner Entrées: $18–$34. Kids: $9–$13.

OVERVIEW With more emphasis on healthy food and fresh, locally sourced ingredients than almost any other restaurant on property, The Wave offers an innovative menu for all three meals. The breakfast buffet is excellent, with a wide array of fresh fruit, made-to-order omelets, a smoked salmon bar, and all the traditional accompaniments like pancakes, sausage, and waffles. Less hungry patrons can order a la carte for not much more than the counter-service Contempo Café upstairs. Lunch focuses mostly on sandwiches, burgers, and salads under $20. Only a few tables are usually occupied unless convention goers take over the space. Dinner brings near signature quality fare at one-credit prices. Same-day reservations are usually easy to secure.

DINING AT DISNEY'S CORONADO SPRINGS RESORT

Las Ventanas

Connected to Rix Lounge on the walk to the convention area

CUISINE Mostly American with some southwest touches. **HOURS** Breakfast 7–10:30am; Lunch 11am–2pm. **DDP** Yes, one credit.

PRICES Breakfast Entrées: $10–$19. Lunch Appetizers: $8–$12. Entrées: $14–$19. Kids: $8–$10.

OVERVIEW Whether the dark, windowless space is small and cramped or cozy and intimate is perhaps a matter of personal taste, but service is surprisingly friendly and food shockingly flavorful at a restaurant that would otherwise seem like an afterthought. Maya Grill serves as the resort's primary Mexican restaurant, so the emphasis here is instead on accessible sandwiches, burgers, and salads at lunch, with southwestern flavors leading a breakfast menu that also includes straightforward entrees like pancakes and waffles. While not a destination restaurant by any stretch of the imagination, we think resort guests that pick it over a similarly-priced meal at Pepper Market will leave impressed for the money. A hidden gem.

Maya Grill

Inside the main building, down the hall to the right of Pepper Market

CUISINE Mexican. **HOURS** 5–10pm. **DDP** Yes.

PRICES Appetizers: $8–$13. Dinner Entrées: $22–$34. Two-Person Platters: $48–$58. Kids: $7–$10.

OVERVIEW Operated by the same company as the so-so restaurants in Epcot's Mexico Pavilion, Maya Grill recently updated its menu to be more in line with La Hacienda de San Angel. In fact, it offers two of the same platters – one featuring steak, chicken al pastor, and chorizo and the other with shrimp, fish, scallops, and vegetables. Other Tex-Mex-style entrees include Beef Short Ribs, Shrimp Tacos, and Fajitas. Kids are unlikely to connect with the restaurant's loosely themed Mayan motifs of fire, sun, and water, but their menu includes some interesting options like a Quesadilla, Tacos, and Grilled Fish, in addition to Chicken Tenders and Mac 'n Cheese.

DINING AT DISNEY'S
FORT WILDERNESS RESORT AND CAMPGROUND
....

Hoop-Dee-Doo Musical Revue

Dinner show at Pioneer Hall, near the boat dock

CUISINE Fried chicken, ribs, and all the fixins. Includes unlimited beer and wine for those 21 and older. **HOURS** Usually three shows daily: 4pm, 6:15pm, and 8:30pm. **DDP** 2 credits.

PRICES Hoop Dee Doo has tables in three price categories. Category 1, which we recommend, is $72 for adults, and $43 for kids. Category 2 ($67/$39) and especially Category 3 tables ($64/38) are more distant from the main stage.

OVERVIEW Run more than 35,000 times over the last 40-or-so years, Hoop-Dee-Doo is as much of a Walt Disney World institution as chicken nuggets and Peter Pan's Flight. While expensive at first blush, your admission includes all-you-care-to-eat fried chicken, ribs, corn, salad, baked beans, corn bread, and strawberry shortcake, in addition to unlimited soft drinks, sangria, house wine, and beer. And, of course, the two-hour, kid-friendly Western musical remains the star of the show. Expect a lot of banjos, sing-a-longs, and audience participation in what ends up being a hokey, joke-filled experience where nobody takes themselves seriously. Take the boat from Magic Kingdom if possible for an easy walk to Pioneer Hall. Those arriving via Disney bus will need to transfer to the internal shuttle for transportation to the show, which can take an extra 20 minutes.

Mickey's Backyard Barbecue

Dinner show and character meal, near Pioneer Hall on the stables side

CUISINE Fried chicken, ribs, hot dogs, hamburgers, and the like. Includes unlimited beer and wine for those 21 and over. **HOURS** Now a year-round offering, shows are usually scheduled at 5:30pm on Tuesdays, Thursdays, Fridays, and Saturdays. **DDP** 2 credits.

PRICES Mickey's BBQ offers tables in two price categories. Category 1, which we recommend, is $72 for adults and $47 for kids. Category 1 guests may enter the pavilion a full hour before show time for exclusive pictures with Mickey and friends and access to the open bar, in addition to reserved seating closer to the stage and a 15-minute head start on the buffet. Category 2 costs $62 for adults and $37 for kids and is open seating.

OVERVIEW Mickey's Backyard Barbecue takes place in a roofed but otherwise open-air (thus not air-conditioned) space. The show features a country band, line dancing, and interactions with Mickey, Minnie, Chip, Dale, and Goofy. Most guests will get more entertainment for their money from Hoop-Dee-Doo; any number of other meals provide better (and less expensive) chances to meet Mickey and friends. Line-dancers and families with young, excitable kids enjoy the experience most. Take the boat from Magic Kingdom for an easy walk to the barbecue. Those arriving via Disney bus must transfer to the internal shuttle for transportation to the show, which can take an extra 20 minutes.

Trail's End

Pioneer Hall, near the boat dock

CUISINE American/BBQ. **HOURS** Breakfast 7:30am–12pm; Dinner 4:30–9:30pm. **DDP** Yes.

PRICES Breakfast Buffet: $21 adult, $12 kid. Weekend Brunch: $25 adult, $13 kid. Dinner Buffet: $32 adult, $17 kid.

OVERVIEW Consistently the cheapest Disney World buffet at breakfast and dinner, Trail's End serves up country cooking in Disney's most casual sit-down restaurant. Breakfast is satisfying with a spread of the usual Mickey waffles, pancakes, pastries, bacon, sausage, etc., in addition to unique items like Pulled Pork Eggs Benedict and Brisket Mash. On Saturdays and Sundays, a weekend brunch is served with many of the same dishes as breakfast, in addition to made-to-order omelets, fried chicken, and macaroni & cheese, for a few more dollars than breakfast. The dinner buffet consists of much of the same food as the much more expensive family-style dinner at Whispering Canyon Café at Wilderness Lodge. Enjoy all-you-care-to-eat peel and eat shrimp, pulled pork, baked beans, chili, brisket, and more. While not necessarily a destination restaurant, Trail's End is a fantastic, economical choice for those staying at the campground.

DINING AT DISNEY'S GRAND FLORIDIAN RESORT & SPA

1900 Park Fare

Character meal, just inside the first-floor entrance on the left

CUISINE American. Character meal with Mary Poppins, Mad Hatter, Alice, Winnie the Pooh, and Tigger for breakfast. Dinner has Cinderella, Prince Charming, Lady Tremaine, Anastasia, and Drizella. All characters may not appear. **DDP** Yes.

HOURS AND PRICES *Breakfast Buffet* (8–11:50am): $32 adults, $22 kids. *Dinner Buffet* (4–9pm): $50 adults, $31 kids.

OVERVIEW 1900 Park Fare's Victorian theme is carried out subtly throughout the restaurant with carousel animals placed around the massive dining room. A calliope, or steam organ, is the focal point, hanging high above the buffet area. The restaurant is otherwise nondescript for the most part—loud, and without windows. Food is quite good for a buffet. Breakfast includes specialties like Lobster Benedict, Smoked Salmon Lox, and Hickory-smoked Ham, in addition to the usual. Dinner brings a large selection of salads and roasted meats, as well as Spice-crusted Salmon, sushi, and Roasted Root Vegetable Gratin. Don't forget the Strawberry Soup. The five very different characters present at each meal otherwise steal the show, as they visit every table taking pictures and mingling with guests.

Citricos

Second floor of the main building, near Mizner's

CUISINE American/Mediterranean. **HOURS** 5:30–10pm. **DDP** 2 credits.

PRICES Appetizers: $13–$18. Dinner Entrées: $30-$49. Kids: $9–$18.

OVERVIEW Citricos is Grand Floridian's best signature restaurant, serving inspired steak and seafood with a Mediterranean twist. Old World furnishings and mosaic-tiled floors invite guests into a restaurant that is just fancy enough that everyone feels welcome, yet an air of glamour and prestige permeates throughout. Shrimp, pork, and veal are done best here with seasonal changes that bring out the freshest flavors. Kids can choose from basics like cheese pizza and macaroni-and-cheese, or go big with Beef Tenderloin or Grilled Shrimp. Views out the expansive windows are pleasant, but don't provide much of a theme park or fireworks view.

Grand Floridian Café

First floor, all the way back on the left

CUISINE American. **HOURS** Breakfast 7:30–11am; Lunch 11:05am–2pm; Dinner 5–9pm. **DDP** Yes.

PRICES Breakfast Entrées: $9–$20. Lunch/Dinner Appetizers: $9–$16. Lunch Entrées: $14–$26. Dinner Entrées: $16–$34. Kids: $10–$12.

OVERVIEW It's usually easy to secure reservations at Grand Floridian's least expensive, most casual restaurant, subtly themed to the Victorian era with charming views of the rose gardens outside. Unlike the signature restaurants, nobody will bat an eye if you arrive wearing fanny packs and Mickey ears. The restaurant is unique in that it serves its entire breakfast and lunch menus from 7:30am through 2pm, so guests have the option of ordering breakfast and lunch options throughout the morning and afternoon. We like the flexibility of being able to order Lobster Eggs Benedict at 1pm or a Shrimp Cocktail at 8am when the mood strikes. You never know when you'll be up late editing a guidebook. Dinner is a relatively inexpensive proposition with most entrees under $25, including Shrimp & Grits and a Lobster Thermidor Burger. We appreciate the relaxed atmosphere and the ease of the overall experience, but it's not necessarily a destination restaurant unless you want to take advantage of some of the resort's other amenities. Kids won't be impressed by the ambiance, but they can get in on the action with salmon, cheese pizza, chicken, and meaty mac 'n cheese.

Narcoossee's

Located outside, near the boat dock

CUISINE Steak and Seafood. **HOURS** 5:30–10pm. **DDP** 2 credits.

PRICES Appetizers: $12–$19. Dinner Entrées: $39–$72. Kids: $8–$17.

OVERVIEW Disney's most expensive signature restaurant is not its best in food quality, service, or ambiance. The windows and waterfront veranda do provide decent, albeit off-centered views of Magic Kingdom and the fireworks, but it's far less impressive than California Grill's 15th floor observation deck. Food is generally on point, but the menu is far less innovative than Citricos, and it's hard to justify a $70+ filet mignon/lobster tail combo when the beef isn't even certified Choice. The atmosphere is otherwise bland at what Disney describes as an "elegant waterfront retreat" with basic wood furniture and standard wood floors. Most diners interested in the fireworks head outside to see them because the patio outside is filled with other guests that block the view from inside the restaurant.

Victoria and Albert's

Second floor of the main building, near Citricos

CUISINE Fine Dining; **HOURS** One seating between 5pm–7:35pm. **DDP** No.

PRICES $185/person seven–course Prix Fixe menu.

OVERVIEW Victoria & Albert's, boasting the AAA Five Diamond Award every year since 2000, is unlike any other restaurant on property. With a seven-course menu that starts at $185 per person, it's also the most expensive. The restaurant does not serve children under the age of ten in the main dining room and there is a strict dress code: men must wear dinner jackets with dress pants or slacks and shoes. Ties are optional. Women may wear a cocktail dress, nice dress, dressy pant suit, or a skirt with a blouse. The 18-table restaurant is otherwise equal parts intimate and opulent, with reliably impeccable service from the inviting staff. Menus change daily, but Chef Hunnel reliably offers Australian Kobe-style beef tenderloin, Holland white asparagus, braised oxtail, Imperial osetra caviar, and other fine ingredients. Desserts, overseen by the venerable Erich Herbitschek, are excellent. While expensive, Victoria & Albert's may be the best value on property. Strongly consider the wine pairings with seven healthy pours of fine wines perfectly paired to each selection. V&A's is not for everyone, but it doesn't get any better than this for those celebrating something special.

DINING AT DISNEY'S OLD KEY WEST RESORT

Olivia's

Next to the gift shop, across the way from check-in

CUISINE American. **HOURS** Breakfast 7–11am; Lunch 12–4:55pm; Dinner 5–10pm. **DDP** Yes.

PRICES Breakfast Entrées: $12–$16. Lunch/Dinner Appetizers: $7–$13. Lunch Entrées: $14–$26. Dinner Entrées: $18–$33. Kids: $10–$11.

OVERVIEW Nautically themed with wooden fish and pictures of past guests adorning the walls, Olivia's is one of the friendliest restaurants on property. Breakfast is excellent with specialties like Crab Cake Eggs Benedict with Key Lime Hollandaise. Standard fare includes pancake, waffle, and egg platters. Lunch and dinner both feature inexpensive burger and sandwich fare, in addition to more expensive steak, scallops, and prime rib served at dinner. Order at least one Conch Fritters. Kids enjoy this colorful, boisterous restaurant with their menu of pasta, salmon, pizza, chicken, hamburgers, and grilled fish. While not a destination restaurant for most visitors, anyone staying here should plan at least one meal back at the resort. Outdoor patio seating is available.

DINING AT DISNEY'S POLYNESIAN VILLAGE RESORT

'Ohana

Character meal (breakfast only), on second floor of main building

CUISINE Character breakfast with Mickey, Pluto, Lilo, and Stitch. Dinner (served family style) is heavy on meat. **DDP** Yes.

HOURS AND PRICES *Breakfast* (7:30am–noon): $34 adults, $20 kids. *Dinner* (3:30–10pm): $46 adults, $26 kids.

OVERVIEW Characters stop by for the Polynesian-themed breakfast served family-style. Scrambled eggs, Mickey waffles, fried potatoes, pork sausage, bacon, and biscuits will all be delivered in copious quantities throughout the meal. It's a limited selection compared to buffets, but it does the trick and the characters are friendly. Dinner starts with pineapple-coconut bread and salad and continues with honey-coriander chicken wings and potstickers. Skewers with sweet-n-sour chicken, marinated sirloin steak, and spicy grilled peel-n-eat shrimp follow with stir-fried vegetables and lo mein as accompaniments. The restaurant is incredibly loud, particularly at dinner when staff members lead kids in games and parades throughout the meal. Very few tables have window views of Magic Kingdom. (Protip: It's 'Ohana. Not O'hana. Or O'hana's. Just, 'Ohana. It means "family".)

Kona Café

Second floor of main building

CUISINE American, Pan-Asian. **HOURS** Breakfast: 7:30–11:15am; Lunch: 12–2:45pm; Dinner; 5–10pm. **DDP** Yes.

PRICES Breakfast Entrées: $13–$18. Lunch/Dinner Appetizers: $8–$16. Lunch Entrées: $15–$25. Dinner Entrées: $19–$34. Kids: $10–$11.

OVERVIEW Kona is too many people's "best kept secret" to count as a hidden gem anymore, but it remains one of Disney's better casual restaurants. We prefer stopping by in the middle of the day for lunch to relax and recharge with less expensive sandwich and burger offerings, in addition to reasonably-priced noodle bowls and other entrees. Dinner upgrades the lunch sirloin for a more-expensive filet mignon and adds heartier dishes like pork tenderloin. Sushi is made with fresh ingredients and elegantly presented from lunch onward. While Kona will probably remain best known for its Tonga Toast (banana-stuffed sourdough French toast rolled in cinnamon sugar and served with a strawberry compote), a stop at any point in the day should satisfy. For breakfast, kids can choose from items including pancakes, French toast, or scrambled eggs along with pasta, hot dogs, fish, chicken, and a cheeseburger available later in the day.

Spirit of Aloha

Dinner show, in dedicated space on the Grand Floridian side

CUISINE American/Polynesian. **HOURS** Usually two shows Tuesday-Saturday at 5:15pm and 8:15pm. **DDP** 2 credits.

PRICES The Spirit of Aloha show offers tables in three price categories. Category 1, which we recommend, is $78 for adults, and $45 for kids. Category 2 ($74/$44) and Category 3 ($66/$39) are distant from the main stage.

OVERVIEW Food is okay at this Polynesian luau and dinner show, which follows the story of a young woman returning home after spending time as a city girl on the mainland. All-you-care-to-enjoy Island pulled pork, BBQ ribs, roasted chicken, and Polynesian rice are served family-style alongside fresh salad with honey-lime vinaigrette, seasonal vegetables, and pineapple-coconut bread. Complimentary beer and wine are served, though it may be difficult to flag down a server for a refill. Kids receive chicken nuggets with tater tots, cheese pizza, and either grilled chicken or mahi mahi with rice and green beans. The show has its moments, with an outstanding fire-dancing and sword-eating finale, but at over two hours, it drags in places. With the amount of better entertainment already seen at the parks, the Luau is going to be superfluous for many, and, at $70/adult, is an expensive proposition.

Trader Sam's Grog Grotto

Past Captain Cook's in the main building and outside on the patio

CUISINE Polynesian, Sushi. **HOURS** 4pm–12:30am or 1am; 21+ only after 8pm. **DDP** No.

PRICES Appetizers/Small Plates: $9–$15.

OVERVIEW Trader Sam's Grog Grotto features two distinct areas married under a single banner. The outdoor, open air Tiki Terrace offers a surprisingly relaxing atmosphere among swaying palm trees, fountains, and live ukulele music. Inside, the bar that officially seats just about 50 people is whimsically themed and full of interactive artifacts from around the mysterious South Seas. Due to the bar's low capacity, Sam's usually uses a pager system to alert prospective imbibers that space is available inside. Wait times can be quoted as high as two or more hours on the weekends, but are usually short or nonexistent on weeknights, particularly after 9pm. Staff will remind those under 21 that they should prepare to leave by the 8pm cutoff. Food tends to be better and more varied upstairs at Tambu Lounge and Kona Café, though you might want to order one of the small bites with drinks inside or out on the patio. Our favorite drink is the souvenir HippopotoMai-Tai, which includes a take-home Tiki glass for around $25. Be careful with the souvenir Uh-Oa, which will run you north of $40, and the Nautilus, which arrives over $50. Other drinks like the Tropical Dark and Stormy are closer to $8, but don't include a souvenir glass.

DINING AT DISNEY'S PORT ORLEANS RIVERSIDE RESORT

Boatwright's

Inside the main building, near the quick service

CUISINE Cajun/American. **HOURS** 5–9pm. **DDP** Yes.

PRICES Appetizers: $8–$13. Dinner Entrées: $19–$36. Kids: $9–$12.

OVERVIEW Loosely themed to a shipyard warehouse with the skeletal hull of a fishing boat suspended overhead, Boatwright's is a casual restaurant just off the main lobby. The menu revolves around typical New Orleans favorites like jambalaya, crawfish etouffée, and catfish, but the usual American steaks, prime rib, and pork chops are also present. Most of the Cajun entrees are under-seasoned and bland. Boatwright's is excellent for guests who unexpectedly find themselves back at the resort, but do make sure you have reservations because waits can be surprisingly long, particularly on weekends in lousy weather.

DINING AT DISNEY'S SARATOGA SPRINGS RESORT & SPA

The Turf Club Bar & Grill

Inside the main building, beyond the quick service

CUISINE American. **HOURS** 5–9:30pm. **DDP** Yes.

PRICES Appetizers: $8–$13. Dinner Entrées: $18–$36. Kids: $9–$12.

OVERVIEW Turf Club is themed to a turn-of-the-century, upstate New York racetrack clubhouse. Wood-paneled walls and dark wood furniture provide a gentlemanly ambiance with views of Lake Buena Vista Golf Club below and Disney Springs in the distance. It's not the most inviting restaurant, particularly with kids, but it's a great choice for couples looking for a more intimate experience, and riders will find the displayed horse tack delightful. Kids may enjoy the covered patio seating outside more. The menu leans toward steak, lamb, and pork. Start with the Turf Club Signature Grilled Romaine Salad and Buffalo Chicken Dip. Kids have the usual burger/nugget/pizza/fish/chicken/pasta options. The Saratoga Cocktail with Maker's Mark Bourbon and Mint Julep with Woodford Reserve are a nice departure from most cocktail menus heavy on flavored vodkas and light rum.

DINING AT DISNEY'S WILDERNESS LODGE

Artist Point

Back of main building

CUISINE American. **HOURS** 5:30–9:30pm. **DDP** 2 credits.

PRICES Appetizers: $13-$20. Dinner Entrées: $30–$50. Kids: $10–$18.

OVERVIEW Specialties of the Northwest are served as guests take in the large, open dining room inspired by national park lodges. Two-story high murals capture the heart and romance of the American frontier as iron lanterns provide the only light. Be sure to request a window table overlooking Bay Lake and Copper Creek Falls, or you risk a lousy view of a walkway or the lobby. The restaurant welcomes kids, but they are unlikely to be transfixed with the restaurant's subtle charm. The restaurant is best enjoyed as a romantic rendezvous. Best are the Smokey Portobello Soup appetizer and anything with buffalo strip or venison loin paired with one of the Northwest wine flights. Don't miss the Artist Point Cobbler for dessert.

Whispering Canyon Café

Just inside the main entrance, on the left

CUISINE American. **HOURS** Breakfast: 7:30–11:15am; Lunch: 11:45am–2:30pm; Dinner: 5–10pm. **DDP** Yes.

PRICES Breakfast Entrées: $11–$19. Lunch/Dinner Appetizers: $9–$12. Lunch Entrées: $14–$24. Dinner Entrées: $19–$35. Kids: $8–$14.

OVERVIEW Whispering Canyon Café is like a Western-themed 50's Prime Time Café. While the antics have been toned down in recent years, guests requesting a bottle of ketchup will find that 25 bottles from around the restaurant appear. Don't be surprised if your drink refill comes in a gallon jug or a two-ounce miniature jar, depending on how generous your server is feeling. All-you-care-to-enjoy platters are the most popular here. Breakfast brings scrambled eggs, Western home fries, bacon, sausage, waffles, buttermilk biscuits, and sausage gravy. A la carte choices include the usual. Lunch and dinner platters include family-style mixed greens tossed in an apple-vinaigrette dressing and freshly baked cornbread. Start with three: smoked pork ribs, barbecued pulled pork, roasted chicken, smoked beef, or sausage, along with vegetables, mashed potatoes, cowboy-style baked beans, and corn on the cob. Bring your sense of humor to enjoy this loud, raucous restaurant, particularly at dinner.

DINING AT DISNEY'S YACHT CLUB RESORT

Ale & Compass Restaurant

Off the main lobby

CUISINE New England-inspired American. **HOURS** Breakfast 7:30–11am; Lunch 11:30am–2pm; Dinner 5–9pm. **DDP** Yes.

PRICES Breakfast Entrées: $9–$19. Lunch/Dinner Appetizers: $9–$15. Lunch Entrées: $14–$20. Dinner Entrées: $17–$40. Kids: $9–$13.

OVERVIEW Ale & Compass opened in place of Captain's Grille in late 2017 with a renewed emphasis on New England comfort food in a slightly upscale setting heavy on royal navy blues and details reminiscent of a lighthouse. All three meals are casual with breakfast bringing delicious entrees like Salted Caramel-Apple French Toast and a Cornbread Waffle, in addition to mainstays like a Ham & Cheese Omelet or American Breakfast. Lunch is our favorite meal, delicious and relaxing with a terrific Fish & Chips and hearty Maine Lobster Roll. Dinner is more expensive and a little less likely to impress with a $40 Coastal Clambake and $36 T-Bone Steak that's not executed quite as well as neighboring restaurants. Still, items like the Fried Chicken & Waffles with Orange-Chili Honey and Seared Scrod with Corn and Lobster Ragoût satisfy for under $25 each. There are more interesting restaurants in the Crescent Lake area, but Ale & Compass is a no-fuss option and has its place if you're looking for an easy, pleasant experience.

Yachtsman Steakhouse

Back of lobby

CUISINE American. **HOURS** 5–9:30pm. **DDP** 2 credits.

PRICES Appetizers: $12–$19. Dinner Entrées: $31–$125. Kids: $9–$17.

OVERVIEW Yachtsman takes its meat more seriously than any other Disney resort restaurant on property, though recent additions like The BOATHOUSE, STK Orlando, and Morimoto Asia to Disney Springs make it much more difficult to definitively award it "best steak". Steaks are aged, trimmed, and hand cut on site before being prepared on an oak-fired grill in the open kitchen. The traditional steakhouse setting is heavy on wood with elegant white linens topping every table. While all steaks come in over $45, the high quality of the meat and the elevated service bring guests back again and again. The restaurant is not the best with young kids in tow, as there's little about the restaurant that will keep them occupied, but they may choose from mac 'n cheese, baked fish, grilled chicken, pasta and meatballs, or a steak skewer. Consider the restaurant for an intimate meal or special occasion, particularly with someone who knows their meat.

Which Tickets To Buy and How Much to Budget

8

In February 2018 Disney World both raised ticket prices and also announced that multi-day tickets for the first time would move to seasonal pricing "later this year." No details of the seasonal price levels or the dates with different prices are yet available. We believe that current ticket price levels will likely represent the lowest ticket prices for 2018. Keep close to easyWDW.com and yourfirstvisit.net, where we will publish more about these new price models when it is available.

"What should we budget?" is the hardest simple question for this book to answer. This is because smaller families, families whose kids are younger, families staying at a less expensive hotel, families going during a less expensive week, and families on shorter trips will pay less. Larger families, families where everyone is over nine, families staying at a more expensive hotel, families going during a more expensive week, and families on longer trips will pay more.

- A parent and one younger child, with three days of tickets and three nights in a value resort during one of the less expensive price seasons, could spend as little as $1,400 in Orlando.
- Add another parent and another younger child and this trip jumps to $2,400.
- Stretch the visit out to the 8 nights and 9 days we recommend for "only visits" and the in-Orlando price exceeds $4,400.
- Stay this long in one of the more expensive deluxe resorts instead, and the price is more than $7,800.
- Shift to the most expensive times to visit at this deluxe resort and add $2,300 more.

(All the figures are before transportation costs and souvenirs.)

The good news is that budgeting for a specific trip is relatively straightforward, with most costs set and paid far in advance of arrival.

This chapter discusses the ins and outs of budgeting. We'll walk you through how to establish what you can expect to pay for each component of your trip, whether it includes just one adult and one child on a tight budget over a few days, or a week-long extended family blow-out.

We open with a discussion of the one major budget issue we haven't discussed yet: theme park tickets with their various add-ons and related costs. The section that follows covers estimating your budget based on your dates, resort hotel, group, etc. Then we cover budgets for "only" trips, several ways to reduce costs, and even a few reasons to spend even more!

Disney World Tickets and Prices

Like most of our budgetary concerns thus far, deciding on the right theme park tickets for your group is simple at first blush and a bit more complicated once we delve into the specifics. Let's break it down.

The Magic Your Way base ticket is Disney's basic theme park admission ticket. The great majority of Disney World visitors will purchase a Magic Your Way ticket, although some guests return with Annual Passes (good for unlimited admissions throughout the year, sometimes with blackout dates) or have a promotional ticket of some kind.

You may purchase a Magic Your Way ticket with one to ten days of theme park admissions. The tickets expire 14 days from their first use at Disney World (the day of first use plus 13 additional days), not from the date of purchase or the date of receipt in the mail, and, in a change starting February 2017, must have their first day of use by December 31 of the year following the date of purchase—so tickets bought in 2018 must have their first day of use by 12/31/19. Should life get complicated and you not be able to use your tickets by then, the value of the unused tickets can be credited to new tickets.

As noted at the beginning of this chapter, later this year Disney World will shift to seasonal pricing for multi-day tickets. All prices in the rest of the Chapter are for currently available tickets, not for the seasonal tickets, whose prices are not yet out.

International visitors, particularly those visiting from the United Kingdom and Europe, may have additional ticket options. For example, Disney offers a 7, 14, and 21-day Ultimate Ticket to UK and some European visitors, good for admission into all four major theme parks, in addition to the water parks and each of the minor parks discussed later in this chapter. The 21-day tickets cost more than $500 each, but for those eligible may be the best option on a long vacation as the only other options for those visiting longer than ten days are Annual Passes or two individual tickets, both of which would likely be even more expensive.

Number of Ticket Days	Adult Price	Price to Add Day	Child Price	Price to Add Day
1	see text			
2	$222.59	$102.24	$209.81	$95.85
3	$324.83	$79.88	$305.66	$77.75
4	$404.70	$15.98	$383.40	$15.98
5	$420.68	$10.65	$399.38	$10.65
6	$431.33	$10.65	$410.03	$10.65
7	$441.98	$10.65	$420.68	$10.65
8	$452.63	$10.65	$431.33	$10.65
9	$463.28	$10.65	$441.98	$10.65
10	$473.93	n/a	$452.63	n/a

COST OF MAGIC YOUR WAY BASE TICKETS

While the cost always goes up to add more days to your base ticket, the cost per day goes down as you add days.

One day tickets are quite unusual. Like other tickets, they cost more for those ten and older than those three to nine years old. As has been true for several years, they also cost more for one day of access to Magic Kingdom than for one day at one of the other three theme parks. Moreover, in late February 2016, Disney instituted seasonal pricing for one-day tickets. As a result, one-day tickets can cost after tax anywhere from $102.24 (child, not Magic Kingdom, value season) to $137.39 (adult, Magic Kingdom, peak season). Current pricing for multi-day tickets of all lengths is shown in the chart, which includes 6.5% sales tax , and assumes that you buy in advance—tickets longer than two days cost an extra $21.30 per ticket if not bought in advance.

As you can see, the cost to add the fourth day is about $78, adding day five is about $16, and each day after that is $10.65. Disney prices their tickets in this way so it is cost-effective to visit the parks for additional days, which means you will be spending more money on food, souvenirs, and hotel rooms, which is where the Walt Disney Company makes even more money than on admission. It also dissuades people from purchasing tickets to other theme parks. After all, the cost to add the 6th day to your Disney vacation is "only about $11", compared to $120+ for a one-day ticket to Universal Studios. Disney keeps its single-day tickets expensive in order to capitalize on those only spending one day at Disney World.

ADDING DAYS TO YOUR TICKET

The Magic Your Way ticket is the bare minimum ticket that can be purchased, but that doesn't necessarily mean you need "more ticket". There are a few rules for upgrading base tickets. First, all upgrades must be done within 14 days of the first use of the ticket. You may also add days to your ticket as needed at the same price as it would have cost had you originally added them. For example, if you're unsure whether you need six, seven, or eight days of admission, you can purchase a six-day ticket and add a seventh or eighth day if you decide that you need them, even after beginning to use the tickets. You would only pay the additional cost per day at the same rate had you originally purchased a seven-day ticket ($10.65 per day, as noted in the chart above). These upgrades must be made before the end of the last day on the ticket. For example, if you've purchased a five-day ticket and would like to add a sixth, you must add it before the end of your fifth day spent in the theme park. Disney uses this policy to cut down on ticket resellers that offer unsuspecting visitors money for their used tickets. The resellers used to take these used tickets to Disney, add extra days for the $10.65 per day cost, and then turn around and resell them as "new" one-day tickets for $50 or more. Reselling used tickets is illegal in Florida, and if you find yourself in the unfortunate situation of trying to use bogus tickets, you'll be refused admission to the parks. Stick with Disney directly or a trusted third party, not the various resellers with strip mall storefronts.

ADDING PARK HOPPERS

The Park Hopper ticket add-on allows the user to visit more than one theme park on the same day. For example, the Animal Kingdom might close at 5pm on the day you choose to visit. With the Park Hopper upgrade, you could exit the Animal Kingdom at any time and travel to and enter any of the other three theme parks to take advantage of evening Extra Magic Hours, a late dinner reservation, or anything else.

Park hoppers on one-day tickets cost from $59 to $66 depending on the park and the price season. For two- or three-day tickets, the cost is $69.23. With a four- to ten-day ticket, the cost is a flat $79.88 per ticket. On a six-day ticket, the cost for the upgrade comes out to $13.31 per day. For another $26.63, you can change to Park Hopper Plus, which adds visits to the minor parks and is described in the next section. (All figures include tax.)

Many guests have what they think is the bright idea of bypassing the expensive Park Hopper upgrade and instead purchase more days of theme park admissions than they need with the idea that they will visit a second theme park on the same day and simply use a second day's admission. For example, a family might be visiting the parks on five days and purchase seven days of admission with the idea that on day five they'll visit Animal Kingdom in the morning and then use a sixth day of admission on the same day to visit Epcot at night. This will not work. Disney is wise to the fact that adding Park Hopper would be almost $80 per ticket, while adding these two additional days is only about $43. In our example, the Cast Member at Epcot would explain the benefits of upgrading to Park Hopper after the ticket was rejected at the scanner.

Many returning visitors purchase park hoppers, but, in most situations, we don't recommend spending the money on the Park Hopper upgrade for first timers, who may not realize how big Disney World is, how much there is to do everywhere, and how long it takes to get from park to park. Remember, Disney will very rarely not take your money and they are more than happy to add the Park Hopper upgrade to your ticket should you deem the cost necessary, even after you've started using the ticket.

Remember that the regular base ticket allows unlimited re-entries to the same theme park on the same day. If you take a recommended afternoon break, you can return to the same theme park later for dinner, attractions, and the night-time entertainment. If your main park for the day closes early, instead of buying a Hopper and pushing on to another park, consider making a dinner reservation at and exploring a nearby resort.

Park Hopper does have its uses, particularly for guests staying at Epcot area resorts or guests visiting for a special event. Guests staying at a resort like the Beach or Yacht Club may wish to start their day at Magic Kingdom, take a break back at the resort, and then simply walk the five minutes to Epcot for drinks, dinner, rides, entertainment, or whatever else.

If you are considering the Park Hopper upgrade, calculate how much it's going to cost and then divide that by the number of times you plan to hop. That's the cost per hop and will give you a better idea if the real additional theme park access options are worth the money.

PARK HOPPER PLUS

In February 2017, Disney eliminated the old Water Park Fun and More ticket add on, but most of its benefits can be added to a Park Hopper ticket by buying a Park Hopper Plus ticket, which is a flat $26.63 per ticket on top of the Park Hopper price. These benefits cannot be added to a standard, non-Hopper Magic Your Way ticket—only to a Hopper.

The Park Hopper Plus add-on grants grants a certain number of visits to the "minor" parks based on the number of days included in the ticket, such as Typhoon Lagoon water park, Blizzard Beach water park, one round of golf at 9-hole Oak Trail, Disney's Fantasia Gardens Mini Golf (before 4 pm), or Disney's Winter Summerland Mini Golf (before 4pm).

The number of entrances you will receive to the minor parks is equal to the number of days on your Magic Your Way base ticket, except for one day tickets, which get two entrances. So if you have one or two day tickets, with Park Hopper Plus you get two minor park entrances; with five day tickets, you get five entrances; with eight day tickets, you get eight.

A single entrance paid at the gate to a minor park will range from $14.91 at mini golf to more than $60 at a water park. So the $26.63 add-on pays for itself almost immediately, and if you were planning, for example, two water park days, more than pays for the Hopper too.

While the water parks and other minor attractions are a lot of fun, we don't usually recommend either the Park Hopper or Park Hopper Plus add-on for a first visit because the major theme parks offer so much to see and do, and hopping between them often takes an hour or more when considering walking to the exit of the original park, waiting for transportation, transit time, and going through security again. For return trips or vacations lasting more than eight days, the Park Hopper Plus is potentially a great value for those planning several visits to the minor parks, and adds the flexibility of the Park Hopper as well.

Estimating Budgets

Now that we've determined the cost of theme park tickets, let's add them to the resort and dining costs discussed in Chapters 5 and 7, and consider the following variables:

- **DATES OF THE VISIT** Walt Disney World price seasons for hotel rooms vary tremendously over the year.
- **GROUP SIZE AND AGE STRUCTURE AT PLANNED CHECK-IN DATE** Kids less than three years old don't require theme park admission and aren't charged at buffets. Kids from three to nine are charged a little less than older folk for theme park tickets, and a lot less for kids' meals and kids' buffets. Kids ten and older as of the check-in date are charged the same as adults for theme park tickets and the Dining Plan. With the exception of the Disney Vacation Club rooms and the Fort Wilderness campground, Disney includes two guests age 18 or older in the room at the base price. Additional guests over the age of 18 will be charged $10–$35 per night extra, depending on the resort level.
- **TARGETED HOTEL** Walt Disney World hotel rooms are available for prices just south of $100 per night to well over $600 per night.

- **TRANSPORTATION COSTS** These vary greatly depending on mode and length of travel.
- **TIPS, SNACKS, SOUVENIRS, AND OTHER EXTRAS** Add about $25 per person, per night.

Now that we have an idea about when and for how long we want to visit, let's input our information and get an idea of how much it's all going to cost. Visit your My Disney Experience account, click at the top Places to Stay and input your check-in date, check-out date, and party size. Pick your desired hotel and room/view type.

The next page lists tickets and the add-ons discussed previously in the chapter. Select the tickets and then click Dining Plan. Note the cost with and without the Plan. While we don't recommend the Dining Plan in most situations, it does give a general idea about what it will cost to eat one quick service and one table service meal per day, in addition to a snack or two. Don't worry if this number seems too high—we'll cover discounts and ways to save money shortly.

Budgeting an Only Visit

For a nine-day itinerary during the Fall 2018 price season, assuming a family of four with two adults, one child younger than ten and one older, budget if possible:

- $8,300+ if you are staying at a monorail deluxe resort
- $5,700 if you are staying at a moderate
- $4,900 if you are staying at a value

Add to this budget the costs of getting the group to and from Orlando. We suggest that a day or two shorter can also work for an "only" visit. For shorter visits, subtract about $450/day if you are staying at a value resort, $550/day at a moderate, and $850/day at a deluxe.

Saving Money on a Disney World Visit

Money-saving opportunities depend on when you go and where you stay:

- When you go matters because Disney changes seasonal pricing roughly 25 times over the course of the year. Staying in the same exact standard-view room at the Polynesian for eight nights during the most expensive time of the year can cost $2,300 more than it would cost during the cheapest period.
- Where you stay matters because Walt Disney World has resorts priced at many different levels. Staying eight nights at the Polynesian instead of Art of Animation during the lower cost season will cost almost $3,100 more.

- Combining these effects—staying eight nights at the Poly during the highest cost time of the year instead of at Art of Animation during the lowest cost time of the year—costs a whopping $5,400 more for the same family with the same theme park tickets!

So the takeaways for the first-time family visitor:

- On a tight budget, consider sticking with one of Disney's less expensive on-property resorts like Art of Animation or Pop Century.
- Think carefully about what is really getting in the way of going during one of the less expensive seasons. Is it possible to pull the kids out of school to visit when crowds and prices are much lower?

Because Disney controls the entire supply of theme park tickets, discounts from reputable sources are slim. Check OFFICIALTICKETCENTER. COM for some of the best discounts on multi-day tickets. Fortunately, major savings may be available on other aspects of your vacation:

- Keep an eye out for deals available to the general public—typically room rate discounts, but sometimes a version of the Dining Plan for free—especially in September. Find them at YOURFIRSTVISIT.NET/DEALS or at Disney World's Special Offer web page as they are announced. These discounts are often available to Disney Visa card holders a few days before they become available to everyone else. Visit DISNEYREWARDS.COM for more information.
- Use special discounts that you quality for, the most valuable of which is the Armed Forces Salute. See MILITARYDISNEYTIPS. COM for more. There may also be discounts for Florida residents, Annual Passholders, international guests, and others.
- Access Disney Vacation Club rooms for a lot less by renting points from owners who won't be using them—this is a particular boon for large families, who have the most difficulty finding Disney-owned accommodations at reasonable prices. Visit DVCREQUEST.COM for pricing and options.
- Consider staying offsite, especially with large groups. As noted in Chapter 5, there are some takeaways on the convenience side of things, but it may be the most viable option for some groups, and the savings can be substantial. It's hard to find reasonably priced Disney-owned options on-site for groups larger than four people, and even more difficult for groups larger than five. You'll find lots of ideas at YOURFIRSTVISIT.NET/LARGE-FAMILIES, but the least expensive way to stay will be offsite.

For groups that will fit into a four person standard Little Mermaid room at Disney's value resort Art of Animation, the chart illustrates what it

Designing to a Target Budget

Art of Animation Nights	1	2	3	4
Base Ticket Days	2	3	4	5
Hotel	*$190*	*$380*	*$561*	*$732*
Dining Plan/Other Food	*$479*	*$775*	*$1,071*	*$1,367*
Park Tickets	*$878*	*$1,280*	*$1,598*	*$1,631*
Extra, Souvenirs, etc.	*$180*	*$270*	*$361*	*$450*
TOTAL: No Extras	$1,547	$2,435	$3,230	$3,760
TOTAL: With Extras	$1,727	$2,705	$3,590	$4,210

Art of Animation Nights	5	6	7	8
Base Ticket Days	6	7	8	9
Hotel	*$903*	*$1,074*	*$1,256*	*$1,446*
Dining Plan/Other Food	*$1,663*	*$1,961*	*$2,256*	*$2,552*
Park Tickets	*$1,704*	*$1,747*	*$1,789*	*$1,832*
Extra, Souvenirs, etc.	*$540*	*$630*	*$720*	*$810*
TOTAL: No Extras	$4,270	$4,782	$5,301	$5,830
TOTAL: With Extras	$4,810	$5,412	$6,021	$6,640

Standard 4-person Little Mermaid room, Fall 2018 price season with Friday arrival; four-person family with one younger than 10; ticket prices as of February 2018.

will cost two adults, one kid older than ten, and one aged from three to nine, to stay for various trip lengths during the Fall 2018 price season.

Spending Even More at Disney World

There's almost no limit to what could be spent on a first visit to Walt Disney World, with a fat enough wallet and sufficient desire to thin it. For example, how about a couple of newly-published authors as really expensive tour guides?

For a fuller list, see "The Comfortable Guide to Walt Disney World" on YOURFIRSTVISIT.NET/COMFORTABLE. But a shorter list of extra spending that may significantly increase comfort levels on a first visit includes the following:

- **RENTING A CAR** Disney's Magical Express (discussed in Chapter 9) will transport your group back and forth from the airport, but it requires that guests return to their resort for pickup no later than three hours before the flight is scheduled to leave. With a car, you can potentially leave for the airport directly from the theme park. On property, Disney's transportation system will get you from your Disney hotel to the parks, but a rental car reduces waits, increases flexibility, and offers a more comfortable, private ride. Transport to all the parks but the Magic Kingdom is faster by car than by Disney bus: it's the only simple way to get from most resort hotels—especially values and moderates—to another for dining, etc.; it's the only easy way to get to the non-Disney parks; and it makes shopping, off-site dining, and other activities much easier.

- **STAYING A FEW DAYS LONGER** Adding two or three days to a trip (and planning on relaxing those days) can make your vacation much more comfortable. A Disney World trip is like a backpacking expedition—lots of walking, lots of energy used, lots of early mornings. A few more days off can make a world of difference.

- **GETTING A MULTI-SPACE ROOM** Even the happiest families can tire of staying together in a single room. Several Disney lodging options—mostly at the expensive deluxe resorts—give you more space. Consider (in order of increasing prices) deluxe rooms at the Wilderness Lodge, one and two bedroom villas at the Disney Vacation Club resorts, and suites at all the deluxe resorts. Much lower priced—but still expensive—multi-room options are Family Suites at All-Star Music and at Art of Animation, and the Cabins at Fort Wilderness. Many—but not all—of these options include full kitchens as well.

None of these are inexpensive...but they might make a real difference to comfort!

Pricing out a Walt Disney World vacation is daunting. The good news is that once you've arrived, most everything is already taken care of and you can let loose and enjoy your trip. In fact, if you've added the Dining Plan, the only additional costs most guests encounter in Orlando is souvenirs (and there will be souvenirs), tips, and a few treats. With the ability to save a substantial amount of money on resort costs and a few dollars on tickets, it's easy to design around just about any budget.

How to Set Everything Up and Get Everything Done

There are three key dates to consider:

- For those staying at a Disney-owned resort, restaurant reservations open for booking 180 days before their arrival date, and can be booked for that date and the next 9 days.
- For everyone else, restaurant reservations open for booking 180 days before a potential dining date
- For those staying at a Disney-owned resort, the Swan or Dolphin, Shades of Green, or a Disney Springs Resort Area hotel booked via an eligible package, FastPass+ reservations can be booked beginning 60 days before their arrival date.
- For everyone else, FastPass+ reservations can be booked beginning 30 days before planned use.

Building a to-do list is keyed to these dates because booking as early as possibly will result in the widest selection of experiences being available.

The first section of this chapter outlines how to sign up for and use Disney's new My Disney Experience mobile app and website. From there, we'll walk through customizing MagicBands and setting up FastPass+.

Tailored to-do lists are available for each of the sample itineraries available at YOURFIRSTVISIT.NET/ITINERARIES. For guests building custom itineraries, the second section of this chapter discusses putting together a to-do list to make sure everything is booked as easily and conveniently as possible.

My Disney Experience, FastPass+, and MagicBands

MY DISNEY EXPERIENCE

If you don't already have a My Disney Experience (MDE) account, sign up for one by visiting DISNEYWORLD.COM and clicking the "sign in or create account" link on the top center of the screen. An account is required to make dining and FastPass+ reservations, in addition to customizing MagicBands and keeping track of each component of your vacation online.

If you already have an account and booked a trip through the website while logged in, you should already see these reservations upon signing in. If not, link them manually by clicking "My Reservations and Tickets" under the My Disney Experience dropdown menu (located in the top right under the search box) and input the confirmation numbers and ticket IDs.

If people on the reservation are missing, click from the same MDE dropdown menu, "My Family and Friends". Once the new screen opens, click the little "Add a Guest" button on the right side of the page. Type the names of the missing people, and, if applicable, their ticket IDs. If you have trouble, try tech support—at (407) 939-5277—and have the ticket and reservation numbers of the missing elements at hand.

BOOKING FASTPASS+ AHEAD OF YOUR ARRIVAL

FastPass+ can be booked in advance by everyone with a valid "Magic Your Way" ticket or annual pass. Guests staying in Disney-owned resorts or other eligible hotels can begin booking FastPass+ 60 days before their arrival date. Guests staying elsewhere can book up to 30 days before planned use. FastPass+ strategy is covered in depth back in Chapter 6.

Booking FastPass+ as soon as eligible is advantageous because the most attractions and times will be available. Each FastPass+ experience has a limited number of slots. Fewer and fewer experiences will be available as a specific visit date approaches because more and more people have gone online and secured their choices.

Read Chapter 6, if you haven't already, and decide which FastPass+ experiences and times you'd like to book. Beginning at 7am, exactly 60 days out, you can sign into your MDE account on DISNEYWORLD.COM and complete the following steps:

- At the top right hover over the words "My Disney Experience." From the drop down that emerges, click FastPass+
- Then you add, one at a time, FastPass+ up to a total of three per ticket per day. You no longer need to book exactly three per day.

- Because not all members of the group are required to select the same FastPass+ experiences, first you select the people for whom you are scheduling for your FastPass+.

- Then you pick the date, and then at the bottom of same page, the park. Rides and possible times for your FastPass+ that day will then show on your screen.

- Note that there are tabs above where you can target morning, afternoon, and evening. Attractions only available in the evening will still show, even if you picked morning. By clicking the rightmost tab, you can even target a specific time.

- By default, the system will show only up to three time choices for each ride. But note that under each ride's name is a link "View Details and More Times." Click it, and if available you'll see a lot more times to pick from. Tap the time you want, and hit the green "Confirm" button at the lower left of the next screen.

- Your FastPass+ may conflict with another time you've picked, or even a set of FastPass+ at a different park. If so, you'll get an error screen. If you lose track of the FastPass+ you've already booked for that day, most pages have a link "My Plans" in the top left. Click that and a pop up of your plans will show up. Scroll down to the appropriate day to see what's conflicting, then X out the pop-up and fix it.

- Once you have a successful "confirm," you will be given the choice of continuing that day or working on a different day. Either way, you will start at the beginning with the people involved for whom you are scheduling a FastPass. Continue until you are done booking all your FastPass+ for everyone!

Times and experiences may be changed as often as wished (limited, though, to what is available at the time you change them), up through the last hour the theme park is open on the day you're visiting. If you run into problems, try tech support at (407) 939-5277.

MAGICBANDS

For those staying at a Disney-owned resort, MagicBands play many roles on a trip. Most importantly, they are room keys, park tickets, the link to using your Dining Plan credits, the link to FastPass+, and, if charging privileges are enabled, a means to charge back to the room.

They contain no personal data—rather, all they have encoded within them is a unique numeric identifier which Disney uses to link up databases in its own systems behind the scenes.

MagicBands are waterproof and hypoallergenic, and don't even need to be worn on a wrist—you can stick them in a pocket or purse and just wave them about when needed. Many need to take them off and wave them about anyway since not all the readers work perfectly when they are on a wrist, especially hotel room locks.

The color and names printed on the MagicBands can be customized online at DISNEYWORLD.COM after booking. To do so, log in to your MDE account at DISNEYWORLD.COM and select MagicBands and Cards from the My Disney Experience dropdown menu. Confirm the shipping address, then select MagicBands one by one for the people in your party. For each MagicBand, pick a color and customize the name, which is limited to nine characters including spaces. So "easyWDW" fits, but not "yourfirstvisit. net". Colors can be the same among your group, so long as the names are different. Well, names can be the same, too...but why would you do that?

MagicBands will be shipped directly to the U.S. address of your choice if they're customized at least 10 days (at press time) before the arrival date. MagicBands customized closer to the check-in date will be available at check-in at the resort. Disney does not ship MagicBands internationally, which means all visitors without a U.S. address will pick up their MagicBands at check-in. If you fail to customize the MagicBands at all, grey MagicBands will be waiting at the resort at check-in.

Those not staying at a Disney-owned resort can purchase MagicBands on site, with current pricing at $12.95 each. The MagicBands of such visitors are linked at the time of purchase to a theme park ticket, and the MagicBand can then be used for FastPass+. Note that a MagicBand is not required to use FastPass+ (a ticket, of course, is required) and off-site guests can simply scan their ticket instead of a Band. There are no charging privileges for off-site guests, so you'll need to keep cash or a credit card handy.

Disney World To-Do List

Tailored To-Do lists are available for each of the itineraries located at YOURFIRSTVISIT.NET/ITINERARIES. For more general guidelines, see below:

More Than 181 Days Before Your Planned Arrival Date

1. Double-check budget (Chapter 8), dates (Chapter 4), intended hotel (Chapter 5), intended dates in each park (Chapter 6), intended dining venues (Chapter 7), and transportation choices and their availability for the planned dates.

2. Make transportation arrangements as necessary, including any flight or rental car reservations.

3. Create your My Disney Experience account and add your group members to it.

4. If staying at a Disney-owned hotel, book your hotel and purchase your tickets. Call 407-939-7675 to book by phone (optimal, because this allows you to tell the reservationist which area at a resort you want to be in, if you have a preference) or go to DISNEYWORLD.COM/PLAN to use Disney's online system. At the same time, you'll have the opportunity to sign up for Disney's Magical Express service that transports Disney-owned hotel guests from Orlando International (but not Sanford) Airport directly to their hotel. Don't worry if you don't have your flight details set. You can come back to this page later or call 866-599-0951 to set it up. Disney hotel reservations can be made over the phone up to 499 days before an arrival date. Online, the system may only show reservations available through the end of the calendar year, particularly if you try to book for the next year more than six months in advance. Call Disney reservations at 407-939-7675 if your dates aren't available online but you are within 499 days of your arrival date.

5. If not staying at a Disney resort, buy your tickets from within your My Disney Experience account—this increases the chance that they will be properly linked. Alternatively, purchase tickets from an authorized reseller and link them manually.

Exactly 6am EST, Exactly 180 Days Before Arrival Date

Log on to DisneyWorld.com/dining by at least 5:50am EST, and have your highest priority reservation all set up on the page. Keep refreshing, as you will be let in as soon as Disney's system decides it is 6am. Make as many of the following hardest-to-get reservations that are on your itinerary, in the order listed:

- Be Our Guest Restaurant [Magic Kingdom]
- Cinderella's Royal Table [Magic Kingdom]
- Chef Mickey's [Contemporary Resort]
- Breakfast with Rapunzel, etc. [Trattoria al Forno on the BoardWalk]
- 'Ohana [Polynesian Resort]
- Akershus Royal Banquet Hall [Epcot]
- 1900 Park Fare Dinner [Grand Floridian Resort]
- California Grill [Contemporary Resort]
- Crystal Palace [Magic Kingdom]
- Hoop-Dee-Doo Revue [Fort Wilderness Campground and Resort]

For other restaurants, booking at 6am 180+ days in advance isn't necessary, but doing so will guarantee a desired day and time.

If you have trouble online, call (407) WDW-DINE (939-3463) to book reservations offline, beginning at 7am EST on the same date.

60 Days Before Arrival Date (If Staying at Disney-Owned Resort or Other Eligible Hotel)

1. Beginning (if you choose) at 7am, go to your My Disney Experience account and set up your FastPass+ selections.
2. If staying at a Disney-owned resort, do online resort check in, requesting any special location or amenity preferences.
3. If staying at a Disney-owned resort, customize MagicBands.

30 Days Before First Park Visit (If Staying Anywhere Else)

Beginning (if you choose) at 7am, go to your My Disney Experience account and set up your FastPass+.

Notes on Packing, Etc., Before You Leave

1. If you have them, bring your MagicBands in your carry-ons or wear them on your wrists.
2. If you use Disney's Magical Express, you do not need to collect your bags at the Orlando airport unless you choose to, arrive late in the evening/at night (between 10 pm and 5 am), or are an international traveler. Disney will obtain them for you (without the bags ever going to baggage claim) and deliver them directly to your room. Your bags will likely arrive at your hotel hours after you do. Plan to pack an appropriate change of clothes for Orlando weather, medications, etc., in a carry-on. Follow the instructions in the Magical Express packet you will receive in the mail regarding both tagging your bags pre-departure and where to go at the Orlando airport to find the bus to your resort. Magical Express check-in is located on the B side of Level 1. If you arrive on the A side or pick up your luggage yourself on the A side, you will need to walk over to the B side. Note that this is only possible on Level 3. There is no way to walk from the A side to the B side on any other level.
3. Bring copies/printouts of your room reservation, confirmation numbers, and any tickets for special events you may have received in the mail.
4. When you arrive at the hotel, if you used Online Check-in, look for the special Online Check-in line, and get into it.

We're almost there! Setting up dining and FastPass+ reservations can be stressful and frustrating, but you're armed with the best possible strategy. Once the reservations are booked, there's little to worry about.

Where to Go Next

Congratulations! You either skipped to the end of the book to find out if the princess really does end up with the prince, or have now read so much great Disney World information that there's really no need to actually go on the vacation. And this book isn't even billed as a money saver. Oh, you still want to go, and you want to be kept up to date on any changes? We weren't expecting that, but we might still be able to help.

First of all, take advantage of our new free update program! We will update this 2018 edition several times between its initial August 2017 publication date and the summer of 2018, when our 2019 edition will come out. For the 2018 edition of this guide, we are offering free updates!

The paperback and Kindle versions are for sale on Amazon.com, and the PDF version is for sale on Gumroad.com.

- If you bought your 2018 edition on Gumroad.com, you'll **automatically** get an invitation to download an updated version of it when it's available.
- If you bought your 2018 edition on Amazon, then **forward your confirming Amazon email** (that is, the email titled "Amazon. com order of The easy Guide to Your Walt Disney World Visit") to easyguidewdw@gmail.com, and then, whenever a new update of the 2018 edition comes out, we will email you instructions on how to get yours (as a PDF).

Then, for changes between updates, bookmark yourfirstvisit.net/easy-guide-2018-changes.

From there, easyWDW.com is your best chance to see what's going on inside the theme parks as it happens. With weekly visits, thousands of pictures, up-to-date info on operating schedule changes, and ideal touring strategies, there's no other website in the world like it. If you'd like to join other WDW fans and have an opportunity to ask Josh questions about your trip directly, sign up for the forums at easywdw.com/forums.

Pay close attention to yourfirstvisit.net for new material aimed squarely at first-timers who both may never return and also don't necessarily want to spend a lot of time planning. Advice there for such visitors is very specific, but always comes with next best options ranked in order for those who can't, or won't, follow Dave's specific advice. The site is particularly helpful for choosing among hotels. Read it, and easywdw.com, too, and your life will be fulfilled.

We sincerely hope this book helped you plan a special trip full of the best that Walt Disney World offers. Get out there and put everything you learned into action. And after you've left Disney World and come back home—leave us comments at yourfirstvisit.net and easywdw. com to let us know how it went!

Acknowledgments

Dave would like to thank those who helped with this book and the years of work that led up to it:

- This book would not have been possible without the encouragement and skills of Bob McLain and Theme Park Press.
- And it wouldn't have been too good without my co-author Josh Humphrey. The best Disney World thinker of his generation, Josh has made this book more than twice as good as it would have been without him, thanks to his capability and stubbornness.
- Gratitude to my family—Amy, Ted, and Alex—who once again let a Walt Disney World project divert my time and attention.
- Many thanks to a list of people whose support over the years made the work that led to this book possible: Steve Bell, Joe Black, Tom Bricker, Lee Cockerell, Mary Conor DeFazio, Beth Pickel Doda, Faith Dority, Mike Ellis, Kristen Hoetzel-Go, Jackie Hutnik, Allison Jones, Linda Stevens Jones, Kathleen Kelly, Karen Landry, Kuleen Lashly, Sarah Harvey Mitchell, Julie Neal, Steve Seifert, Len Testa, Carl Trent, and Jodi Whisenhunt.
- Last, but not least, thanks to the readers of YOURFIRSTVISIT. NET—more than ten million of them—you all inspire me every day.

Josh would like to thank:

- My mom and dad for smiling as their (favorite) son crossed the country to try and chase down yet another dream.
- Dave Shute for bringing me this posh book deal, in addition to providing the foundation and structure for everything in it.
- Everyone that's ever recommended easyWDW to a friend, colleague, family member, or fellow DISboards member. Your continued support is what drives everything I do. Thank you.

About the Authors

Dave by day is a strategist and problem solver for clients ranging from the Fortune 500 to local not-for-profits. At night and on weekends he writes yourfirstvisit.net, and, lately, Disney World guidebooks. All the time he's a husband, dad, son, and brother. He has a BA from the University of Chicago, and both an MA in English Literature and MBA from the University of Virginia, where he also completed the majority of work for a PhD in English Literature. He spent almost a decade as a strategy consultant at McKinsey & Co., Inc., and since then has largely operated as an independent strategy consultant. He founded yourfirstvisit.net in 2009—the first Disney World site aimed squarely at first-time visitors who may never return. He visits Disney World six to ten times a year, and in 2017 he stayed in his 150th different Disney World-owned hotel room.

Josh grew up in Seattle, Washington, the only known city to adequately prepare a person for Orlando's wet summers. He was fascinated by Disney theme parks long before his first visit to Disneyland at age eight. He started easyWDW.com in the spring of 2010 as an outlet to help visitors maximize their theme park experience with practical, hands-on advice. He lives just 15 minutes from Magic Kingdom's gates and records more than a hundred theme park visits every year, each with the express intent of uncovering ways to better enjoy everything the parks offer. In his spare time, he enjoys dressing his Duffy the Disney Bear in fabulous outfits, taking his dog to the park, and the occasional single malt scotch.

About Theme Park Press

Theme Park Press publishes books primarily about the Disney company, its history, culture, films, animation, and theme parks, as well as theme parks in general.

Our authors include noted historians, animators, Imagineers, and experts in the theme park industry.

We also publish many books by first-time authors, with topics ranging from fiction to theme park guides.

And we're always looking for new talent. If you'd like to write for us, or if you're interested in the many other titles in our catalog, please visit:

www.ThemeParkPress.com

. . . .

Theme Park Press Newsletter

Subscribe to our free email newsletter and enjoy:

- ◆ Free book downloads and giveaways
- ◆ Access to excerpts from our many books
- ◆ Announcements of forthcoming releases
- ◆ Exclusive additional content and chapters
- ◆ And more good stuff available nowhere else

To subscribe, visit www.ThemeParkPress.com, or send email to newsletter@themeparkpress.com.

26134894R00178

Made in the USA
Columbia, SC
07 September 2018

Now in Its 5th Edition!

You don't need an 800-page gorilla of a guide to plan your Walt Disney World vacation. Beat the crowds, the cost, and the chaos with Dave and Josh's up-to-date, comprehensive, step-by-step advice for the perfect Walt Disney World vacation.

It doesn't get any *easier* than this:

Pick the Best Time! Pick the best time to visit Walt Disney World with our exclusive month-by-month calendars of cost, weather, crowds, and special events.

Stay at the Best Hotel! Rest easy with our analyses and comparisons of all Walt Disney World resorts, for any budget, plus floor plans and recommendations.

Eat the Best Food! Learn how to take advantage of Disney's new dining plan, then plan your meals with our succinct reviews of every Walt Disney World restaurant.

Conquer the Lines! Experience all the attractions you want, with short waits and no hassles, thanks to our detailed touring plans and the ultimate FastPass+ guide.

Save Money! Save thousands of dollars on everything from theme park tickets to Disney hotels by following our proven, time-tested advice.

If planning your Disney vacation has put the pain into your pixie dust, this is your magic wand to make it go away. Whether it's your first trip to Walt Disney World or your fortieth, *The easy Guide* will make it your best. Don't go see Mickey without it.

Dave Shute has been the webmaster of yourfirstvisit.net since 2008. He began the site to help people who may visit Walt Disney World only once in their lives.

Josh Humphrey has been the webmaster of easywdw.com since 2010. Living just 15 minutes from Magic Kingdom, he visits Walt Disney World over 100 times per year.

www.ThemeParkPress.com